CW00502056

NEW DIR

PEER POLITY INTERACTION AND SOCIO-POLITICAL CHANGE

PEER POLITY
INTERACTION
AND
SOCIO-POLITICAL
CHANGE

EDITED BY COLIN RENFREW
AND JOHN F. CHERRY

The right of the
University of Cambridge
to print and sell
all manner of books
was granted by
Henry VIII in 1534.
The University has printed
and published continuously
since 1584.

CAMBRIDGE UNIVERSITY PRESS
CAMBRIDGE
LONDON   NEW YORK   NEW ROCHELLE
MELBOURNE   SYDNEY

CAMBRIDGE UNIVERSITY PRESS
Cambridge, New York, Melbourne, Madrid, Cape Town, Singapore, São Paulo, Delhi

Cambridge University Press
The Edinburgh Building, Cambridge CB2 8RU, UK

Published in the United States of America by Cambridge University Press, New York

www.cambridge.org
Information on this title: www.cambridge.org/9780521112222

First published 1986
This digitally printed version 2009

A catalogue record for this publication is available from the British Library

Library of Congress Cataloguing in Publication data
Peer polity interaction and socio-political change.
(New directions in archaeology)
Bibliography: p.
Includes index.
1. Social archaeology–Addresses, essays, lectures.
2. Political anthropology–Addresses, essays, lectures.
3. Social interaction–Addresses, essays, lectures.
I. Renfrew, Colin, 1937–   .II. Cherry, John F.
III. Series.
CC72.4.P44 1986   930   85-24321

ISBN 978-0-521-22914-2 hardback
ISBN 978-0-521-11222-2 paperback

v

CONTENTS

CONTRIBUTORS

Gina L. Barnes, Department of Archaeology, University of Cambridge.

Richard Bradley, Department of Archaeology, University of Reading.

David P. Braun, Department of Anthropology, University of Southern
    Illinois at Carbondale, Illinois, USA.

Sara Champion, Department of Archaeology, University of
    Southampton.

Timothy Champion, Department of Archaeology, University of
    Southampton.

Robert Chapman, Department of Archaeology, University of Reading.

John F. Cherry, Faculty of Classics, University of Cambridge.

David A. Freidel, Department of Anthropology, Southern Methodist
    University, Dallas, Texas, USA.

Richard Hodges, Department of Archaeology and Prehistory, University
    of Sheffield.

Colin Renfrew, Department of Archaeology, University of Cambridge.

Jeremy A. Sabloff, Department of Anthropology, University of New
    Mexico, Albuquerque, New Mexico, USA.

Stephen Shennan, Department of Archaeology, University of
    Southampton.

Anthony Snodgrass, Faculty of Classics, University of Cambridge.

PREFACE

Archaeology is still not very good at dealing with two themes which are increasingly seen as central to an understanding of human societies and of change in them: style, and communication. Indeed, it is a measure of our failure to analyse them successfully that they are generally regarded as separate subjects and treated in very different ways. 'Style in civilisation' is an old topic, with an extensive literature, but one which is unsteadily sustained by the hidden assumptions of various disparate schools of thought and indurated with the common sense of earlier ages. Style is often seen as something personal, to be judged on a subjective basis, a topic which the more robust spirits of the archaeological community often avoid. Communication, on the other hand, associates readily in the mind with information theory and with aspects of efficiency in very large systems: these are matters susceptible to precise measurement, and often avoided by those who seek sensitively to intuit meaning from the relics of earlier days.

In reality, however, these are two sides of the same coin. Style is invariably an aspect of expression: without communication between individuals there can be no style, in whatever field. At the same time, communication has to occur, if it is to take place at all, through a channel, in a medium. In the case of communication between humans (rather than, for instance between machines linked electronically), that channel involves one or more of the senses. Style is an indispensable component of the communication system, along with the messages themselves. Just as there can be no style without communication, so communication when it occurs also generates or utilises style.

There are issues here which are crucial to archaeology: they underlie most of the discussions in this volume. For the subject matter is communication, and the effects of communication between nearby communities. What are the nature of the interactions between them, and the consequences of these interactions? On what scale do they operate?

These questions are of course not new to archaeology. On the contrary, they represent some of the first which archaeologists set out to tackle. In the early days, research was undertaken with almost automatic recourse to theories of invasion and migration. It was then pursued for many decades under the general rubric of the 'diffusion of culture'. More recently, it has been conducted with greater emphasis upon autonomy and on local innovation. But although these were among the first interpretive problems tackled by anthropologists and archaeologists, they have not been satisfactorily resolved. Indeed, so familiar have they become that it is difficult to take up any major issue in archaeology or prehistory without soon becoming ensnared in their ramifications.

The papers in this volume present what we feel is a

radical new initiative to break out of some of the constraints of the traditional mould while avoiding the new, rather stereotyped reactions against it. Just as it is no longer enough to explain changes in the society and in the material culture within a specific area by vague reference to the 'diffusion' of ideas from another, so the alternative claim of autonomy is generally an insufficient response. In the same way, the simple assertion of the operation of a 'world system' is sometimes little more than a reiteration of the old diffusionist model, ill-concealed in a new jargon which has replaced 'focal centre' or 'hearth' (*foyer de civilisation*) with the new 'core', and 'barbarian fringe' with 'periphery'.

The framework presented here is a simple one and, as indicated in the first chapter, it is essentially a structure within which the discussion of various cases can conveniently be set. It is an approach, not a solution. It does, however, possess the important characteristic that it directs attention to such matters as style and communication in a systematic and structured way which allows the integration of these with other aspects of the culture system, thus forming a coherent view. It can do this without our claiming to know or understand the full content of the communication, without pretending that we can intuit the meaning of all the messages.

The underlying idea of peer polity interaction was developed first in the attempt to establish a convenient framework for discussing the early emergence of state societies within the Aegean. It became clear that while the diffusionists might emphasise the significance of 'influences' from outside the region, and while some theorists of state formation would instead concentrate entirely upon social and economic processes within a single territory or polity, both of these views were in fact missing some of the most important processes and interactions. These, occurring as they did between neighbouring societies, were being overlooked in many theoretical formulations. The question is thus largely one of scale, and it has to be hammered out using concrete cases of well-defined territorial extent.

It was with this aim in view that the theme was made the subject of a symposium at the 27th Annual Meeting of the Society for American Archaeology, held at Minneapolis in April 1982. Most of the papers included here were first prepared in draft for that meeting.

David Freidel was invited to contribute to this volume following his interventions in the symposium, and Anthony Snodgrass agreed to write a paper following later discussion, as did Richard Bradley and Robert Chapman. Henry T. Wright presented a paper to the symposium, 'Peer polity interaction in early Mesopotamia', which we would have liked to include here, and the two symposium discussants, David Grove and Antonio Gilman, also made interesting contributions; we would like to thank all three for the stimulus of their interest.

At the symposium we were very much impressed to see how far, in the analysis of processes of development in quite different areas, issues which were effectively variations on the same themes, arose again and again, although in very different guises. The discussion and the analysis was able to proceed at a genuinely cross-cultural level, yet without losing a clear focus upon, and a precise definition of, the specific features in each individual case. This applied as much to the papers discussing state formation (early Greece, Japan, the Maya, and Anglo-Saxon England) as to those considering interactions at what might be considered a less complex level (Hopewell, and three cases from European prehistory).

The common link in each instance is the emergence of influential symbolic systems, seen to operate over quite wide areas. These are viewed, however, within a processual context. They are not claimed as the 'essence' of the cultures or civilisations in question, as they might be in some idealist sense. They are accompanied in most cases by economic and social changes evidently of considerable importance. It is ultimately the link between these various spheres of activity which deserves to be explored, and which has hitherto largely escaped successful analysis. In our view it should not be necessary to make a choice between an approach favouring the symbolic and the stylistic on the one hand, and one favouring the material and the technological on the other. Both aspects are seen as acting and interacting within a specific social matrix. It is not enough, however, simply to assert that this is so; the essential is to investigate these relationships in specific cases. This is what the papers in this book set out to do; we believe that conclusions of wide and general interest emerge from the undertaking.

Colin Renfrew
John F. Cherry

Chapter 1

**Introduction: peer polity interaction and
socio-political change**
Colin Renfrew

Introduction

The concept central to this paper—peer polity interaction—is a process in terms of which the familiar problem of
the growth of socio-political systems and of the emergence of
cultural complexity can be examined in a fresh and original
way. Simply to name a process in itself, of course, establishes
nothing. If, however, it brings new problems into clearer focus
and offers an avenue towards their investigation, it can prove
its usefulness. My claim is that the concept of peer polity
interaction does that by bringing to the fore the question of
the development of *structures* in society—political institutions,
systems of specialised communication in ritual, conventionalised patterns of non-verbal language—and even of the
development of ethnic groups and of languages themselves.

Peer polity interaction designates the full range of interchanges taking place (including imitation and emulation,
competition, warfare, and the exchange of material goods and
of information) between autonomous (i.e. self-governing and
in that sense politically independent) socio-political units
which are situated beside or close to each other within a single
geographical region, or in some cases more widely.

The framework of analysis has two obvious properties.
It avoids laying stress upon relations of dominance and subordination between societies, although such relations are
indeed common enough and their discussion is, in the
archaeological literature, the most frequent approach to
questions of culture change. This is seen from the early days of

the analysis of the 'diffusion' of culture, through the later
treatment of 'primary' and 'secondary' states, to more recent
investigations in terms of 'core' and 'periphery'. These are of
course all terms which are valid in specific situations, but they
have been applied very much more generally than the evidence
sometimes warrants.

Secondly, the discussion here, by definition, does not
simply consider the socio-political unit in isolation. *Die
isolierte Stadt* is a concept whose examination has indeed
yielded useful insights, and within which questions of the
intensification of production and of the emergence of
decision-making hierarchies in the face of increasing
population density and other factors, can profitably be
discussed. But the *form* of these control hierarchies and of the
institutions by which intensification is achieved cannot so
effectively be considered in isolation.

Spatial relations and power relations

The underlying principle is conceived here primarily
with reference to fairly complex societies (developed
chiefdoms or early states), although it no doubt applies in
many other instances of both lesser and greater scale and complexity. When we consider most early states, for instance, we
find that they do not exist in isolation. On the contrary, it is
possible to identify in a given region several autonomous
political centres which, initially at least, are not brought
within a single, unified jurisdiction. It is such autonomous

territorial units, with their administrative centres which together constitute what is often termed a civilisation. They may be recognised as iterations of what I have called the *early state module* (ESM). Often the ESMs—which in any given case tend to be of approximately the same size—conform to a modular area of approximately 1,500 sq.km. In many early civilisations their number is of the order of ten, within a factor of two or so (Renfrew 1975: 12–21; Fig. 1.1).

To say this is to draw attention to the distinction, in spatial terms, between an *early state*, and a *civilisation*, seen here as a group or cluster of states sharing a number of common features. These usually include closely similar political institutions, a common system of weights and measures, the same system of writing (if any), essentially the same structure of religious beliefs (albeit with local variations, such as a special patron deity), the same spoken language, and indeed generally what the archaeologist would call the same 'culture', in whatever sense he might choose to use that term. The individual political unit—the states—are often fiercely independent and competitive (Fig. 1.2).

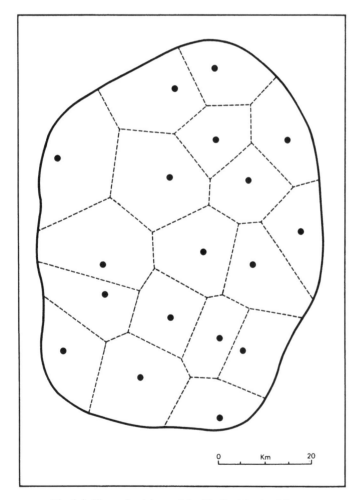

Fig. 1.1. The early state module: idealised territorial structure of early civilisations showing the territories and centres of the ESMs within the civilisation (i.e. the area of cultural homogeneity).

Indeed, not uncommonly, one of them may come to achieve political dominance over the others, ultimately uniting the cluster into a single larger unit frequently coterminous in its extent with that of the entire 'civilisation'. This is a *nation state*, sometimes even an *empire*. The individual political units at the time of their independence are the peer polities of our title, whose interactions are the subject of our study.

The same general phenomenon may be seen at other scales, or to put it another way, at other levels of socio-cultural complexity. Precisely the same configuration may be recognised in almost any case where the archaeologist or the anthropologist speaks of chiefdom societies. The separate chiefdoms are effectively autonomous in terms of their power relations (Fig. 1.3), yet they do not exist in isolation for they have a large number of neighbours, among which each has much in common with the others. That is not to say that such societies cannot exist in isolation. The case of Easter Island shows that sophisticated chiefdom society is not incompatible with remoteness (although even here the local region was usually divided territorially into a number of peer polities). It demonstrates only that such societies would be different if they did.

Nor is this configuration restricted to stratified or ranked societies. Among supposedly 'egalitarian' agricultural societies individual, politically autonomous units can usually be distinguished, whether as villages or tribal units. And at a greater territorial scale than these are those larger entities identified by many archaeologists and ethnographers where specific features or groups of features have a distribution sometimes taken to define a 'cultural' or ethnic unit. The problem of identifying such units (Clarke 1968: 367) is so acute that the utility of the archaeological concept of the 'culture' has been questioned (Renfrew 1978a: 94; Shennan 1978). Nonetheless, the adjacent small polities do share a number of features: often a common language, and generally other symbolic systems, including belief systems. Their recovery from the archaeological record undoubtedly presents many problems. The difficulties are more acute in the case of less complex societies, which generally possess a more narrow range of symbolic expression and less formalised institutions. But ethnographic experience suggests that in nearly all cases of such societies, the extent of these structured symbolic systems is greater than the power span of the individual polities.

It should be clearly understood that the term 'polity' is not in this context intended to suggest any specific scale of organisation or degree of complexity, but simply to designate an autonomous socio-political unit. One of the first questions to face the archaeologist in any context, whether he is dealing with band societies or empires, is the scale of the autonomous unit. The polity is here conceived of as the highest order socio-political unit in the region in question. In many farming societies it will simply be the village or (with a dispersed settlement pattern) the neighbourhood. In others, the various villages or neighbourhoods may be aggregated into a larger unit

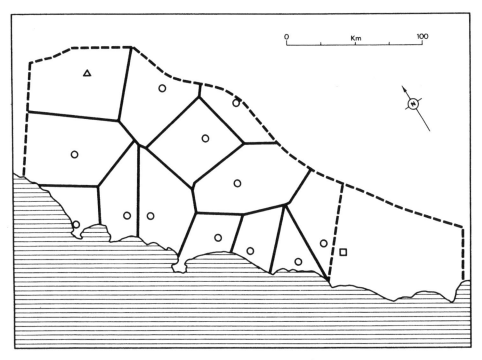

Fig. 1.2. The early state module in Etruria: the twelve cities of ancient Etruria (circles) with hypothetical territorial boundaries. Rome is indicated by a square and Fiesole by a triangle. The Etruscan cities competed and were not united under a single rule till Roman times.

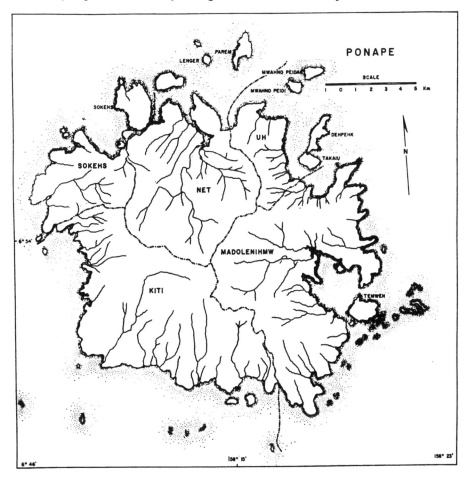

Fig. 1.3. Peer polity interactions at chiefdom level: territorial divisions between the five independent tribes of the Pacific island of Ponape in the Caroline Islands (after Riesenberg 1968:9).

with some socio-political coherence; such units are often termed 'tribes'. But it is now very clear that not all relatively egalitarian farming societies can realistically be termed 'tribal', nor do some of the loose aggregations or associations which have at times been referred to as tribes have any effective political institutions (Helm 1968). Chiefdoms, on the other hand, certainly do.

In hierarchically structured societies the term 'polity' is likewise reserved for the highest politically autonomous unit. The subordinate units, which may themselves have been independent polities at an earlier time, are often simply administrative or territorial subdivisions. Thus a nation state will normally contain several local areas or 'counties' which, at an earlier stage, may themselves have enjoyed independent status as early states, at that time ranking as polities.

It does not follow that a polity has to be territorially based or defined: many band societies and other egalitarian groups are formally defined in kinship terms. But the polity and its constituent members will nonetheless occupy a pre-ferred area of land and will often enjoy privileged access to resources within it. Nearly all human groups, and hence nearly all polities, thus show territorial behaviour even when they are not formally defined in territorial terms. Nor need a polity

display any notably developed or differentiated system of government or of administration; it is sufficient that there should exist procedures for decision-making which habitually work, and which in practice do modify or otherwise affect the behaviour of most of the members. Such a definition applies as much to a hunter–gatherer band as to an early state. It follows that a polity is not subject to the jurisdiction of a higher power.

Structural homologies

So far the general observation has been made that autonomous political units do not generally exist in isolation, but have neighbours which are analogous in scale to them. But that assertion does not in itself make the simple and evident point that these neighbouring polities display a remarkable range of structural homologies in any specific case. Although this idea may be obvious it has not often been stressed, and it may prove to be remarkably important.

To take a familiar example, a typical Maya ceremonial centre consists of a central complex which is organised around a group of plazas, courtyards and platforms, surrounded by stepped pyramids (Fig. 1.4). The pyramids are generally approximately square in plan, and each was surmounted by

Fig. 1.4. The Maya ceremonial centre: a reconstruction of the site of Copan, Honduras, in the Late Classic period. (drawn by Tatiana Proskouriakoff).

a platform. At the more important centres carved stone stelae are found, bearing recognisably similar glyphs, which show the same system of numeration and other similarities.

Now *why* should this be? Why should we find these same *structures* (in the architectural sense) repeated throughout the region of this civilisation? Why are the architectural features of the sites in some respects homologous? Why do the numeration systems display a complete structural homology? Why do the writing systems show similar homologies? These are, we may be sure, simply the material manifestation of further homologies in social organisation, and in the belief system.

There is nothing in biological evolutionary theory that says we should expect such pronounced structural homologies in behaviour among members of a species within a given region, when at the same time finding a very different set of behaviour patterns among members of the same species in a different region. Of course, it could be argued that the various communities where these homologies of behaviour are observed are all the direct lineal descendants of a common ancestor community, whose behaviour patterns they have to some extent conserved. But such a simple explanation, except in a straightforward colonial situation, is rarely valid. Often the different communities developed simultaneously and their structural homologies developed with them. No individual centre can claim primacy for them all.

It would theoretically be perfectly possible for neighbouring early state modules (ESMs) to differ greatly in all these respects. Or at least they could differ as much between themselves within the ambit of a single civilisation as do ESMs when chosen for comparison from different civilisations. In the biological case that would often be so. Communities of a given species of social insect, for instance, show much the same structural homologies when compared with near neighbours as with other communities spatially remote from them. But this is not the experience with human societies.

Evidently the structural homologies which we see among the ESMs of a civilisation are the product of the interactions which have taken place between them, in many cases over a long time period.

In a strictly ecological sense we might regard some of the features which these societies share as necessary adaptations. These would be features which might have evolved quite independently in response to the similar environment in the different communities, each faced with analogous practical problems. Thus we might expect analogies in house structure among communities in arid lands, where mud is the only obvious building material. The *pisé* structures of the early Near East show many similarities with the adobe constructions of the American South-west, and a broadly 'functional' explanation along those lines could easily be constructed. If we are not surprised by similarities between Near Eastern and South-western structures, we have no cause to be any more so by comparable similarities between

structures at different sites within the South-west.

Some social forms may be discussed and perhaps 'explained' in the same way. In a general sense, the recognition of the emergence of 'state' societies in different parts of the world implies the assertion of some measure of structural homology. And since the different areas were (in some cases) not in significant contact with the others, the homologies in these instances cannot be ascribed to interaction.

The homologies upon which we are here commenting are, however, very much more specific than these in terms of structure. We are talking in terms of *specific* architectural forms, *specific* numerical systems, *specific* symbolic systems, and indeed, a very wide range of homologous structures which are seen within the social and projective systems of a given area.

The important question which we are asking is this: To what extent was the very emergence of such systems significantly determined by the interactions whose operation we may infer from the specific structural homologies observed? The distinction here is not a trivial one. We are concerned to explain certain important developments, such as the emergence of a particular governmental form, or the inception of specialised places of worship of monumental scale. In the cases which we have under consideration, these structures took on a specific form—specific, that is, to the civilisation in question, but shared among the constituent ESMs. The explanation for the shared elements within the civilisation, that is to say for the structural homologies, comes from the interactions between the polities—the peer polity interactions. To what extent were these peer polity interactions an indispensable and necessary element in the emergence of such systems, whatever their specific form?

The analysis of change

The approach advocated here differs from many earlier ones, where the dynamic for change is often viewed as operating outside the area and thus outside the societies which are the subject of study; this is exogenous change. Alternatively, several scholars have studied a single polity, effectively in isolation, and sought there the dynamic of change within the subsystems operating inside that polity or between those subsystems; this is endogenous change. It is relevant to note some of the properties of these two perspectives. Both offer useful approaches to the study of change, but they omit precisely that factor which is singled out for consideration here, namely the interactions of neighbouring polities of equivalent scale and status.

Exogenous change

Many analyses of societal change have utilised what may be termed 'models of dominance', where the changes within the area in question are explained largely in terms of the influence of, or of contact with, an adjacent area where the socio-political organisation is seen to be in some sense more 'advanced'. It is hardly necessary to recall the many early analyses of state formation and other processes of organisational growth conducted in terms of the 'diffusion' of culture. Morton Fried's use of the terms 'pristine' and 'secondary' to classify state societies into two categories, namely independent (parthenogenetic) and derivative, depending on the degree of purity and autonomy in their antecedents (Fried 1967: 231), is a popular and widely followed example of recent diffusionist thought. Another is the closely related idea of areas which are designated as 'core' and 'periphery' within a broader economic entity or 'world system', to use the terminology of Wallerstein (1974). Such concepts have been found useful in discussing the impact of the Western colonial powers in recent centuries upon what today is sometimes termed the 'Third World'. In my view, however, there are risks in projecting too vigorously onto the prehistoric past the particular circumstances of society, economy and transport which may make these terms appropriate, for instance, to the West Indies in the eighteenth century AD.

It should be noted that an emphasis upon exogenous change is not restricted to the 'cultural historical' school, which traditionally has favoured explanations based upon diffusion, nor to their neo-Marxist successors, in whose works a number of the same ideas are curiously reflected. Some of those advocating a systems approach likewise insist on looking outside the system for their explanatory thrust. Thus Hill (1977: 76) has written: 'no system can change itself; change can only be instigated by outside sources. If a system is in equilibrium, it will remain so unless inputs (or lack of inputs) from outside the system disturb the equilibrium.' Likewise, Saxe (1977: 116) writes: 'the processes that result in systematic change for all systems are and must be initiated by extra-systemic variables'.

It is not, of course, part of the case of Hill or Saxe that the outside sources instigating change need themselves be more complex societies than those under study, whereas that is precisely what the diffusionists and some of the neo-Marxists do argue. But either way, the exogenous approach, while entirely appropriate in those cases where the dominance relationship can clearly be demonstrated, is not an appropriate general model for all early socio-political change. In the words of Gordon Childe (1956: 154) it 'has the effect of relegating to the wings all the action of the prehistoric drama'.

There is a further class of models which may be considered here with the straightforward exogenous ones. These are the ones where there is a major regional diversity which the society manages to exploit. In such cases, the diversity may well be outside the territory of the society, but the organisational response is an internal one. Flannery's explanation for the rise of the Olmec (Flannery 1968), and those of Rathje (1973) and Tourtellot and Sabloff (1972) for the rise of the Classic Maya, fall within this category.

Endogenous change

At first sight the alternative to an emphasis on external forces or influences acting upon the area in question, and

leading to transformations within the society which is under study, is to look at the territory and at the polity which it contains, considered in isolation. This has, in effect, been the approach adopted by many workers attempting 'processual' explanations, whether or not the idea of isolation is deliberately introduced as a positive feature of the model.

Many, although not all, of the 'prime mover' approaches hitherto proposed operate in this way. For instance, irrigation and the accompanying intensification of agriculture are often seen to relate functionally with certain organisational changes within the society, and a growth process is sustained by this interaction. In other models population increase is a 'prime mover', and accompanying it there is the ever greater efficiency of economies of scale and of administrative hierarchies, which favour more effective information flow as the number of units to be co-ordinated increases. Many of the most interesting growth models recently proposed, such as those of Wright (1977b), of Johnson (1978), and indeed the processes indicated by Flannery (1972), are essentially of this kind.

A systems approach can harmonise admirably with this view; there is absolutely no need for it to lay stress only upon homeostasis, as the authors cited in the previous section do. Maruyama (1963) long ago emphasised the importance of positive feedback leading to morphogenesis, and I have myself (Renfrew 1972; Cooke and Renfrew 1979) used this notion as the major explanatory mechanism for the emergence of complexity in the Aegean. The treatment has often been essentially an endogenous one.

Peer polity interaction

The peer polity approach is intermediate, from the spatial perspective, between the two preceding ones (Fig. 1.5). Change is not exogenous to the system as a whole in the region under study, as it generally is when agencies of 'diffusion' are invoked. Nor is it necessary to define the system so widely as to include whole continents, as is so often the case when 'world systems' are brought into the discussion. But, on the other hand, the locus of change is not situated uniquely within the polity under study, as sometimes seems the case with the endogenous approach.

Instead, change is seen to emerge from the assemblage of interacting polities, that is to say it operates in most cases at the regional level. Interactions at this scale have been largely ignored in many discussions of state formation, where, as noted above, the consideration has often been in terms of 'secondary' states (i.e. exogenous change) or 'pristine' states (where the change is often regarded as endogenous). Interestingly, it is in the discussion of non-state societies that more careful consideration of significant contacts at the intermediate scale has taken place, notably with Caldwell's useful notion of the 'interaction sphere', initially applied to the North American Hopewell finds (Caldwell 1964).

While analysis at the local level, in terms, for instance, of the intensification of production, it always necessary, and

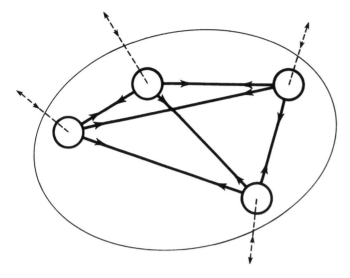

Fig. 1.5. Peer polity interaction. Strong interactions between the autonomous socio-political units within the region are of greater significance than external links with other areas.

an assessment of the significance of long-distance contacts equally desirable, it is suggested here that in many cases it is the intermediate-scale interactions between local but independent communities which are perhaps the most informative and certainly the most neglected. For it is at this level that those uniformities emerge which sometimes seem to have a significant role in determining the future pattern of development. The significant unit is thus seen, in this perspective, to be the larger community beyond the polity level, comprised of loosely related, yet politically independent, interacting groups. It is here, for instance, that the processes of ethnic formation must in many cases operate, and here too that the foundations for the later emergence of the nation state are laid.

Using the concept

The real interest of this analytical perspective will emerge below. But it is first necessary to examine the risks of circular reasoning which a careless or loosely defined application of the notion of peer polity interaction can readily carry with it. The risk of circularity is most acute when the aim is not primarily to examine change, but simply to explain the existence in the archaeological record of the rather wide-spread distribution of a particular feature or trait.

In such a case the first stage might be the recognition and definition of the wide spatial distribution of the feature in question. This distribution, particularly if it is greater in areal extent than other comparable distributions at that time or earlier, clearly stands in need of explanation. It might be thought tempting, then, to assert the operation of some principle of peer polity interaction to explain the distribution—perhaps countering other diffusionist suggestions that the distribution is the result of contacts with some other area. Evidence for the operation of this process of peer polity

interaction is then sought, and prominent among the supporting arguments is obviously the widespread uniformity in question.

This, however, is a purely circular argument. In effect, it has been possible to equate the *explanandum* and the *explanans* by separating them by means of a single hypothetical construct, namely peer polity interaction. The distribution is at once seen as explained by peer polity interaction and constitutes the evidence leading us to propose peer polity interaction as an explanation. Such an explanation is empty of meaning.

On the contrary, it is essential to bear in mind that our aim is the explanation of a temporal pattern, namely the changes which have taken place in the degree of complexity in the organisational aspects of a given society; simple trait distributions are not the appropriate subject of the explanatory exercise. And change in complexity must evidently be documented by some measure of complexity.

The causal role of the process of peer polity interaction can more legitimately be asserted when we have evidence of contact prior to the change in question in terms of information flow or the movement of goods, as well as at least the outline of some mechanisms whereby the interaction can be seen to have some role in facilitating the observed change. These circumstances may not be sufficient to document the explanation or even to make it entirely plausible, but they will at least save it from circularity.

Such then are the necessary conditions for the concept of peer polity interaction to be used as an explanatory or interpretive framework. Accompanying this general framework come some empirical observations, which it is worth setting out. For in this volume there is the opportunity to consider several interesting cases where the notion of peer polity inter-action may be used. It is desirable therefore to make some positive statements which can be tested.

1   Within a given region with a human population, we shall term the highest order social units (in terms of scale and organisational complexity) 'polities'. It is predicted that, when one polity is recognised, other neighbouring polities of comparable scale and organisation will be found in the same region. (This is simply a statement of the early state module observation, which applies to other and simpler organisational forms, too.)

2   When a significant organisational change, and in particular an increase in complexity, is recognised within one polity, it is generally the case that some of the other polities within the region will undergo the same transfor-mation at about the same time.

3   Leaving out of account the specific criterion which may be used in statement 2 above to recognise organisational change, we can predict that several further new institutional features will appear at about the same time. These may include architectural features, such as monumental buildings of closely similar form; con-

ceptual systems for communicating information, such as writing or other sign systems (including systems of mensuration of number, length, weight and time); assemblages of specific and special artefacts which may be associated with high status in the society in question; and customs (including burial customs) indicative of ritual practices reflecting and perhaps reinforcing the social organisation.

4   The observed features will not be attributable to a single locus of innovation (at least not in the early phases of development), but, so far as the chronological means allow, will be seen to develop within several different polities in the region at about the same time.

5   It is proposed that the process of transformation is frequently brought about not simply as a result of internal processes tending towards intensification, nor in repeated and analogous responses to a single outside stimulus, but as a result of interaction between the peer polities, which we can examine under the headings of:

> (a)   competition (including warfare), and competitive emulation
>
> (b)   symbolic entrainment, and the transmission of innovation
>
> (c)   increased flow in the exchange of goods

6   Moreover, this general assertion—that many organisational transformations may be explained in terms of peer polity interaction—may be elaborated to make a further prediction. In a region with peer polities which are not highly organised internally, but which show strong interactions both symbolically and materially, we predict transformations in these polities associated with the intensification of production and the further development of hierarchical structures for the exercise of power.

The nature of the interactions
The nub of the matter, and the real focus of interest, lies in the *nature* of the interactions between these peer polities and *between whom*, precisely, they operate.

The emphasis here is not primarily upon interaction in terms of the exchange of material commodities, but rather in the flow of information of various kinds between the polities. The importance of information exchange as a fundamental component of exchange systems has been made elsewhere (Renfrew 1975: 22–3), but here we can go further and consider the importance of such symbolic exchange even in the absence of trade in material goods.

It may be suggested that the emergence of new institutions in society can often profitably be considered in terms both of intensification of production, and of peer polity interaction. Many significant social transformations are accompanied by increased production (of foodstuffs and other materials), which permits not only increased population density but also the accumulation of pro-

duction beyond subsistence (PBS), which in turn allows the employment of craft specialists and other personnel at the behest of the élite, which in some cases controls that PBS. Within that framework, any interactions which serve to promote intensification of production are relevant to the discussion.

Warfare, to the extent that it uses up resources (whether as a result of destruction and looting, or in supporting an army), will promote intensification if it takes place on a sufficiently prolonged basis. (On the other hand, if it results in a great many deaths, so that food production can in consequence be substantially reduced, the converse is the case). Warfare (Fig. 1.6) is clearly one form of interaction between peer polities which may favour both intensification and the emergence of hierarchical institutions (initially for military purposes) within the various polities (Carneiro 1970; Webster 1975).

Competitive emulation is another form of interaction where neighbouring polities may be spurred to ever greater displays of wealth or power in an effort to achieve higher inter-polity status. There is a clear analogy here with individual behaviour, for instance in the well-known case of gift exchange, where positive reciprocity can be used to enhance status. The same process operates at group level in the familiar example of the potlatch, where the chief of a group engages the status of the whole group in the munificence of his feast-giving and gift-giving. This is a process favouring intensification, in that the resources utilised fall within the category of production beyond subsistence. But in an interesting way the emulation consists not only in the making of expensive gestures. The magnitude of these gestures has to be measured along some scale, and the gestures are thus similar in kind. If status is achieved, for instance, by erecting a particular kind of monument, the neighbouring polity will most readily acquire greater status by doing bigger and better.

There is reason to think that this is a significant factor in peer polity interaction. In several cases where there are concentrations of surprisingly large monuments — for instance the image *ahu* of Easter Island (Fig. 1.7) or the stone 'temples' of Malta—competitive emulation may help account for their otherwise rather puzzling scale. Within the present context of discussion it may in part also help explain the structural homologies of their form.

It would be wrong, however, to think of all the relevant interactions as essentially competitive. There is another process, perhaps of greater relevance, which I should like to term *symbolic entrainment*. This process entails the tendency for a developed symbolic system to be adopted when it comes into contact with a less-developed one with which it does not strikingly conflict. For one thing, a well-developed symbolic system carries with it an assurance and prestige which a less developed and less elaborate system may not share. These remarks apply, for instance, to the adoption of writing systems (Fig. 1.8) as much as to the adoption of systems of social organisation (such as some of the institutions of kingship).

Fig. 1.6. Warfare: a *condottiere* of Renaissance Italy, depicted outside a well-fortified hill town (Guidoriccio da Fogliano, in the painting attributed to Simone Martini in the Palazzo Pubblico, Siena).

Fig. 1.7. Competitive emulation: an image *ahu* of Easter Island, with colossal statue. The *ahu* were focal points within tribal territories.

We may imagine, for instance, in the Mesopotamia of the Protoliterate period, that several cities had centralised economies where an adequate system of recording would be a bureaucratic advantage, and indeed where some steps towards such a system had independently been taken. A really effective system developed in one would find ready adoption in many of the others.

A similar view may be developed for the adoption, or at least the parallel growth, of a political or administrative system, including that of kingship itself. The very existence of such a social order in one polity could tend to further the stability of a similar order in a neighbouring one. For it is the very nature of power that it is held by a few and accepted by many. The act of acceptance implies a sort of willing suspension of disbelief, an acquiescence in a belief structure or political philosophy, which neighbouring belief systems can do much to influence.

The *transmission of innovation* in a sense embraces symbolic entrainment within its scope, but refers also to innovations which are not, or do not at first seem to be, of a symbolic nature. Such innovations are perhaps 'transmitted' within the peer polities of the interacting group, and at first sight this would seem to be an example of the familiar process of 'diffusion'. Yet it differs from the standard view of that process, not only in that the peer polities have the status of more-or-less equal partners (which is not the case in most studies of diffusion), but, as I have argued elsewhere (Renfrew

Fig. 1.8. Symbolic entrainment: writing in early Mesopotamia emerged in a number of cities, probably simultaneously—Protoliterate tablets of limestone found at Kish, c. 3500 BC, length c.6.4. cm.

1978c) the crux of the matter, the true innovation, is not the original invention of the new feature or process but rather its widespread acceptance by the society or societies in question. Acceptance of an invention in one society may facilitate or even sanction it within another in which the invention itself may have occurred at an earlier time.

Although the emphasis here is primarily upon the exchange of information, there is no doubt that an *increased flow in the exchange of goods* can itself further structural transformations. For, clearly, if a society acquires an increasing proportion of its gross annual turnover from outside its own territory, those engaged in exchange are likely to become more numerous and new institutions may develop to cope with the reception, allocation and distribution of goods. The same applies to exports as to imports, and here the significant feature may be the increased level of production required to produce the materials to be exported. This may favour craft specialisation, perhaps mass production, and certainly other organisational features not hitherto required. All this is, of course, simply the familiar process of economic growth based partly on a developing import and export trade, and there is nothing very specific to peer polity interaction about it. Indeed, it applies to, and has been used with equal validity on, dominance models, where a more developed socio-political organisation enters into economic relations with, and perhaps 'exploits', a less developed one. Here we return to the neo-Marxist 'world system' approach. But economic growth is not an exclusive property of unequal partnerships. Moreover, with that growth and with the development of new organisational institutions, there is plenty of scope for the processes of emulation and symbolic

entrainment to operate and hence to influence the specific forms and structures of these emergent organisations.

These observations only begin the task of considering the range of significant interactions operating between polities. And while the discussion has, for the sake of example, dealt primarily with early state societies, many of these points apply also to less highly structured social formations.

They also hint at problems as yet hardly broached by archaeologists, and rarely by anthropologists. One of these relates to the formation of ethnic groups. How do such groups form, sometimes over a long time period, and what governs their scale and extent? The same questions are pertinent to the understanding of the behaviour of specific languages. What determines the area over which a particular language is spoken and the number of people who speak it, and the expansion or contraction in its linguistic boundaries? There are few ready answers to such questions at present. Yet we are approaching them when we consider and seek to explain the widespread distribution in space of certain archaeological phenomena, such as Beaker burials, or Hopewell ceremonial behaviour. Our approach, however, specifically does not make assumptions about the equivalence of linguistic or ethnic or 'cultural' groups. It seeks instead a fresh grasp of the interaction processes underlying them.

An example

The trajectories of development in the Greek islands at different times offer an appropriate example of the relevance of this approach. During the first millennium BC many individual and rather small islands achieved the explicit organisational structure which since the time of Plato and Aristotle has been the paradigm instance of the state—in this case the Greek city state. These islands, despite their small size, were self-governing, had a well-defined constitution, were subject to explicit law, issued coinage in the case of Naxos and Paros, and were famed for their accomplishments in sculpture (Figs. 1.9, 1.10). Yet it should be noted that the population of each was generally not more than 5,000 persons, and there was often little hierarchy of settlement since the population was generally concentrated in a single urban centre. Analogous developments can be seen in the third and second millennia BC, culminating in the second millennium in the emergence of small urban centres which lasted until the general organisational collapses in the Aegean before 1000 BC.

In the past, attempts have been made to represent both the Greek city states, and their Bronze Age predecessors in the Minoan and Mycenaean periods, as representing a 'secondary' civilisation, with states of earlier origin in the Near East or Egypt seen as 'primary'. But this view has increasingly been

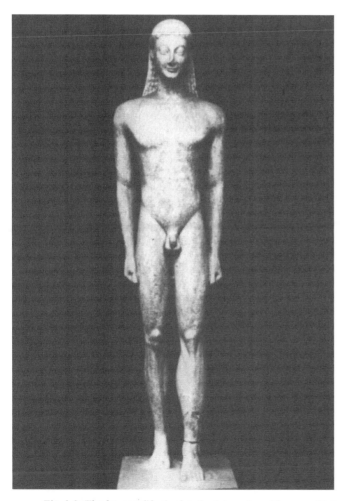

Fig. 1.9. The *kouros*: life-sized male statue of marble seen widely in the city states of Greece in the sixth century BC. The form is highly standardised, which illustrates a high degree of interaction between the independent cities. (From Melos).

called into question (despite undisputed evidence for trading contacts with the Near East). Instead, it is possible to see the course of development in this area as fundamentally an Aegean one, a response to a number of processes which can be analysed primarily in Aegean terms, without denying a real role to external trade.

In this early period—certainly in the first millennium, and perhaps earlier—the communities in question were politically independent, although they were later incorporated into a larger political unit, dominated by Athens.

Attempts to explain the emergence of the state for any individual polity, considered in isolation, soon run into difficulties, however. In the case of Melos (Renfrew and Wagstuff 1982), for instance, it is possible to identify some of the processes of agricultural and industrial intensification which accompanied and underlay state formation, and to identify some of the political and cultural institutions involved. But while the intensification may in a sense be endogenous to Melos, the social, cultural and religious framework in which it took place is to a large extent shared with other islands (the peer polities) and other city states in the Greek world.

An entirely autonomous, endogenous explanation falls down: it is difficult to think of Melos, for instance, had it existed in magnificent solitude (the Easter Island scenario), beginning the move towards statehood. But at the same time Melos is not secondary to any identifiable primary centre. (The dominance of Athens then lay in the future.) The small states of Greece emerged *together*, pulling each other up by the bootstraps, as it were. What they shared were the common elements of Greek civilisation: language, religion, shared history, similar (but not identical) institutions, equivalent agricultural and commercial practices. If the exogenous and the isolated—endogenous explanations fall down, the focus must be upon the interactions among these peer polities which made possible what in some ways was a shared trajectory of development (notwithstanding their jealously guarded political independence). And while there were local variations in resources—marble in Paros, gold in Siphnos, particularly good grapes in Naxos—the model for growth cannot be based upon intra-regional diversity, any more than it can rest primarily upon inter-regional trade with areas outside the Aegean.

The interactions which merit study in this case are largely of a symbolic nature. For in the first millennium BC the new and emergent features, which ultimately came to characterise Greek civilisation as a whole, were not primarily technological. The solid agricultural base had been established centuries earlier (Renfrew 1982a). Instead, it is the new institutions that gave the civilisation its character and shaped its eventual trajectory. The importance of the Greek temple (Fig. 1.11) as the focus of religous expression is one such element. Pride in civic autonomy is another, and this found significant commercial expression in the development of silver coinage throughout much of the region.

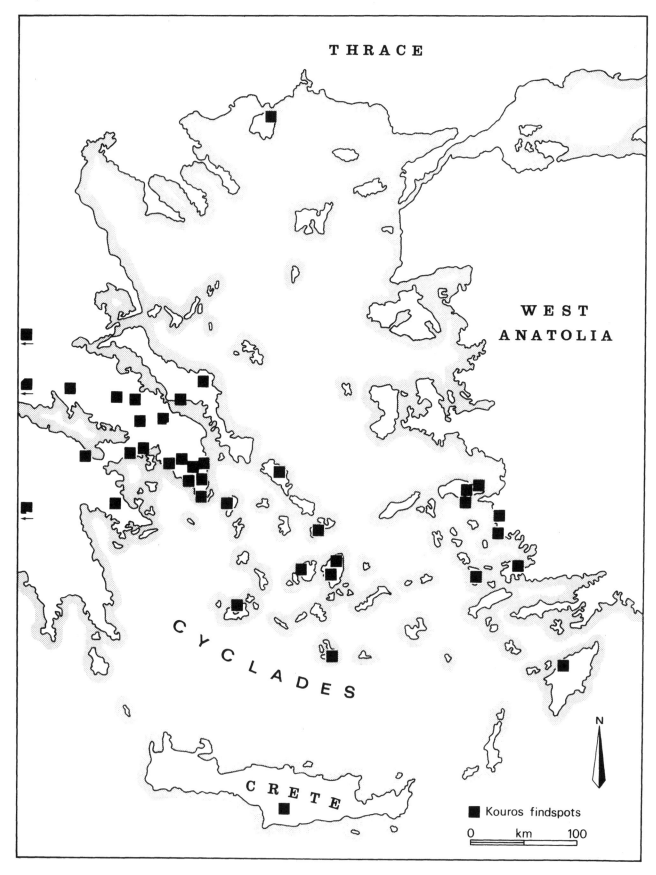

Fig. 1.10. The distribution of *kouroi* in the Aegean: one indication of the extent of symbolic interaction in the sixth century BC. (Nine finds outside the Aegean, notably from Italy and Sicily, are not shown.)

Fig. 1.11. The Doric temple, the most striking civic manifestation of Greekness: The 'Temple of Concord' at Akragas (Agrigento) in Sicily.

The interactions operating here undoubtedly included warfare, of which the earliest records certainly speak, and there are plenty of examples of competitive emulation—for instance in the magnificent treasuries and monuments which the richer islands (including Naxos and Siphnos) erected at pan-Hellenic sanctuaries such as Delphi and Delos, in an expression of civic pride (Fig. 1.12). But most of the simultaneous developments throughout this region can conveniently be subsumed under the term 'symbolic entrainment', as a first step in the discussion. To do so, however, simply underlines the need to understand the cultural dynamics by which important innovations, such as coinage, or large sculpture, or the adoption of the alphabet, came to be taken up so vigorously in so many different small and autonomous centres. There was a ferment of activity in the seventh, sixth and fifth centuries BC, which only at the end of that period resulted in the dominance of the Athenian or the Spartan state. Similarly, in the third millennium BC it is possible to speak of an 'international spirit' (Fig. 1.13) operating *within* the Aegean, which culminated five hundred years later in the emergence of the various centres of the Minoan and subsequently the Mycenaean civilisation.

In the first millennium, and perhaps earlier, there are underlying ethnic patterns, whose role in channelling these developments has not yet been analysed in a processual framework. It is, of course, common enough to stress the significance of the Greek language and to assert the 'Greekness' of Hellenic civilisation. But hitherto these have been particularistic statements, claims—perfectly warranted

Fig. 1.12. The Treasury of the Athenians at the sanctuary at Delphi: an outstanding example of civic pride and display, and dedicated to the god Apollo.

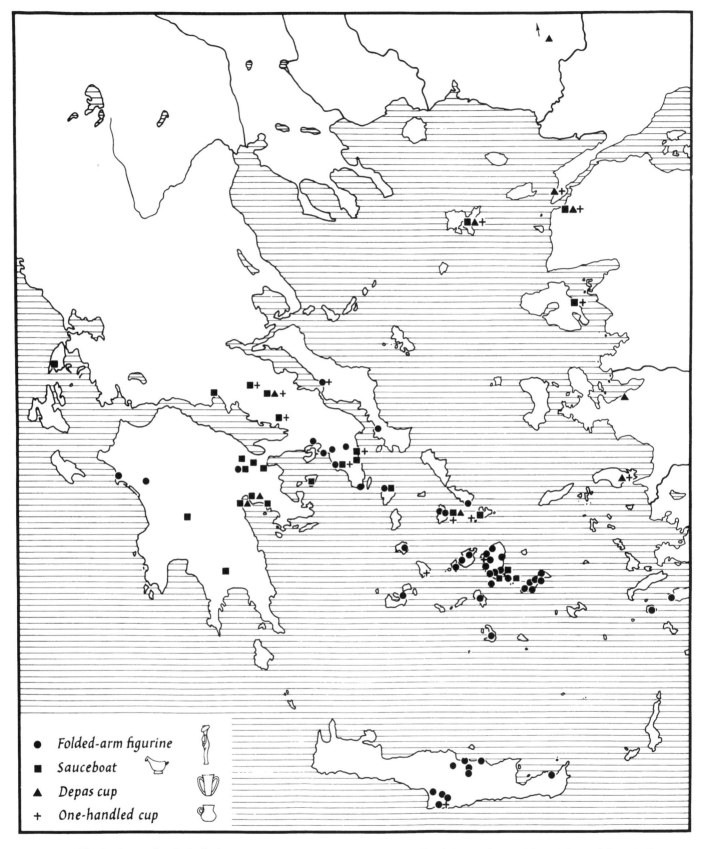

Fig. 1.13. The 'international spirit' of the third millennium BC Aegean, whose small-scale interactions anticipated those of the early Greek cities by two thousand years. The most characteristic products of the Cycladic Islands were symbolic: the marble folded-arm female figurines whose distribution is shown. But no region of Greece was dominant at this time.

claims, in a sense—of uniqueness. At the same time, one can now see them more clearly as a rather good example of the processes which are here under consideration. Their further investigation may prove rewarding on both the general and the specific level. Snodgrass, in his contribution to this volume, has developed a number of the relevant ideas, some of them already introduced in his earlier works.

The emergence of structure

The foregoing example perhaps illustrates the need for an analysis of this kind, at a level intermediate between that of a close examination of processes within a single polity on the one hand, and gross inter-regional, 'core—periphery' comparisons on the other. But in doing so, and in focusing attention on the importance, for an understanding of the processes of change, of the specific institutions and symbolic systems involved, it still leaves several questions unasked, let alone answered.

In particular, the precise nature of the interactions, in personal terms, remains to be explored. For instance, in the case of acts of competitive emulation—such as the construction of the Treasury of the Siphnians at Delphi—exactly

who, or what group of people, reached the decision to construct it? And in precisely what way were these persons influenced by earlier comparable acts of conspicuous community display (for instance the construction of earlier treasuries there)? Whom did they hope to impress, both inside their own polity (i.e. Siphnos, which is far from Delphi) and amongst the various peer polities? Of course the data of archaeology, or indeed of early history, are not able to supply precise answers to all these questions. But it is pertinent to ask them if we are to frame an adequately detailed model of the working of the system.

These very questions suggest that one obvious and important nexus is the limited group of persons who are influential in making decisions, and who, in a decision-making hierarchy, are located at a high level. Within the agonistic framework set out by Marx, these individuals are conceived of as manipulating resources, symbols and people in such a way as to strengthen their own position within their society with respect to other classes or social groups. This is clearly a legitimate framework of analysis: to examine their control of communications, and hence of interactions, in essentially self-interested terms. But it does not complete the analysis; even if

Fig. 1.14. The investment of resources in the media of internal communication: the great Ziggurat of Ur in southern Mesopotamia, photographed during excavation.

they were acting purely altruistically, they would remain the decision-making group. It is relevant to explore how the actions, including the symbolic actions of other peer polities, impinge upon them and how their own actions come to be known and perceived by the members of other polities. The distinct and related question as to how the interactions between the polities are seen and interpreted by others within them who are less centrally placed in the decision-making process, and how their reactions nonetheless affect that process, is also an interesting one. Nor is this as abstract as it at first sounds: most early state societies invested substantial resources in the media of internal communication (Fig. 1.14), and all the great buildings and large-scale monuments erected within them can be interpreted in this way.

If we are studying peer polity interaction, it is thus of particular importance to consider the circumstances in which individual members of different polities are likely to have met, circumstances where competition and emulation could operate (Fig. 1.15), and where symbolic utterances or displays could have their effect. Obviously this could happen on neutral ground, and one may suggest that the whole phenomenon of pan-polity gatherings is one of special interest (Fig. 1.16). The

pan-Hellenic games and festivals at centres such as Olympia, Isthmia, Nemea, Delphi and Delos (Fig. 1.17) are an excellent example, and no doubt many other early state societies had some kind of framework where members of different polities came into contact. Even warfare can operate in this manner: the way in which war in some New Guinea societies often takes place without serious consequences of territorial loss or gain, and sometimes without great loss of life, emphasises that war can be a channel for communication as much as for destruction. The role of the warrior as a communicator, for instance in heroic societies like those of the Celts, would prove an interesting field of study.

Such questions as these need to be asked. Until we have some clearer idea of the way communications within and between non-literate (and early literate) societies are structured, we shall not properly understand the change and development of their institutions. Yet happily, since those communications were to a large extent effected by means of material symbols, the archaeological record has much to offer about them.

In discussing these differential patterns of communication within and between social groupings, we are, of course,

Fig. 1.15. Investment in communication through games: the Late Classic Maya ball court at Copan, Honduras.

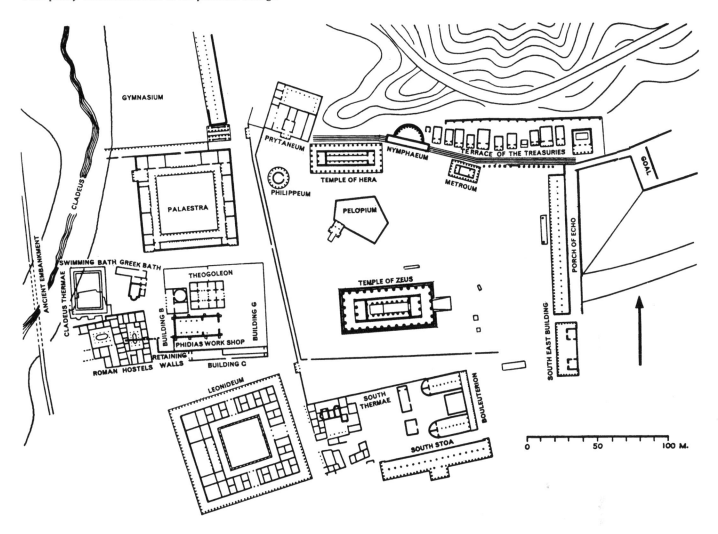

Fig. 1.16. Plan of the great pan-Hellenic sanctuary, dedicated to Zeus, at Olympia, indicating (at the top) the treasuries dedicated by the individual city states whose athletes regularly competed and won there (after Mallwitz).

Fig. 1.17. Reconstructed elevations of three of the treasuries at the pan-Hellenic sanctuary of Apollo at Delphi, dedicated by the citizens of Cnidus, Massalia and Siphnos. Siphnos was an independent island state with a population of less than 4,000 people (after Dinsmoor 1950: Fig. 50).

impinging upon a field which has been considered by sociologists. Barnes (1969), for instance, has considered decision-making in terms of a social network approach, utilising graph theory. Network analysis studies (Boissevain and Mitchell 1973) have the merit of applying formal and quantitative techniques to the examination of specific aspects of social groups. Braun (this volume: Ch. 9) and others have advocated a network approach of rather a different sort, which perhaps stands closer to that used by contemporary geographers (e.g. Haggett and Chorley 1969). Simulations of a related kind have indeed been conducted in considering examples of morphogenesis in self-organising systems, such as the development of urban structure (Allen 1982).

In a sense, of course, any pattern of interactions can be regarded or defined as a network, and, as Braun indicates, to do this establishes a useful relationship with work undertaken in other fields. Such an approach is perhaps most effective when the network is a relatively undifferentiated one—when the nodes, for instance, may be visualised as single individuals, or perhaps as small village communities, which stand in a symmetrical relationship one to another. With very simple polities of this kind the network need not be too over-poweringly complicated. But when the polities themselves are more complex, as Braun indicates, with pronounced hierarchical structures within them, the degree of differentiation of activities—or of subsystems of the culture system—is such that the linkages between individuals within the polities can no longer be represented as single edges in a simple network. They become multidimensional, and an appropriate network diagram would need to show several different channels linking each pair of interested individuals. It is precisely with this differentiation in channels of communication, with the different *kinds* of interactions, between individuals and between polities, that we are concerned here. And in my own view the problem for research, to which the peer polity interaction approach is designed to respond, is not so much the examination of the spatial configuration of the interactions, which the network approach is well equipped to undertake, but rather their very nature. Who impresses whom, and how, and what effect does that have upon the future actions of both? That question has already been posed by some workers within the framework of the endogenous approach, and indeed answered in a rather simplistic way by others within the framework of the exogenous approach, where, for instance it has been hypothesised that petty chieftains have used imported manufactured goods to amaze the rural populace and thereby enhance their own status. It becomes a more interesting and complex problem when considered within the context of the emerging symbolic and communication systems which are shared by a number of peer polities.

In each of the papers which follow there is a concern with what I have termed the structural homologies visible between neighbouring and autonomous polities, and in the interactions responsible for them. This emphasis on forms, and on symbolic interactions, distinguishes our approach to some extent from that of Barbara Price (1977), with whose cluster interaction model the present approach has otherwise much in common.

It could be argued that our emphasis on specific structures makes our approach a 'structuralist' one, and in a sense this is so. We are concerned with social and symbolic forms which are specific to human society, and are the product of the specifically human ability to conceptualise. Our very emphasis on structural homologies may to some evoke comparisons with French *structuralisme*. But our work differs fundamentally from that approach in its concern with diachronic processes, with specific development through time. Our observations, like those of all archaeology, are rooted in the material world and this, for all its obvious limitations, gives to them a certain concreteness not always obvious in the discussion of myth and oral tradition.

Our aim, however, is not to ascribe labels, or to define new 'isms', but to ask fruitful questions. These do indeed pertain to human beliefs and human symbolic systems, and to the way human societies have sought to conceive their world in order to shape it more effectively. The framework which we have chosen to adopt allows the same questions to be posed in relation to societies in different parts of the world, and of very differing degrees of complexity. The intention is to develop a cross-cultural approach, with the hope of obtaining general insights.

Acknowledgements
The following are gratefully acknowledged as sources or as copyright holders for the illustrations to this chapter: Fig. 1.3, Copyright, Smithsonian Institution, Washington DC; Figs. 1.4 and 1.15, Peabody Museum, Harvard; Fig. 1.8, Ashmolean Museum, Oxford; Fig. 1.9, National Museum, Athens; Figs. 1.11, 1.12, 1.16 and 1.17, Thames and Hudson, London, and Hirmer Verlag, Munich (from Berve and Gruben 1963); Fig. 1.14, British Museum.

Chapter 2

**Polities and palaces: some problems in
Minoan state formation**
John F. Cherry

Introduction

The model of peer polity interaction sketched by
Renfrew in the preceding chapter stems from an empirical
generalisation that commands widespread support among
archaeologists and anthropologists. In many instances of
state formation (including those of the so-called 'pristine'
states), the initial stages in the process do not involve the rise
of a single, monolithic, socio-political unit in splendid
isolation; on the contrary, the normal pattern suggested by the
archaeological record is one that implies a group of relatively
small-scale entities in synchronic and interdependent
evolution. Frequently, these political units display a strongly
theocratic cast (Webster 1976b), lack the highly structured
control hierarchies typical of nation states and empires
(Flannery 1972; Wright 1977: 220; Johnson 1978), and are
not characterised by mutual relations of dominance and subordination (as emphasised, for instance, by Haas 1982).
Nascent states of this sort often (but not always (cf. Fisher
1985)) occur together within a given region in groups which
exhibit a degree of equivalence in territorial size and central-
place separation, implying comparable population levels,
comparable settlement hierarchies, and comparable conditions
of communication and transport. This aspect of modular
regularity has been reified in Renfrew's (1975: 12–21; 1978a)
term 'early state module' (ESM) and in Prices's (1977) notion
of 'cluster component'; the 'Asiatic States', as defined by
Friedman and Rowlands (1977: 220), involve reference to the
same recurrent pattern. Equally important, however, is the
fact that such early formative states do tend to share a number
of features—political, ideological, linguistic, symbolic, and
material—at a level of specificity which does not find ready
explanation in terms of common descent or environmental
constraint. This appears to be a valid observation even in those
cases where it is possible to document considerable political,
or even military, antagonism among the individual members of
such a cluster of states.

These statements, of course, are so general that they are
somewhat obvious and, indeed, they lurk close to the surface
in much previous writing on state origins. Moreover, just as is
the case with any cross-cultural generalisation, they are open
to falsification in individual cases. Nonetheless, they represent
a body of ideas that has not so far been put to work as a
systematic framework for dealing with certain classes of socio-
political change. In an earlier discussion of the spatial aspects
of small-scale states (Cherry, J.F. 1978: 422–3), I noted:
'When combined with appropriate exchange models, this construct [sc. ESM] can provide some insight into the manner in
which a cultural and ideological *koine* can develop over a wide
region which has not itself yet come under political
unification.' It is precisely the purpose of the peer polity
interaction approach to explore that challenge.

This chapter offers a preliminary, yet fairly detailed
illustration of the framework outlined by Renfrew (this
volume: Ch. 1), together with some of the operational and

theoretical problems it poses, in the case of the emergence of complex societies in the prehistoric Aegean. As the first of the series of temporally and geographically wide-ranging case studies that follows, this region is of special significance, for it was with Greece and the Aegean above all in mind that the ESM and peer polity interaction concepts were originally formulated (Renfrew 1975: Fig. 3; 1977: 115–18; 1982a: 279–89), even though they were envisaged from the outset to be of very much wider applicability.

Odd though it may seem, considering the long history of research into Classical and pre-Classical Greece, this is an area so far largely neglected by archaeologists and anthropologists in most general studies of the formation of complex societies. Several factors have no doubt contributed to this neglect. One is the relatively late appearance of states of any sort in the Aegean, at least by the standards of several other parts of the Old World; the extension of theorising about state origins into contexts other than the handful of earliest 'pristine' states is surprisingly recent (e.g. Claessen and Skalník 1978; 1981). Another factor is the small scale of the Bronze Age polities and later Classical *poleis* of Greece, whose modest populations, limited territorial extent, and lack of highly developed settlement hierarchies create difficulties for the direct application of certain modern archaeological characterisations of state-level societies (e.g. Wright and Johnson 1975). Yet a third factor is that many of the classic causal models of state emergence founder on the hard data from the Aegean (see, for example, the discussion in Renfrew 1982a: 283–6; Cherry 1984: 19–24), a problem considerably exacerbated by empirical ambiguities and variant opinions about the degree to which the Aegean in the formative period of the third millennium BC was influenced by, or even in direct contact with, developed states farther east. If these considerations have led anthropological archaeologists to shy away from the Aegean, then, conversely, the Classical and Art Historical training of the majority of the archaeologists actually working there has generated a disinclination to generalise, a belief in the uniqueness of Greek culture history as the fountainhead of Western civilisation, and even a failure to see the rise of states in this area as a significant problem demanding explanation (Cherry 1983a; 1984).

In this chapter, therefore, the application to the pre-historic Aegean of some of the ideas enshrined in the concept of peer polity interaction is an exploratory attempt to steer a path through some of these obstacles by emphasising some recurrent features in the emergence of socio-political complexity which, at the same time, are not incompatible with the known or inferred facts of the Aegean case. The island of Crete—the main focus of this chapter—offers, moreover, certain advantages as a test case for ideas of this sort. In the first place, it provides the special benefits of all islands as 'laboratories for the study of culture change' (Evans 1973; Cherry 1980): as an isolated, neatly self-defining, bounded unit, it allows—at least in principle—the separation and measurement of the types of internal and external interactions which are crucial to the approach. Secondly, since the

beginning of this century when the Bronze Age palatial centres at Knossos, Phaistos and Mallia first began to be explored, excavations and (more recently) field surveys have been accumulating information. The resultant data base is large and the prehistoric sequence well understood in outline, although it has to be admitted that nearly all this work has been directed to culture history, which requires an explanation rather than providing one (Snodgrass 1985: 5–7). Thirdly, complex societies have arisen more than once in Crete: in the early second millennium BC with the palatial polities of the Minoan (and, later, the Mycenaean) civilisation, and again after the Dark Age of Greece in the form of the many independent, historically attested city states that emerged from about the eighth century BC (this volume: Ch. 3). In searching for causal regularities in the political process, therefore, it ought to be possible to conduct a useful exercise in cross-cultural comparison by considering the effects of similar processes operating under much the same constraints, but at different times (Renfrew and Wagstaff 1982; Cherry 1984: 18–19).

Peer polities in Minoan Crete

This section presents a necessarily terse summary of relevant culture-historical background to the case study that forms the focus for this chapter. It should be understood that, even at this very general synthetic level, many ostensibly factual statements are in practice still the subject of intense archaeological debate within the field.

For the reasons just noted, the initial definition of the region encompassing the polities under consideration poses no difficulty: we are concerned with the island of Crete as a whole, a topographically highly differentiated landmass of some 8,000 sq. km separated by more than 100 km from the nearest mainland. First colonised by man no earlier than the seventh millennium BC according to the available evidence (Cherry 1981), Crete witnessed the florescence of a complex society—Minoan palatial civilisation—for more than 500 years during the second millennium BC (for recent overviews, see Hood 1973; Warren 1975: 67–110; Cadogan 1976; Hiller 1977). At its height during the *New Palace* period (c. 1700–1450 BC), Minoan civilisation encompassed, or at least was very influential upon, a larger area including many islands of the south-central Aegean and the southern Greek mainland (Fig. 2.1), although it is often unclear in individual cases whether this 'Minoanisation' reflects the stimulus of contact, the existence of strong exchange ties, the establishment of colonies or trading enclaves, or even political subjugation (Hägg and Marinatos 1984; Branigan 1981). Far-flung trade relationships, whether direct or (more often) indirect, moved Cretan objects as far as Qatna in the upper Orontes valley of Syria and Abydos or Aswan in Upper Egypt, and gave the Minoans access to materials such as tin, amber, lapis lazuli and ostrich eggshell, which were available only in very distant regions. In its earlier phases of development, however, Minoan civilisation was a very much more restricted, insular phenomenon.

There is general agreement that the foundations of

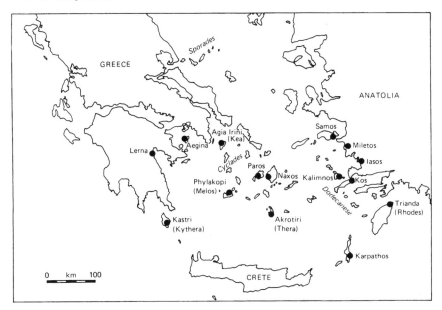

Fig. 2.1. The island of Crete in its south Aegean context. Filled circles indicate some of the most important places with significant quantities of Minoan imports or with other strongly 'Minoanising' features; there is considerable controversy about whether they may have been under Minoan political control during the period of the New Palaces.

palatial Crete lie in the formative (*pre-palatial*) period of the third millennium BC (Branigan 1970), not least because of the high degree of continuity in Minoan material culture (and perhaps also language and ethnicity) from the inception of the Bronze Age until the collapse of the palace system near its end (Warren 1973a). A consensus does not yet exist on whether the development of social complexity there is best characterised as a protracted, progressively developing process, or rather as a swift quantum leap forward (Cherry 1983a), nor on the importance (if any) of contact with pre-existent Near Eastern states (Watrous, in press)—both matters of some relevance to a peer polity approach, as discussed below. What is beyond doubt, however, is that a major change in the scale and nature of socio-political integration on Crete took place in the twentieth century BC (probably c. 1950–1930 BC), a change signalled most visibly by the construction of several political/religious/economic central places, or 'palaces' (Fig. 2.2). This critical moment of transformation, in the Middle Minoan IB ceramic phase, marks the beginning of the

Old Palace period in Crete, c. 1950–1700 BC (Cadogan 1983).

Unfortunately, the palaces at Knossos, Phaistos and Mallia are not yet well understood in their Old Palace phase, since they were totally remodelled and extended two centuries later (the beginning of the neo-palatial phase) following destructions probably caused by earthquakes. At Kato Zakros, in extreme eastern Crete, the excavations of the past two decades, which have uncovered a splendid palace of the neo-palatial period, have not yet indicated decisively whether there existed a proto-palatial predecessor; and the presumed palatial centre beneath the modern town of Khania in western Crete has only recently begun to be explored. The picture is further confused by the existence of sites such as Gournia, where a small provincial town has a central building complex of palatial character, albeit in microcosm. Moreover, as the discovery of Kato Zakros reminds us, it is quite possible— though a possibility that is dwindling as the pace of field surveys increases in Crete—that other palaces still remain to be discovered. Nonetheless, current evidence suggests that, in

Fig. 2.2. Map of Crete, showing places mentioned in the text and hypothetical palatial territories. Palatial centres are indicated by stars within circles, other sites by smaller filled circles.

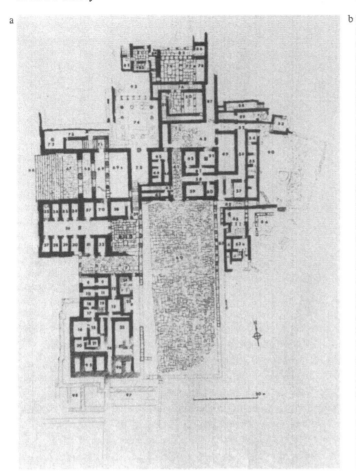
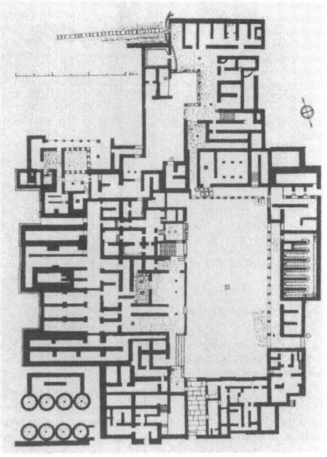
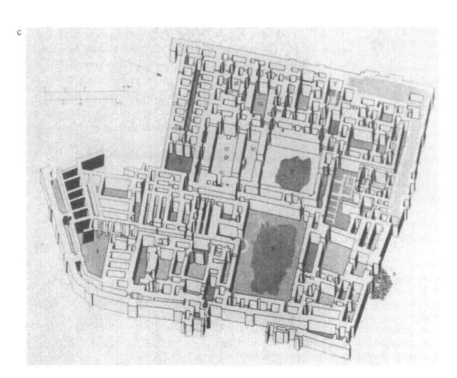

Fig. 2.3. Comparative plans of the palaces at (a) Phaistos, (b) Mallia, and (c) Mari in Syria (reproduced by permission of Princeton University Press).

the New Palace period at least, there existed no more than half a dozen such central places (Graham 1969: Fig. 1; Renfrew 1972: Fig. 14.4; 1975: 14). The average separation between adjacent palaces would thus be c. 35–40 km, with notional territories of the order of c. 1,000–1,500 sq.km (Fig. 2.2), though much land is marginal mountain country. These palatial sites, which appear in most cases to have had large residential settlements or 'towns' surrounding the palace itself, stood–in the New Palace period–at the head of a settlement hierarchy that included country residences (some of which served as second-order administrative centres), non-palatial towns, small-scale rural establishments, and a variety of functionally specific sites, such as ports and locations devoted solely to religious observance. At an earlier stage in the development of the palatial system, however, it seems likely that there existed both fewer palaces and a less structured organisation of regional settlement.

The palaces differ among themselves in a number of detailed respects, including both developmental history and overall layout (Evans 1921–35; Levi 1976; Van Effenterre 1980). Yet there also exist many remarkable points of close similarity or even near-identity (see below) and these demand explanation. At a very general level, the palaces can be regarded as a type of regional centre which has parallels not only within Crete itself, but also in a range of western Asiatic palace–temples or temple–palaces of the later third and second millennia BC as far east as the Tigris–Euphrates area (Graham 1964; Fig. 2.3.). This, however, does not necessarily say anything about origins, since generically similar centres may have evolved in response to the similar organisational demands of elite/ceremonial/redistributive systems in a largely non-urban context. Indeed, Bintliff (1977: Fig. 25) has gone yet further in pointing to a number of interesting close *functional* similarities between the Minoan palaces and certain early medieval monastic complexes in Europe. Whatever the case may be, there are no special difficulties involved in the normal interpretation of the Minoan palaces as multifunctional complexes serving as the highest-order centres integrating economic, political and ritual activity within the regions each of them controlled. As Halstead (1981: 201) put it: 'Apart from their role as elite residences, the "Minoan palaces" seem to have served a multiplicity of functions, combining under one roof the equivalents of Buckingham Palace, Whitehall, Westminster Abbey and, perhaps, even Wembley Stadium.' Yet it is important to bear in mind that the detailed evidence on which such a view rests often represents a conflation of data drawn from more than one stage in the history of the palaces.

Most of the palaces and other important sites in Crete were destroyed violently and/or abandoned c. 1450 BC, in the Late Minoan IB period (probably *not*, as once widely supposed, the direct result of the volcanic eruption of the island of Santorini some 60 km to the north (Doumas 1978)). There ensued a period whose duration is a matter of intense dispute (see Hooker (1977: 70–80) for a summary,

with references), during which the indications are that most or all of the island was under the control of Mycenaeans from the Greek mainland, with Knossos as the chief (perhaps sole) surviving palatial centre (Hallager 1977; Niemeier 1982). Even experts in the field are baffled by the complexities of the data and its political interpretation during this so-called 'post-palatial' period; but it has considerable importance as the time at which the Linear B tablets, in an early form of the Greek language, were written both at Knossos and at various Mycenaean palaces on the mainland (Fig. 2.4), giving unrivalled insight into the organisation of administration in Late Bronze Age Aegean polities (Ventris and Chadwick 1973). It is clear, at any rate, that it is *not* appropriate to think at this stage of a number of independent centres and of interacting polities in Crete, and it is therefore with the situation in the earlier second millennium BC that we are concerned here.

Independent polities?

Before we turn to consider possible forms of interaction that may have relevance for understanding the rise of socio-political complexity in Minoan Crete, it is necessary to deal

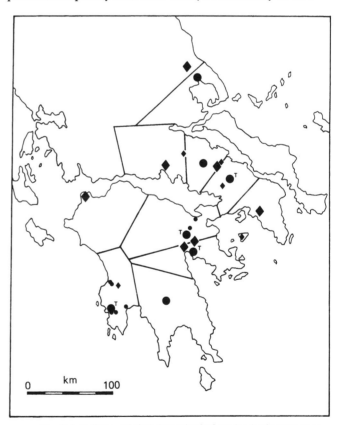

Fig. 2.4. Polities and their hypothetical territories in Mycenaean Greece. Palaces are indicated by large dots, major fortified strongholds by large diamonds; smaller dots and diamonds represent other sites with large, possibly 'palatial' buildings and fortifications, respectively; sites with Linear B tablet archives are denoted by the letter T (after Renfrew 1975: Fig. 3, with additional data from Hope Simpson and Dickinson 1979: 426–7).

squarely with an important operational difficulty. In the preceding discussion, there is a tacit assumption that each of the palatial centres, with its dependent hinterland, was a discrete and fully independent unit, exhibiting the two values most jealously prized by Greek city states of Classical times: political self-determination (autonomy) and economic self-sufficiency (autarky). Is this a sound assumption to make? Some Minoan archaeologists would certainly wish to maintain the opposite: that the island was politically unified from earliest palatial times, with the other palaces attached by relations of dependency to one pre-eminent central place— Knossos. If it is impossible to document whether the palaces were politically equivalent (i.e. true 'peers') or, conversely, were affiliated to, or controlled by, some superordinate centre, then naturally the application of the peer polity approach is bound to be hedged with uncertainties. (Moreover, it may well be the case that the relationship between the Minoan palaces did not remain constant throughout the five or more centuries of their existence, so that it becomes important to be clear about the point(s) during their emergence and subsequent history for which the peer polity approach is claimed to be relevant.)

In the case of fully literate states with historical records, as other chapters in this volume indicate, the problem scarcely arises. Rulers may be named explicitly and their promulgation of law-codes, official decrees, or coinage for their domain often makes its political independence a self-evident matter; state archives or exchanges of diplomatic/commercial letters may likewise refer to territorial boundaries or frontier problems, thus defining the polity in relation to neighbouring, contemporary polities; gravestones may declare the citizenship or political affiliation of the deceased; and so on. Such types of evidence are not available for the Minoan civilisation, despite its literate status. The small corpus of written documents of Old and New Palace date involves scripts (Hieroglyphic and Linear A) which have thus far defied complete and satisfactory decipherment. In any case, their brevity and format, together with many obvious similarities to the Linear B tablets (which *can* be read), make it plain that these are laconic records of purely internal economic matters, holding out little hope of information on inter-polity relations. The Aegean civilisations, before the fourteenth century BC, are thus effectively fully prehistoric.

In the absence of political self-declaration of the sort just noted, it is tempting to infer the existence of discrete political entities from the mute data of artefact distributions and patterns of fall-off in overall similarity of cultural traits (of the sort, for instance, studied by Frankel (1974) in Middle Bronze Age Cyprus). A number of cultural geographers, and some archaeologists too, have investigated the suggestion that political boundaries may act as barriers to interaction and that the edges of polities may thus be reflected in diffusion patterns (Gould 1969; Soja 1971; Hodder 1978). But here also there exist problems. Firstly, much recent work in ethnographically or historically controlled contexts has

shown that the circumstances under which political, ethnic or linguistic boundaries find clear expression in material culture are highly variable and very complex (e.g. Hodder 1977b; 1978: 199—269; 1982a; De Atley and Findlow 1984). Secondly, it is the considerable degree of cultural *homogeneity* throughout Crete (and indeed beyond it), rather than marked regionalism, that is one hallmark of the Minoan civilisation at its height. Thirdly, recourse to cultural distributions carries with it the risk of circularity, by invoking the very similarities cited in a peer polity approach as evidence of interaction, in order to define the interacting units themselves. There is, after all, a paradox involved in the idea (Renfrew, this volume: Ch. 1) that interaction among peer polities accentuates the resemblances already existing among them, yet at the same time enhances their differentiation as competing units. Obviously, what is required is the development of archaeological means for detecting political or social boundaries, territoriality and ethnicity in prehistoric situations (De Atley and Findlow 1984; Green and Perlman 1985), quite independent of the 'intermediate' flows (Renfrew 1975: 18) of goods and information between hypothesised peers; historical case studies necessarily form a critical link in the development of such methods, but insufficient work has yet been done in this area (cf. Sabloff, this volume: Ch. 8).

A more useful approach to the problem is perhaps to be found in considering the closely related question of *Mycenaean* (rather than Minoan) political geography, for here it becomes possible to draw not only on archaeology, but also on the Linear B tablets, on Homer and on later Greek tradition. It is a straightforward matter to plot the obvious highest-order central places of Mycenaean Greece, the palaces and fortified citadels (Hope Simpson and Dickinson 1979; Skoufopoulos 1971); this does not in itself assume that these sites and their territories are either autonomous or equivalent in status. If that assumption *is* allowed, then—with minor adjustments—each central place can be set in a notional territory indicated by Thiessen polygons (Fig. 2.4). Renfrew, who first conducted this exercise (1975: Fig. 3), noted that although this map is certainly an extremely crude approximation of Mycenaean political geography, no doubt distorted by missing data and false assumptions, it nevertheless clearly suggests a landscape of equivalent, relatively small territorial units. The Linear B tablets, disappointingly, seem to say nothing about relations with neighbouring polities. But in one or two cases—notably the territory in Messenia in the southwest Peloponnese controlled from the palace at Pylos—there exist sufficient topographic clues in the tablets to infer the size and extent of an evidently autonomous kingdom (Chadwick 1972; 1976; Cherry 1977), and this harmonises very well indeed with the hypothetical territory indicated for it in Fig. 2.4. It may therefore be the case that the other Mycenaean mainland centres, especially those with archives, controlled equivalent autonomous realms.

Further help is forthcoming from the Homeric 'Catalogue of Ships' in *Iliad* 2, a section of the epic poem that lists the peoples or polities sending contingents to aid the Greek expedition against Troy (Hope Simpson and Lazenby 1970). Despite being set down in writing some centuries after the period to which ostensibly it refers, the 'Catalogue' yields a picture of the Mycenaean kingdoms (Page 1959; Hope Simpson and Lazenby 1970: Map 1) which, with some minor and interpretable exceptions, is strikingly similar, both in scale and relative disposition, to that of Fig. 2.4 (Renfrew 1977: 115–18). Whether this similarity arises from a direct and continuous oral tradition spanning the five or more centuries between the Mycenaean and Homeric worlds, or rather from some underlying processual regularities in the spatial organisation of segmentary, centralised societies in the Greek landscape, it is not possible to pursue here. The important point to emerge from the general conformity of these several sources of information is that it permits a measure of confidence in the main outlines of the political geography described elsewhere in the *Iliad* and *Odyssey* (and with which the 'Catalogue' is not significantly in conflict). Renfrew (1977: 115) characterised this as:

> a patchwork of autonomous small states, governed by independent rulers (often related by kinship or marriage) sharing a common language and customs but united politically only on occasion and in a loose associative way, under the charismatic leadership of the ruler of Mycenae. His authority over the inhabitants of other states and their leaders was valid only while they were associated in a great military expedition, and there is no suggestion that he had any territorial jurisdiction over their own states at home, but simply over their soldiery while on the expedition overseas.

The evidence from the epic, as might be expected, is not always internally consistent with this generalised picture: at one point, for instance, Homer describes Agamemnon (of Mycenae) as 'lord of all Argos and many islands'. But there is certainly no indication of a *single, permanently unified* Mycenaean state, nor yet of the Near Eastern style 'Mycenaean empire' some modern scholars have wished to imagine (cf. discussion in Betancourt 1984).

What, then, of palatial Crete? Is it appropriate to think in terms of a similar regional breakdown of the island into separate principalities? Its central places are as large and impressive as those on the mainland, and their inferred territories of comparable scale. Moreover, just as Homeric and later tradition associated specific rulers with individual sites or kingdoms (Atreus and Agamemnon at Mycenae, Herakles and Diomedes at Tiryns, Akrisios at Argos, Menelaos at Sparta, Nestor at Pylos, Odysseus at Ithaka, etc.), so too in Crete, Minos, Rhadamanthos and Sarpedon are mythical dynastic figures (also, admittedly, brothers) associated with Knossos, Phaistos and (perhaps) Khania or Mallia (Strabo X.4.8; Diodorus Siculus 5.78–9). Are there, then, any convincing arguments *against* the assertion that the major palatial sites enjoyed a significant degree of political independence, even if their élites were perhaps closely linked by ties of kinship or

dynastic intermarriage, as, for instance, with the Aztec or Mayan ruling lineages in Mesoamerica (Adams 1977a: 35–6, 282; Molloy and Rathje 1974)?

Some scholars have written in terms that presuppose that Knossos had control over Crete as a whole, at least at the height of the New Palace period in Late Minoan I. It is worth enumerating briefly the types of evidence that have encouraged this supposition:

1   The lack of city walls or other defensive works protecting rich palaces, together with the existence of undefended luxurious 'country houses' (Hood 1983), has suggested to some (including Thucydides) a *pax Minoica*, possible only with political unification and centralisation; this is all the more striking in an island notorious in later times for its endemic inter-state warfare and separatist rebellions (Llewellyn Smith 1965). While there is a real contrast with the mainland, where the scale and pace of citadel fortification in the later thirteenth century BC might almost allow one to speak in terms of an 'arms race', it should be remembered that there were also major Mycenaean centres (Pylos, Orchomenos, Iolkos) apparently without fortifications.

2   The 'Minoanisation' of a number of islands and coastal settlements in the southern Aegean during palatial times, and especially in Late Minoan I, has been taken to imply colonisation and control from Crete; moreover, numerous Classical writers speak of Minoan naval power and colonial rule of the islands, specifically by Minos from Knossos (Starr 1955; Branigan 1981). This tradition of a Knossian island empire, if its historicity were unquestioned, would constitute useful support for a politically unified Crete. However, the 'thalassocracy of Minos' is a concept first set down in writing many centuries later, partly to make political capital, and there are many obvious distortions and exaggerations (see papers in Hägg and Marinatos 1984). In any case, Minoanisation itself in no way necessarily implies colonisation or any form of political intervention, and either could have involved more than a single palace or polity in Crete.

3   In the neo-palatial period, Knossos grew to become one of the largest settlements in the Late Bronze Age Aegean, with a built-up residential area of perhaps 50 hectares including élite tombs, and residences such as the 'Little Palace', the 'Royal Villa' and the 'Unexplored Mansion'; the palace itself at this stage was almost double the size of that at Mallia and two-and-a-half times that at Phaistos (Cadogan 1976: 50–91; Hood and Smyth 1981; Hood and Taylor 1981). Such a differential might indeed imply a more than purely regional significance for Knossos. Yet Knossos, partly as a function of its exceptionally long settlement history (Evans 1971), was a precociously large site *before* any of the palaces were built (indeed, even in the Neolithic),

when there can be no question of island-wide domination (Whitelaw 1983).

4   The discovery of neo-palatial clay sealings, impressed by the same or very nearly identical seal-stones, at Knossos and at sites scattered throughout central and eastern Crete (Tylissos, Agia Triada, Sklavokampos, Gournia, Kato Zakros: Fig. 2.2), has been regarded as evidence of Knossian bureaucratic activity in the provinces on the part of officials travelling from the centre (Betts 1967). Hood (1983: 132) goes yet further in proposing that such evidence would be unsurprising if a single Cretan ruler owned several palaces, as did pharaohs like Ramesses III or Amenhotep III in Egypt. But, obviously, links between different palaces or country houses in various parts of the island, indicated by sealings or indeed any other artefact type, could as well arise from commercial or gift-exchange relationships between wholly autonomous polities and do not *ipso facto* imply central rule.

5   For much of the palace era, Knossos can reasonably be regarded as pre-eminent in many cultural and artistic areas, such as fine pottery production, wall painting or architecture; this is understandable, given the size of the palace and thus the scale on which it was able to support specialised artisans and provide craft workshops. However, our chronology is insufficiently precise in most cases to be able to say with confidence whether an innovation spread from Knossos to other centres and lower-order sites, or arose simultaneously in different places. It is equally dangerous to take the finds of Knossian fine-ware pottery at other major sites both on Crete (e.g. at Agia Triada, Phaistos, Kommos, Kato Zakros) and on other islands (e.g. Kythera, Kea, Melos, Thera, Rhodes) as an instance of cultural imperialism which implies political domination: not only were transactions in many cases two-way, but styles formerly thought to be exclusively of Knossian production (e.g. the Late Minoan IB Marine Style) are now being shown to have been manufactured at other Minoan centres too (e.g. Niemeier 1979) and even abroad (e.g. Mountjoy *et al.* 1978).

It thus appears that none of these lines of argument, which have mostly been applied to the New Palace period, provides decisive indications that Minoan Crete was politically unified or that one or more large sites dominated other large sites, militarily or politically. One reason why scholars have attached special significance to Knossos is that in the late fifteenth and fourteenth centuries BC, to judge from the toponyms in the Knossian Linear B archives (Wilson 1977), it probably *did* control a large proportion of the island and certainly seems to have been the only site functioning as a true palace at that time (Hallager 1977; Bennet, in prep). This observation, however, must be set in the more general context of the Mycenaean polities discussed above: Mycenaean Crete as a whole, with its central place at Knossos, was merely one member of this larger group of interacting polities. On the mainland, the distribution of written documents correlates with the central places of independent principalities (Fig. 2.4), so that the occurrence of a Linear B archive at Knossos alone goes some way towards confirming that the island was organised as a single political unit at that time. In contrast, the multiplicity of Minoan sites that have produced Linear A documents (Fig. 2. 9b) should imply multiple autonomous centres (although obviously not every site with tablet finds can properly be considered as the administrative centre of an independent kingdom). A similar argument could be deployed with regard to the finds of documents written in the Hieroglyphic script at each of the three Old Palaces (Fig. 2.9a).

At present, therefore, given our very limited inter-pretative controls, the most conservative hypothesis remains that consistently favoured by Renfrew (1972: 366–70; 1975: 14; 1977: 114; 1978b: 419–20; 1982a: 279–89), namely that each palace centre with a written archive functioned within an autonomous polity of the sort also seen on the Greek main-land a little later in Mycenaean times. The suggestion could also be extended to certain smaller-scale Minoanising island polities (Renfrew 1978b; Renfrew and Wagstaff 1982), in which the use of writing may likewise suggest the existence of an institutionalised central authority, albeit of much smaller scale (e.g. Thera, Melos, Kea, Kythera). This, of course, is not to overlook the *caveat* sounded by Wiener (in press):

> Whatever the case regarding central rule in LM I, it is highly unlikely that the relationship between the Minoan palaces remained constant for 500 years. If the palaces were independent at the outset, then differing effects of plague, of drought and of malaria, the accidents of individual longevity affecting rule and succession, rivalry between the palaces, and the consequences of dynastic intermarriage would likely have resulted in shifting alliances and borders and differing degrees of central authority. Palatial rule from MM IB to LM IB must have reflected not only patterns of continuity but also processes of change.

Even were it accepted that at some stage in Minoan civilisation the island as a whole were politically united, it is inherently unlikely that this came about immediately in the Old Palace era, since such a supposition would involve an implausibly massive transformation of the small-scale and relatively non-complex socio-political systems of the Cretan Early Bronze Age.

Inter-polity homologies

The preceding excursus has been necessary to demon-strate, if not the certainty, then at least the likelihood, that close cultural similarities or homologies of the sort to be discussed below did indeed arise and coexist simultaneously in more than one Minoan ESM. This is an important assumption whose validity will be accepted in the argument that follows. Much confusion in understanding the nature of political organisation in Minoan Crete has resulted from an apparent 'problem': that a number of highest-order social units in the island not only form a cultural *koine* or unified civilisation, but have some remarkably specific features in common. For this reason, indeed, most writing about Minoan archaeology is pitched at the level of the civilisation as a whole, rather than of individual polities within it. Yet it is clearly incorrect to suppose that an area of homogeneous culture reflects, or correlates exactly with, some overarching, consolidated political system. It is precisely on the existence of such exact parallels in related, but distinct, socio-political units that the peer polity approach seeks to lay emphasis. This section provides a few examples.

Two preliminary comments are necessary. Firstly, it should be remembered that, for the reasons mentioned earlier, our best evidence comes from the New Palace, rather than the Old Palace, period. In some cases, therefore, it can at present only be inferred that features seen in neo-palatial times (and the types of structures and interaction which they may be taken to imply) also existed, in the same form or to the same degree, at an earlier stage in the history of the palatial systems; this is a problem to which I shall return later.

Secondly, it is noteworthy that while instances of imitation and emulation, competition, and exchange of material goods and information can readily be seen, one class of interchange noted by Renfrew in his introductory statement (this volume: Ch. 1) and discussed more fully by Freidel in the case of the Maya (this volume: Ch. 7) is conspicuous by its absence: warfare. To some extent, the allegedly peace-loving nature of Minoan society can be seen as an instance of modern myth-making (Bintliff 1984), comparable to Rousseau's conception of the 'noble savage' or Gauguin's reaction to the cultures of Polynesia; some understandable reaction to this view has now begun (e.g. Alexiou 1979; Walberg 1983: 151–2). Yet it remains true that the sorts of hostilities between rival warring city states, so characteristic in later Greek history, are hard to see in the Minoan world—no walled cities or fortified citadels with provision for siege warfare, no defensive earthworks or border fortifications, little military equipment or evidence for standing armies, few burials with traumatic injuries, and so on. This contrasts sharply with the militaristic character of the Mycenaean kingdoms. In Crete, one can speak in terms of 'warrior aristocracies' (Renfrew 1972: 390–9; Hood and de Jong 1952) only in the later phase of the Late Bronze Age when the island was under strong Mycenaean influence/ control. The naval power of King Minos, remembered in later tradition, may well have deterred enemies elsewhere in the Aegean, but it cannot account for the lack of *internal* evidence for the military expansionism and exercise of naked force seen in nearly all early states (Claessen and Skalník 1978). It may be suspected that the archaeological record has more to reveal here.

Palatial design and layout

The twentieth century BC saw the appearance, in several

regions of Crete, of complex monumental buildings (i.e. palaces) of closely similar form (Fig. 2.3), the material embodiment of radically new institutional features and major changes in the organisational basis of Minoan society (Graham 1969; Cadogan 1976; Shaw 1973a). Precise parallels exist between them not only in terms of overall conception (as large, multi-storied blocks of rooms ranged around an open, central, porticoed courtyard, with a further courtyard to the west), but also in technical innovations (e.g. the extensive use of large sawn ashlar blocks, downward-tapering columns), in characteristic architectural design features (e.g. pier-and-door partitions, light wells, lustral basins, monumental stairways, major public rooms on upper floors, etc.), and in functional arrangements (e.g. substantial provision for storage, craft workshops, ritual areas along the west side of the central court, archive rooms, etc.). Some of these features can be seen as a response to a mixture of functional requirements which also find expression in other Near Eastern palaces of the second millennium BC (Graham 1964; Hägg and Marinatos, in press), although strenuous efforts have been made—with some success—to find a purely Minoan pre-palatial ancestry for certain elements (e.g. Branigan 1970; Press 1973; Zoes 1982; Warren, in press).

Such similarities in *individual elements* appear all the more impressive when one considers the very considerable differences, from site to site, in the detailed treatment of the *overall designs* of the palaces, which show sprawling structures revolved about the central court in a manner quite distinct from the highly regular plans of many Egyptian and Mesopotamian palaces, such as Tell el Amarna or Mari (Graham 1969: Figs. 148–9). Moreover, recent improvements in knowledge of the form of the first palaces have shown that each developed architecturally in its own locally distinct way, although much is still conjecture. For instance, the earliest monumental construction at Knossos, at the end of MM IA, includes features such as the original outer walls and the deep pits of the north-west area (Pendlebury 1939: 36–7), which, together with earlier features, partially define the size, shape and orientation of the palace in its later form; this includes the central court, itself an Old Palace feature, as also at Phaistos (Levi 1976: Pls. B and C), Mallia (Pelon 1982–3) and Kato Zakros (Platon 1974: 222–6), though in this last case it forms part of a substantial complex aligned quite differently from the later palace. Phaistos has revealed a complex sequence (Fiandra 1961–2), indicating the development during MM IB–II of a central court with blocks of storage and cult rooms in the west wing, which has a most impressive west façade against another paved court; elements such as storage magazines and rooms for cult purposes are early features, better understood here than elsewhere. Mallia is very different again. The earlier palace is poorly understood, although recent excavations have revealed monumental architecture and cult areas beneath the later Quartiers III and IV. Elsewhere at the site there are impressive houses of MM IA–B date, and further to the west there existed separate major 'public' buildings such

as the 'agora', the 'hypostyle crypt' and Quartier Mu—the
latter a large, multi-storied complex of MM II date containing
palatial features such as a paved court, a shrine, lustral basins,
storerooms, craft workshops, and written clay documents. One
has the impression that at Mallia all the functions of a palace
were served from an early stage in scattered blocks of buildings
which were not brought within a unified architectural frame
until rather later. All the palaces, moreover, seem to have
developed as central features in what were already relatively
large and complex settlements (Whitelaw 1983).

Several general points emerge from these data. Each
palace followed its own distinctive developmental course: they
are not repetitions of some formal design copied from (or
imposed by) some single centre on Crete, or derived directly
from Near Eastern prototypes. Given our present coarse
chronological control, monumental architectural expression
of the concept of the palace appears at essentially the same
time in several sites spread widely throughout the island. This
point applies with equal force to individual elements within
that overall concept: the Minoan column, for instance, was
present by MM II at Knossos, Phaistos and Mallia (Warren, in
press: n. 13). Nevertheless, there exists such a multitude of
detailed points of similarity linking the palaces in separate
polities that it becomes very difficult to imagine how such a
circumstance might have arisen, except under conditions of
sustained and intensive interaction between them throughout
the period of their emergence. Such homologies, moreover,
are not only of a generic kind, but extend also to parallels of
an extraordinarily precise nature. Two examples will
illustrate the point.

Casual inspection of the plans of the new palaces shows
that their central courts are in each case of rectangular shape,
with the long axis oriented approximately north—south. This
intriguingly similar orientation has been studied by Marinatos
(1934) and, more recently, by Shaw (1973b), whose careful
measurements show that the three larger palaces are aligned
within 15° of each other and slightly east of true (Polaris)
north (Fig. 2.5). Kato Zakros, a smaller, and for the most
part later, foundation, has a rather more easterly alignment.
These parallels take on added significance, as Shaw (1973b:
48) notes, because the Old Palaces (or fragments of their
plans) have exactly similar orientations, while earlier non-
palatial buildings on the same sites are laid out quite
differently from the later palatial establishments superimposed
on them. The use of such a uniform convention is immediately
reminiscent of the extremely accurate orientation, to the
cardinal points, of the corners or sides of many religious
buildings in Mesopotamia and Egypt, where later texts reveal
the ritual importance of astronomical sightings in laying-out
ceremonies (e.g. Edwards 1961: 254—96). Shaw prefers to see
the east—west, rather than north—south, alignment of the
Minoan palaces as significant and possibly connected with

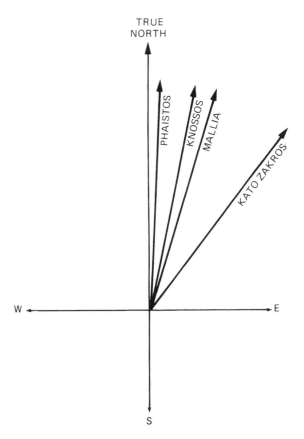

Fig. 2.5. Comparison of the orientations of the central courts of
the palaces at Knossos, Phaistos, Mallia and Kato Zakros (after
Shaw 1973b: Fig. 1).

illumination by the rising sun of the east-facing ritual rooms
along the west side of the central court. There is the further
factor (discussed below) that the palace orientations, certainly
at Knossos and Phaistos (Fig. 2.6), and possibly at the other
palaces and some non-palatial sites, too, are to be associated in
a general way with sacred mountains on the skyline to north
or south (Mt Iuktas, Mt Ida). All these interpretations stress
the role of architectural forms and their placement in space as
an embodiment of a particular world view, of some ideational
system—architectural design, that is, as shared information. A
growing literature on the symmetrical and cosmological
ordering of site plans or site distributions, seen as complex
symbolic systems, provides examples as scattered as the
Maya (Marcus 1973; 1976), the prehistoric pueblos
of the American South-west (Fritz 1978; Lekson 1981), and
early historic Chinese cities (Wheatley 1971). What is
significant in the present context, of course, is the inference
that the same ideational system or belief structure found
simultaneous expression in several discrete Minoan polities,
and from the earliest stage in their existence.

The second example also concerns an aspect of palatial
design and, once again, the evidence relates to all the palaces

Fig. 2.6. View of the central court at the palace of Phaistos looking north to the twin peaks of Mount Ida, immediately below which lies the Kamares Cave (reproduced by permission of Hirmer Verlag).

in both the Old and New Palace periods. Graham (1960; 1969: 222–9) advanced the suggestion that the palaces reflected the use of a foot, valued at 30.36 cm, as the unit of linear measure. His careful measurements of certain symmetrically arranged architectural details (e.g. the exterior west façade at Phaistos in both its Old and New Palace versions) convinced him that both they and many of the longer dimensions of palace layout were regularly planned around a system of proportional whole numbers of 'Minoan feet' (Fig. 2.7). The evidence for the existence of some such latent unit of mensuration appeared to be placed on a firmer basis with the discovery that the principal dimensions of the central court at Kato Zakros (excavated *after* Graham's proposal was first published) could be interpreted as 100 × 40 Minoan feet (Graham 1969: xi-xii). A recent 'quantum-hunting' computer study (Cherry 1983b) has shown that the strictly statistical support for a 30.36 cm foot is weaker than Graham supposed, although there *is* good evidence for some latent unit. Moreover, even if there were no highly accurate unit in use throughout Minoan Crete, but rather some inherently variable standard (for instance one related to a measure taken from

the human body), there remain unambiguous signs of a widespread concern for measured symmetry and pro-portionalities in both minor and major aspects of palatial design from the very beginning in all the palaces. This is not merely 'the archaeological evidence for deliberate action carried out to a preconceived design' (Renfrew 1982b: 21), with all the cognitive implications that carries with it, but a developed symbolic system shared by several polities. Once again, our chronology does not permit a clear view on whether or not such a system did develop in one centre first, from which it was subsequently transmitted to others, perhaps by the process which Renfrew has termed 'symbolic entrainment'; still, one may readily imagine how the prestige and efficiency of the successful development and application of such a system in one palatial polity might facilitate or even sanction its acceptance in others.

The ideology of peak sanctuaries

One of the most striking features of the archaeology of the Old Palace period is the sudden proliferation in MM I of a new class of site: the so-called 'peak-top sanctuary'. These

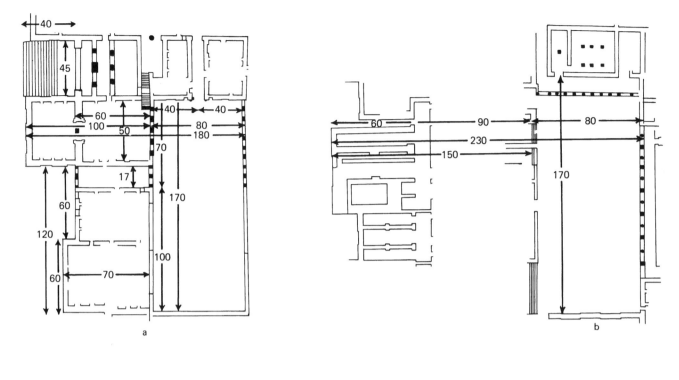

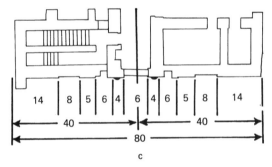

Fig. 2.7. Plans of parts of the palaces of (a) Phaistos and (b) Mallia, showing J.W. Graham's interpretation of their layout in terms of dimensions in round numbers of 'Minoan feet'; (c) shows the detailed proportions of the north façade of the central court at Phaistos (after Graham 1969: Figs. 144, 146, 145).

are ritual areas, located on or near the summits of mountain- or hill-tops with commanding views, in which are regularly found thick layers of greasy ash from sacrificial bonfires, large numbers of whole or fragmentary small-scale votive objects, and—a relatively rare and late feature—the remains of stone-built structures ranging from enclosure walls to elaborate multi-roomed structures (Rutkowski 1972: 152–88; Peatfield 1983; in press). Fieldwork, especially since the 1950s, has produced an island-wide distribution of over fifty certain or probable sanctuaries (Fig. 2.8). Only a small proportion of these has been excavated, but surface material indicates clearly that most were established in MM I, remained in use throughout the MM period, and came to an end soon after the close of the Middle Bronze Age; Late Minoan finds are scarce and mostly of LM I date (Cherry J.F. 1978: 429 and Fig. 1; Peatfield, in press). There is thus a chronological

correspondence between the emergence of state-like polities in Crete and the appearance of a new type of cult site throughout the island (Majewski 1955).

An important aspect of the archaeology of Minoan peak sanctuaries is the close correspondence in the types of objects found at widely separated sites. Clay figurines form by far the commonest class of object, both miniature and large size, whole and fragmentary (with representations of parts of bodies, such as heads, arms and legs). Both humans and animals are represented, the latter including not only the full range of domesticates (especially bovids and ovicaprids), but also tortoises, fish, birds, beetles, lions and other less readily identifiable creatures. Clay or stone vases, particularly cups or miniatures, occur frequently, together with objects such as bronze tools or weapons, whetstones, lamps, small clay balls, altars or offering tables, double axes, horns of consecration,

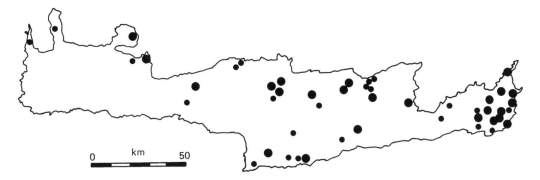

Fig. 2.8. The distribution in Crete of sites claimed to be peak sanctuaries. The larger dots indicate those sites which are definite or very probable (after Peatfield 1983: Fig. 1).

and so on. Statistical analysis of these assemblages indicates that there is as much similarity between sites at opposite ends of the island as there is between nearest neighbours. We are thus dealing with a new, pan-Minoan form of ritual practice at a time when there is no evidence that the island was itself politically unified.

Both Faure (1969) and Rutkowski (1972: 184–5) have suggested that peak sanctuaries originated in eastern Crete, since this region has the highest density of such sites and EM III pottery has been found on some of them. There is a chronological difficulty here, however, in that EM III styles continued in use there well after the introduction and use of pottery in MM I styles elsewhere (Cadogan 1983). Other attempts to push back the history of peak sanctuaries into the pre-palatial period likewise involve stretching the defining criteria to an unacceptable degree (e.g. Branigan 1970; Warren 1973b). At present, it appears safer to regard these sanctuaries as a phenomenon beginning in the MM I period and thus coincident with the emergence of the Old Palace polities.

The argument can be taken a step further, however, for there exists evidence (for the most part, admittedly, of later date) that links the ritual activities seen at peak sanctuaries with the political and economic special interest groups responsible for the palaces themselves. Firstly, most items of cult apparatus found at the peak-top sites correspond closely to those particularly common in the palaces: double axes, horns of consecration, libation and offering tables, portable altars, bull's-head rhyta, etc. Secondly, at least 19 objects from seven sites have been found to bear inscriptions in Linear A, a script which is otherwise represented only at the palaces, at settlements of a strongly palatial character, or at other sorts of ritual location (Fig. 2.9b); in a period of apparently highly restricted, palace-controlled literacy, this is a significant connection. Thirdly, neo-palatial iconographic representations of peak-top ritual occur in the palaces and on clearly élite objects. Examples include the steatite rhyton from Kato Zakros showing a mountain shrine topped with horns of consecration and flanked by mountain goats; a Knossian stone vessel with a relief scene in which a human at a mountain sanctuary makes an offering in a large bowl; a number of precious rings and seals showing a female deity

worshipped by animals or humans on mountain peaks; and, in the miniature frescoes at Akrotiri on Thera, an apparent depiction of worshippers ascending to a Minoan-type mountain shrine (Nilsson 1950: 358–62; Marinatos 1974: Colour Pl. 9).

Elsewhere (Cherry, J.F. 1978: 429–31), I have suggested that this peak–palace nexus reflects a deliberate attempt by the political and economic special interest groups in Minoan polities to consolidate their power by the communal performance of ritual activities revolving around unverifiable sacred propositions. Other writers too (e.g. Bintliff 1977), noting parallels of more recent date in Greek Orthodox religion, have stressed the integrative role of peak sanctuaries and discussed the ways in which common symbols made visible in ritual might serve to unify an increasingly hierarchically organised society. As Wheatley (1971: 315–16), writing of early Chinese history, puts the matter:

> [Kings or a secular élite] . . . were prone to use religious authority not only as a means for consolidating their own social position, but also as a primary instrument for the achievement of autonomous political goals beyond the ethical conceptions of an ascriptively organized society, and for the validation of a concentration of power beyond that sanctioned by the moral order of a folk community . . . Palaces and tombs, and many more besides, are eloquent testimony to the massive concentrations of social and political power commanded by monarchs invoking sacrally sanctioned authority in the pursuit of essentially secular goals.

There can be no doubt, as for instance Coe (1981) and Keatinge (1981) have recently emphasised, that religious sanctions and ideology, in the absence of naked coercive force in early state societies, offered a primary means for the development of political centralisation—what Claessen and Skalník (1978: 615) have termed 'the Functional Principle of Legitimation'. What is important here, however, is that *a number* of centralised polities emerged simultaneously in Minoan Crete, and that they were united by participation in a belief structure existing at a scale *larger than any one of them* (and not obviously emanating from any single religious centre). It is difficult to understand how such a circumstance might have arisen in the absence of sustained and intensive interaction among them.

Writing systems

The development of literacy in early states allowed humans to share and transmit information over space and through time, independent of an oral context. Despite the fact that only a tiny percentage of the population was literate, literacy nonetheless effected radical transformations, since those few who could read and write were primarily responsible for programming the activity of their societies. The relation between state formation and the development of written script is not coincidence: access to large bodies of information strengthens the focal position of central persons, increases their powers of organisational control, and may imbue those who can write with a certain mystical power.

As with other significant technological changes, such as the agricultural or metallurgical 'revolutions', the widespread adoption of an organised and accepted system of writing is often preceded by a significant period of invention, experimentation and development (Renfrew 1978c): such is certainly the case in the Aegean and southern Balkans. A wide variety of incised or impressed marks or signs on third-millennium-BC sealstones, clay sealings, spindle whorls and pottery vessels testifies to the local use of idiosyncratic systems of signification, if not of writing proper (Renfrew 1972: 411−12). Pottery marks have not received the attention they deserve, but the best recent studies (e.g. Bikaki 1984) confirm earlier suggestions that they have a long history leading to an apogee in the Middle Bronze Age, at just the time when true writing was developing in Crete.

In Crete itself, there is considerable evidence (Branigan 1969) for the use of meaningful notations during the protracted pre-palatial period, some of them clearly ancestral to ideograms employed in the more systematic writing systems of the Middle and Late Bronze Age (Branigan 1965). However, the written documents of the Old Palace period are themselves a complex matter, since they are short in length, few in

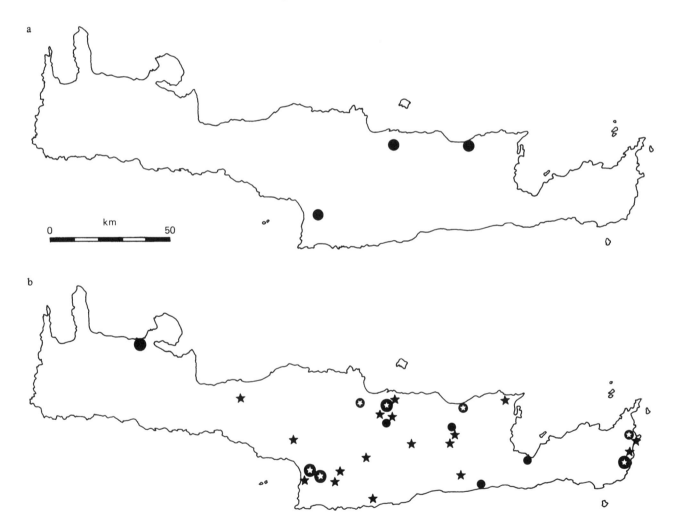

Fig. 2.9. The distribution in Crete of inscriptions in (a) the Hieroglyphic script, and (b) Linear A. In (b), filled circles denote finds of archival material, stars finds of non-archival material, stars within circle finds of both types at a single site; the larger symbols represent sites where major archives have come to light.

number, undeciphered, and evidently represent several systems in simultaneous use. Despite these overwhelming difficulties, it is quite clear that writing was extremely limited in extent (being confined almost entirely to palace contexts) and restricted in its use to three main areas: (i) recording economic data for administrative purposes, (ii) marking commodities with an indication of their origin, nature, destination or ownership, and (iii) brief ritual or religious inscriptions. The confinement of literacy to the palaces and its use as part of a bureaucratic system of palatial economic organisation puts Minoan practice in generic relationship with that of the Near East (Fiandra 1975). But the specific sequence of development in the Minoan polities is worth further attention.

The earliest true script, the Hieroglyphic, is found only at Knossos, Phaistos and Mallia (Fig. 2.9a) and is characterised—as the name implies—by very short texts (Fig. 2.10) employing pictorial signs and a decimal system of numerals inscribed on three- or four-sided seals and their sealings, as well as a few clay tablets and labels (Evans 1909). Notwithstanding its extreme simplicity, it had a long history, beginning early in MM I and continuing in use until MM IIIB (i.e. about half a millennium), although the first group of what might be called texts—the Hieroglyph Deposit from Knossos—is dated towards the end of the Middle Minoan

period, when it is possible to detect a more developed version of the script. As Fig. 2.10 shows, there are some precise parallels in the forms of signs used in each of the palaces. During the period of the script's use, however, there were clearly other systems in operation. The most famous, but also the most puzzling, is the 'Phaistos disc', found in the north part of the palace in a MM IIIB context; its clay, as well as the unique arrangement of 45 different stamped signs arranged in a retrograde spiraliform pattern, indicate that the piece is almost certainly an import, although similar signs, possibly evidence of the same script, have been found on a bronze axe from the Arkalokhori Cave in east-central Crete. Earlier, and more useful, evidence is provided by the huge series of nearly 3,000 clay sealings of MM IB/IIA date from Phaistos (Levi 1958; Fiandra 1968), which reveals a notational system which is not only distinctive and coherent, but whose signs display affinities with the early Hieroglyphic script, with Early Minoan sealstones, and with Linear A itself.

The majority of the Linear A documents (Figs. 2.9b, 2.11) are of New Palace date, but the discovery of early Linear A texts in the ruins of the first palace at Phaistos has pushed back the date of this script's first appearance to MM IIA, or even MM IB. This means that it may be almost as old as

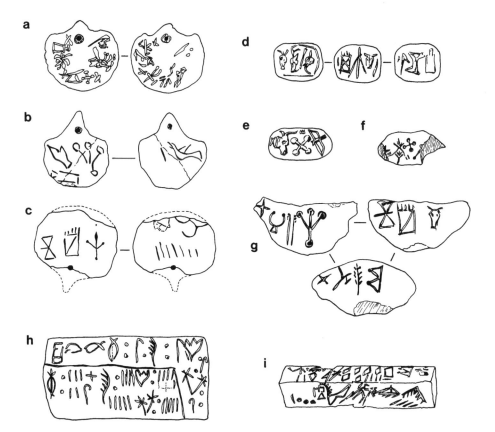

Fig. 2.10. Hieroglyphic inscriptions from proto-palatial Knossos, Phaistos and Mallia: (a)–(c) clay labels or 'roundels'; (d) and (e) sealstones; (f) and (g) clay sealings; (h) clay tablet; (i) clay bar; (a), (f), (g) and (i) are from Knossos; (b)–(e) from Mallia; (h) from Phaistos. Note the close similarity of pictorial signs used on different media and at different sites (after Evans 1921: Fig. 208; Chapoutier 1930; 18, 20; Evans 1909 164; Ventris and Chadwick 1973: Fig. 5).

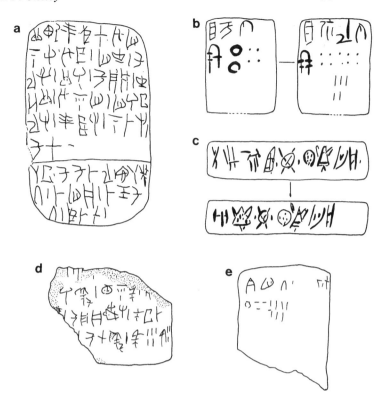

Fig. 2.11. Comparison of Linear A documents from five Minoan sites: (a) Agia Triada, HT 117a; (b) Knossos (Temple Repository), KN 1a–b; (c) Mallia, MA 1a–b; (d) Phaistos, PH 3 1a; (e) Kato Zakros, ZA 1b (after Godart and Oliver 1976).

Hieroglyphic itself and did not develop from it, despite the close resemblance of almost a third of the Linear A sign forms to those occurring in Hieroglyphic; certainly the two systems were in use concurrently. Linear A, however, is more developed, in that it uses a syllabary of c. 85 signs with extensive use of ligatures; it is graphic in character, is read uniformly from left to right, and never appears on sealstones. Texts on clay tablets have now been found at 13 sites (including two outside Crete), with major archives at Agia Triada, Khania, Phaistos and Kato Zakros, and, when other types of inscription are taken into account, the total number of find-spots stands at almost 30 (Fig. 2.9b). What might broadly be described as 'archival' inscriptions (i.e. those on tablets, nodules, roundels, or sealings) occur at all the palaces and at a few second-order sites, such as villas (e.g. Agia Triada, Pyrgos and Tylissos) or towns with quasi-palatial features (e.g. Arkhanes, Gournia, and Palaikastro), indicating the extension of bureaucratic procedures a little way beyond the confines of the palaces themselves. The remaining inscriptions exist on a startlingly wide range of materials: on libation tables, a door-jamb, and spoon-shaped ladles of stone; on a gold ring, silver and gold pins, and a miniature gold axe; on a bowl, a tablet, and several ingots of bronze; on lead weights; incised on pottery vessels and on stucco; and written in cuttlefish ink on the inside of a clay cup. Such non-archival inscriptions are usually very short and occur on objects or in contexts of a ritual nature, such as peak sanctuaries, sacred caves or tombs.

Even from such a sketchy summary of the data, several very significant points become apparent. Firstly, Minoan writing evolved locally, no doubt from pre-palatial notational symbols, under the stimulus of palace emergence and without apparent external models. Secondly, it was in the three palaces in the centre of the island and at essentially the same time that it first arose, only later spreading to embrace a wider range of sites, both geographically and functionally. Thirdly, at least three distinctive systems of writing are more or less simul-taneously attested in the Old Palaces and, as Figs. 2.10 and 2.11 illustrate, instances from different sites reveal striking similarities not merely in the use of individual signs, but in the whole conception of the writing system. Lastly, the evolutionary convergence from early Hieroglyphic, through its more conventionalised 'B' form, to 'proto'-Linear A and, finally, its developed version (which includes elaborate signs, including those for fractional accounting, which may be of Near Eastern type), can be traced at several central places.

In short, if it is accepted that these forms of writing existed in a number of separate polities, then the only plausible inter-pretation of the parallel developments over the course of 500 years or more is—once again—that there occurred sustained interactions between these peer polities, interactions of a sort that led to the mutual adoption of a well-developed (if locally varying) symbolic system. As Renfrew noted in the previous chapter, the existence of a truly effective system of recording in one polity could tend to further the development of similar systems in neighbouring ones.

A related example will serve to emphasise this point.

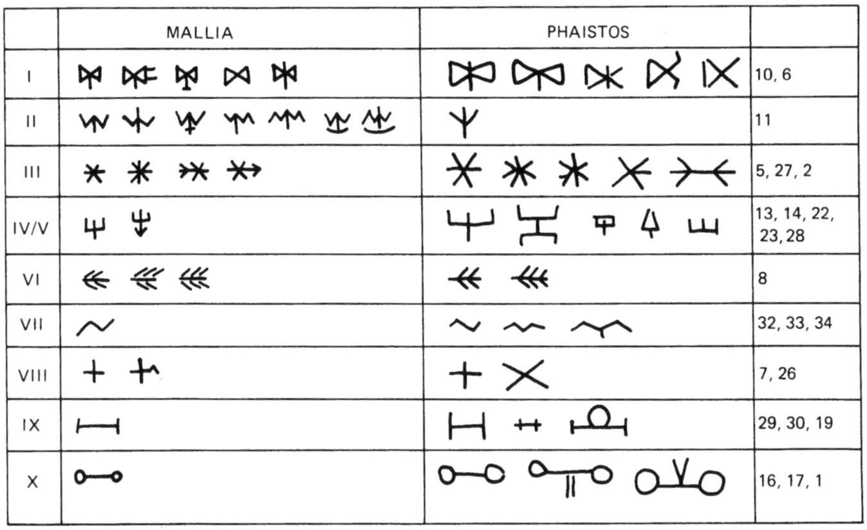

	MALLIA	PHAISTOS	
I	⋈ ⋈ ⋈ ⋈ ⋈	⋈ ⋈ ⋈ ⋈ ⋈	10, 6
II	⋎ ⋎ ⋎ ⋎ ⋎ ⋎ ⋎	⋎	11
III	✳ ✳ ✳ ✳	✳ ✳ ✳ ✳ ✳	5, 27, 2
IV/V	⊔ ⊔	⊔ ⊔ ⊔ ⊿ ⊔	13, 14, 22, 23, 28
VI	≪ ≪ ≪	≪ ≪	8
VII	∿	∼ ∼ ∼	32, 33, 34
VIII	+ +	+ ✕	7, 26
IX	⊢⊣	⊢⊣ ↔ ⊔	29, 30, 19
X	⚬⚬	⚬⚬ ⚬⊤⚬ ⚬⊻⚬	16, 17, 1

Fig. 2.12. Comparison of mason's marks found in the palaces at Mallia and Phaistos (not drawn to scale). The numbers at either side refer to the typologies devised for Mallia by Pelon (1980: 181) and for Phaistos by Pernier (1935: 407–9).

Scattered throughout the four excavated palaces, and also in at least a dozen other sites, are found signs cut into the surfaces of architectural blocks (Fig. 2.12). By analogy with practice in later Classical times, these are known as 'mason's marks', although there is no real evidence that their function was as guides for the placement and orientation of the blocks on which they are cut. In fact their interpretation is problematic (Shaw 1973a: 109–11; Sakellarakis 1967), since for the most part there seems to be no logic governing the frequency and distribution of different symbols on a single block, within a room, or even within an entire palace, and in some cases the marks could not have been visible at all once the building was complete. The marks themselves, of which some 600 are known at Knossos and 300 at Phaistos, are quite simple—star, cross, trident, double axe, branch, thunderbolt and other less easily describable forms—and cannot be considered as writing in the true sense of the word, despite some resemblances to Linear A and B (Ventris and Chadwick 1973: 29). Nonetheless, they have a history equally as long as the writing systems discussed above (MM I–LM I) and a comparable pattern of distribution. For present purposes, therefore, their function (probably religious, but likely to remain enigmatic) is a side issue. The important point is that, despite the greater popularity of some marks at certain sites, or the obvious inconsistencies in their size and shape even within the same site, mason's marks are consistently the same wherever they occur. Thus, it can be asserted confidently that they reflect a system of signification to which *several* polities subscribed, apparently from the very outset of the palatial era.

Elite pottery styles

Many recent archaeological studies serve to illustrate the mutually reinforcing relationship between an increased flow in the exchange of goods and information on the one hand, and structural transformations in the societies involved on the other. New institutions and new organisational features may emerge to foster economic growth of this sort and to cope with its logistic demands. The rise of palatial polities in Middle Minoan Crete offers a striking instance of such intensification, as I emphasised recently (Cherry 1984: 28–9). A significant feature of the early palace societies is their markedly greater scale of 'capital investment', manifested not only in the building of the palaces themselves, but also in aspects such as the support of craft specialists and their associated technologies within the palaces (requiring long-distance resource procurement, workshops, storerooms, and accounting devices to handle the output of mass production). This intensification of production allowed the development of institutionalised forms of exchange involving prestigious objects which, to judge from their occurrence in the Near East, were of interest to distant exchange partners. The peer polity approach, however, seeks to lay emphasis not on the imbalanced relationships of international trade between somewhat unequal partners, but rather on the intermediate-level interactions between clusters of polities *within* a single culture area or civilisation.

An excellent example is afforded by pottery production in the Old Palaces, which has been the subject of recent detailed study (Andreou 1978; Walberg 1976; 1978; 1983). Distinctive, wheel-thrown pottery with polychrome, curvilinear decorative motifs was first discovered in quantity before the turn of the century at the sacred cave called Kamares, just below the horn-like twin peaks of Mt Ida, which are clearly visible from the central court at Phaistos; shortly thereafter, it was realised that this 'Kamares ware' is the quintessential fine ceramic type throughout the Old Palace period (Fig. 2.13). Andreou's careful study of closed pottery deposits from a number of central and east Cretan sites has

Fig. 2.13. Examples of Kamares pottery from various sites in Crete: (a) Kamares Cave, bridge-spouted jar; (b) Knossos, bridge-spouted jar; (c) Phaistos, pithos; (d) Phaistos, beaked jug (photographs courtesy of the Museum of Classical Archaeology, Cambridge University).

elucidated the development of several local traditions, in the context of which Kamares pottery represents the special development of certain features whose origins go back to the (pre-palatial) EM III and MM IA periods. In MM IA (Walberg's pre-Kamares phase), there begins the use of white and red/orange polychromy in a light-on-dark style, experimentation with a peculiar form of relief decoration known as 'barbotine', an increase in curvilinear motifs, and a greater degree of regionalisation of ceramic style. Some MM Ia pottery, or imitations of it, occurs at coastal sites of the eastern Greek mainland—virtually the first Minoan material discovered abroad.

It is in MM IB, however, contemporary with the establishment of the first certain palaces, that decisive developments took place. Of these, the most significant is the introduction, after more than four millennia of hand-made pottery, of the fast wheel, allowing the creation of sophisticated shapes, standardisation and mass production. Marginally later, in the early eighteenth century BC, comes the development of 'eggshell' Kamares, a ware with walls so thin that it was probably mould- rather than wheel-made, perhaps in imitation of precious metal vessels (as other features such as crinkled rims, central bosses, clay 'rivets', and a high black-gloss finish also imply). Polychrome decoration becomes more complex, as also does the syntax of motifs, which include spirals, curves, trefoils, pendents and other stylised plant designs (Walberg 1978). New shapes were introduced, for instance the hemispherical and carinated bowls, the Keftiu cup and the bridge-spouted jar, which retained their popularity throughout the remainder of the Minoan civilisation. In short, ceramics became a major art form, attaining a level of technical and artistic excellence scarcely equalled at any later stage in the Aegean Bronze Age. Such may also have been the opinion at the time, for finest-quality Kamares ware pottery is found from the MM IB period as imports at a number of sites in the Cyclades, the Dodecanese, coastal western Anatolia, Cyprus, the Levant and Egypt (Kemp and Merrillees 1980): 'it was the finest pottery of its time in the whole East Mediterranean' (Cadogan 1976: 31).

It was also an exclusively élite style, extremely rare in Crete outside the palaces, except in certain cult contexts such as the Kamares Cave itself. As Walberg (1976: 126) notes:

> The Kamares style is a sophisticated palatial style and could only have been produced in the social surroundings of the palaces. Their organisation and economy could give the potters and painters opportunities of specialising and experimenting and relieved them of the need to devote themselves to dull mass production.

Indeed, she remarks (1976: 21) that there are far more individual variations of shape and decoration than in other classes of pottery, so that it is practically impossible to find two exactly identical specimens. Furthermore, although few scientific provenance analyses have been carried out and other ceramic production centres of 'palatial' character may have existed, it seems quite clear on present evidence that true Kamares pottery was an exclusive product of workshops at Knossos and Phaistos. Very significantly, neither site can be regarded as the originator of the style: it emerged with the palaces themselves *in more than one polity*.

Identifiable exports of Knossian/Phaistian Kamares ware, other than those found abroad (as noted above), are extremely rare, occurring at present on no more than a handful of sites (Walberg 1983: 90, 96, 112, 130–1). On the other hand, provincial Minoan sites, particularly in south and east Crete, yield plentiful imitations of Kamares pottery, although this influence is mostly apparent in specific motifs (e.g. at Mallia, radiating and whirling patterns, antithetic J-spirals (Walberg 1983: 68)) or in details of shape and design, and it does not change the character of the various local styles. This is a point of great interest in itself. In MM IIA/B, there is a strong contrast between the uniformity of Classical Kamares pottery from Knossos and Phaistos and the regional heterogeneity of close provincial imitations of it, from Khania in the west to Palaikastro in the east. This applies even to another of the palaces, Mallia, where pottery from MM II Quartier Mu

> is similar to Classical Kamares pottery from Knossos and Phaistos, but has at the same time a clearly different character. The style could only have been created in a workshop where the Kamares style from Knossos and Phaistos was known. It is, however, not merely an imitation, but an independent creation, which has to be analysed and distinguished from Kamares' (Walberg 1983: 2).

At Kato Zakros, in the extreme east, it is apparently not until a late stage (MM IIIB) that there occurs pottery in styles recalling Kamares. Indeed, Walberg (1983: 151) comments that there is a marked progression from considerable regional differentiation of pottery styles in MM I to great stylistic uniformity at the end of the Middle Minoan period, as purely provincial production came increasingly under the influence of Kamares-inspired shapes, motifs and decorative syntax; by MM III, it is 'not necessary to distinguish between palatial and provincial pottery' (*ibid*).

These data are complex and not yet fully worked out, but several important conclusions emerge. At the time of the construction of the palaces at Knossos and Phaistos, a distinct palatial pottery style was developed, drawing extensively on existing features traceable back to the Early Minoan period, but exploiting the opportunities for experimentation possible in palace workshops and exploring new technological devices such as the fast wheel, polychromy, moulding and relief. That Kamares ware was a truly élite style is indicated in several ways: by the restriction of its production to palace workshops, by its relationships to precious metal vessels (known to have had significance as prestige gifts and items of standardised value in Near Eastern societies), by its very limited distribution at other Minoan sites, and by its widespread occurrence as luxury exchange items abroad. The style was one to be emulated: elements of it were rapidly copied in other production

centres, including palatial ones, so that by the end of the Old
Palaces the saturating inspiration of Kamares had largely broken
down the regional distinctions visible in the pottery of two or
three centuries earlier, a change which resulted in the stylistic
koine we think of as so characteristic of the Minoan civilisation. Much the same pattern, incidentally, can be observed at
later stages of Aegean culture history, for instance with the
LM IB Marine Style or the LM II Palace Style. And by the
developed Mycenaean Age (Late Helladic IIIA/B), similar
processes of stylistic interaction between independent polities
spread over a far wider geographical range led to a quite extraordinary uniformity in pottery production from southern Italy
to the Levant (even when allowance is made for regional
variability in the relative popularity of shapes and decorative
motifs).

External interactions and the Near Eastern connection

The main thrust of this paper so far has been to present
detailed arguments in support of two main propositions. The
first is that there coexisted in Minoan Crete—probably during
the Old Palace, and possibly also in the New Palace period—a
number of regional political units of the sort Renfrew has
termed 'early state modules'. These seem to have emerged at
approximately the same time and to reflect closely comparable
organisational systems (although the detailed trajectories of
local political development in each case may well have been
rather different, as contrasts in the patterns and rates of
development of the palatial centres themselves perhaps
imply). As we lack good evidence for the existence of any
overarching political control or for relations of dominance and
subordination among these regional units, it is appropriate to
examine them as 'peer polities'. The second proposition is
that they were bound together and developed in a nexus
of mutual interaction, since they exhibit a number of
extremely specific homologous features in areas as diverse as
architectural design, mensuration, writing and other notational
devices, ceramic style, and ritual systems. This list by no
means exhausts the cases where an analysis in these terms
would be possible: the manufacture of sealstones, fine stone
vases, or human and animal figurines; craftsmanship in
materials such as ivory, faience and metal; the use of a
common system of weight measurement; mortuary practice
(and especially the development and spread of the chamber
tomb); domestic architecture; the regional structure and
hierarchical organisation of settlement systems; details of
bureaucratic procedure; many aspects of religious ideology
and the material provision for ritual practice, both in palatial
and non-palatial contexts—these are just some of the further
instances in which it is possible to document striking com-
parabilities at a scale greater than the individual polity. The
examples discussed in the previous section have been chosen
as particularly clear-cut cases, where the homologies in
question can, for the most part, be referred to the earliest
stages in the history of palatial culture and where no individual
polity can be singled out as the originator.

Taken together, these two propositions provide strong
empirical support for the sorts of process argued, at a
theoretical level, by Renfrew in the preceding chapter. If it can
be accepted that several autonomous polities existed in
Minoan Crete, then the shared elements among them, at various levels of specificity, scarcely allow their development in
splendid isolation as a realistic idea. It has to be supposed that
their nature—indeed, their very emergence—was conditioned
by intermediate-scale symbolic interchanges and by flows of
information between them, even though evidence for the
inter-regional movement of material commodities among
polities is thin on the ground. As Renfrew (this volume: Ch. 1)
has emphasised, the appropriate locus of analysis and
explanation is the cultural emulation and political competition
taking place beyond the polity level within the larger unit
comprising loosely related yet politically independent
interacting groups.

The sceptical reader may well see this as unsurprising.
After all, has not most previous analysis been conducted at
the level of Minoan civilisation *as a whole*? And who has
seriously sought to maintain that different parts of Crete
controlled from palatial centres were *not* in sustained contact
and that such contacts helped determine the overall nature
of Minoan culture? These are perfectly valid points, of course.
Much of the literature on Minoan archaeology, however,
readily assumes that Crete was ethnically, linguistically and,
to a large extent, culturally differentiated from its
neighbours for centuries or millennia before the palatial
era; it therefore often tries to interpret palatial civilisation
itself as governed by these pre-existing ethnic and linguistic
affiliations, seeing it as the product of distinctively Minoan
ways of doing things or of 'the Minoan genius'. The present
approach reverses the analysis by seeking to identify some
specific, archaeologically visible processes of interaction,
within the area of Minoan civilisation, which could have
generated such a homogeneous culture and fostered an
ethnicity which transcended political divisions. In other
words, it lays emphasis not on some quasi-psychological
appeal to the *uniqueness* of the Minoan personality, but
rather on a specific class of interactions *generalisable to
other comparable contexts*.

To this our sceptic might respond that it is merely
an assumption that the structural homologies and
organisational transformations in question resulted from
interaction between polities within Crete: why could they
not be the outcome of repeated and analogous responses to
a single outside stimulus? Specifically, what about the
influence of the Near East? Renfrew has already
commented, in the previous chapter, on the general weaknesses of both purely endogenous and purely exogenous
models of change. There is no need to dwell here on the
problems associated with the former—that is, with an
interaction model at the scale of the isolated, individual
polity, emphasising microecological diversity and focusing on
transformations brought about by interchanges between a

central place and its hinterland and by the dynamics of feed-backs within the system (Renfrew 1972). Such voluntaristic benefit models have received much critical comment, both in an Aegean context (Renfrew and Wagstaff 1982: 279–89; Cherry 1984) and more widely (e.g. Gilman 1981), and seem unlikely to be able to explain the sorts of phenomena we have in view here at the multi-polity level. External contacts, however, merit closer consideration, since they have formed such an important component in accounts of the rise of palatial civilisation on Crete for most of this century. Does the adoption of a peer polity approach entail denying the importance, or even the existence, of any stimulus from abroad on local Cretan political intensification?

So far as connections between Crete and the rest of the Aegean in the later Early Bronze Age and the Old Palace period are concerned, the situation depicted by Renfrew in *The Emergence of Civilisation* (1972: 89, 94, 449–60) has not been much modified by subsequent discoveries and analysis (see Rutter and Zerner (1984) and Stucynski (1982) for more recent listings). Significant quantities of Minoan material (mostly pottery) outside Crete begin to be found from the MM IB period, although the pervasive Minoanisation of the south Aegean, reflecting the cultural dominance of palatial societies, is largely a New Palace phenomenon; only relatively slight amounts of MM IA pottery have turned up, at sites on the east Greek mainland and in the east Aegean islands. For the third millennium BC, the evidence is much more exiguous and does not indicate any sustained strong influence on Crete from any other part of the Aegean. Cretan interaction with the Greek mainland in pre-palatial times, for instance, is documented at present merely by three sealstones and a few fragments of painted pottery, themselves quite possibly exchanged via intermediaries in the Cycladic islands. Not surprisingly, it is with the culture area closest to hand, namely the Cyclades, that the closest links seem to have existed: Cretan imitations or imports of Grotta-Pelos bottles (Renfrew 1972: Pl. 5) take the relationship as far as the Early Bronze I period, while later in the third millennium BC the quantity of finds of Cycladic character at sites on the north coast of central and eastern Crete has even led some scholars to propose the presence of Cycladic settlers on the island. Such evidence, however, must be considered in the larger con-text of the Aegean-wide interactions in the mid-third millen-nium BC, reflecting what Renfrew (1972: 454 and Fig. 20.5 (cf. this volume: Fig. 1.13)) has termed the 'international spirit' of the time. The complex web of short-haul sea-routes linking different regions of the Aegean coasts and islands cer-tainly resulted in the vigorous adoption at many small and independent sites of new technologies, materials and styles, with important consequences for economic and socio-political development. This is clearly one aspect of the background to state formation in Crete. Yet no single region—and certainly not Crete—was pre-eminent economically or more complex than the others in institutional terms. Nor is there anything specifically Cycladic in the character of the Old Palaces. And,

most important of all, it is Crete, and Crete alone, among these regions which had earlier been in interaction, that forged ahead in the first centuries of the second millennium. There is, in short, no reason to consider the parallel developments in the early palaces as a common response to the stimulus of external contacts with other parts of the Aegean.

When we turn to the Near East, the picture is rather different and more complicated. On the basis of present evidence, it can be stated flatly that there is no early Bronze Age Minoan material—indeed, no Aegean material at all—from Sumer, the Levant or Egypt, nor have undoubted Near Eastern or Egyptian finds yet come to light in Early Bronze Age contexts in mainland Greece or the islands. Only in Crete are objects of certain or possible Near Eastern manufacture and third millennium BC date found, but these are beset with interpretative and chronological difficulties. They include Pre-dynastic to First Intermediate period Egyptian stone bowls (it is not certain that any of them were imported to Crete at the time of their floruit in Egypt); ivory seals and amulets (some of them have proved to be of bone, antler, or boar's tusk); beads and a bowl of faience (the date of the inception of Minoan faience manufacture is unclear); and exotic stones such as amethyst or Cappadocian obsidian (not necessarily obtained direct from their sources). Quantitatively, this material is slight. Moreover, much of it comes from contexts either chronologically confused or still receiving deposits of materials well into the Old Palace period.

Even if we ignore these difficulties, it remains the case that the evidence for Minoan interaction with the Near East *before* the Old Palaces came into existence is minimal. Branigan (1973), in a striking revision of his earlier (1970) views, has argued convincingly that there were *no* definite contacts between Early Minoan Crete and Old Kingdom Egypt. Some links between Crete, Cyprus and coastal Syria are hinted at by the identification of Minoan dagger types from Lapithos and Vounous in Cyprus (Branigan 1968: 61), probable Byblite metalwork in Cyprus and Crete (Branigan 1966), two EM III/MM I vases in Cyprus (Catling and Karageorghis 1960), and an Early Cypriote III vase in an EM III/MM IA context at Knossos (Catling and MacGillivray 1984); but these are merely straws in the wind. For those unfamiliar with the history of Minoan scholarship, it is worth stressing how much current views of the matter—including some which in my view are inflated (e.g. Warren 1981)—differ from the diffusionist ideas of earlier generations, who regarded it as almost self-evident that the rise of palatial civilisation on Crete was attributable to intense foreign influence from Egypt and the Levant during pre-palatial times, and even wrote of Egyptian colonists and Minoan ambassadors in foreign ports (e.g. Evans 1921: 14–20, 75–93, 122–6, 286–300; Xanthoudides 1924: 128–32; Pendlebury 1939; Childe 1957).

On the other hand, enough evidence exists to be reasonably confident about the existence of sustained long-distance exchange in high value/low bulk goods between Crete and the Near East *throughout* the Old Palace period. In the

Near East, the data consist mostly of central Cretan fine palatial pottery exports at such sites as Karmi in Cyprus, Ras Shamra, Qatna, Beirut, Byblos and Hazor in the Levant, and Lisht, Harageh, Kahun, Abydos and Aswan in Egypt (Cadogan 1983: 514). In Crete, there is an increasing flow of exotic imports: a good many scarabs, Egyptian faience, (probably) the first Egyptian stone vases, north African ostrich eggshell, and even objects bearing the name of an Egyptian pharaoh or official. Near Eastern palace archives, such as those at Mari in Syria, begin to make explicit reference to Cretans as participants in this sort of élite exchange network. The result was a growing internationalism of style. For instance, a highly specific vase shape, the 'crinkle-rimmed kantharos' (Fig. 2.14), particularly common in the later Old Palace pottery at Mallia and other east-central Cretan sites (Andreou 1978: 134–63), occurs in both clay and silver (Davis 1979), is imitated in the Minoanising pottery at Harageh and Kahun in Egypt, and appears to be modelled on metal vases of similar shape at Kültepe and other sites in eastern and central Anatolia c. 1850–1750 BC. This example, incidentally, suggests that by this time centres such as Mallia were successfully emulating the example of Knossos and Phaistos in establishing their own imprint in eastern exchange systems. Phaistos itself, moreover, provides evidence of stylistic links pointing in the same direction but in a different medium altogether, to judge from the several seal impressions there which have exact counterparts at Middle Bronze Age Karahöyük (Levi 1969).

For the critical intervening 'formative' period (EM III–MM IA), the data are frustratingly sparse, consisting at present merely of some poorly defined links in metalworking, a single north-central Cretan vase in Cyprus, and half a dozen Egyptian scarabs from central Cretan sites (Cadogan 1983:

513). The political instability of the Levant in the late third millennium BC may have been a factor here. The masted, plank-built sailing ship first appears on Minoan sealstones of just this date, and the motive for its introduction must surely have been a greater interest in overseas contact. Certainly, a *coherent* pattern of interaction with the Near Eastern seaboard in general can only be documented after the first Minoan palaces had come into existence. But, on the whole, it has to be admitted frankly that for Minoan Crete, just as for so many other early instances of state formation, the quantity and chronological resolution of the evidence is simply insufficient to discriminate adequately between external trade as a contributory cause or as a consequence of increased political complexity; to put it very crudely, whether trade follows the flag, or vice versa (Webb 1975).

In a very recent paper, however, Watrous (in press) has rightly cautioned against the deterministic assumption that 'a certain amount and type of material goods in trade is a prerequisite for a flow of ideas' and that a mere quantitative listing of imports/exports can allow an adequate assessment of the significance of interactions between politically distinct regions. This understandable reaction is entirely in harmony with the approach adopted here, in which the emphasis 'is not primarily upon interaction in terms of the exchange of material commodities, but rather in the flow of information of various kinds between polities . . . *and* . . . *the importance of such symbolic exchange even in the absence of trade in material goods'* (Renfrew, this volume: 8; emphasis added). Watrous considers a number of radically new features (including some of those discussed in the previous section of this paper) which he ascribes to EM III–MM IA Cretan society and regards as reflections of the adoption of Near Eastern religious and political institutions. Among them are several

Fig. 2.14. The crinkle-rimmed kantharos in silver from Gournia (Heraklion Museum 201; height 8.1 cm, maximum diameter 10.1 cm; from House Tomb II, Gournia).

wheel-made, specialised new vase shapes imitative of Near Eastern vessels; worship at peak sanctuaries and other details of cult and divine iconography; and many of the distinguishing aspects of palatial complexes, such as their monumentality, the presence of writing, a complex administrative system of sealings, specialised production, etc. Rightly noting that these innovations are not random traits, Watrous argues that they should be understood as elements of a single administrative system 'introduced together into Crete from the Near East as part of the institution of kingship'.

There exist objections of various kinds to this proposal. Several of the features adduced are attested in Crete no earlier than MM IB, at which time we know that the socio-political institutions supported by the apparatus of the palaces had already evolved in two or three Minoan polities. In at least one case—worship and cult sacrifice at peak-top sanctuaries— the Minoan instances are of substantially greater antiquity than those in the Near East, from which they are alleged to have been derived; the existence of Hittite, Canaanite and other Near Eastern cults of mountain gods does not, of itself, constitute a compelling argument. Similarly, the use of seals and sealings reaches back to the Neolithic period in the Aegean and there is nothing specifically Near Eastern about their use in Minoan palace bureaucratic procedures (even if such devices are in fact nearly ubiquitous in palace– temple institutions all the way from the Aegean to the Indus valley). The introduction of the fast potter's wheel is likewise understandable as a common and repeated response to the increased demand for specialised and/or mass-produced ceramics in a centralised, redistributive economy. Too many of Watrous's claims involve the uncritical adoption of the standard diffusionist position that any features known earlier in area A than in area B must therefore have been introduced from A to B. Yet there are also insights here on which we may profitably build.

First of all, it would be both counterintuitive and counterproductive to deny the existence of contact, however indirect and however scanty the tangible material evidence for it, between the urban societies and small royal kingdoms with palace centres in Anatolia, the Levant and the Near East on the one hand, and Crete in the later centuries of the pre-palatial period on the other. With the genesis of the Minoan palaces, however, there was a marked stepping-up of the scope and regularity of such long-distance, directional trade, which probably involved both gift exchanges between élite centres and merchant trade, conducted under treaty, for basic resources such as metals. This was a general development in the Near East at this time (Sherratt n.d.; Cherry 1984: 36), but in the Aegean, Crete alone was involved, at least initially— no doubt partly a function of its obvious advantages as a jumping-off point for voyages from the Aegean which linked up with east Mediterranean coastal routes. Secondly, for all the gaps in the data base, it seems certain that already in EM III–MM IA some Cretan sites, notably those later to develop as palace centres, experienced major growth in settlement extent and population size (Whitelaw 1983: Fig. 72; for Knossos, see Hood and Smyth 1981: 8). As Whitelaw has argued, such demographic concentration (which approaches the lower range for some of the smaller city states of the Classical world) must imply some degree of complexity in societal organisation; it may well be the rise of powerful individuals (or families or lineage groups) that lies behind the appearance at this time of individualising, rather than communal, burials, some of them with clear wealth disparities suggestive of differential status within the community (Cherry 1984: 31). Increasing competition between emergent élites of this sort could well be reflected in the progressive regionali-sation of late pre-palatial culture, and even in site destructions late in EM II (Alexiou 1979).

While these are somewhat speculative suggestions, it nonetheless appears entirely reasonable to think of Minoan society on the threshold of the palatial era as incipiently stratified and also aware, to some extent, of the nature of royal authority and its legitimation in the Near Eastern kingdoms. If this is so, then, as Watrous has suggested, one natural way for Cretan rulers to consolidate their own authority and power-base would be by emulation of certain characteristics of Near Eastern royal institutions. Exchanges of prestige goods between foreign élites can confer higher status at home and lead to further inequalities by way of the development of monopolies over long-distance trade in other classes of commodities; they can also convey information and conceptual constructs of special interest to the limited group of persons at the highest level in a decision-making hierarchy, as Renfrew (1975; this volume: Ch. 1) has emphasised. To assert this, is not to relapse into out-and-out diffusionism of the Childean sort, whereby the Minoan polities are regarded as straightforward instances of secondary state formation resulting from exchange contacts with pre-existing states (Childe 1936: 169–70); nor is it to embrace a macro-regional, core–periphery perspective (e.g. Sherratt n.d.). The important point is not so much that Crete engaged in interactions with altogether different regions, but rather that *several* Minoan polities did so. In this view, exposure to the institutions and apparatus of Near Eastern states did not *cause* the rise of state-level polities in Crete, but it did provide some, at least, of the 'currency' of competition, in which élites in neighbouring Minoan polities sought to secure higher inter-polity status for their own system—a sort of 'symbolic intensification', paralleling (and also encouraging) the more material forms of intensification of production seen in most early states. A specific example may help to illustrate this idea.

As discussed briefly earlier in this chapter, the Minoan palaces were multi-purpose buildings serving many of the same functions as their contemporary or earlier equivalents further east. Not surprisingly, therefore, there are many generalised points of similarity; but attempts to see the Minoan palaces as direct copies of Near Eastern ones have not been successful (Graham 1964) and there are elements which clearly derive from local architectural traditions. In Cretan terms, what principally makes the construction of the palaces such a radical new departure is their very size (far greater than any previous single building or building complex) and their monumentality; these were edifices to impress, expensive gestures on a grand scale. One way in which their monumental character finds expression is in the extensive use of ashlar masonry, especially in elaborate ashlar orthostate façades (Hult 1983: 46–7; Shaw 1973a: 83–92; 1983). Good Old Palace examples survive at Phaistos (Fig. 2.7c; Levi 1976: 5), at Mallia (e.g. van Effenterre 1980: 241–7), and at Chrysolakkos (Shaw 1973c), an elaborate, probably élite, funerary complex a few hundred metres north of the palace at Mallia. Such masonry, often cut with great bronze saws, is highly labour-intensive and would no doubt have been doubly impressive as something quite new on the Aegean scene (Fig. 2.15). But as Hult's (1983) recent comprehensive survey of the evidence has shown, ashlar masonry became widespread in the Levant at this same time; the specific orthostate construction technique seen at Mallia finds precise parallel in the Middle Bronze I palace and city at Ebla in Syria, as also in palaces of Middle Bronze Age date at Alalakh, Tilmen Hüyük and Ras Shamra, so the technique may have been developed in that country (Hult 1983: 66–70). While there is nothing inherently Near Eastern about monumental architecture, at least one technical device (namely, ashlar masonry) for building this way in Crete seems certainly to have been in imitation of Near Eastern prototypes, carrying with it, one supposes, some of their symbolic over-tones. The point at issue is that not just one, but *all* the

Fig. 2.15. An example of the Minoan ashlar orthostate building technique: the façade flanking the Minoan road at Kommos, looking south-east; probably Late Minoan I (Shaw 1983; Fig. 2; photograph reproduced by permission of Professor J.W. Shaw).

palaces followed suit: indeed, ashlar masonry rapidly became a common feature in Minoan Crete, but one reserved for more important buildings (primarily palaces, but also luxurious residences, some sanctuaries, and a few tombs). Renfrew has commented that if status is achieved, for instance, by erecting a particular sort of grand building, then there must exist some scale for measuring its grandeur, one to which all subscribe; the competitive temple-building of Archaic Greece, discussed by Snodgrass in Chapter 3, offers a striking instance.

What this example serves to illustrate is the considerable care that is called for in interpreting the impact of contacts between developed states and a group of peer polities at the time of their emergence or early development. The material evidence of such contact can indeed be a primary feature of the archaeological record at the time in question (see, for example, the exotic finds from the Mediterranean world in late Hallstatt and early La Tène Europe (discussed by the Champions in Chapter 4)). But it is inadequate either to assume, on the one hand, that the transmission of information and commodities in this way directly 'caused' change, or, on the other, simply to assert that the importance of such external contacts was minimal in comparison to inter-polity processes themselves. Both, of course, are quite legitimate ideas, but they require careful specification as hypotheses which carry with them testable implications for the archaeological record, and this the peer polity approach seeks to do. My own reading of the Minoan case suggests that the Near Eastern exemplars emulated by different Minoan polities provided a *medium* for competitive display and self-aggrandisement, yet they were not the *cause* either of such competition or of the rise of the competing political entities themselves. Whatever the circumstances that led objects to be exchanged, traits to be borrowed, or technologies and even institutions to be adopted, the focus must remain firmly on their roles within internal processes—internal, that is to say, to the group of polities, rather than to any individual member. In this sense, it could prove to be the case that the peer polity approach is better suited for explaining why the institutions and symbolic structures of the Minoan polities took the forms they did and why they look so strikingly similar from one polity to the next, rather than for giving an account of why they came into being at all.

Further problems

In this final section I wish briefly to discuss three theoretical or operational issues raised by the Aegean case considered in the present chapter.

(1) The first of these is a matter posed squarely by Renfrew in the preceding chapter. Asserting that our aim is the explanation of changes over time in the degree of complexity in organisational aspects of society, he asked (this volume: 5): 'To what extent were these peer polity interactions an indispensable and necessary element in the emergence of such systems, whatever their specific form?' Likewise, we can ask here in what way the peer polity approach helps explain

the rise of palatial civilisation on Crete and, if it does not, whether this seriously reduces the validity and usefulness of the approach. Renfrew demands as necessary conditions for a successful *causal* peer polity explanation (i) that a number of autonomous highest-order polities can be recognised within a defined area; (ii) that there is evidence of contact between them (whether movements of goods or flows of information) *prior* to the change in question; and (iii) that there can be specified some mechanism which relates such interactions to the observed changes.

As the discussion earlier in this paper has indicated, it is certainly possible to define a number of putative highest-order polities within Crete, although to demonstrate that they were wholly autonomous, particularly later in their history, is very much more difficult. These, however, are the ESMs or polities which existed *after* the process of state emergence in Crete and, indeed, which help to define that process. So where and what were the political entities whose interactions are asserted to have helped generate the palatial organisations themselves? Here we encounter severe difficulties because our understanding of the society of pre-palatial Crete in the late third millennium BC is so poor. Yet it is scarcely possible to speak of large central places dominating entire regions, even allowing for the enigmatic large EM II buildings at Palaikastro (Branigan 1970: Fig. 6), Agia Triada (Laviosa 1973) and Knossos (Evans 1972). On the contrary, all the evidence points to the extended family as the likely maximal social unit, living in many small communities of a few dozen (or at most a few hundred) individuals, and burying their dead in communal tombs without marking obvious status distinctions (Whitelaw 1983). Nor are there signs of the actions of central persons, for instance in regulating and administering the institution-alised circulation of foodstuffs or other commodities on an intra- or inter-regional basis. Naturally, such small residential groups are likely to have been in communication with each other, at least on a local basis; indeed, widespread cor-respondences in features such as metallurgical techniques or mortuary practices, as well as actual instances of exchange in commodities such as ceramics, assure us that this was the case. One could argue, with Renfrew, that the village is in this case the highest-order socio-political unit in the region in question. But generalised patterns of interaction between such units existed throughout the one-and-a-half millennia of the Cretan Early Bronze Age and even earlier during the Neolithic period. Why then was it only in the two or three centuries immediately preceding palace emergence that there begin to be seen the first signs of incipient stratification and regional differentiation (Cherry 1983a)? What mechanisms link the development of complexity with the existence of local contacts of the sort to be seen in almost any early agricultural society? And how can we account for other 'null cases' (Cherry 1984: 21) in the Aegean—that is, the *failure* of other regions with highly developed networks of interaction among similar village farming communities (e.g. Halstead 1985, for Thessaly) to follow the Cretan path of increasing socio-

political elaboration? To base the argument on interactions among small-scale autonomous villages is not, it seems, a promising line of attack.

In his book, *The Emergence of Civilisation* (1972), Renfrew proposed the argument in a rather different form when he stressed the interactions that took place within the Aegean at large during the formative period of the middle third millennium BC and indicated, using a systems frame-work, how positive feedbacks would lead to growth. In this view, the interacting polities that provide the explanatory focus would be cultural regions, i.e. much larger entities, defined primarily by the distribution of specific material features, but whose socio-political coherence is debatable (as, for instance, in the cases studies of Braun, Bradley and Chapman, and Shennan in this volume). But again there are difficulties. One is that the types of object used to define this so-called 'international spirit' (Fig. 1.13) are either very generalised (e.g. one-handled cups) or tend to be artefacts more at home in the Cyclades (e.g. marble folded-arm figurines, 'frying pans', chlorite schist vases, bronze tweezers, etc.) than in any of the other regions. Another is that, in purely quantitative terms, Crete's participation in this inter-regional network seems slight and restricted to imports found at a few sites on or near the north coast, from the immediately adjacent Cycladic islands. Lastly, if each of the several regions of the Aegean is regarded as having developed *pari passu* as a result of such interaction, then the 'null case' problem arises again: Crete alone advanced rapidly to state-hood at the beginning of the second millennium. One is forced to assume either that similar processes led to different end results, or that special factors operated in the case of Minoan Crete.

It thus appears extraordinarily difficult to detect either in Crete or the Aegean during the pre-palatial period a group of polities and a set of circumstances that meets Renfrew's necessary conditions for a non-circular explanation in peer polity terms. This may, of course, simply be a function of the inadequacy of the archaeological record, or of our present knowledge of it. Nor does it imply that more satisfactory causal applications of the approach are not possible in other cases, as papers elsewhere in this volume perhaps suggest. It may be, nonetheless, that the chief insights provided by this framework relate to the understanding of the mutual dynamics of clusters of early states *already in existence*, rather than of state formation in general. Here it certainly has considerable explanatory power, as the instance of Minoan Crete illustrates rather well: it not only accounts for the existence of structural homologies and symbolic convergence, but also provides a model for the further political growth of the system. Once the balloon (i.e. a state system of organisation) is launched, as it were, the processes of peer polity interaction do not simply help keep it aloft, but actively encourage its further inflation and elevation. Indeed, those who posit the existence of independent states in Old Palace Crete and their unification as a nation state under

Knossos in neo-palatial times (e.g. Hood 1983: 131–2)–a perfectly reasonable, if unproven, scenario with plentiful parallels in other ESM clusters–might gain much from considering the steps in this process in terms of peer polity interaction.

(2) The institutional changes for which explanation is sought in the case of Crete and the Aegean in the later third and early second millennia BC constitute a specific instance of the general problem of state formation. In any such case there is the need to provide a satisfactory account of the processes whereby the natural fissioning tendencies of small-scale political units came to be overridden by fusion and integration within larger institutional structures, despite the obvious inequalities of access to power and resources that this inevitably entails. Naturally enough, therefore, most state formation studies concentrate on the attempt to isolate one or more new or altered factors or conditions that have changed the structure of the system, or shifted the balance of power between competing components or groups. (This, it need scarcely be emphasised, is not to suggest that we should revert to a search for some mystical prime mover to explain all instances of state formation, nor indeed to insist on exogenous origins for all change in socio-cultural systems.) At an even more general level, there is the problem not merely of why states evolved at all, but why states or state-like forms of institutionalised central government evolved in so many parts of the world within such a relatively short period.

In Minoan Crete, this last problem is especially acute since major organisational change seems to have occurred there quite rapidly, following several millennia of relative stability under non-state modes of organisation. The pace of change is perhaps partly a matter of perspective (compare Cherry 1983a and 1984 with Warren, in press). We are dealing, certainly, with change over several centuries either side of c. 2000 BC, a sufficiently long period perhaps for political consolidation and the rise of powerful élites not to be patently obvious to any single generation (though the implications of a material action such as the building of a palace must have been clear enough). Nevertheless, these three or four critical centuries represent a ferment of change when we set them beside the four or five millennia during which settled agricultural communities had existed on the island.

The normal sense of a satisfying explanation in archaeology is that it makes a set of facts in some sense intelligible by demonstrating that they seem 'natural' when viewed from the perspective of a certain framework of thought. In practice, this is often taken to mean that it becomes possible to 'predict', retrospectively, that certain events would occur. This the peer polity approach claims to attempt by proposing a number of testable predictions, as set out very clearly in the section of Renfrew's discussion (this volume: 7–8) entitled 'Using the concept'. Yet very often an explanation of this sort will simply take the form of an assertion that–given some specified processes, appropriate initial conditions, and sufficient elapsed time–certain

transformations will take place. It can hardly be denied that such a formulation, if it found adequate empirical support, would constitute a major step forward. It would, however, remain a loose explanation, in the sense that it offers no immediate insight on the questions of *when* and *how fast* such transformations might take place–important aspects, surely, of explanation couched in an historical framework.

The question, then, is whether the concept of peer polity interaction, as an implicitly gradualist approach, can deal adequately with sharp disjunctions in the rate and scale of change. My feeling is that it cannot and that some further theory-building is called for. I would suggest, tentatively, that evolutionary ideas–by which I mean the fundamental concepts of variation and selection in Darwinian terms, rather than teleological, cultural evolutionism–might have some role to play.

The basic problem tackled by the peer polity approach is the causes underlying the widespread evidence of 'selection for' centralised polities (whether in clusters of ESMs or not). Selection in evolutionary theory may stem not only from physical, environmental pressures, but also from competition between or within species, especially in a social species like man for whom social behaviour is an integral component of adaptive strategy. There is thus no conflict between the role of intra-specific competition in evolutionary theory and the emphasis on ranking, domination, power and exploitation seen in most archaeological discussions of change during the past 10,000 years or so (Halstead 1982); moreover, there is much in common with the peer polity interaction framework which, again, is largely about competition. Often, however, archaeologists writing about change under circumstances of competition between individuals or between groups, invoke unjustifiable and untestable additional assumptions about man's inherently acquisitive, ambitious or aggressive nature (the models of systems growth in the Aegean proposed by Renfrew (1972: 479–85) provide a good example). A more appropriate approach would be to treat such characteristics not as *universal,* but as *recurrent,* features of human behaviour, and then to consider the circumstances in which that kind of behaviour might be favoured by selection (Halstead 1982). This would go some way towards strengthening one aspect of the peer polity concept by making concrete the links between the sorts of interaction and competitive behaviour so important to the concept and the types of change they are assumed to have engendered and encouraged. It would have the further function of clarifying the general problem (raised above) of understanding the temporal context of socio-political change by specifying clearly where, in time and space, the selective advantage of such behaviour is likely to be significant. The heuristic value of the approach can only be reduced if it relapses into a general interaction model applicable to *all* times and places.

(3) The final problem is closely related to the previous one, in that it also concerns chronological matters. It will already be apparent from earlier sections in this chapter that

the chronological framework for Crete in the third and early second millennia BC is far from precise. Radiocarbon dates are relatively few in number, are associated with standard deviations of the order of 50 to 100 years either way, and present various problems of interpretation, although they do provide a firm understanding of sequence and relative duration. Dates based on external cross-links, involving stylistic comparanda or exports, are even fewer and shakier as a result of problems of time-lag and contextual disturbance, and usually give only a *terminus*. Consequently, Cadogan (1983: 507), in the latest review of Early and Middle Minoan chronology, felt compelled to warn at the outset: 'I am skeptical of chronologies or, rather, chronologists, who venture beyond half-centuries to suggesting decades . . . To suggest anything else for these early times implies a precision we do not have.' Yet more recently, Snodgrass (1985: 7) rightly pointed out: 'It is surely clear that any kind of "historical" narrative, for a culture in which any of the dates may be even fifty years out, let alone two hundred, in either direction, is an impossibility'.

This degree of chronological imprecision presents a real impediment to the application of the peer polity framework, in the Minoan case, in the detail that is really necessary. The core of the concept, after all is interaction between living individuals or societies. As Renfrew put it (this volume: 18): 'Who impresses whom, and how, and what effect does that have upon the future actions of both?' While resolution to the level of the individual is scarcely ever possible in fully prehistoric contexts, one might at least hope to be able to work with a chronology that allowed the study of the material record of *contemporaneous* social groups in different places (i.e. a single living generation). So loose is the chronology, however, that we must count ourselves fortunate if we can tie down some object or innovation to a century (i.e. three or four generations). It is important to know, for instance, whether the inception of palace construction was a simultaneous event in several polities or, conversely, whether a single polity had clear priority; in the later Greek world (Snodgrass this volume: Ch. 3), emulation in monumental construction often occurred within a generation or even less. A further requirement, moreover, is to obtain greater chronological precision not simply for the culture as a whole, but for its regional manifestations. In Crete, it is becoming increasingly clear, particularly as a result of detailed pottery studies such as those by Walberg (1976; 1983) and Andreou (1978), that there existed significant time-lags between different parts of the island in terms of the rate of diffusion or adoption of ceramic styles. This in itself tells us something about the directions and strengths of the interactions we seek to study. Peer polity interaction, in short, may be an abstract concept, seemingly far removed from the archaeological record itself, but it has the virtue of encouraging detailed factual research stimulated by fresh questions.

Acknowledgements

I am very grateful to Alan Peatfield, Peter Warren, Vance Watrous, and Malcolm Wiener for allowing me to read and make use of articles in advance of publication. Special thanks are due to Sue Alcock for help in collecting data from the literature and for her critical input. The costs of travel to Minneapolis, where the original version of this paper was delivered, were met in part by a grant from the Travelling Expenses Fund of the University of Cambridge.

Chapter 3

Interaction by design: the Greek city state
Anthony Snodgrass

Peer polity interaction, like many concepts recently
under discussion in archaeological circles, is by no means the
exclusive property of archaeology. On the contrary, one
could argue that its best chances of validation will be found in
cases like that dealt with in the present chapter, where it can
be in part documented by historical evidence, which can show
certain stages of the process in more or less unquestioned
operation. Yet the presence of documentary evidence, in this
case at least, no more brings about an immediate dissolution
of the difficulties than does that of material evidence. An
important stage in the history of any state is the stage of its
formation; and one of the problems on which the model of
peer polity interaction could be expected to throw light is
that of the origins of the Greek (or any other) form of
state. But for this epoch in Greek history an abiding
difficulty—which is merely a facet of the general difficulty of
applying modern concepts to past institutions—is that it is
doubtful how far, if at all, contemporary consciousness of the
emergence of a 'state' existed.

This may sound improbable. Could a people be unaware
that, by setting up a central government to which it would
owe certain obligations and from which it would expect
certain benefits, it was taking an important new step? Furthermore, later citizens of these same Greek states were acutely
aware of their distinctive characteristics, and some of their
extensive writings on these matters survive. Yet these same
writers, who offer us a range of confident statements about
the foundation and early history of cults, about early warfare,
oracles or legislation, are reduced to virtual silence on the
question of the emergence of the entity of which they claimed
citizenship. This would appear to suggest that that process had
not made an indelible impact on their ancestors who had lived
through it. Indeed, the very concept corresponding to our
term 'statehood' is not one that is apparent in Greek political
writings, even of the full Classical period.

How much does this matter? Very little, I would argue.
The operations of peer polity interaction are by no means
confined to fully-fledged states. For the sake of accuracy, it
will be better to replace the familiar phrase 'city state', which
I have used in my title, with the Greek term *polis*, denoting in
its strict sense a polity consisting of a settlement and its
territory, politically united with one another, and independent
of other polities. But whether or not we choose to credit the
polities of Classical Greece with 'statehood', with the
specific attributes given to that term in the last few centuries
of modern political thought, the fact remains that they
represented a striking, innovatory and advanced system by the
lights of their own age: if that had not been so, they would
not have had such a profound impact on later Western
thought. As such, they must have emerged at some time, and
the earlier we date the beginning of that process, the more
remarkable we are implying that the phenomenon was. We

return, therefore, to our previous difficulty: the ancient Greek political analysts appear to throw little light on the origins of what they were analysing.

Such evidence as they do offer on the age and ancestry of the Greek *polis* has come to seem, in the light of modern research, extremely difficult to accept. Let us take one of the best-informed and most judicious of them, Thucydides of Athens. True to his aim of tracing events to their causes, he offers by implication (II. 15.2) an explanation of how the political organisation of fifth-century Attica came into being: it was Theseus, he says, who persuaded its people to give up their local political centres and adopt Athens as their centre of government. There is no suggestion that later generations had ever gone back on this act of 'synoecism', so that the origins of the Classical *polis* of the Athenians are thus firmly placed in the Heroic Age. This in turn implies that the decisive step had been taken some 800 years before Thucydides' days, and he shows by references elsewhere that he himself would have endorsed this modern calculation of the interval of time. Nor is this the only passage in Thucydides which carries the implication that the *polis* system was of such great antiquity. In the introduction to Book I he finds it necessary, in order to establish the unique historical importance of the contemporary war whose history he was writing, to give a

searching critique of the accepted view of the greatest conflict of the Heroic Age, the Trojan War. He does this in quantitative and logistic terms; and since the commander of the Greek forces, Agamemnon, was king of Mycenae, this in turn involves him in a comparison between Agamemnon's capital and a contemporary *polis* like Athens (Fig. 3.1). The fifth-century *polis* of Mycenae had become a very small place; yet Thucydides assumes without question that he can use it as a measure of the size and power of Agamemnon's capital, and thus make a fair comparison with contemporary Athens. This suggests that he believed in the essential continuity of the *polis* of Mycenae over a period, once again, of about eight centuries (I. 10.1).

In these same chapters, he discusses the sea-power of Minos of Crete in language completely appropriate to the world of the *polis*, which gives a further hint of the same attitude (I. 4; I. 8.2). Beside Thucydides' account, we can set many more uncritical statements of ancient authors, particularly those in which they retail the foundation legends of Greek cities, usually giving them a setting in the Heroic Age, and never betraying any recognition that important structural changes might have occurred subsequently.

Why is it that modern scholarship has come to reject the

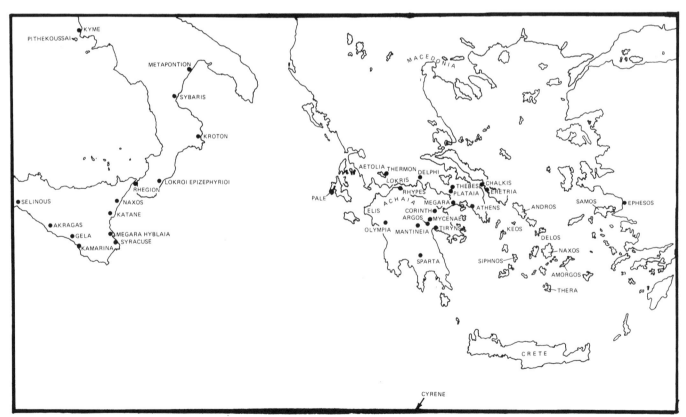

Fig. 3.1. Map of the Aegean and Magna Graecia indicating places mentioned in the text.

implication that the political system of Classical Greece essentially goes back to the Heroic Age? To begin with, the last hundred years have given us some considerable independent knowledge of that 'Heroic Age' by showing it to have its historical basis in what archaeologists call the Late Bronze Age. This knowledge, although imperfect, is quite enough to show that the political systems of the Aegean world at that time were very different from those of the Classical age. The political units conform to the model which is best described as 'redistributive': relatively large, heavily centralised, minutely bureaucratic, they leave little scope for an independent citizenry. Extravagant and laborious steps are taken to secure the prestige and power of the rulers, to an extent which is not matched even in the most deferential Archaic cities of, say, the seventh century BC. Production and distribution were, it seems, closely monitored (Renfrew 1972: 297–307, 462–5 etc.).

Next, there is the evidence of the Homeric poems. Here it is not so much the few and faint memories which, even on the most positive view, Homer betrays of the political realities of the Late Bronze Age Aegean; rather, it is the general (though not quite total) absence from Homer's world of any awareness of the systems characteristic of Greece in the Classical period. It is usual to conclude, on this and on much other evidence, that a complete interruption had taken place between the Late Bronze Age kingdoms and the rise of the *polis*; that the Homeric poems, which portray a system that resembles neither the one nor the other when examined in detail, are giving us a glimpse of one or more stages within the period of the interruption; and that the emergence of the *polis* is likely to have begun only at the time when the poems were reaching their final form, that is, probably in the eighth century BC (Snodgrass 1980: 27–31).

Such, at least, is the view taken here, and the main emphasis of this chapter will be on developments which took place between approximately 750 and 650 BC. For the reasons given above, there will be certain difficulties in extending these developments to include the actual emergence of the Greek polities, though the attempt may still be made. But whether or not it succeeds, there is a whole range of further processes, only slightly later in date, which seems to me to illustrate the interaction of peer polities in an unusually clear way. Some of the evidence advanced will be archaeological, some historical; it will cover issues ranging from the fundamental question of the size and nature of the Greek *polis* itself, to such details as law-codes, warfare, burial practices, temple architecture and the production of painted pottery.

According to the model under consideration in this book, it will be maintained that an entity like the Greek *polis* is 'legitimised in the eyes of its citizens by the existence of other states which patently do function along comparable lines' (Renfrew 1982a: 289). Perhaps the first quality of the Greek *polis* which might stand in need of such legitimation is its small size. It has not been characteristic of the Greek-speaking world at other periods of its history that it should be composed of such a proliferation of small, mutually independent units. This is true not only (as would be expected) of the periods when Greece has been under the control of a major power, whether external (the Roman and Ottoman Empires) or in some sense internal (Macedon, Byzantium), but also of the other eras in which the Greek world has comprised a number of independent states. The Mycenaean kingdoms, for example, do not appear to embody the Classical principle that each major town and its territory should be autonomous (Gschnitzer 1971); nor, in the two-and-a-half centuries after the Fourth Crusade, when a series of independent baronies grew up in the Aegean lands, was any of these of such small compass (Miller 1964). To establish the political and—subject to a certain degree of inter-dependence—the economic viability of the numerous Greek *poleis* must have been an initial problem. But it is hard to believe in any general principle, applied at the time or even invoked later, such as would justify the more extreme cases of local fragmentation. Some representative figures for the territory sizes of Greek *poleis* are given by Ehrenberg (1969: 27–8). But it remains difficult to detect the rationale by which, for example, the small Cycladic islands of Keos (131 sq.km) and Amorgos (124 sq.km) each have their territory divided, at least in the earlier stages, between four and three separate *poleis* respectively, when larger neighbours such as Andros (380 sq.km) comprised a single *polis*, and when the *polis* of Naxos probably incorporated the archipelago of very small islands around it, in addition to its own 430 sq.km. Outside the Cyclades, these upper and lower limits of size were comfortably exceeded in either direction; but this very divergence in size of territory and in population is, in its way, a testimony to the strength of the '*polis* idea'. Later, towards the middle of the fifth century BC, more than two hundred of these once independent polities around the Aegean coasts became tributary allies of Athens (Fig. 3.2).

We may, in general, have little independent evidence as to how this and other formative steps in the emergence of the Greek *polis* were taken; but there is fortunately one large exception—that of the early Greek colonies. We know enough about several dozen of these in their early years—approximate or accurate date of foundation, identity of founding city, partial excavation of sites and cemeteries, occasionally more circumstantial accounts of the original settlement—to be able to make certain observations about them (see Hammond 1967: 657–60 for a table of dates and founding cities). One is that, if we set on one side a very few settlements which were emporia of a rather cosmopolitan kind, virtually every Greek colony was a *polis*. This at first sight predictable fact is made more interesting by two factors. First, the earliest of these colonies were sent out at a time when the *polis* system was, at most, a newly established feature of the Greek homeland; Sicilian Naxos, in 735 BC, may be the first colony for which we have a plausible and exact foundation date, but Pithekoussai (Ischia) and Kyme in the Bay of Naples were both appreciably older than that. Secondly, not every Greek

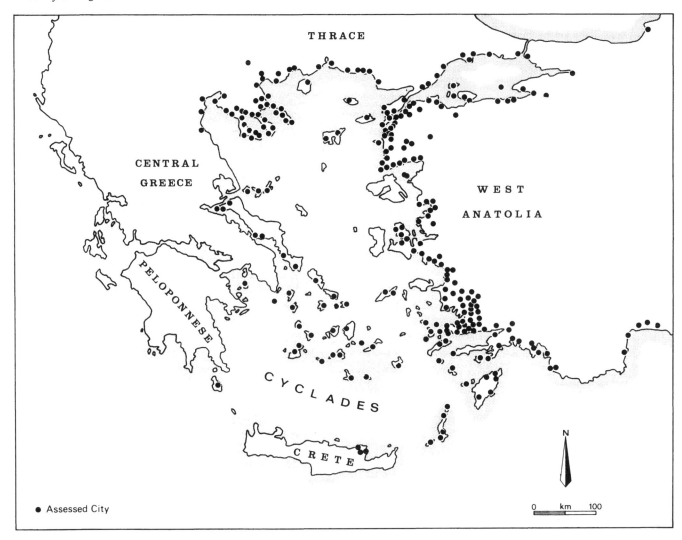

Fig. 3.2. Map of the Aegean showing the distribution of polities assessed in the Athenian tribute lists during the later fifth century BC.

in the homeland lived in a *polis*, either then or later; what is more, a number of important colonies in the west (Sybaris, Kroton, Metapontion, Lokroi Epizephyrioi) were actually settled from the regions of Achaia and Lokris, which were among those areas where the *polis* idea had not been adopted (Fig. 3.3). Instead, the inhabitants lived in scattered village settlements, linked by some more or less loose form of alliance which, in later centuries, became formalised into a confederation or league. The very fact that the founders of these colonies were recorded merely as 'Achaians' and 'Lokrians', rather than as coming from an individual town or district, must imply some capacity for concerted action, even in the early days, on the part of these regions of the homeland. Yet these 'ethnic' colonists seem to have adopted without hesitation the model of the *polis* when establishing their new settlements, complete with city, territory, individual land-plots constituting the title to citizenship, official cult of the patron deity, law-code and all the other appurtenances. There were of course incentives, at least initially, for doing so: only a

concentrated settlement would stand a chance of surviving its early years on a fairly distant and potentially hostile continental shore. Nevertheless, this assimilation to the *polis* model does give an example of the kind of interaction that we are looking for. The very earliest colonists in the west had come from places—Chalkis and Eretria, Corinth and Megara—where the *polis* idea was accepted: their successors apparently followed the same practice because it had been seen to work in the colonial context, irrespective of whether or not they found it appropriate to their own circumstances at home.

Irrespective too, one might add, of a larger consideration: would not other and larger political units have proved even more effective in the colonial west? Whatever geographical determinants might be held to justify or explain the prevalence of small autonomous polities in the Greek homeland, such as the fragmentation of good farming land by the pervasive and barren limestone, they apply much less obviously to the landscape of southern Italy and Sicily. To take an immediate instance, why did not the three Achaean

Fig. 3.3. Mainland Greece and the Aegean: the extent of the *polis* system (shaded areas) in the Archaic period.

colonies of Sybaris, Kroton and Metapontion, strung out over more than a hundred miles of coastline along the 'instep' of Italy, come to form a single federal state, as their Achaean homeland was later to do? The answer must be in part that, at the early date when they were founded, the appeal of the *polis* to Greek minds was too strong to be resisted. Greek colonisation, in other words, exhibits in rapid succession two of the modes of interaction between peer polities that can occur in the context of emigration: first, the political systems of the earliest colonists are 'exported' and reproduced in a new geographical setting; second, the interaction between overseas polities of different stock becomes influential enough to over-ride the native affiliations of later arrivals on the scene. In this case, only a single generation intervened between the two stages.

One part of this phenomenon, that is the weakening of native ties, seems to be a cultural equivalent of the 'founder principle' of genetics, recently discussed in the context of island colonisation by Cherry (1981: 61–2): an off-shoot of a larger parent population almost invariably becomes genetically distinct in its new habitat because it does not represent fully the gene pool of the parent population. But it is the other part, the assimilation to each other of groups of different origins coming together in the new environment, which, as Renfrew points out (this volume: Ch. 1), lacks obvious biological analogies and remains accordingly mysterious. One further illustration of this second process in the Greek colonial world may be given, from the field of burial practices. Within the general prevalence of the rite of inhumation among the early colonists (some of whose mother-cities favoured cremation), we may note a more particular phenomenon: the use of a form of crude sarcophagus,

hollowed out from a single block of stone, into which the body was placed. This form of interment was popular in Corinth and, so far as we know, only in Corinth among the colonising cities. It is not unexpected, therefore, that it proves to have been equally popular in Syracuse, Corinth's colony. What is more interesting is that it is later found in the other Sicilian colonies of Megara Hyblaia, Gela, Selinous and Kamarina, of which only the last-named is linked with either Syracuse or Corinth; the others were founded from cities where the practice seems to have been unknown (Snodgrass 1971: 175–6, 199 n. 19).

The western colonies, like the pan-Hellenic sanctuaries (cf. Renfrew, this volume: 16), are a valuable testing-ground for the concept of peer polity interaction, in that they provided an area in which the members of different Greek polities came into contact. But it is time to leave them and return to the Greek homeland, where we may not be able to follow the process of the emergence of the *polis* to its very beginnings in the same way, but where episodes not very much later in date can be used to illustrate the same overall concept.

No clearer illustration could be given of the sheer power of *polis* rivalry and emulation than that of early Greek warfare. The emergence of the Archaic heavy infantryman (*hoplite*), with the attendant changes in equipment, tactics, social stratification and political obligation, stands close to the heart of the idea of the *polis* (Snodgrass 1980: 99–107). The notion that all citizens above a certain property qualification should be obliged to serve in the army of the *polis*, equipped at their own (considerable) expense, and that by so doing they secured certain minimal rights as citizens, arose sufficiently soon after the emergence of the *polis* itself to constitute, in many cases, our earliest and most positive proof of its reality. The hoplite phalanx was the embodiment of the *polis* idea translated into action (Fig. 3.4). At the same time, hoplite warfare, as has often been observed (e.g. Adcock 1957), had a strong element of the conventional, even of the ritualistic about it. In the Archaic period especially, armies were used in the main for a single tactical purpose (the pitched battle on level ground) and in a single formation (the close-order phalanx). Campaigns were decided by a single engagement, whose verdict was invariably accepted by both sides; there were no reserves worth mentioning since it was essential to field one's maximum strength for the first encounter, and the training of other arms, apart from the heavy infantry, was neglected. The use of long-range missiles was considered contemptible, winter campaigning unthinkable. The two-handled shield or *hoplon*, in which the hoplite engaged his left arm and from which he took his name, was a symbol of duty and at the same time a badge of privilege for the well-to-do citizen.

The rules of this game were apparently accepted without question by every Greek *polis*. The experience of foreign wars can only have served to reinforce this conviction, for hoplite armies fought with signal success against Etruscans, Persians and Carthaginians, and Greek hoplite mercenaries were in

Fig. 3.4. The close-order phalanx of Greek heavy infantry in action. Late Protocorinthian jug, Rome, Villa Giulia Museum, c. 640 BC.

demand in many countries: a mere boat load or two of them, landing in the Nile Delta, were enough to tip the power struggle in Egypt in the 660s BC, according to Herodotus (II.152). True, the economic basis for this system, a settled population of prosperous farmers, was not at the disposal of every Greek state; backward ethnic groups like the Aetolians might fight by different rules (Thucydides III.94), and they could occasionally spring a surprise on the hoplite army of a *polis*. It was from a similar background that, centuries later, the Macedonian kings, with their strong cavalry, their lighter-armed troops using a pike held with both hands, and their winter campaigns, brought about the downfall of the hoplite system.

As long as success attended this form of warfare, however, the Greek polities conformed to it with what seems an excess of zeal. In many states the proportion of the free adult male population which qualified for hoplite service was of the order of one-third; this will have meant that, of the *total* population, something in the region of one-fifteenth would have been available for effective warfare. If a *polis* was small, therefore, it might produce an effective army of a really tiny size. We have a poignant illustration of this when the united army of the allied Greek *poleis*, representing something approaching their full muster of hoplites, took the field against the Persians at Plataia in 479 BC. The by now insignificant cities of Mycenae and Tiryns fielded a joint force of four hundred men; the *polis* of Pale in Kephallenia sent just two hundred. On this occasion, taking their place alongside the ten thousand Spartans and the eight thousand Athenians, their contribution was valued; but one is bound to wonder about their role in the much commoner circumstances of warfare against other Greek states. A city that

could muster only two hundred men at arms would be utterly dependent on alliances with more powerful neighbours; logically, one would have thought, some other tactical system which could involve a wider section of the population would seem preferable. But a hoplite army had become a symbol of *polis* status, and that was enough. Here again, the neglect of wider considerations seems to underline the strength of the urge to conform to the practices of one's peers, even when it was only in order to fight them. War had indeed become 'a channel for communication' (Renfrew, this volume: 8).

A second essential principle of the *polis* system was the existence of codified law. By its mere existence and, even more important, by its exhibition in public, a law-code represented a major step in the advance of the *polis* idea, establishing that element independent of both ruler and ruled which is a necessary ingredient of statehood (Fig. 3.5). We do not know the sequence by which the Greek cities came to adopt this advance, but one thing is clear: interaction between cities played a large part. The commonest medium was that of a prominent individual who, having acquired a reputation as a lawgiver, was then called upon for his services by cities other than his own. There are some surviving inscriptions with Archaic law-codes, but for the very earliest stages we have to rely on the statements of writers who, however authoritative (Aristotle's *Politics* is the most fruitful source), lived several centuries later. The first, rather isolated case is that of an exiled Corinthian nobleman, Philolaos, who was invited by Thebes to devise a law on adoption. The motive for the invitation, 'to preserve the number of land-holdings', is one that lies at the very heart of the *polis* system, where 'citizenship' at first consisted of no more than the possession

Fig. 3.5. Fragment of a law-code inscription from Dreros in Crete, late seventh century BC. (photograph courtesy of Miss L.H. Jeffery.)

of a plot of land; if we can accept the dating of Philolaos' visit to the 720s BC, then it gives early confirmation of the adoption of the system at Thebes, and by implication at Corinth too. But this episode falls short of attesting a full codification of the law; and the tradition that Philolaos was an exile also detracts from his claims to represent an institutional-ised structure. Our next body of evidence derives from the years towards the middle of the seventh century BC, and two areas figure prominently in it, the western colonies and Crete. Zaleukos of Lokroi Epizephyrioi (one of the colonies dis-cussed above), who became the most famous lawgiver of his day, is said to have been taught by a man who had learned his law in Crete, and the island is certainly the richest source of Archaic law-code inscriptions. Later in the century, Epimenides the Cretan was called in by the Athenians to purify their city after an unsuccessful *coup d'état*; while, in the west, two pupils of Zaleukos established law-codes for their own cities, Rhegion and Katane. In the next century, Demonax, from Mantineia in Arkadia, was called in to reform the constitution of Cyrene; other examples can be found in, for instance, Jeffery 1976: 41–4, 145–6, 188–90. These activities once again suggest that the Greek *poleis* kept an alert eye on the constitutional progress of their peers, and were ready to learn from them.

In two of the fields which we have been considering, colonisation and codification of law, a prominent part was played by the pan-Hellenic sanctuary at Delphi and by its oracle of Apollo. Whatever rationalist interpretation we may care to put upon the oracular utterances of Apollo's priestess, their prestige, and the range of expertise with which they were

credited, are undoubted facts. The function of the Delphic oracle is perhaps seen at its most remarkable in the context of colonisation (Forrest 1957). Most important Greek colonies boasted a foundation legend which began with a consultation of the oracle. Not only are many of the reported responses specific and well-informed about distant coastlines but, more striking still, the oracle frequently emerges not merely as an adviser but as an initiator. A typical story concerns, yet again, one of the Achaean colonies of southern Italy. Myskellos, an Achaean from the small town of Rhypes, went to consult the oracle about a private matter, his own childlessness; he was told that he would be granted children, but only when he had founded Kroton, an enterprise for which, not unnaturally since the place did not yet exist, he needed further directions. Following these, and finding the already established colony of Sybaris, he asked Delphi's permission to settle there; he was refused, and eventually Kroton was founded, traditionally in about 708 BC (Anderson 1954: 78). Even when due allowance is made for political manipulation, the role of the oracle remains an important one. Delphi was evidently acting as the main central clearing-house for information of a geographical and political kind which was of potential value to many different cities and their governments; it was also being used as an instrument of persuasion by pressure groups, and here too it could act across the lines of division between states. When, for example, the instruction to found a colony came as a surprise to a city's rulers and was unwelcome to many of its citizens, we may suspect that the pressure came ultimately from outside; such were the circumstances in our best-documented case of a colonial settlement, the foundation of Cyrene from Thera in the 630s BC (Herodotus IV. 150–8).

With legislation and codification, likewise, the Delphic oracle did not merely approve proposals—it initiated them. Sometimes, indeed, it is represented as taking a dangerously interventionist line, as when a Corinthian from outside the ruling circle of his city was encouraged to 'put Corinth straight'; he was Kypselos, who became the first Corinthian tyrant and the most powerful individual ruler in the Greek world of his day. The story of the oracle *might* indeed be dismissed as a propagandist invention, by Kypselos or his supporters, to justify his seizure of power. In the same way, the promoters of a lasting constitutional reform at Sparta, at about this time (perhaps the second quarter of the seventh century BC), presented their measures as having been initiated by Apollo, whereas it is much more likely that a pre-arranged 'package' was presented to the oracle for divine ratification. The fact remains, however, that in both these cases it was thought worth while to obtain the seal of Delphic approval; and in neither case did Delphi disown its attributed words. This must mean that, before 650 BC, Delphi had acquired great prestige as an arbiter who in some sense stood above the authority of any single *polis*; and this prestige in turn must have been at least partly based on the only earlier episode in which it had played a leading role, that of colonisation. One thing that all these activities had in common was success: the Greek colonisation of Sicily and southern Italy created polities which not only survived, but in several cases grew to overshadow their founding cities; Kypselos established a dynasty which ruled for 74 years and brought Corinth to the zenith of its power; the Spartan constitution became a by-word for political stability.

But, given that its initial successes were the foundation of its subsequent prestige, how was Delphi able to embark on this career in the first place? Like the Pope, it had no divisions, yet the most powerful cities felt the need of its sanction. If its role had been exclusively a religious one, and if the motive for soliciting its approval had been only piety, it seems unlikely that it could have played so complex a role. The explanation must surely be that a culture so politically fragmented as Archaic Greece was very much in need of a common arena, in which the innovations, advances and attainments of each individual *polis* could be rapidly communicated to others, when desired, or could, more simply, be displayed for admiration. The alternative of direct interaction, when there were more than two hundred separate polities, often many days' travel apart, would have required an extremely elaborate network of communications.

Delphi, although its possession of an oracle gave it an early primacy in certain spheres, was not the only inter-state sanctuary which could fulfil such a function. Its athletic festival, for example, was eclipsed by that of Olympia and was of much later foundation. But both sites show a parallel development. In the early days, there is evidence for geographical or political bias: the responses of the Delphic oracle may betray a partiality for Corinth and its allies (Forrest 1957), while the earliest Olympic victors were drawn from a restricted area of the Peloponnese. Already, however, the dedications show that *individuals*, some of them well-to-do, were being attracted from further afield (the Athenian tripods at Olympia, for instance, or the Cretan bronzes at Delphi). As the Archaic period advanced, the fact that both sanctuaries were relatively remote from the most powerful and innovatory centres of the Greek world came to matter less, and the advent of inscribed dedications proves that polities, as well as individuals, were cultivating Olympia and Delphi. The process reaches its peak with the construction of the treasury buildings in the later Archaic and Classical periods (Figs. 1.12, 3.8 and 3.9)—a dozen at Olympia, at least 28 at Delphi. Whereas to muster a hoplite army was one way of staking a claim to be a fully fledged *polis*, to erect a treasury at a pan-Hellenic sanctuary was to put one's city forward as belonging to an élite among the *poleis*. Just as both activities were clearly inspired by the example of the peer polities, so both had the effect of impressing those peers: when little Siphnos, with its territory of 75 sq.km and its population of perhaps two to three thousand, built its splendid treasury at Delphi, it was directly challenging comparison with Corinth, which was more than ten times the size in both categories.

Some of the smaller dedications, and some surviving historical anecdotes, throw a little more light on the question of *how* these sanctuaries acted as media for interaction. The Olympic festival, in particular, was clearly the place at which to make any appeal, over the heads of the individual *polis* governments, for the adoption of a pan-Hellenic policy, or more simply for recognition outside one's own *polis*. Only after his overwhelming reception at the Olympic games of 476 BC, for example, did Themistokles feel that he had reaped his due harvest of honour for having played a leading role in delivering both Athens and Greece as a whole from Persian conquest, four years ealier. The policies of an individual city could be held up for condemnation, as when Lysias' speech at the festival of 388 BC provoked a riot against Dionysios, the tyrant of Syracuse, for his brutality and treachery towards fellow Greeks in the west. These examples from later history show that Greeks came to regard the great sanctuaries as offering a forum, superior to that offered by the channels of normal diplomacy, for communication with the citizens of other *poleis*. Can we detect any signs from the earlier, mainly archaeological evidence, for the exercise of a similar function?

The prominence of dedications of hoplite armour at Olympia (and to a much lesser extent at Delphi and other sites) suggests one answer (Snodgrass 1980: 105–7). The very fact that armour and weapons were dedicated at sanctuaries is important, for down to about 700 BC it had been a common practice to bury them with their owner in the grave, and this custom desists just as the dedications at Olympia begin. In a general way, this merely shows a switch of emphasis and loyalty from the individual and the family to the *polis*; but there was a second, concurrent change in that it now became

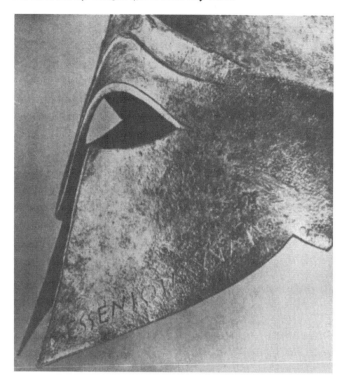

Fig. 3.6. Inscribed helmet dedicated at Olympia, recording a victory of the *polis* of Messana over that of Mylai, both in north-eastern Sicily, early fifth century BC (photograph courtesy of Deutsches Archäologisches Institut, Athens.)

the tendency to dedicate not one's own, but one's defeated enemy's arms. Such dedications were quite often inscribed, to rub home the message that they were intended to convey (Fig. 3.6). At a fundamental level, it is not unlikely that this contributed something to the spread of hoplite equipment and tactics across the Greek world; much more certainly, it will have impressed the citizens of other *poleis* with the prowess of one's own. The same message could be transmitted in a less obvious way through other types of dedication. Of the 24 statues of Zeus which the traveller Pausanias records his having seen at Olympia, for instance, one was (not unfittingly for a pan-hellenic sanctuary) a memorial to the

victory of the allied Greeks over the Persians at Plataia, another commemorated the Eleans' successful expulsion of the Arkadians from Olympia itself, after the latter had temporarily seized control of the festival, while yet another was a supplicatory offering for the intended suppression by the Spartans of the serious internal revolt in 464–456 BC (Pausanias V. 23; V. 24.1; V. 24.3–4). In all these cases the choice of an inter-state sanctuary is surely designed to communicate with other polities and their individual members; one's own fellow citizens or subjects could be more easily impressed by the commissioning of a fine building, a statue or an armour dedication at home—as is shown by the fact that all three (and other) forms of dedication are common in the state, as well as the inter-state, sanctuaries.

In one respect at least, the pan-Hellenic sanctuaries can be said to have developed more slowly than those of the individual cities: this is in the acquisition of monumental temples. The earliest temples at Delphi, Olympia or Delos are relatively small and unspectacular. But at the same period, the most prosperous states were building more pretentious temples at home, and one feature of these shows how they, too, could act as a medium of rivalry between peer polities (Table 3.1). Two of the very largest temples known from the eighth century BC are the first temple of Hera on Samos and the long, apsidal temple of Apollo at Eretria. The Eretria temple is certainly the later of the two, and its slightly larger dimensions could be seen as dictated by a desire to outdo the Samians; there is other evidence that the two cities were mutually unfriendly, and by the end of the century they were almost certainly at war. A similar comparison may be made between two smaller structures of approximately the same date, the building which overlies the Mycenaean palace at Tiryns and is best interpreted as a temple of Hera, and the structure at Thermon in Aetolia, which almost certainly became a temple of Apollo, even if it was not originally built as such. The comparison of dimensions in these two cases may seem inconclusive, but as so often in Greek history one can strengthen the inference by appealing to later and clearer

Table 3.1. *Comparative measurements of certain Greek temples*

Temple	Length (m)	Width (m)	Area (sq. m)	Approximate date
Hera, Samos (first)	33.50	6.70	224	c. 800 BC (?)
Apollo, Eretria	35.00	7.00 (façade)	c. 240	c. 750 BC (?)
Hera, Tiryns (?)	20.90	6.90	144	8th century BC (?)
'Megaron B', Thermon	21.40	7.30 (at rear)	c. 150	8th century BC
Artemis, Ephesos (first)[1]	109.20	55.10	6,017	550 BC
Hera, Samos (fourth)[1]	111.00	54.40	6,038	530 BC
'GT', Selinous[1]	110.12	50.07	5,538	540 BC
Olympian Zeus, Akragas[1]	110.09	52.74	5,806	480 BC

[1] Measurements taken from Lawrence 1957: 331, 95, 325 and 326, respectively.

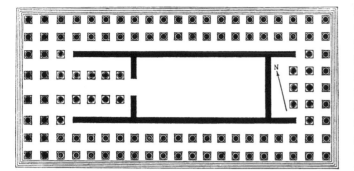

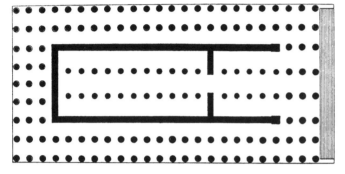

Fig. 3.7. Competitive emulation in monumental temple-building: (top) the Archaic temple of Artemis at Ephesos, c. 550 BC; (bottom) the fourth temple of Hera on Samos, c. 530 BC.

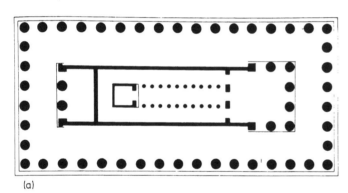

(a)

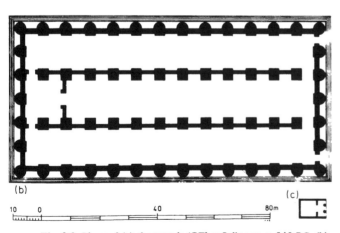

(b)   (c)

Fig. 3.8. Plans of (a) the temple 'GT' at Selinous, c. 540 BC, (b) the temple of Olympian Zeus at Akragas, c. 480 BC and (c), for comparison of size, the treasury of the Athenians at Delphi, c. 500 BC.

instances. The two largest Archaic temples in the Ionic order were the 'Old' temple of Artemis at Ephesos and the fourth temple of Hera at Samos (Fig. 3.7). Here again, we know that the larger temple—the ground area at Samos comes out at 6,038 sq. m as against 6,017 at Ephesos—was begun later, while mythology and geography alike suggest a tradition of political rivalry between the two cities. Among the western colonies, meanwhile, a similar competitiveness seems to have operated in the designing of giant temples in the Doric order. The temple known as 'GT', at Selinous in western Sicily, was begun in about 540 BC and held the field for about two generations until the neighbouring city of Akragas laid out a temple of Olympian Zeus with almost exactly the same length and a marginally greater width (Figs. 3.8 and 3.9). Yet again, there is a record of hostile political alignment for these two Sicilian cities. If the degree of geometrical nicety imputed by this view to the Archaic temple-builders seems improbable, it become less so in the light of the fact that Herodotus, in the following century, rightly describes the Samian temple as 'the largest of all those known to us' (III. 60.4)—a difficult point to establish had there not been a clear local tradition to this effect, and a deliberate intention behind it.

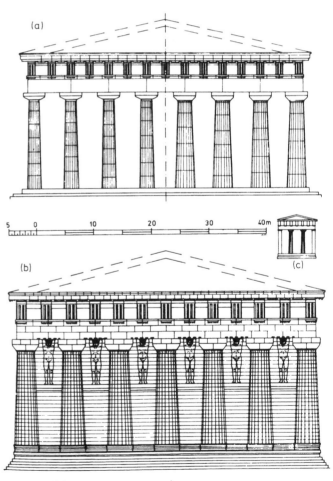

Fig. 3.9. Reconstructed façades of (a) the temple 'GT' at Selinous, (b) the temple of Olympian Zeus at Akragas, and (c) the treasury of the Athenians at Delphi (cf. Fig. 3.8).

All the examples so far given are concerned with the activities of governments, rulers, rich patrons, or at least (in the case of hoplite warfare) the more prosperous land-owners—that is, in the main, of the policy-makers within the Greek states. But the material evidence indicates that comparable effects were taking place at the level of craftsmanship and art style; it can also show that these effects began to operate well before the emergence of the *polis*. Take, for example, the long series of changes in the method of decorating painted pottery, between the eleventh and the eighth century BC. We see in succession the adoption of the compass and the multiple brush, and of a range of motifs to which these aids lent themselves and which go to make up the style called Protogeometric; then more than a century later a new style, the Geometric, emerged, distinguished by the use of new motifs like the meander and the swastika, and new devices like the cross-hatching of outline shapes; finally, the silhouette figure, human or animal, is adopted as the most important decorative element (Fig. 3.10). Each of these changes, as it happens, is believed to have originated in Athens; but each in turn is taken up by other local schools, one after another, the

circle widening at each stage until the final change of fashion produces echoes from Sicily to Ionia (Snodgrass 1971: 45–94, 418–19). To attribute the changes to purely commercial competition, in these early centuries, would be quite inappropriate (Cartledge 1983); taste, if not deeper psychological needs (see e.g. Himmelmann-Wildschütz 1968), is likely to have counted for more than pursuit of profit. But the tastes were collective ones: groups of craftsmen, living in settlements whose political organisation was as yet primitive, were already emulating other groups in other such settlements. With sculpture, the case is changed somewhat by the fact that the client, rather than the artist, tended to be the greater arbiter of convention and change; but one can still point to the later spread of the *kouros* type of statue (Figs. 1.9 and 1.10) as evidence of the way in which the patron in one city was influenced by the taste of his counterpart in another.

The case of Classical Greece has thus, in my view, proved able to furnish a series of fairly concrete instances of the operation of peer polity interaction. It shows the process taking place before, during and after the emergence of a political unit, the *polis*, which at the least has some of the

Fig. 3.10. The appearance of figures in Greek Geometric art. Attic Late Geometric krater, National Museum, Athens, c. 740 BC (photograph courtesy of Deutsches Archäologisches Institut, Athens).

attributes of statehood. The Greeks' espousal of a small-scale polity in which the community of citizens could act in concert, later so resonant in the pages of Plato's *Republic* and *Laws* and Aristotle's *Politics*, appears to have been a strong factor from the very start; indeed, so widely unquestioned were the assumptions behind it that later Greeks appear to have forgotten how the idea first came into being. The Greek case has also served to show the interaction of peer polities at several different levels of activity: the formation of state policy, patronage of the arts and architecture, and the field of the individual craftsman himself.

But can the study of the Greek *polis* do more than that? Can it serve to enhance the model of peer polity interaction, rather than merely exemplifying it? Here I am more doubtful, save perhaps in one respect. The Greek example seems to me, in more than one instance, to indicate that peer polity interaction could be a *conscious* process. The people responsible for the foundation of the western colonies, for the formation of the early hoplite armies, for the marginal surpassing of the measurements of their rivals' temples, or for the equally direct provocation of setting up their city's treasury in a pan-Hellenic sanctuary, must have been aware not only of the structure within which they were operating, but of the scope which it gave for internal comparisons. In this case at least, therefore—and there are certainly other, if mostly much later, instances—the idea of peer polity interaction is seen to be not merely a modern intellectual concept imposed on its unsuspecting subjects, but something which those subjects were themselves practising, with some acumen and deliberation of purpose. There are not many models of which one can say as much.

Chapter 4

Peer polity interaction in the European Iron Age
Timothy and Sara Champion

In this paper we propose to consider the value of the concept of peer polity interaction in the explanation of cultural homogeneity, with particular reference to three case studies from the European Iron Age. In all cases we would argue that the concept is of considerable importance, though there are serious difficulties inherent in attempts to apply it to the static archaeological record as it is at present constituted. In all three cases the cultural homogeneity is easy to demonstrate—it is indeed the phenomenon that we are seeking to explain—but the definition of the polities and the monitoring of interaction between them, as distinct from the homogeneity of the system as a whole, are more difficult to accomplish. In our first example, polities can be discerned but the independent evidence for interaction between specific polities is slight. In the second, there is more evidence for such interaction but the polities themselves are more difficult to define. In the third, as in the first, the polities can be defined, and the availability of ethnohistorical evidence enables the nature of some of these inter-polity interactions to be defined, though archaeological correlates are currently almost lacking.

Complex chiefdoms in the Early Iron Age

Central Europe in the Iron Age (700–1 BC) is generally characterised as a chiefdom society, identified by ranking in settlement types and within cemeteries but, until its final phase, without the institutionalised political and military organisations characteristic of a state. The complexity of these

chiefdoms varied considerably in time and space. In particular, between 600 BC and 450 BC in the area covered by eastern France, southern Germany and Switzerland (Fig. 4.1) there emerged fairly rapidly a series of polities of a similar nature as far as their material culture, settlement and burial types, economic and industrial organisation (though with differing regional specialities), and, less tangibly, ritual procedures, as

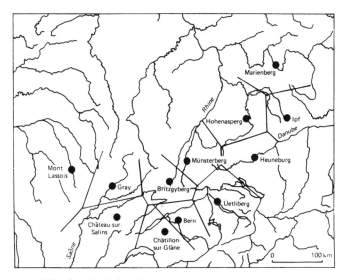

Fig. 4.1. Possible polity network in Early Iron Age central Europe (after Härke 1979).

recoverable from burial practices, are concerned. While within each polity, centred on a major settlement site, there is evidence for social hierarchies, the main sites themselves and the polities they represent do not appear to be part of a hierarchy, but to be of equal status. This archaeological pattern, it is suggested, can best be interpreted as the result of the interaction between these polities.

The archaeological evidence for this network of polities is limited and variable, with a distinct bias towards burials. Discussion (summarised by Härke (1979: 67–148)) has frequently revolved around the definition and applicability of such interpretative terms as *Fürstensitz* (princely residence) or *Adelssitz* (noble's residence) rather than concentrating on functional or social similarities between sites. In the circumstances it is somewhat difficult to establish a catalogue of peer polities with any certainty or precision, but, following approximately Härke's (1979: 119) proposed criteria, we believe it is possible to suggest with some confidence a list of twelve major sites, characterised as he proposed by abnormally rich burials, imported Mediterranean goods and prominent, defended topographical locations, which served as the centres of polities; the territorial extent of these polities could then be established by the fitting of notional boundaries between sites, assuming that the political landscape was completely packed. There is also, of course, the question of the peer status of these sites. Frankenstein and Rowlands (1978), for instance, assumed a greater degree of hierarchisation, with one site, the Heuneburg, paramount for at least part of the lifespan of these sites, but the recent discovery of an early and extremely rich burial at Eberdingen-Hochdorf (Biel 1982) in the vicinity of the neighbouring site of the Hohenasperg, allows the possibility that the two sites may have existed simultaneously as peers throughout their occupation. We would prefer to regard all these sites as peer polities for the sake of this analysis, though this does not imply that there were not real variations in the power or authority of individual polities from time to time. The network of polities established in this way would have had centres at an approximately regular spacing in the range of 50–120 km and territorial extents of 6,000–10,000 sq.km (Fig. 4.1).

Excavation and research have concentrated on the central sites of the polities and more particularly on their associated burials; burials have been recorded from other sites, but almost nothing is known about lesser settlement sites within the polities. Even among the central sites, only one, the Heuneburg, has been extensively excavated in recent years and it must therefore serve as a model for the rest. The excavations at the Heuneburg (Kimmig 1975; Gersbach 1976; Härke 1979: 91–7) revealed a complex sequence of defences and an even more complex series of internal settlement phases. The defences were destroyed and rebuilt at frequent intervals, and were obviously the subject of considerable expenditure of effort. They were mostly in traditional local styles of stone and timber, but in one phase, Period IVb, they were remodelled in a Mediterranean style

using Mediterranean materials; sun-dried mud-brick was used to construct a defence which incorporated bastions along one side. Mud-brick would have been singularly inappropriate building material for the climate of temperate Europe, and its combination with the exotic feature of bastions suggests either a Mediterranean architect or a local builder familiar with Mediterranean styles. A similar concern with the maintenance of massive defences seems evident at other sites too, and, though the Heuneburg remains the only certain example of imitation of exotic architectural styles, Härke (1979: 92) suggests that it might possibly have been a more widespread phenomenon.

The internal organisation of the Heuneburg was evidently complex, but is as yet far from clear. No single building of distinctive type has yet been recognised; on the contrary, in some phases the occupation seems to have consisted of residential structures and granaries of standard types. In one phase there is evidence for a specialist craftsmen's quarter. The range of activities documented on the site is of the greatest interest; they include the working of exotic raw materials such as coral and cardium shell from the Mediterranean, amber from the Baltic, and lignite from central Europe. Iron and bronze were also worked; among the items produced was a copy of an Etruscan bronze jug-handle (Kimmig and von Vacano 1973). There is no actual evidence for the production of pottery on the site, but a new type of painted pottery is closely associated with the site and its accompanying burials (Dämmer 1978). Evidence for the production of a similar range of items could also be suggested for at least one other site, Mont Lassois in eastern France (Joffroy 1960). It seems clear that one of the functions of these central sites was the production of items of high social status, especially personal ornaments. Where they are observed in the archaeological record, these items are found particularly in the richest graves and were therefore of restricted social circulation (Champion 1982).

The archaeological evidence therefore suggests that the intensification of production was primarily in the fields of defensive architecture and high-status items, but the polities may also have owed some of their power and wealth to increased exploitation of local resources. Salt and metal ores in particular may have been used in this way, though they have left little trace. Certainly, these central European polities were in a position to engage in exchange with the Mediterranean world, through which they received luxury manufactured goods, especially pottery and metalwork (Frankenstein and Rowlands 1978; Wells 1980). What items were given in return is not known, but they may well have included raw materials, as well as foodstuffs and human beings in the form of slaves or mercenaries.

The burial evidence is much fuller. It shows firstly a considerable degree of homogeneity in material culture, especially in such items as personal ornaments; in particular, it shows the widespread and apparently simultaneous adoption of new brooch types during the sixth century BC

(*Schlangenfibel, Bogenfibel* and later *Paukenfibel* and *Doppelpaukenfibel* (Mansfeld 1973; Fig. 4.2)). In weaponry, too, there was a widespread innovation: throughout most of later European prehistory the sword was always the prestige weapon, but in the sixth century BC it was temporarily abandoned in favour of a short dagger.

The burials also demonstrate a broadly similar set of rites. The construction of wooden chambers and the inclusion of waggons in the richest burials had already been widespread practices in the seventh century BC, and these continued. The burial mounds themselves were frequently of very large size, such as those near the Heuneburg (Riek and Hundt 1962). Imported goods from the Mediterranean were also commonly placed in the very richest graves, and were sometimes of enormous size, such as the krater from Vix (Joffroy 1954) or the bronze, wheeled couch from Eberdingen-Hochdorf (Biel 1982) (Fig. 4.3). Contact with the Mediterranean can also be seen in other aspects of the burials. The grave mounds at Hirschlanden (Zürn 1970) and Eberdingen-Hochdorf were surrounded by low stone walls in a manner similar to Etruscan graves: at Hirschlanden the mound was topped by a stone statue. This statue has usually been considered to be of

Fig. 4.2. Groups of similar fibula types, Early Iron Age: (a), (h) Heuneburg, Germany; (b) Neunform, Switzerland; (c), (d) Wangen, Switzerland; (e) Esslingen, Germany; (f) Amondans, France; (g) Asperg, Germany; (i) Mont Lassois, France; (j) Lunkhofen, Switzerland.

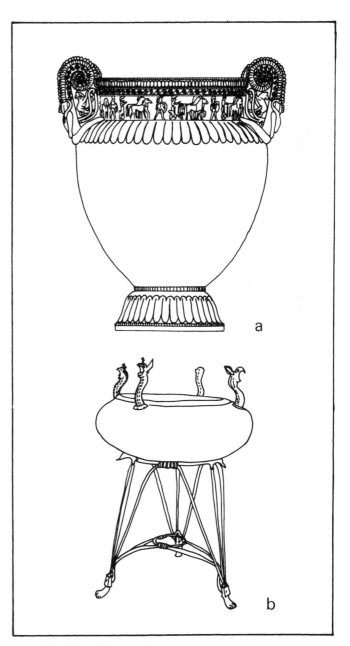

Fig. 4.3. Mediterranean imports to central Europe: (a) krater (ht. 1.64 m), Vix, France; (b) cauldron (diam. 70 cm) and tripod (ht. 57 cm), Ste Colombe, France.

local manufacture, though ultimately inspired by a knowledge of the Archaic Greek *kouros* style, perhaps transmitted via Italy; it has now been suggested, however, that it may actually be an imported Greek *kouros,* modified locally (Beeser 1983).

Explanations of this phenomenon, whether they invoke conquest from outside (Kimmig 1969) or the exploitation of opportunities for exchange with the Mediterranean world (Wells 1980), have concentrated on the rise of the system as a whole and not on the very marked similarities between the individual polities. Nevertheless, one of the most striking features of the archaeological record of this period is the network of similar sites and the high degree of comparability in such areas as settlement types, burial rites and material culture (particularly high-status ornament types) that characterises it. Behind this archaeologically observable pattern there lay the reality of a period of greatly enhanced social ranking, which also seems to have been shared by all the polities. It is suggested here that the precise similarity of these developments can best be understood as the result of inter-action between these polities.

It may also be possible to suggest some of the specific forms which this interaction took. The precise homogeneity of weapon styles suggests warfare as one possibility, as any new fashion in weaponry or fighting methods, especially if militarily more effective, would tend to be rapidly adopted by all the polities involved. Such a suggestion might be con-firmed by other evidence for raiding: the repeated destruction of the defences of the Heuneburg, for example, could well be used to support this argument.

Competitive emulation between polities may also be demonstrated in this archeological record. The greatly increased size of burial mounds, the sheer quantities of goods deposited in some graves and the conspicuous consumption of imported Mediterranean items, sometimes of surprisingly large size, all suggest that burials were one focus for competitive display. Another was in the construction of defences: the sun-dried mud-brick wall and bastions of the Heuneburg Period IV defences surely represent the ultimate in such competition—bigger, better and different.

Discussion of central European contacts with the Mediterranean world at this period (e.g. Wells 1980) have largely concentrated on the exchange mechanisms and their control, rather than on the way in which Mediterranean goods and ideas were used in European societies. Possession and consumption of Mediterranean goods and imitation of Mediterranean styles clearly played a twofold part in central European Iron Age society. On the one hand, within a polity they were a symbolic code which served to distinguish the élite from the rest and, on the other, they were the major focus for competitive rivalry between the élites of different polities. Bonfante (1980) has perceptively discussed the role played by Etruscan styles, especially of art and dress, in northern Italy, and the peculiar receptivity towards these styles shown both in Italy and in central Europe no doubt

owes much to the way in which they were used locally in the transformation of social organisation.

Other forms of interaction are rather harder to document archaeologically. Some methods of interaction had certainly existed in earlier periods since a broadly uniform pattern of material culture is known throughout the area covered by these polities in the sixth century BC. Contem-porary evidence for interaction, however, which is independent of the patterns of homologous development to be explained, is difficult to find. The occasional finds of objects which can be shown to have been manufactured in one polity and found in the territory of another may be important in this connection, and the study of inter-regional exchange of goods at this period, hitherto much neglected, could well repay serious attention.

This evidence, however insubstantial, suggests that through interaction these central European polities responded in a similar manner to similar internal and external stimuli; perhaps most important was the spirit of competitive emulation, for it may well have been competition between individual polities for access to the wealth offered by exchange with the Mediterranean world that initiated the growth of the whole system. This suggestion, furthermore, is supported by the nature of their collapse. In the fifth century BC changing priorities for their southern neighbours probably led to less intensive contacts between central Europe and the providers of their imported goods. Greece turned more to the Black Sea region for its supplies of raw materials and food-stuffs, and the Etruscan cities were being eclipsed by the rise of Rome. At the same time it is possible that socio-political changes locally in central Europe contributed to the disruption of the system described above. Whatever the causes, most of the rich central sites came to an end rather suddenly within a period of about fifty years, suggesting that though competitive emulation and other forms of interaction had actually helped these sites to flourish in the short term, their institutions were not stable; even the local infrastructure seems in many cases to have disappeared, as evidenced in the abandonment of many burial sites. Such central sites as survived the initial phase of collapse did not survive it for long, at least in their original form, and they appear not to have been able to take advantage of the decline of their neighbours through the annexation of additional territory, though evidence to demonstrate such an event might be difficult to adduce. The collapse was like that of a house of cards: the interaction was essential for their common survival, and once one succumbed, they all did.

Cultural homogeneity in the Middle Iron Age

The second case study concerns the immediately succeeding phase of the European Iron Age, the so-called La Tène period, where there is archaeological evidence for widespread interaction at several levels between different regions of Europe, but as yet little understanding of the social organisation of the period, on which a reconstruction of polities could be based. The La Tène culture which emerged at this time eventually extended in some form from Ireland to Rumania, and is commonly referred to ethnically and linguistically as Celtic (Fig. 4.4). The archaeological evidence is in many areas derived almost exclusively from burials, and little is known of settlements, let alone settlement hierarchies. In the circumstances it is difficult or impossible to define polities, though some regional cultural groupings are apparent. This is in fact one specific example of the general problem of defining polities which lack archaeologically observable centralised political institutions (others might be early Christian Ireland or early Anglo-Saxon England). This is particularly unfortunate since the concept of peer polity interaction seems of considerable relevance to understanding the rapid adoption of similar material and ritual practices over such a wide area.

The regional groups demonstrate a homogeneity of cultural features—burials, ornaments, weapons, pottery, and particularly art style and symbolism—which implies constant interaction at many levels. The new form of inhumation burial in a flat grave not marked by a tumulus, and the grouping of many of these graves together in large cemeteries, frequently of hundreds of graves, demonstrates not only a change in social organisation, at least as it pertained to burial, but also in ritual procedures, which became universally accepted across mainland Europe. Similar types of personal and dress ornament were used in all areas (Fig. 4.5), though regional variations in style allow the identification of objects involved in exchanges between groups, and their number is greatly increased since the previous phase.

The most striking common feature of the decorated artefacts is the art style, the so-called 'Celtic art', which is used on stone, metal, pottery and, where it has survived for retrieval, wood and leather (Jacobsthal 1944; Megaw 1970).

The appearance of this style in the fifth century BC, with its roots in Greek, Etruscan, Oriental and European art, has been the subject of many studies; what has never been in doubt has been the speed with which it was acquired, developed and used by craftsmen all over Europe (Schwappach 1973). An additional feature of the regional groups was their common adoption of certain symbols which, with remarkably little variation, evidently became widely used throughout the area. The most striking is the human/god head, whether carved in stone or wood, cast as a terminal for a metal ornament, or engraved between the coils of decoration on a bronze plaque. In many cases the head bears what has been called a 'leaf crown', which may in fact represent a specific form of hair-style, an emblem found on heads in Czechoslovakia, Germany, Switzerland, France and Britain. It is possible that these heads have a connection with those severed skulls found in southern French ritual structures of the Later Iron Age. Other common symbols of this period are the boar, the ram, the ox and the stag, and a series of man-beasts that include the horned god Cernunnos. In addition to such visual symbols, this area was also united at this time by the use of the Celtic language. The correlation of such a linguistic entity as Celtic with the archaeological record has for long proved an intractable problem and, though the full question cannot be pursued here,

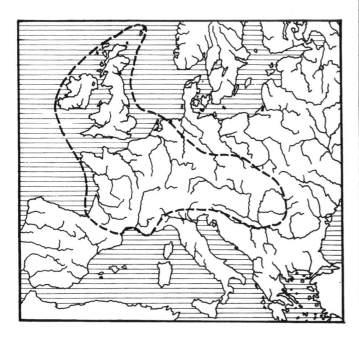

Fig. 4.4. Extent of developed La Tène culture in Europe.

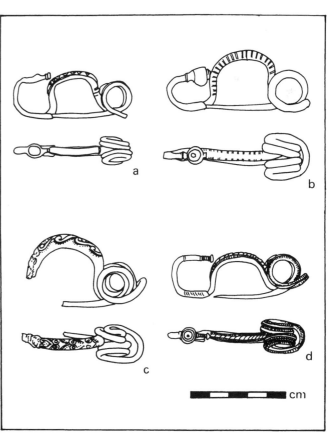

Fig. 4.5. Early La Tène fibulas of similar type: (a) Dürrnberg, Austria; (b) Bussy-le-Chateau, France; (c) Hunsbury, England; (d) Darshofen, Germany.

it is possible that the traditional explanation for the development of Celtic through diffusion by migration (a concept largely derived from nineteenth-century archaeological thought) should be reconsidered.

For symbols of this nature to be so widespread among groups with different environmental and indeed social backgrounds (for not all the areas now included in this system experienced the sixth century BC phenomenon described above) implies a vast network of channels for the exchange of information, raw materials and manufactured items. The adoption of art styles, rituals, symbols, language and material types over such a wide area and with such speed is what has given the impression of a 'civilisation' and has led to its equation with an ethnic group, the Celts. The issue that Renfrew has raised, in his introductory chapter in this volume, of the way in which ethnic groups form and what governs their scale cannot be answered here, or with such inadequate evidence; but given that the correlation with the Celts is correct, then it is a teasing question as to whether all the groups accepted the new symbols, rituals and art style because they already felt part of a larger ethnic group, or whether in accepting the symbols and styles, unable to reject their potency, they recognised themselves as a 'people' for the first time.

The emergence of the state

The third case study concerns the final phase of the Iron Age before the Roman conquest, that is, the La Tène III period of the late second and early first centuries BC. The archaeological record includes evidence from a wider range of contexts than in previous centuries, including settlements, ritual sites and burials, is reasonably plentiful and, as before, has a solid chronological framework. There is now also the addition of literary evidence, for the so-called barbarians figure more prominently in the historical, geographic and ethnographical literature of the Classical world. Although this record is somewhat patchy and frequently obscure, we have sufficient surviving fragments from the independent testimony of different authors writing at and about different periods (especially Polybius, Posidonius and Caesar (Tierney 1960; Nash 1976a)) to be able to construct at least the beginnings of a diachronic ethnohistory, a distinct advantage compared with the written evidence from other contact phases between literate and non-literate societies.

This period of the Iron Age saw the emergence of a substantially homogeneous Late La Tène 'culture' (or perhaps even 'civilisation') across western and central Europe from France to Czechoslovakia and Hungary, a distance of about 1,000 km. This homogeneity can be most visibly demonstrated in the realm of material culture; it was long ago noted, for instance, that some brooches from Mont Beuvray in central France were indistinguishable from some found at Stradonice in Bohemia. There was also a widespread

similarity in the shapes and decoration of pottery, for example in the painted pottery (Maier 1970) (Fig. 4.6).

There was, furthermore, a broadly shared development of economic intensification. Though little is known of agricultural production at this time, in other fields there are clear signs of change. Increasing craft specialisation can be suggested on the basis of burials with craft tools as a symbol of personal identity (e.g. a blacksmith (Taus 1963)) and of a much wider range of specialised tool forms (Jacobi 1974a). New technologies were also being adopted, most obviously in the production of pottery: wheel-turned vessels now formed a considerable proportion of the entire output (Pingel 1971) and the adoption of the kiln represented a significant investment in new production facilities; these kilns are frequently found in some numbers, as at Sissach, Switzerland (Frey 1935), or in a specialist potters' quarter at Gellerthegy-Taban, near Budapest, Hungary (Boní s 1969).

There was also a widespread development in the settlement pattern of the area with the growth of large, densely occupied, frequently defended sites, described by Caesar and other writers as towns (Collis 1975). Though there was considerable regional variation in the precise form and location of these sites, they acted as local centres, not least of specialised production and exchange; the range of industries documented is very wide, including pottery, metalwork, carpentry and leatherwork (Wyss 1974; Collis 1976: 10–12).

Writing, or at least a system of notation, was widely adopted (Jacobi 1974b) and standard systems of weights were in use throughout western and central Europe (Schwarz 1964). Coinage had come into widespread use throughout Europe in about the third century BC (Allen 1980), but from the early part of the first century BC new issues of low value coins were becoming common, and were particularly associated with the new urban sites; whatever the original purpose for which the coins were minted, by the end of the Iron Age they were playing a significant role in facilitating the conduct of exchange.

There were also generally similar trends in ideological and ritual activity. The burial rites which had prevailed in much of this area for the previous three centuries were abandoned, though it is far from clear what new rites took their place. At about the same time a new type of site became common throughout the area; this was a small, rectangular, ditched enclosure (*Viereckschanze*), best interpreted as some form of shrine (Planck 1982). These are the first known structures of purely ritual function in the Iron Age of this area, and must represent an important and widespread new direction in ritual activity and ideology.

It has long been thought that the general context for this phase of social, economic and political transformation was the contact between the societies of central and western Europe and the expanding Roman world. Roman control over northern Italy had been secured by the late third century BC, and

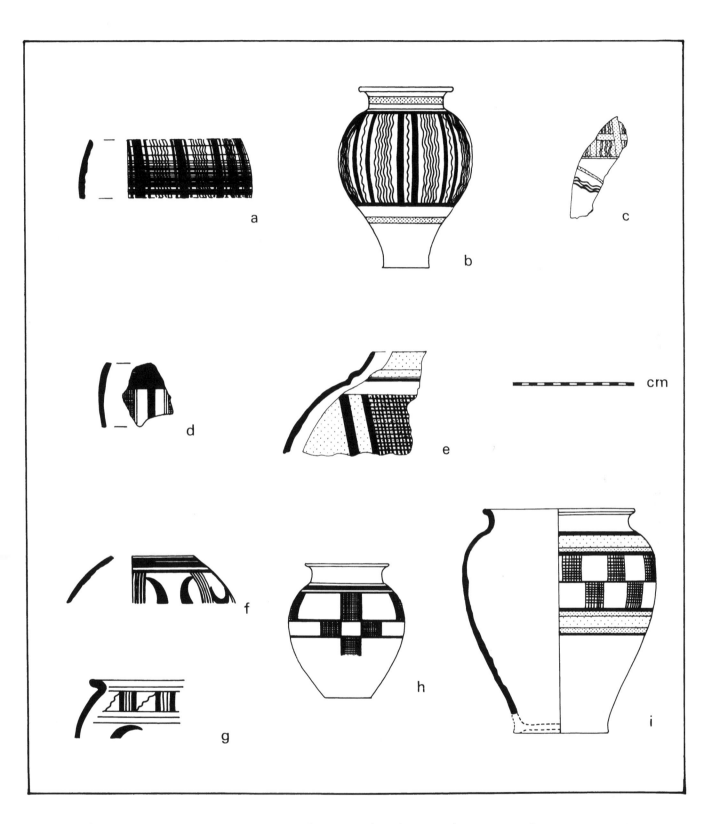

Fig. 4.6. Painted pottery of similar types from Germany, Switzerland and France: (a), (d), (f), (i) Manching, Germany; (c), (e) Basel, Switzerland; (b) Magalas, (g) Ensérune, (h) St Rémy de Provence, all France.

from 154 BC onwards Rome took a progressively greater interest in the affairs of southern France, until by 121 BC a Roman province was established. This expansion offered Rome's northern neighbours a new stimulus to economic intensification, as well as new opportunities for exchange, perhaps in particular for the supply of slaves, and for the enhancement of status by those able to control and manipulate this exchange and the consumption of Roman imports, especially wine and drinking equipment (Peacock 1971; Werner 1954). The rise of the 'culture' or the 'civilisation' as a whole, therefore, conforms to a well-recognised pattern, but in this particular case the additional ethnohistorical evidence can offer insights into what has not been satisfactorily studied or explained, the relationship between the individual polities within the whole system.

This historical evidence is important firstly because it allows the individual polities to be defined with some clarity. Caesar's eye-witness account of France in the 50s BC makes it clear that the polities were territorially defined units, and frequently contains enough information to make possible the detailed reconstruction of these boundaries (Rice Holmes 1899; Nash 1976b; 1978a). This task of reconstruction is, in fact, made much easier by the recognition that for much of central France these pre-Roman boundaries were preserved in the Roman and, later, diocesan divisions up to the French Revolution.

Secondly, the evidence tells us something of the nature of these polities (Nash 1978b). Latin authors use the word *civitas*, which can mean 'state' as well as 'citizenship' or 'nationality', but to the Greek writers the appropriate term was not *polis*, the city state, but *ethnos*, a term used, for instance, for such other Greek states which did not conform to the model of a city state (as, for instance, the Macedonians). They were thus recognised as polities possessing the characteristics of a state, but not the Classical city state. It is also clear, however, that these polities, though recognisable entities, were not entirely stabilised. Each state appears to have consisted of a number of territorial subgroups (*pagi*), perhaps four or five, and the degree of control over these subdivisions could fluctuate considerably. The states themselves, though independent and of equal importance for our analytical purposes, could vary considerably in actual political status and authority; the Aedui, Arverni and Sequani, for example, were autonomous polities, but each at various times held positions of varying prestige with respect to the others. As well as the major polities, there were also smaller groups who could sometimes be considered as constituent parts of a larger state, and sometimes as autonomous, but inferior, polities.

Thirdly, the historical evidence gives some indication of the development of social and political organisation. Accounts of Celtic social organisation are totally united on the division of society into warrior nobles, a learned priestly class of Druids and the common people. Relations between the nobles of a society were carried on primarily through competition for status and power, achieved partly through the institution of clientage. Status could be measured by the ability to mobilise clients acquired by military success or promises of wealth, and the Celtic greed for wealth used to promote status in this way was notorious in the Classical world. There is no mention of centralised political institutions in the earliest accounts, especially those of Polybius and Posidonius, which refer to the period from the fourth to the late second century BC, but thereafter there were two important transformations of political organisation. The first was the emergence of kingship as a widespread institution. When this happened is far from clear, but the references to past kings in Caesar and other authors, and their absence from earlier accounts, suggest that it was probably happening in the second half of the second century BC.

By the time of Caesar in the 50s BC, a second transformation had been achieved, at least in the western part of the area under discussion, where our documentary evidence is fullest. How far other areas were affected is unclear, though there are some indications to suggest that this was a phenomenon of restricted occurrence, and the argument must therefore proceed on the basis of evidence from western Europe. Though kingship still survived in some places, in a large block of land from western France to Switzerland the characteristic institutions of a state had appeared. Supreme power was in the hands of a magistrate, elected annually according to publicly known laws, and the powers of the assembly of nobles were greatly strengthened. There were strict safeguards against the retention of power by an individual or his family, and attempts to re-establish a kingship were forbidden and severely dealt with. Broadly comparable institutions are known, and appear to have evolved simultaneously in at least three, and possibly in as many as eight, states (Fig. 4.7). The polities sharing these similar institutions were roughly equal in size, though at approximately 15,000 sq. km they were substantially larger than Renfrew's early state module (Renfrew 1975).

The particular value of the historical evidence for this phase of political development is that it contains an account of the nature of the political relations between the nobles both *within* a polity and also *between* polities. The evidence is derived particularly from Caesar and therefore applies especially to the latest phase of this development, but there is no reason to suppose that it is not equally valid for the earlier phase, with due allowance made for the different nature of the political institutions involved.

Within the polity, power was firmly in the hands of the nobles, and competition between them was focused around two main themes, one internal and one external. Internally, the political struggle was typically in the form of one powerful noble against the rest, realised in attempts, on the one hand, to restore supreme power to a single individual as king and, on the other, to uphold the newly established institutions of oligarchic government, which at least guaranteed a share of supreme power to all nobles: Celtillus

Fig. 4.7. Probable early states in central Gaul, first century BC (after Nash 1978a).

of the Arverni, for example, failed to establish himself as king in this way, as also did Orgetorix of the Helvetii, despite being able to mobilise 10,000 supporters (Caesar: *De Bello Gallico* VII.4; I. 2–4). Externally, the attitude to be adopted to Rome was a conveniently important question which served as a focus for dissension and rivalry; among the Aedui the competitive brothers, Dumnorix and Diviciacus, were respectively regarded as the leaders of anti-Roman and pro-Roman factions (Caesar: *De Bello Gallico* I. 18–20).

Political relations between polities were also marked by a spirit of competition. The aggressive recruiting of clients by an individual noble was paralleled by the acquisition of minor polities in a form of alliance, and convenient local issues were found as the focus for competitive rivalry, sometimes to the point of open warfare. The Aedui and the Arverni were for a long time rivals for the premier status in central France, until the defeat of the latter by Rome in 121 BC; thereafter, the Aedui and the Sequani were rivals, contesting in particular the right to control tolls on the River Saône, which flowed between them (Strabo IV.3.2). The Sequani eventually called in mercenaries, but in the ensuing conflict the erstwhile rivals appear to have joined forces against the mercenaries as a common enemy. Rival states could also have sharply opposed attitudes towards Rome, for instance the Aedui and the Arverni.

Perhaps most important was the possibility of alliances between individuals in different polities. The clearest case concerns the attempt by Orgetorix to establish personal

power among the Helvetii (Caesar: *De Bello Gallico* I. 2–4). He formed alliances with similarly minded nobles in other polities, Dumnorix of the Aedui and Casticus of the Sequani, thus bringing together powerful and ambitious men from different states all intent on overthrowing the established oligarchic institutions. To quote Caesar, Orgetorix

> convinced them that it was easy enough to accomplish such endeavours, because he himself (so he said) was about to secure the sovereignty of his own state. There was no doubt, he observed, that the Helvetii were the most powerful people in all Gaul and he gave a pledge that he would win them their kingdoms with his own resources and his own army. (Caesar: *De Bello Gallico* I. 3)

Such connections with allies in neighbouring states served to promote the interests of both, and could also be useful in helping to provide a safe refuge for those who found exile necessary. These political alliances could be sealed by marriages—Orgetorix and Dumnorix were connected by marriage in this way. Dumnorix, indeed, was at the centre of a web of such political marriages and owed much of his power to them. To quote Caesar again:

> his power was extensive not only in his own state but also in neighbouring ones. To secure this power he had given his mother in marriage to the noblest and most powerful man among the Bituriges, he had himself taken a wife from the Helvetii [i.e. the daughter of Orgetorix] and had married his half-sister and his female relations to men of other states. (Caesar: *De Bello Gallico* I. 18)

These alliances could range over long distances, as shown by the marriage of Ariovistus, from eastern France, to the sister of Voccio, the king of Noricum, in modern Austria, more than 600 km away (Caesar: *De Bello Gallico* I. 53).

In this way, rivalry for power within a society and the specific arguments through which this rivalry was practised were carried on through a network of alliances which transcended the borders of individual polities. In this specific case, therefore, the political institutions of the state were adopted by some late Iron Age polities as a device to control the power of single individual nobles—a trade-off which balanced the loss of the chance to achieve supreme power with the certainty of not being subjected to it, but being able to share in it for at least a limited period. This type of constitution was adopted, however, as the result of a political struggle which transcended the boundaries of the individual polity. Success in one polity would greatly increase the chances of success in another, and hence similar constitutional arrangements could be expected to occur very rapidly in neighbouring polities.

Though our evidence is limited to the later phases when kingship was giving way in some polities to oligarchic institutions, there is no reason to think that similar mechanisms of alliances between individuals across polity boundaries were not at work earlier. They may also underlie the apparently rapid adoption of kingship as the central political institution, perhaps in the second century BC, and help to explain the uniformity seen in the patterns of ideological reorganisation, with new burial modes and new ritual structures, which were used to reinforce the new social order. The widespread adoption of a large-denomination coinage (Allen 1980), which had taken place rapidly at a time which cannot be fixed with precision, but probably in the third century BC, is perhaps also best seen as a similarly shared means of implementing central control of wealth and its circulation.

Four possible trajectories might be suggested for a system of polities interacting in this way. Firstly, the attempts to control the ambitions of the powerful nobles might be successful. In fact this is broadly what happened, at least for a short time, since no cases are known where the new constitutional arrangements were overthrown, except at the time of the Roman conquest. A network of relatively stable peer polities would thus survive. Secondly, these arrangements might fail. There are several known cases of attempts to restore the kingship and to build a single, larger political entity, some of which have been described above, but, although they all failed, it would not appear that such unification into a higher-order polity was impossible. Thirdly, the main stimulus to the economic intensification and political development of these societies—the opportunity for interaction with the Roman world—could be cut off. This might well have led to the collapse of the system as a whole because of the close interaction between its constituent elements. Fourthly, the polities could be incorporated into a larger entity. This again is what happened. At the time of Roman conquest this part of central France proved one of the easiest to assimilate, perhaps because of its long contact with Rome, its high degree of political centralisation, the emergence of pro-Roman factions, and the relatively large size of the polities, which continued to play a significant part in the political organisation of the area. What factor or factors determined which trajectory was followed is not clear; what is clear is that, because of the inter-polity ties, the whole cluster of polities did behave, or probably would have behaved, as a single unit.

Assessment

This last case study has drawn on the historical evidence to demonstrate not only how, in this particular case, peer polity interaction did play an important part in the widespread adoption of certain specific political institutions, but also that it could have played a similar part in the general development of centralised political authority. But it is one thing to show the utility of the concept in understanding a specific proto-historic case, quite another to develop methods to test it or to generate a body of theory to bridge the gap between the dynamic process of peer polity interaction and the static archaeological record. We have tried to stress some of the problems encountered in applying the concept in these various cases, and it is worthwhile to review them again briefly.

Two problems in particular have to be faced. Firstly, the polities themselves can be difficult to define where historical or ethnographic evidence is lacking. The cultural homogeneity of the cluster of polities as a whole can be so great that it effectively masks the local variations specific to individual polities. Two possible solutions have been found useful here. Analysis of settlement hierarchies, using spatial patterning, might provide a notional model of polity structure, once socio-political development had reached a level visible in this way. This was, in effect, possible in our first case study, and rank–size analysis might also be profitable. Secondly, an archaeological correlate of centralised authority might be recognised. The highly clustered distribution of burials of the sixth century BC containing high-status objects, including Mediterranean imports, would be one example, while in our third case study the second-phase coinage of central France, which used a small number of varieties specific to each polity and was produced for that polity's fiscal purposes, is also of interest; there is a high degree of correlation between some of these coin distributions and the historically known territories of polities. Neither of these suggestions, however, would be of much use in the analysis of networks of societies with a comparatively low level of socio-political development, as, for instance, in our second case study. The difficulty experienced in defining polities in that case is largely due to an excessively chronological and typological approach to the study of the relevant archaeological record, and is not necessarily insuperable. Study of the material in terms of social organisation, which has scarcely begun, might well bring a greater understanding of the nature of social ranking and the degree of political centralisation. The nature and scale of regional grouping would also repay study.

The second problem is that independent evidence for interaction between polities is hard to discern. Though the comparative economic, material, social and political homogeneity of a system could well be explained by the concept of peer polity interaction, that explanation needs testing against the evidence for interaction between the constituent parts of the whole system. In our case studies this evidence was either rare or non-existent. Possible instances of such inter-regional exchange have frequently been noted in passing, but the study of such flows of goods on a more than local scale has not formed a major theme of research.

The application of the concept of peer polity interaction to the three case studies described above has proved enlightening but somewhat inconclusive. Although a full assessment of its utility will not be possible until the archaeological record has been more rigorously investigated in appropriate ways, the concept has attractive possibilities for the explanation of a series of socio-political changes in later prehistoric Europe.

Chapter 5

Peer polity interaction and socio-political change in Anglo-Saxon England
Richard Hodges

'Catatonic obscurity' is how one eminent Anglo-Saxon historian recently described the terminology of the New Archaeology (Wormald 1982). Yet, like it or not, the terminology used by archaeologists and anthropologists has to be employed if definition is to be given to 'notional units of the past' (Harris 1968: 359). The terms refer to concepts and, although they may be readily challenged, these concepts possess a definition which should stand the test of usage. Archaeology, however, is passing through a period of self-analysis after a phase of vigorous creativity, and many terms recently in vogue are not withstanding the test of time (Renfrew 1982c). Consequently, this might seem an inappropriate occasion to introduce another term to archaeology; but, of course, it too must stand on whether it enables us to discuss meaningfully the processes responsible for units of the past.

In our consideration of this matter, it is perhaps useful to keep in mind the poverty of conceptualising in early medieval history. Unlike historians of later periods, early medievalists have resisted the use of anthropological or other terminology to give some finer definition to the beginnings of medieval society. As a result, the central problems of early medieval history have lapsed into what some archaeologists might call a 'long sleep' (Renfrew 1982c). In part, this period of tranquillity in the great Mansion of History can be attributed to the difficulty historians face when wishing to measure behaviour before the advent of abundant taxation documents, in the Renaissance. The *Annales* school of history at the Sorbonne developed a methodology for post-Renaissance history which satisfactorily measured behaviour, but this has not proved so satisfactory for the patchily documented earlier periods. Early medieval history instead comprises a range of individualistic observations of those times: there are saints' lives, the biographies of kings, land charters and a collection of wills and laws. Archaeology, it can be justifiably claimed, offers the best means of measuring those different rhythms of history before AD 1500 that have been identified by Fernand Braudel. These rhythms amount to the history of man's relationship with his environment, the history of groups and groupings, and the history of individuals. History, as Braudel views it, is divided into three different times (Braudel 1975: 20—1) and each can be measured by archaeology. To achieve this, however, archaeologists have to make full use of the record at their disposal. The interactions between settlement systems, production—distribution systems, as well as cultural and cognitive systems, must be defined. In total, these constitute the material record of documented societies. Hence, archaeological and documentary data will reveal the pattern and scale of behaviour and how these were regarded at the time. In the early medieval period, as I shall attempt to illustrate, peer polity analysis adds fresh definition to important processes that can be documented using archaeological and historical sources. Enhanced definition of these processes enables us to comprehend more clearly the three rhythms of history.

In this paper I wish to use the archaeology of the Anglo-Saxon period to illustrate the point outlined above and to demonstrate the merits of peer polity analysis. In this first part of the paper I shall sketch the history of the period between the Roman withdrawal from Britain and the formation of the English nation. This span of five-and-a-half centuries passes through what I shall term three political horizons. The first consists of the Early Saxon period from c. AD 400–600; the second encompasses the century between AD 600–700 when Christianity was adopted by the English; and the third horizon lasts from AD 700–878. The period from AD 878 until the English kingdoms were fully unified in 954 is a period of state formation which I shall also briefly describe. In the second part of the paper I wish to examine the merits of peer polity interaction model in greater detail using this case study. In particular, I wish to look at each of the 'positive statements' which in combination constitute the essence of the peer polity approach. It is in the context of a well-documented period such as the Anglo-Saxon one that a concept like peer polity analysis can be most effectively tested. I also hope to illustrate briefly how archaeological definition enables us to comprehend the intersecting rhythms of history in complex pre-state conditions.

The beginnings of English society

A picture of Britain in the immediate aftermath of the Roman occupation is difficult to imagine. The shock and bitterness felt by the British after the withdrawal of the provincial Roman government is captured by the sixth-century chronicler, Gildas; his account has left a vivid impression of the cataclysm that befell the native population. The legends of King Arthur, the gallant Christian stemming the pagan tide, have been embroidered by medieval and Victorian poets to accentuate the brutality of this period. Yet it is the archaeological record, not the fleeting gasps of contemporary observers, which provides a source of data on the pattern and process of the Anglo-Saxon conquest of southern and eastern Britain (Alcock 1972).

The first political horizon spanning the Early Saxon period was a time of climatic deterioration following a period of stable weather conditions. The North Sea littoral was inundated on the German side and, as recent surveys in Lincolnshire show, on the British side as well. Surveys in the Pennines also indicate withdrawal from upland areas of Britain during this period. It was a time of change, most blatantly reflected in the deserted towns and ruined Roman-period farms which littered the countryside. To the migrants these were the work of giants whose achievement was awesome but not replicable. The rhythm of man in the landscape altered quite dramatically in the later fourth century with the withdrawal of the Roman (economic) will to command the

landscape and, through taxation, a population of a million or more Britons.

The formation of the earliest English political units is a matter of some controversy. How many Britons remained after the Romans departed? How large were the migrations by the Angles, Franks, Frisians, Jutes and Saxons? How did the British and migrant communities adapt to each other? These are questions which archaeologists will answer only when they behave as archaeologists rather than as illustrators of the margins of history (Hills 1979). At present, however, the period of fiercest interaction between these communities is an enigma. Only at the end of the fifth century can we begin to identify political units. In the British sectors, these units appear to be ranked, but far from complex in their organisation. The sub-Roman world of King Arthur consisted of fortified, nucleated settlements which have no obvious ranking: minimal indication of agricultural and industrial production; and a modest participation in long-distance trade (indicated by fragments of Mediterranean amphorae) with Roman communities which were still flourishing. These were the communities which met the Anglo-Saxons at the battle of Mons Badonicus and, after a short-lived victory, were gradually overwhelmed by the Germanic invaders. For two centuries these sub-Roman polities maintained their own material culture, interacting over great distances as they evidently forged their resistance to the migrants.

The warbands of the Germanic polities encountered at Mons Badonicus early in the sixth century are better documented. C.J. Arnold (1980) has sketched the outlines of the evolution of ranking in Early Saxon England using cemetery data. Arnold has made use of the cremation and inhumation cemeteries which are found in most parts of southern, eastern and central England and has argued that at least four tiers of ranking can be detected within the sixth-century Anglo-Saxon cemeteries. The uppermost tier, which becomes most apparent by the middle of this century, is characterised by specialised warrior equipment such as swords, shields and fine, indigenously manufactured jewellery. These social groupings, however, seem to be in contrast with the archaeological evidence of the rest of the settlement system. A number of villages dating to this period have been excavated and none disclose the same marked ranking (Rahtz 1976; Pader 1981; Dixon 1982). Unlike the sub-Roman fortified settlements, often on hilltops, the Anglo-Saxon settlements were undefended clusters of farms that frequently occupied the best environments previously worked by Roman villas. As a rule, moreover, these communities amounted to four or five farms, each about the same size and each with a farmyard defined by a ditch or fence. This contrast between the archaeology of life and that of death is intriguing. The stratification and, indeed, the warrior ideology encapsulated in the funerary rite complemented the simple political system as well as the largely peaceful character of these times.

The existence of peer polity interaction as soon as

ranked societies exist can be demonstrated in the funerary rite. The objects interred with the dead indicate the adoption of a symbolic system within the communities that practised cremation which is similar to the system within those that practised inhumation. The information displayed on the burial accoutrements encompassed the migrant community as a whole, although it evidently had no meaning for the stead-fastly Christian, sub-Roman British. Cost-control changes, as information-handling became more centralised—leading to increasing quality in these funerary accoutrements—cannot be ascribed to any one area. For example, highly decorated funerary urns were made by a number of potters in eastern and south-eastern England during the central decades of the sixth century. J.N.L. Myres, who has studied these pots, has not ascribed the introduction to any one locality, but instead regards the proliferation of skilled craftsmen as evidence of competitive emulation spurring them on to greater status-giving displays (Myres 1977). Indeed, the striking feature of Early Saxon culture is its insular character. There are very few imported objects to lend status to the uppermost tier within the patchwork quilt of polities. Instead, individual craftsmen drew upon traditional artistic schemes and through interaction with other artists developed highly characteristic insular symbol systems. The eighth-century chronicler, Bede, throws a little additional light on this interaction within the Anglo-Saxon region when, at the end of the sixth century, he resumes his history of Britain (after omitting the later fifth and most of the sixth century) and highlights the warfare and the alliances between the emergent Anglo-Saxon aristocracy, as also the impact made by the Christian Mission which had been sent from Rome and was accompanied by Franks. This is the time when individuals and events first appear on the stage, when the *histoire événementielle*, as Braudel calls it, of the English, begins.

The second political horizon begins about the time of the conversion of the English by St Augustine in 597, if not a decade or so earlier (cf. Hodges 1982a: 34), and closes about a century later. During this period the environment of England gradually changed as the climate slowly improved after the later Roman deterioration. Recent surveys show budding-off movements far out into the Lincolnshire fens, and there are burials and place names from this period in the southern part of the Pennines (Ozanne 1962). The Anglo-Saxons also altered their exploitation of the environment, as I shall show below.

During this century, the history of English social groupings takes an important new direction. The settlement system indicates the emergence of individualised leadership, and the historical record confirms the existence of fewer, but larger, polities. This leadership is also apparent from changes in the production—distribution system, and from the advent of a new spiritual order, the Church.

During the sixth century, rich warrior graves, sometimes demarcated within the cemetery, are regarded as an indication of an emergent élite (Arnold 1980). Towards the end of the

century and during the seventh century, the cemeteries take on a new appearance. First, prominent individualised burial comes into fashion (Shepherd 1979). Burial mounds contain rich—sometimes spectacular—grave goods, including gold-and-garnet jewellery (the index of the new fashions), imported drinking equipment, imported clothes and, as a rule, an array of elaborately ornamented weaponry. This individual pro-minence, which I shall attempt to explain in the second part of the paper, accompanied the adoption of Christianity and the development of trading alliances with the Frankish kingdoms on the Continent. Sutton Hoo, the great ship burial found near Ipswich in Suffolk and a display of royal East Anglian power, is the finest of these barrows. But similar barrows promoting the same ideology are found in nearly all the polities of the seventh century. Individualised barrows, however, occur in a phase of comparatively richly furnished cemeteries where earlier traditions are maintained—before the sudden abandonment of this funerary rite and the occurrence of graves without accoutrements. Individualised leadership has also been identified in the settlement pattern. The first 'palaces' occur in the seventh century; Yeavering in Northumberland, for example, is transformed from a small cluster of buildings into a highly distinctive élite centre early in the seventh century (Hope-Taylor 1977). Similarly, the Church—the other pillar of society, as Chaney (1973) has called it—built its own élite centres. Bishops' residences and churches were constructed in the ruined Roman towns, where building materials could be found and where the ideology of the traditional Roman Church could be best promoted. Monasteries were also constructed in the country-side, often on top of, or close to, Roman settlements (Cramp 1976). At this time changes were made to the structure of the settlement pattern itself. In particular, many Early Saxon settlements were deserted, creating what field archaeologists term 'the Middle Saxon shuffle'. Arnold and Wardle (1981) have accounted for this shuffle (occurring in many polities at roughly the same time) as an adaptation to new social and economic demands. The Church, after all, needed land and by c. 700 owned 25 per cent of England. The élite, as a few early charters from the period indicate, were also building up their holdings. Indeed, the competition between the polities is most explicitly illustrated by the great dykes, like Wansdyke in Wiltshire and Devil's Dyke in Cambridgeshire, which date to this period. The mobilisation of labour to construct these great earthworks must have necessitated the kind of management that is well documented by the later eighth and early ninth centuries (Brooks 1971). By then, labour services (to be precise, bridge- and fortress-building work) were a form of taxation owed by almost everyone.

Individualised leadership also gave rise to the exchange of prestige goods between several English kingdoms and their Frankish counterparts. The earliest of these exchange systems probably dates to the 580s, when Kent made a trade pact with the Neustrians (northern French Merovingians). But the first gateway community to have been found is at Ipswich. It served the East Anglian kingdom and gives an impression of the scale of trade. Austrasian (Rhenish Franks) traders came there and, to judge from their pottery, stayed awhile as the exchange was slowly transacted (Hodges 1982a). This was not an exploitative exchange system of the kind postulated by the neo-Marxists (cf. Friedman 1982). As I have shown, early medieval trade in prestige goods was a balanced, administered affair serving the élite, who needed to produce these commodities to stabilise their positions within their own polities. Hence, for example, the Anglo-Saxons obtained gold bullion and garnets, which they used to manufacture jewellery that, for instance, imitated the Frankish brooches of the time, but far exceeded them in quality. This jewellery became the fashion of the early Christian generations. With it, however, came clothes and other luxuries as well as a Frankish metrological system, Frankish builders and glaziers and, of course, a Roman/Frankish cognitive system–the Church.

The emergence of an élite also gave rise to the dynasties and individuals which are the substance of an *histoire événementielle*. The great Anglo-Saxon chronicler, Bede, gives us a very colourful and highly partisan view of these early kings (Wormald 1977). Great emphasis is placed upon King Ethelbert's achievement, as he was responsible for permitting the Christian missions to land and to operate in 597. He had, it seems, a Christian Merovingian royal wife, and hence the alliance between the Franks and the Kentish kingdom was established; but how he came to have this wife is not known. Bede, naturally, emphasises the virtues of the other Anglo-Saxon kings who espoused Christianity, and, as he does so, he charts the succession of militant confrontations which are the other main events of the period. From his history we can follow the shift from elected leadership (Wallace-Hadrill 1971) towards dynastic leadership. We also gain a colourful impression of the competitive emulation between the aristocracy, which becomes an increasingly significant factor in the political geography of Middle Saxon England.

The third political horizon in which peer polity interaction can again be observed begins symbolically, towards the end of the seventh century, with a fiscal survey known as the Tribal Hidage (Fig. 5.1a), and ends just as symbolically on the windy Wiltshire ridge where King Alfred settled half of England with Danish Vikings, keeping half for himself. During these two centuries the climate gradually became a little warmer than present, reaching its optimal point in the tenth to early twelfth centuries. By the early to mid-ninth century the prospects for extending the confines of cultivation became apparent, although the significant movements into what might be termed 'marginal landscapes' are a feature of the tenth century in all parts of western Europe from Italy to Norway. Population–that other dimension of Braudel's 'timeless history'–appears to have grown at a slow rate from the sixth or seventh centuries onwards; we have no means of measuring it satisfactorily as yet. However, it has been estimated that

there were a million people in early fourth-century Britain, and a million in 1086 when the Norman Domesday survey was prepared. The archaeological evidence suggests that the population of southern and eastern England doubled and possibly trebled between c. 900 and 1086. Hence, we might estimate a population of about half a million when King Alfred died, and possibly around half that number when St Augustine landed in 597, although this last figure is extremely difficult to gauge (Wailes 1972). The fact that the land under cultivation in 1914 was about the same as that farmed in 1066 and that nearly thirty times as many people were being supported during the wartime economy illustrates (no more) the underdeveloped character of the Middle Saxon economy.

The political configurations of eighth- and ninth-century England are comparatively well documented. The Tribal Hidage and the later Anglo-Saxon Chronicle offer a fairly accurate account of the Middle Saxon polities. The Tribal Hidage, in particular, provides a perspective of six of the seven major kingdoms (it omits Northumbria), as well as of some 24 satellites. These territories have been recently considered as a three-level size hierarchy (Davies and Vierck 1974). The largest territories were in excess of 7,000 hides (over 3,360 sq. km) and include only four of the six major kingdoms; the intermediate units range between 3,500 and 7,000 hides (1,680–3,360 sq. km) and include nine territories, of which two were autonomous kingdoms during this period; lastly, there were seventeen small units ranging in size between 300 and 1,200 hides (144–576 sq. km). In other words, the largest category was roughly the size of two notional ESM's and the intermediate territories were about the size of one ESM (Renfrew 1975). During the course of the eighth century, the kingdom of Wessex gained a paramount ascendancy in the first two decades, after which Mercia maintained supremacy over the other kingdoms–or so the historians of this period indicated (Fig. 5.1b). Mercia retained this supremacy over the other polities until the death of King Coenwulf in 821; after that, Wessex achieved the status of the paramount kingdom and was in this position when the Danish Vikings began their conquest of England in the late 860s (Campbell 1982). The many intermediate and small units were gradually swallowed up by these two great kingdoms, although Northumbria remained independent of both until the Vikings overran it in 866.

The archaeology of this period reflects the increasing political authority invested in kingship; its most explicit expression is to be found in the two great gateway communities of Middle Saxon England. Southampton was laid out around 700. A deep ditch was cut, enclosing about 46 ha of low-lying ground, and a grid of gravelled streets was constructed. Thereafter, for just over a century, the emporium accommodated traders from northern French courts and monasteries, who brought prestige goods for the West Saxon hierarchy. It has been estimated that some 5,000 people were in the emporium at the beginning, and the total, though

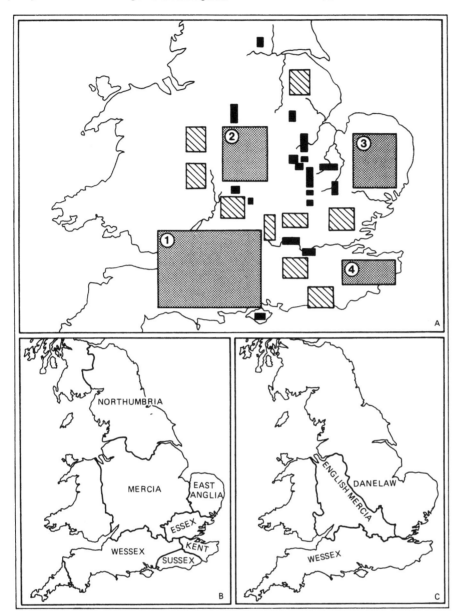

Fig. 5.1. Anglo-Saxon England between the seventh and later ninth centuries. (A) A schematic presentation of the Tribal Hidage, a seventh-century tribute list probably prepared by the king of Mercia. The map shows the location of the kingdoms recorded in the document and their relative tributes. Twenty-nine kingdoms are listed, and can be divided into three tax categories, with Wessex (1), Mercia (2), East Anglia (3) and Kent (4) being assessed at the highest level of taxation. (B) The approximate political configurations of England under kings Offa (of Mercia) and Egbert (of Wessex) between the late eighth and early ninth centuries. In this era, royal power was emerging as an important feature of Anglo-Saxon society. (C) The division of England in 878 between King Alfred of Wessex and the Danish leader, Guthrum, resulted in the Danelaw—the kingdoms of eastern England under Danish and Norwegian control. The eventual defeat (in 954) of the Scandinavian chiefs led to the unification of England and the sanctification of the West Saxon dynasty.

fluctuating with the changes in political figures, probably remained at about this level until a civil war in the 830s destroyed the Carolingian Empire (Hodges 1982a). Ipswich was approximately the same size and almost certainly served the East Anglian hierarchy (and, through them in all likelihood also the Mercians). The imported pottery indicates that its trade connections were with courts and monasteries in Flanders and the Rhineland (Hodges, in press). The interesting feature of these emporia, which were ten times larger in areal terms than the next largest settlements and had populations that were fifty times larger than any other settlements, is that they were planned and created on this scale. Hence, if the trade in prestige goods was intended to stabilise the political position of the élite (cf. Friedman 1982), this was on a very large scale virtually from its inception. Indeed, so large was the scale of the transactions that the kings must have found it difficult to administer these emporia ruthlessly. Their position, in other words, must have been secure enough to accept that some of these imported materials might by-pass the royal

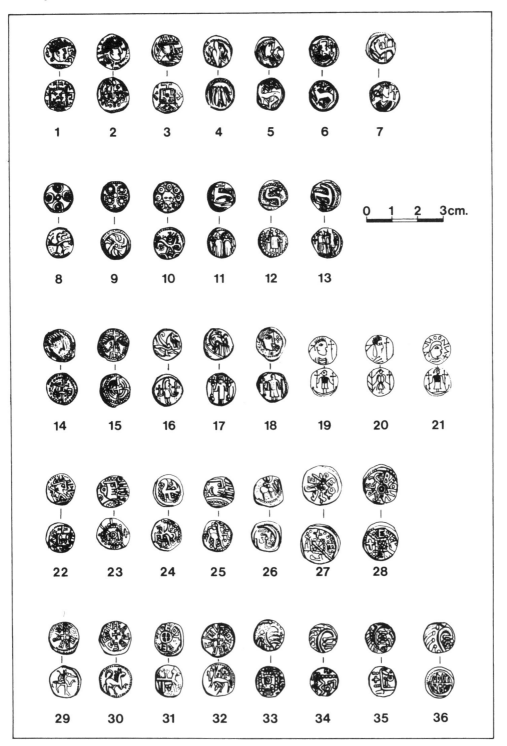

Fig. 5.2. Anglo-Saxon sceattas. The sequence of late seventh- to mid-eighth-century silver pennies is contentious. It is commonly believed that a primary series (nos. 1–3) was followed by a regionally diversified secondary series in c. 720 (nos. 4–36). The primary series were exclusively issued in Kent; these bear Continental symbols and may be related to a formal prestige goods exchange. The symbols on the secondary sceattas are more diverse, and may have been employed as low-value media in élite-controlled exchanges of regional commodities. The jumble of symbols are difficult to discriminate between. They are as follows: Kent (nos. 4–7), Wessex (nos. 8–13), Mercia (including Hwicce) (nos. 14–21), East Anglia (nos. 22–8), Northumbria (nos. 29–32). Nos. 33–6 are known as porcupines and may be Frisian coins, or English copies of Frisian sceattas.

network and thus ostensibly threaten the underlying rationale for the commerce in terms of alliances made between the ecclesiastical and secular élites in Britain and on the Continent (cf. Smith 1976: 314).

Another feature of this horizon is the growing importance of coinage, and its development in metrological terms in line with Carolingian currency. However, the initial series of coins, known as sceattas (Fig. 5.2), and the later pennies were minted as weights and with prominent designs that owe little to Continental symbol systems. Both types of coin have a strong Anglo-Saxon character, showing the existence of structural homologies. The same point can also be made as far as works of art (Fig. 5.3) and architecture are concerned. During the early part of this period, Anglo-Saxon missionaries were part of the consignments taken to the Rhineland in return for Rhenish luxuries (Levison 1946). These missionaries spearheaded the Carolingian annexation of the pagan territories to the north and east of the Rhine. They also introduced some of the quite spectacular ecclesiastical arts to the Continental monasteries. However, towards the end of the eighth century, the Carolingian Empire generated a cultural *renovatio* to express the vibrant new ideology of the Frankish Roman Church (Ullmann 1969). It is interesting to trace what elements of this *renovatio* reached England, whilst bearing in mind that within the Empire itself the movement

Fig. 5.3. The Fuller brooch. A classic illustration of early ninth-century Anglo-Saxon workmanship. This brooch illustrates the highly capable and creative artistic capabilities of the Anglo-Saxons and the vibrant figurative elements typical of Carolingian silversmithing at this date. Like many silver pieces dating from this epoch, the Fuller brooch reflects the integration of two dominant styles at a time when the Carolingian ideology was endeavouring to impose itself upon Christian and political thinking in England.

was as vigorous in central Italy as it was in the Rhineland (Hodges and Whitehouse 1983: 103–11). It appears that in Mercia the Anglo-Saxons adopted some aspects of the new Roman formalism (e.g. arches over portraits); the same features were also incorporated in the most magnificent of all early medieval works of art, the Book of Kells, painted around 800 in Iona. But in both cases insular symbol systems were rampant in the pictures and friezes. The West Saxon sculpture of this period and the great array of metalwork are even more insular in style. A case can be made out, however, *contra* Biddle (1975), for interpreting the Old Minster at Winchester— only 12 miles from Hamwih (Saxon Southampton)—as an adaptation of Carolingian architectural ideas in an Anglo-Saxon context. In short, the artists of the period resisted the full weight of the *renovatio* while acknowledging the importance of the new ideology. We might note that only once does an Anglo-Saxon king call himself Emperor, in imitation of the title of the Carolingian leader, and even then only titles himself Emperor of Mercia (Yorke 1981: 177).

Archaeology appears to reveal the growing status of kingship, although the lineage system, as well as the Church, prevented kings from the grandest aspirations. However, the collapse of the trading systems and the Viking menace altered the fundamental character of Middle Saxon England. The next political horizon in many ways is the most fascinating.

In the 860s the Danish Vikings suddenly changed from being pirates to being conquerors. There are many reasons for this, but the result was momentous (Hodges and Whitehouse 1983: 102–22). Kingdom after kingdom fell to the Danes until only Wessex stood before the Danish leader, Guthrum. In 878 the West Saxon king, Alfred, and the Danish king led their forces into battle at Etheldun. The outcome of this battle suggests that the West Saxons managed, just, to gain the upper hand. Alfred ceded half of England to the Danes, thenceforth known as the Danelaw, and he retained command of the other half. The political configuration of Anglo-Saxon England was altered on that day (Fig. 5.1c). The polities had been fused into two territories. Alfred almost at once planned to take back the Danelaw. Within eight years he had embarked upon a programme of fortress-building and military preparation. These fortresses became refuges for the community, which he later transformed into market-places (Biddle 1976; Davis 1982). The militia system was replaced by a small permanent army and the first English navy. At the same time King Alfred enhanced the legal status of kingship, and as a result of his resistance to the Danes he achieved a position unrivalled until then in Anglo-Saxon history. To him can be attributed, in the 890s, a system of markets and the development of regularly spaced manufacturing industries (Hodges 1982a: 162–84). It seems to be no coincidence that in the same decade the Viking kings instigated the same market ventures. Unlike the West Saxons, however, the Danes had to import ideas either from Wessex or the Continent; these markets and their new manufacturing industries were in fact initiated by captured or willing Continental craftsmen.

The tenth century witnessed the astonishing development of the Anglo-Scandinavian economy. Despite the intermittent wars between the West Saxons and the Danes up until the unification of England in 954, the market system flourished as settlement, production—distribution systems, and the evidence for churches dating to this period indicate. In this period the two polities transformed their underdeveloped economies without recourse to international trade (at least of an archaeologically detectable sort). After 954, when the last Viking king fled York, the unified nation under the West Saxon dynasty experienced a quite remarkable economic expansion, with a comparable expansion of the population also occurring in this period. At the same time, distinctive regional art styles developed in the heart of the West Saxon kingdom (known as Winchester style), and in the heart of the Viking kingdom around York. These owed only a little to Continental art (Parsons 1975), and indeed the pattern of Anglo-Saxon art and architecture before the Norman conquest was as insular and as vigorous in its creativity as was the fast-expanding regional market system. Strong, centralised kingship and the very apparent wealth of England were the incentives for Duke William to invade the island in 1066.

Peer polity interaction and socio-political change

The existence of a number of autonomous polities interacting with each other can be documented in Anglo-Saxon England from approximately the end of the fifth century until England was divided into two at Etheldun in 878. However, there are three horizons within this period in which the socio-political circumstances developed step by step towards the formation of a nation state. Throughout this period we can detect homologies encompassing these polities and, with the fine historical chronology available to us and with a sometimes useful historical record, we can also begin to comprehend the interactions which led to shared structures. We should note, of course, that the polities shared a common language, although from the eighth or ninth centuries dialects can be identified. Similarly, common house forms exist for the polities until the later ninth or tenth centuries, when regional variation becomes increasingly prominent (Addyman 1972; Dixon 1983). But the real interest of Anglo-Saxon England lies in the mediation that existed between the interactions of the polities and those Continental influences which might be crudely defined as an example of a core—periphery relationship. To illustrate this important point more fully I now wish to examine each of the six characteristics which Renfrew suggests as attributes of peer polity interaction (this volume: 7—8).

(i) It is predicted that, when one polity is recognised, other neighbouring polities of comparable size and organisation will be found in the same region. In the evolution of Anglo-Saxon society through the three pre-state horizons, this statement is well endorsed. In the earliest horizon small tribal territories competed with one another. Most were between about 500 and 1,500 sq. km in area, as far as we can tell. Trade relations with the Frankish kingdoms, as well as

inter-polity competition, led to the emergence of seven major kingdoms in the second political horizon, spanning the seventh century. During this time many Early Saxon polities were swallowed up by kingdoms like Mercia, Northumbria and Wessex, although the Tribal Hidage clearly indicates that many more small, migration-period territories continued to exist as autonomous polities until the eighth century. This process of mergers continued in the eighth century—the third political horizon. Four kingdoms dominated the political history of England immediately before the Vikings: East Anglia, Mercia, Northumbria and Wessex (Fig. 5.1a). The ninth-century (West Saxon) *Anglo-Saxon Chronicle* colourfully records the expansion of each of these polities as the last of the smaller Early Saxon polities were consumed by the great kingdoms. Finally, we should note that none of these kingdoms could gain absolute ascendancy over the others, although for long periods in the later eighth and ninth centuries Mercia, and then Wessex did dominate the other three. The unification of the kingdoms was made possible by the political upheaval created whilst the Vikings overran most of the country.

(ii) and (iii) Organisational change with concomitant institutional features will occur in all the polities at about the same time. This is borne out by the Anglo-Saxon evidence, although the impact of Frankish prestige exchange upon the English élite has to be kept in mind. In the earliest horizon, the development of a hierarchical structure has been identified by cemetery analysis; the emergence of an élite, for example, has been documented in Deiran, Kentish, East Saxon and northern West Saxon cemeteries, all at about the same time (Arnold 1980). This organisational change, however, can be seen much more clearly in the second horizon, in the seventh century, when the rich graves are either dated by imported gold coins or by the fineness of the gold in the jewellery found with the dead (Kent 1975). Hence we can chart the spread of the Frankish—Christian burial rite. It seems that the earliest Anglo-Saxon kings recognised the status this Frankish ideology bestowed upon them. Their fathers had been elected to power by the aristocracy within the kingdom, but they themselves evidently aspired to establishing dynasties, as Bede illustrates for the Mercian and Northumbrian houses (Wallace-Hadrill 1971). The Church offered a means of altering the social rules, while traditional legitimacy was endorsed by a final, quite spectacular burial rite (as at Sutton Hoo) when the son sought recognition for his rights through the lavish disposal of traditional and Frankish—Christian imported goods in a pagan ceremony. Thereafter, the Church safeguarded the rights of the dynasty which supported it, and the status of the dynasty was promoted by the living king rather than by his politically insecure successor. Kingship and the Church, in other words, were intertwined as the élite sought a means of securing power for their families. The advent of this individualised leadership as it passed through the critical phase of securing long-term dynastic power is clearly documented in the archaeological record in the form of the brief spell of rich seventh-century

burials, followed by an equally brief spell of church-building—the churches being constructed by alien architects (Arnold 1982). This social engineering occurs in Kent first, then in Essex, then in East Anglia and Deira, then in north Wessex and Mercia. By the later seventh century, gold-and-garnet jewellery—the symbol of this brief period—becomes a sign of the past. Such objects are no longer worn and are no longer buried with the dead. However, the latest piece to have been found comes from the coffin of St Cuthbert, who died in 697; his pectoral cross had been mended many times. From this time forward personal wealth was promoted within the churches.

In the third political horizon, we can distinguish the same dialogue between the polities on the one hand, and between specific kingdoms and their Frankish contacts on the other. Coinage provides a useful illustration. In the later seventh century the Franks abandoned the traditional Roman metrological system and devised their own, based on Germanic mensuration. Almost at once the kingdom of Kent imitated the new silver pennies, possibly because an exchange system linked the Austrasian Franks and Kent. Since their first pennies are almost indistinguishable, it seems that the Kentish court simply imitated the Frankish coins. However, the concept was gradually found to be useful by other Anglo-Saxon polities, as interaction between themselves, and with Franks, developed. These 'secondary sceattas', first minted in Wessex and Mercia, followed a different course. Their form was the same as the Kentish sceattas, but their weights and designs were altogether different. A decade later the Northumbrian court began to use these coins, and its sceattas are quite different again (Hodges and Cherry 1983). The pattern of coinage in every respect became highly insular and, while few secondary sceattas occur on the Continent, there are many primary sceattas. By contrast, the pattern of secondary-sceatta distribution within England is an excellent illustration of peer polity interaction, contrasting with the highly concentrated Kentish distribution of primary sceattas (Fig. 5.2). The process, in fact, was repeated once more when the Frankish court decided to reform their coinage in 757. This time, however, the initial imitative coins were minted in East Anglia, then Kent, then Mercia, then Wessex, However, Northumbria never adopted this type of reform penny and was still minting a highly degraded form of sceatta when the Vikings conquered the kingdom in the 860s. The peer polity model in these instances mediates between the neo-Marxist concept of core—periphery relations and the concept of indigenous development. Interactions between the Anglo-Saxon kingdoms were responsible for their receptivity to Frankish concepts; those within England, however, qualified the acceptance of these alien concepts.

(iv) The locus of the observed features will be seen to develop first within different polities within the region.
This contradicts the multilinear evolutionary trajectories proposed by the neo-Marxists (e.g. Friedman 1982; Gledhill and Rowlands 1982). The statement also runs counter to

many historical expectations, yet, as I have just illustrated, the point is confirmed within the Anglo-Saxon context. Possibly the most interesting illustration of this point from this period focuses upon prestige goods exchange. Historians and some uncritical archaeologists have always assumed the paramount role of the Kentish court in Anglo-Frankish trade throughout this period. Yet we can now demonstrate that East Anglia was managing its own trade connections at the same time as Kent was inviting Christian missionaries to its court. We can also document the rise of West Saxon trade on a remarkable scale at the end of the seventh century and its persistence during the mid-eighth century, a period in which it is the Mercian kings who have commanded historians' respect. Equally, we can document the rise of Ipswich, the gateway community for East Anglia, linking that kingdom to the Carolingian court at a time when the Carolingians were participating in an international trading system (Hodges and Whitehouse 1983). Yet the East Anglian court remains a complete enigma to historians of this period. These massive trading settlements, we might conclude, reflect the will of individuals and the highly individualistic pattern of their relationships. These were not exploited secondary states readily plundered of raw materials, but sensitive participants in balanced commerce, as an exchange of letters dated to the 790s between the great Carolingian king, Charlemagne, and Offa of Mercia illustrates (Whitelock 1955: 781—2).

To illustrate this point in another respect, we might briefly consider the two most famous Anglo-Saxons, from a European perspective, before Alfred: Bede and Alcuin. Both were Northumbrians, and as a result they have accorded that kingdom a historical status in political terms that is not borne out by archaeology. Yet these men were responsible for considerable Frankish investment being made in the Northumbrian kingdom and contributed beyond all doubt to one of the finest cultural movements in the medieval period. In short, the role of the individual in complex pre-state circumstances constitutes an undoubtedly important variable in the development of that society.

(v) The process of transformation can be attributed to the interaction between the polities, which may be examined as (a) competition, (b) symbolic entrainment, and (c) increased flow in the exchange of goods. To begin with the third point first, it is extremely difficult to document the flow of inter-regionally exchanged goods within a collection of polities such as Anglo-Saxon England. The historical data on this matter are poor and the archaeological record is not fine enough to detect the movement of food-stuffs, for example, which probably was the principal feature of these interactions. Systematic regional research programmes involving survey and excavation to recover the settlement and production—distribution systems are needed, but how rare are such programmes! Instead, archaeologists have contented themselves with central places and surveys of their environs (Hodges 1982b). In Anglo-Saxon archaeology we are beginning to witness a positive attempt to carry out pro-

grammes of this kind, but it will be a decade before we shall be able to consider the results.

However, we can examine core—periphery relations as exemplified in the prestige goods exchange. Excavations at Southampton, for instance, indicate no signs of the *increased flow* that Renfrew predicts. Instead (as at other European gateway communities) these settlements began on a level which was more or less maintained, depending upon the relations between participating élites. Their role was to achieve a level of economic stability, and many factors prevented an increased volume of trade. One obvious one in the Anglo-Saxon period was that the boats of the time had very restricted cargo capacities, and only a major technological improvement or many new craft could enable the volume of goods to be increased (Hodges 1982a: 94–100). The population was evidently increasing at a slow rate, and the gradual improvement in the climate allowed agrarian resources to expand. But of one matter we can be sure: regional production increased slowly and élite wealth increased at the same pace. Social change leading to the formation of the nation state transformed the bases of society, and population, production and regional distribution increased on a scale that is readily detected even by second-rate archaeological programmes.

By contrast, competition and symbolic entrainment were evidently key factors governing political change. Competition between polities and the slow increases in agrarian production provided the foundations of political change, but the transformation itself seems to have been effected with the support of an exogenous ideology. Hence, Christianity was the means by which seventh-century kings changed the social order, but the Church itself, of course, made use of the developments which preceded its arrival, as well as the interaction between the polities accentuated by its arrival. We have yet to establish the context for the massive increase in long-distance trade at the end of the seventh century, but we can be sure that the West Saxon trade and the Northumbrian renaissance (responsible for such masterpieces as the Lindisfarne Gospels) are part of an important change in the *structure* of Anglo-Saxon society. We can be in no doubt that ideology was a critical variable in medieval society, one appreciated by Alfred and so in all likelihood not lost on early Anglo-Saxon kings. The use of new concepts, like the use made of great scholars, was often as machiavellian as the political gamesmanship with which we are familiar (cf. Ullmann 1969). To detect this, however, we must be able to place the cognitive and cultural aspects of the archaeological record in their systemic context. Peer polity interaction seems to emphasise this point *contra* many recent polemical statements on cognitive archaeology (cf. Hodder 1982b).

(vi) We predict transformations in these polities associated with the intensification of production and the further development of hierarchical structures for the exercise of power. Here, Anglo-Saxon archaeology

indicates quite the opposite. Instead, at the point of political transformation (in each horizon), it is possible to show the existence of moderately increasing production before and after the moment of change. However, the management of resources appears to change at the inception of a new political horizon. The 'Middle Saxon shuffle', like the incidence of land charters, is a mark of this development. The complex laws of Ina, King of Wessex, written down as Hamwih was being created, may reflect further managerial changes at the end of the seventh century. The Tribal Hidage is another index of changing managerial attitudes to resources. But there is no evidence of an increased volume of agrarian produce, and if we use other archaeological measures, such as coinage or pottery, as a means of illustrating the pattern of production during the Middle Saxon period, we must seriously doubt any archaeologically detectable phase of 'intensification' as such. Intensification, however, most clearly occurred in the tenth century, on a scale which transformed the character of the land. As I have shown elsewhere (Hodges 1982a: 185–98), production was organised to meet the needs of the political élite. The number of specialists (in the Church, on the land, in the royal administration etc.) was extremely small before the creation of the state, at which time a new energy system came into being with all the ramifications that that entailed (Gall and Saxe 1977).

Conclusion

Peer polity interaction is a valuable concept for the Anglo-Saxon period because it directs attention to two important aspects of this epoch. First, it emphasises the circumstances upon which socio-political transformation can be built; it focuses on the systemic interactions which make change possible. Secondly, it qualifies the useful models proposed by neo-Marxist anthropologists and geographers. On the one hand, it emphasises the existence of balanced trade in the substantivist framework (Dalton 1975), as opposed to the exploitative frameworks that form the guiding principle of the core—periphery model used by Wallerstein 1974), Smith (1976) and Friedman (1982). On the other hand, it underlines the mediation between the polities and the imported ideas as well as the luxuries, which in these circumstances often proved to be a critical variable in stabilising political change. This concept, therefore, draws attention to the interaction between processes and individual action. It emphasises the stepped (or punctuated) evolution of complex societies and the systemic consequences of this transition. To appreciate such a complex trajectory, however, calls for sound archaeological data and a fine chronology, as I have indicated. In these circumstances, the concept of peer polity analysis enhances our comprehension of the interaction between the three levels of history defined by Braudel; it compels us to investigate the relations between archaeology and history; and, above all, it sheds light on the processes of the past which are too often reduced in a meaningless manner when such concepts are lacking (cf. Adams 1974).

Chapter 6

Jiehao, tonghao: peer relations in East Asia
Gina L. Barnes

One of the most pressing problems in East Asian archaeology today is the assessment of the relationships between China, Korea and Japan (Fig. 6.1) in bringing about complex social development in the Yellow Sea region. North China developed relatively early: by 1200 BC there was a highly stratified society known as the Shang, indicated archaeologically at Anyang by elaborate shaft-tomb graves, craft specialisation in bronze, jade and ceramics, and the beginnings of literacy and administration, seen in the oracle bones (Chang 1980). Competition and then warfare between the feudal states of the Zhou period, which developed in the wake of the Shang civilisation (Table 6.1), characterised much of the first millennium BC. Unification of these feudal states under the Han Dynasty in 206 BC marked the beginning of an expansionist empire. Chinese military outposts were established on the continent around the periphery of the empire, including Luolang and Taifang on the Korean peninsula, drawing local populations into a complex system of trade and exchange (Yu 1967). Furthermore, the courts of Han and Wei, a subsequent dynasty, frequently dispatched envoys to distant lands to record the customs of local inhabitants. As a result, we are given our first historical glimpse of life in the Japanese islands during what is known archaeologically as the Yayoi period. Island envoys to the Chinese court are also recorded from AD 57 onwards in the Chinese dynastic chronicles, and by the mid-third century AD, 30 'countries' (*kuni*) in Japan

were said to be maintaining relations with the Chinese court (Tsunoda and Goodrich 1951: 8).

Because of the undeniable fact of the incorporation of the Korean peninsula and the Japanese islands into the greater Han cultural sphere, the development of complex societies in these areas has often been explained away as a secondary manifestation of Chinese culture. For example, it has been standard practice to derive the formation of the four Korean kingdoms of the middle first millennium AD—Paekche, Kaya, Silla and Koguryo—directly from the military occupation of the peninsula by the Chinese beginning in 108 BC, although there is currently a trend to reject this interpretation (Pearson 1979). In turn, the impetus for Japanese state formation has been characterised by some as the conquest of the islands by a horse-riding élite from the Korean peninsula (Egami 1964; 1967; Ledyard 1975).

These explanations explicitly embody a core–periphery, superior–inferior framework for looking at cultural development, first in the case of China versus Korea and then in the case of Korea versus Japan. In both cases, reliance on the concepts of diffusion and colonisation prematurely obviates any investigation of the possibility of an indigenous elaboration of social organisation. Furthermore, it ignores the fact that states are intricate forms of social organisation, requiring economic and political foundations that are more than diffused traits and that cannot be created overnight. The

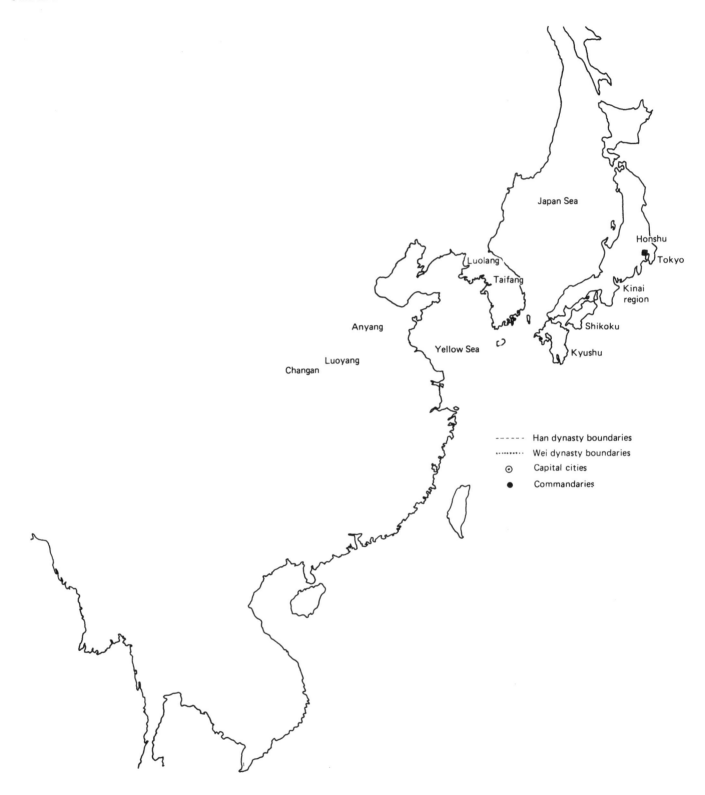

Fig. 6.1. Yellow Sea interaction sphere: north China, Korean peninsula and western Japanese islands.

Table 6.1. *East Asian chronological chart*

	Chinese mainland	Korean peninsula	Japanese islands
BC			
1700			
1500	Shang civilisation	Chulmun (mesolithic)	Jomon (mesolithic)
1300			
1100			
900	Zhou period	Bronze–Iron Age	
700			
500			
300			
	221 Qin Dynasty		
	206		
100		108 Establishment of Luolang commandary	Yayoi (agriculturalists)
AD	Han Dynasty		
100			
	220		
300	Three kingdoms		
	Six dynasties	Three kingdoms	Kofun
500		Koguryo Paekche Silla	(Mounded Tomb culture)
	581 Sui Dynasty		
	618		
700	Tang Dynasty	668	
		United Silla	710
			Nara period

qualitative transformation of a simple society into one with the complexity of a fully-fledged state occurs through time within a systemic context, and involves changes in basic socio-economic variables which can be monitored archaeologically. These include demographic changes, increasing specialisation in crafts and agricultural production, increasingly hierarchical organisation, and the development of specialised administrative facilities.

Although societies in both the Korean peninsula and the Japanese islands were constantly subject to influence from the central Chinese area, their trajectories of social development, in terms of the above variables, are more similar to each other than to China. In particular, the emergence of state-like polities occurred at approximately the same time in both Korea and Japan, namely around the fifth century AD. This suggests that the development of complex society in these two areas occurred as part of a single process involving both of them equally, a process which can and should be segregated from the more generalised influences of China on each. Several facts support this line of thinking:

1   Archaeologically identifiable polities in Korea developed four to five centuries after the initial Chinese colonisation, so the latter's influence on actual state formation must have been of secondary importance.

2   The simultaneous appearance of strong Japanese and Korean polities took place at a time when China itself was divided into smaller contending states, none of which pursued a policy of foreign aggression or intervention such as had occurred during the Han Dynasty.

3   Early Japanese polities utilised objects derived from the continent for the symbolic expression of political relations; however, the relations expressed were not those between China and Japan, but those between polities in Japan itself.

4   The peninsular and insular kings mentioned in the early chronicles maintained contact with China, and their relations with the Chinese court might be characterised as hierarchical. However, as Hirano (1977: 72) emphasises, 'the relations [between Korea and Japan] are more properly described by the frequently repeated terms [in the Chinese accounts] for peer relations, *jiehao* and *tonghao*'.[1] Military conflicts between various kings are also attested to in stele inscriptions on the peninsula (Szczesniak 1952), as well as in the early Japanese chronicles covering the period in question (Aston 1896).

Thus, it is possible to view the developments in Korea and Japan in the context of a nexus of interactions which were tangential to China proper. While the presence of core—periphery relationships between China and Japan/Korea is acknowledged, I am suggesting that they were not of prime importance in bringing the peripheral states into existence. Instead, it can be postulated that the crucial relationships occurred within the Korea—Japan subregion and took the form of interaction between political groupings that were essentially 'peer' to each other.

The developmental sequence in this subregion can be divided into two stages: (a) when polity interrelations were conditioned by, and confined to, interactions within Japan and Korea respectively, and (b) when the major polity interactions took place between Japan and Korea. The first stage encompasses the second to fourth centuries AD, while the second stage covers the fifth and sixth centuries. Before examining the details of this developmental sequence, it is necessary first to clarify how I understand the concept of peer polity interaction and how I will be using it to illuminate the East Asian case.

Us verus them: a model for élite interaction

Although in Renfrew's formulation of the peer polity interaction model (this volume: Ch. 1) the units in interaction may be anything from the autonomous village to the state, here I will confine my definition of 'polity' to those social units with formal political structure—that is, centralised societies occupying hierarchically organised territories. Within these centralised hierarchical polities, it is interaction at the upper social levels that I see as the crucial driving force for social development and organisational elaboration. Thus, in this paper I will use the concept of peer polity interaction only in the sense of interaction among élites of equivalent political groupings.

Peer polity interaction is judged to be an effective concept for organising the East Asian data primarily because, unlike earlier formulations of interaction, it specifies the unit of social activity: the stratified polity. In doing so, it avoids the assumption of undifferentiated social space implicitly built into diffusionist models of interaction, and it avoids the assumption of 'through flow' in network models of interaction, where the social unit is merely a node through which interaction activities pass. (Compare Irwin-Williams (1977) and Ammerman and Cavalli-Sforza (1979) with Alden (1979) and Struever and Houart (1972).) The peer polity concept places the focus of interaction squarely on the different status groups of people occupying the polity.

The peer polity concept as originally defined does not provide a model for élite interaction, since it was designed to be of use in a wide range of social situations; thus it is first necessary to develop such a model. In this section I will draw on concepts from three existing spheres of investigation in order to construct a synthetic model of how interaction between peer polities can foster organisational elaboration. These existing concepts are (i) that for determining social identity, (ii) that for interest group formation, and (iii) that

for prestige goods production and distribution. First, a formulation of interpersonal social relations derived from Japan may be useful in structuring an approach to élite interaction: this is the concept of in-group(*uchi*)/out-group(*soto*) relations (Nakane 1970). Commonly applied to account for patterns of interaction in modern Japanese society, this concept specifies individual identity in terms of us/them relations. At any particular moment, individuals interact with an 'in-group' as participating members and everyone else is considered part of the 'out-group'. However, the composition of both groups will change at different moments according to the identity needs of the individual; they may shift focus, or expand or contract in size. The concept focuses on the individual and can be extended to include first the family, then the neighbourhood, the place of work, the region of residence and finally the nation state. Depending on the particular needs of the moment, individuals may place themselves as members within any one of these units. The two important aspects of this concept are (i) that membership identification is continually shifting between small and large groups and (ii) that people who are considered as outsiders at a lower level of inclusion ('my family versus your family') are often considered as insiders at a higher level ('our neighbourhood versus that other neighbourhood'). The level of group identification is determined by social context and not by absolute or invariant criteria.

This insider/outsider concept is clearly not related to a particular level of social organisation; nevertheless, it can serve to clarify what may be happening during peer polity formation. An important element in the formation of hierarchical polities is the emergence of an élite. Current models of social evolution postulate that in some cases this may be effected by a particular lineage assuming the role of representatives of the ancestors, mediating access by the other lineages to the ancestral (and territorial) spirits (Friedman and Rowlands 1977). The élite at the apex of such conically arranged societies are thus very much involved, as the deities' major representatives, with the internal structuring, scheduling and functioning of activities. Nevertheless, personal interactive ties are established outside the conical unit with the élite of other similar social formations. The élite therefore have the choice of identification with either their own local polity or a supralocal élite grouping.

The intensity with which members identify with one or the other may determine whether élite objects and social 'structures' are shared between polities or whether local differences are stressed to maintain identity differences. If identification is essentially local, then interaction may lead to the trading of certain ideas or material items between polities, but these are then reinterpreted in a local context. Elite interests directed internally, therefore, may lead to 'balkanization' (Freidel 1981a), with a number of shared traits but no coherent integrative system connecting the polities. On the other hand, if identification is with the supralocal grouping, then interaction may lead to the retention and reproduction of traded items and ideas with minimal reinterpretation. A homogeneous symbolic content is maintained because it represents membership in the wider, élite group; it is also the key to that membership and ensures its continuation. Elite interests directed externally, then, will result in activities and social 'structures' having considerable homogeneity and conformity through space. This conformity is predicated on participation and a feeling of membership, not on anonymous transactions.

The formation of an élite subculture is essentially the objectification of social stratification in material terms. Stratification or the formation of social classes has long been a crucial concept in the study of state origins; yet in the study of modern society, where the concept of 'class' has been most used, it is falling into disfavour as an analytical concept. Instead, attention is coming to be focused on smaller 'interest' groups (Cohen 1974). Cohen stresses that membership in, or identification with, an interest group is always accompanied by the manipulation of symbolic forms—material symbols as generalised as style of dress, and non-material symbols including language, dialect, accent, etc. It is by these symbols that members recognise each other and proceed to communicate or interact, knowing that they share similar value systems and basic background information.

It is my perception that the crucial step in the formation of an élite subculture is the development of qualitatively different material objects that symbolise élite group membership. Thus the formation of a supralocal élite interaction network is postulated to coincide with the creation of prestige goods which are subject to sumptuary rules. These prestige goods are more than indicators of wealth; they are the material symbols of group membership. Therefore, the distribution of the objects through social space reflects not merely the ability to acquire them through trade relations, but reflects even more the restrictions against acquiring them without belonging to the 'in-group'. These sumptuary rules pose a problem, namely the maintenance of restricted access to those goods during both production and distribution. Essentially, such goods may be acquired in one of two ways: they may be extracted from, or obtained through, exclusive trade arrangements with social units which are not part of the élite membership group; or they may be produced locally under élite control. These conditions will have differing effects on the structural elaboration of society: the former may lead to the territorial expansion of the élite group to include those from whom it obtains its needed goods; and the latter may lead to greater craft and administrative specialisation within the local polity.

Combining these three concepts—of insider/outsider identity distinction, interest group formation, and prestige goods production—we arrive at a model which specifies that the degree to which the élites of particular polities identify themselves on a supralocal basis will correlate with the degree of homogeneity of material goods manipulated or utilised by the élites. Greater homogeneity of goods implies standardisation—that is, control over the production of the goods. Whether this control is in the form of adherence to social convention or explicit specifications of dimensions and design is unclear. But either convention or regulation is implied by this model for both prestige goods production and their distribution limiting the accessibility of the final product.

This argument gives theoretical underpinning to the archaeological interpretation of homogeneous élite cultural assemblages as representing the extension of political authority. This is a standard interpretation of the expansion of the Mounded Tomb culture in protohistoric Japan (Kobayashi 1961). I would argue, however, that the 'political authority' in question was not a centralised one controlling the entire broad region of the Mounded Tomb culture, but took the form of the establishment of a network of political relations based on group identity. The nodes in this network, the individual polities, were then available for rearrangement into hierarchical orderings at a later date when one or more became dominant over their peers. In the succeeding sections, we shall investigate the nature of polity formation in protohistoric Japan and the evidence for élite interaction, together with its effects on production.

Polity identification

Our first task in investigating peer polity interaction in Japan is to identify the polities that form the basis of our analysis. Two sources of data can be exploited to that end: ethnohistorical records in the Chinese chronicles and archaeological evidence in the form of mounded tomb distributions. The Chinese dynastic history for AD 221–65, the *Wei Zhi* (compiled between 233 and 297), provides evidence for the presence of centralised territorial groupings, as described below, but it is difficult to determine whether these territories were hierarchically organised in a spatial sense. The *Wei Zhi* states that 'The people of Wa [Japan] . . . formerly comprised more than one hundred communities. During the [Later] Han Dynasty [Wa envoys] appeared at the Court; today thirty of their communities maintain intercourse [with us] through envoys and scribes' (Tsunoda and Goodrich 1951: 8). Further ethnographic accounts of these communities include the data given in Table 6.2.

The transliterations of place names and official positions given here, taken unchanged from Tsunoda and Goodrich (1951), are of dubious accuracy for various reasons; still, it is occasionally possible to make tentative identifications between places mentioned in the *Wei Zhi* and known locations in ancient Japan. Most of the 'countries' (*kuni*) from Tsushima to Toma in Table 6.2 are thought to have existed in or near Kyushu, the southernmost of Japan's main islands and the closest to Korea. The location of Yamadai/Yamatai, however, has been a raging historiographical controversy for the last millennium (Young 1958). Essentially, the proponents are divided between the Kyushu theory and the Yamato theory, the first locating Yamatai in Kyushu's Fukuoka Prefecture and the second putting it at the head of the Inland Sea in Yamato (present-day Nara Prefecture) (Fig. 6.2). I do not propose to

Table 6.2. *Wei Zhi data on third-century polities in Japan*

Size	Country	Chief official	Next-in-rank	Households
400 sq. *li*	Tsushima	hiku	hinumori	1,000 +
300 sq. *li*	?	hiku	hinumori	3,000
–	Matsuro	–	–	4,000 +
–	Izu	niki	semmoku, hekkuko	1,000 +
–	Nu	shimako	hinumori	20,000 +
–	Fumi	tamo	hinumori	1,000 +
–	Toma	mimi	miminari	50,000
–	Yamadai	Queen Himiko	ikima, mimasho, mimagushi, nakato	70,000 +

continue the arguments here, but only to point out that Japanese society of the time, as seen through Chinese eyes, consisted of several important components:

1 spatially defined political units with
2 centralised leadership and
3 fairly large populations

In general, the data on polity sizes are inadequate. Using the Han and Wei Dynasty values for the *li* (Han *li* = 346.5 m; Wei *li* = 415 m (Young 1958: 35)), we can calculate that Tsushima's area of 400 sq. *li* would correspond to roughly 48 or 69 sq. km, and the unnamed polity would have been about 36 or 52 sq. km in area. The *Wei Zhi* also gives the distances, in *li* or days, between these various polities; but at the present stage of historiographical knowledge, these figures must be adjudged too imprecise (or even apocryphal) to be of use to us. The further list of neighbouring 'countries', however, at least gives an idea of the multiplicity of polities in Japan at that time. Countries beyond Yamatai to the north and under its queen's dominion were Shima, Ippoki, Iza, Tsuki, Minu, Kasoto, Fuku, Shanu, Tsusu, Sonu, Koyi, Kenusonu, Ki, Iigo, Kinu, Yama, Kushi, Hari, Kiwi, Wunu, and Nu. To the south and not under the queen's dominion was Kunu, 12,000 *li* (between 4,000 and 5,000 km) from Yamatai, with a chief official called *kukochi-hiko*.

It is unclear from these historical data whether the polities recorded actually consisted of territorial hierarchies. The problem is linguistic and involves the interpretation of the semantic components of the names listed in Table 6.2 for the next-in-rank. The word *hinumori* is used in four cases, and Tsunoda suggests it is related to *hinamori*, whose components mean 'outlying' (*hina*) and 'to guard over' (*mori*) (Tsunoda and Goodrich 1951: 17). This interpretation suggests the existence of secondary settlements, or the guarding of the border (Miller 1967: 20), where individuals of secondary rank had their operation base. In contrast, if *hinumori* is broken into three semantic components (*hi-nu-mori*) instead of two, and if the *hi* is interpreted as the same component as in the words *hi-me* (*hi*–female = princess), *hi-ko* (*hi*–male = prince) and hi-miko (*hi*–shaman), the meaning of *hinumori* changes to something like 'protector of the *hi*', the connective *nu* being

a possessive. One of the meanings of the native word *hi* is sun; knowing that the later imperial line claimed descent from the sun goddess, we may interpret the *hi* element as meaning 'sun', in reference to both the ruler and the goddess. Such a concordance of meaning agrees well with theoretical predictions of ruler–deity identity (Friedman and Rowlands 1977). This interpretation is at least as likely linguistically as *hinamori* ('outlying' and 'guard over') (D.W. Hughes, personal communication); however, it does not support territorial hierarchisation, only hierarchical role differentiation.

Queen Himiko/Pimiko is recorded by the Chinese as having had a mound '100 paces in diameter' erected over her grave (Tsunoda and Goodrich 1951). This passage in the *Wei Zhi* is the source of great historiographical controversy, since the first of the mounded tombs in Japan is not reckoned to have been constructed until 50 years later than the Chinese dating of Himiko's death. Nevertheless, more Japanese archaeologists today are considering the possibility that the Mounded Tomb culture began earlier than hitherto supposed in Japan (K. Terasawa, personal communication), and I think it reasonable to use the archaeological evidence traditionally dated to the fourth century to complement these documentary data for the mid-third century.

The archaeological evidence concerning polity size is less ambiguous than the historical evidence; hierarchically organised territories are indicated by mounded tomb distributions at least in the Nara Basin, one of the two possible locations of the Yamatai polity mentioned in the Chinese histories. In examining tomb distributions, I shall focus mainly on those mounded tombs that are keyhole-shaped in ground plan. They are just one of several tomb shape-types; others include round mounds and square mounds.

The existence of keyhole tombs (Fig. 6.3) around the edge of the Nara Basin has been known for a considerable time (Date 1963); however, the data have not been used very efficiently in identifying regional groupings. Instead of treating all keyhole tombs together, as in past studies, I have endeavoured to divide them into size groups and map each group separately. The segregation of tombs into distinct size classes (Fig. 6.4), based on measurements given in the 1970s

Fig. 6.2. Alternative locations of the legendary Yamatai in western Japan.

survey lists (Nara-ken Kyoiku Iinkai 1974), is statistically supported (Barnes 1983). By mapping only the large-sized keyhole tombs from the Early Kofun period (fourth century), we find that the tombs appear to be clustered into two groups: a northern and a south-eastern group (Fig. 6.5). It will be noted that the south-eastern group is strung out along the eastern basin margin; however, the distances separating the elements of that group are insignificant when compared to the gap between the northern and southern groups as wholes. Mapping the medium-sized keyhole tombs from the Early Kofun period produced spatially discrete clusters, some in the areas not occupied by the large tombs (Fig. 6.6).

If two assumptions are made concerning the assignment of meaning to the tomb size distributions, then the above patterns can be interpreted as representing the central foci (the large keyhole tombs) and the outlying centres (the medium

Gina L. Barnes   86

Fig. 6.3. Large keyhole tomb of Emperor Suinin, fourth century AD, Japan, Nara Prefecture (photograph courtesy of Shibundo Publishing company).

keyhole tombs) of a territorial hierarchy. The necessary assumptions are that tomb size is a direct reflection of rank in the socio-political hierarchy and that the tomb locations represent settlement locations. Currently, there is no unequivocal data on the distribution of actual settlements in the basin that are contemporaneous with these tombs, but the centres of gravity of the large keyhole tomb clusters coincide with important areas of activity attested by archaeological excavation (at the Makimuku and Saki sites) and literary references to important personages ('Prince Saho' and the Sujin line of kings) living in these respective areas (Barnes 1983). The size–rank assumption, moreover, is not merely

based on calculations of the availability of labour resources for construction, but is also supported by sumptuary rules governing tomb sizes recorded in the early chronicles of Japan (Aston 1896).

If these assumptions are allowed, then not just one, but two, territorial groupings are indicated in the basin, focused on the large keyhole tomb clusters and probably composed of three hierarchical levels: centre, subcentre and village. By splitting the distance between the centres of gravity of the two large-sized tomb clusters, one can posit two non-overlapping territories with radii of 8 or 9 km (c. 225 sq. km each). There is, however, no real reason to assume these territories were either circular in shape or equivalent in area; given the geographical layout of the basin, the northern polity might have been half the size of the southern polity. In any case, the

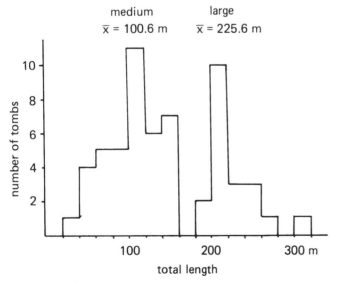

Fig. 6.4. Early and Middle Kofun period keyhole tomb lengths in Nara.

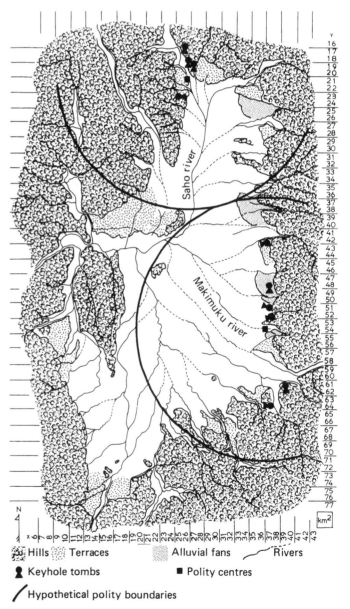

Fig. 6.5. Early Kofun large-sized keyhole tomb distributions and postulated territories in the Nara Basin.

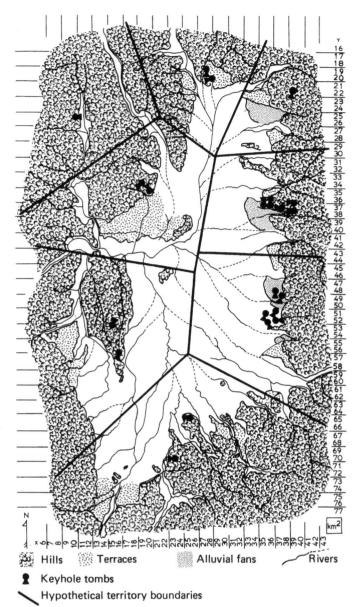

Fig. 6.6. Early Kofun medium-sized keyhole tomb clusters and territories in the Nara Basin.

size of the basin containing both of these polities, measuring 750 sq. km to the surrounding mountain tops, with 320 sq. km of arable, is far smaller than the 1,500 sq. km calculated by Renfrew (1975) for early state modules.

I contend that the first stage of protohistoric polity development that is known from both literary and archaeological evidence in Japan is represented, in size and structure, by the territorial units centered on the two-tiered Early Kofun keyhole tomb distributions. Polities of this size could easily have been duplicated thirty times in the Inland Sea area; therefore the Chinese accounts of the existence of various 'countries' in Japan are not unreasonable from a logistical point of view.

In the fifth century, during the Middle Kofun period, there is evidence for higher-order integration. No longer

were the Nara tombs the largest in the size hierarchy, for much larger structures were being built in the Osaka plains area to the immediate west: the Nintoku mausoleum reaches 486 m in length. This gives us good reason to suppose that the Nara polities were integrated into a supra-basin hierarchy. Nara's tomb distribution shows a surprising shift at this juncture; the location of the southern large-size tomb cluster shifts from the eastern to the western side of the basin. It is not known whether this represents the superseding of a former polity by a newer one or merely the removal of a polity centre, but I think it possible that proximity to the higher-order centre on the opposite side of the mountains may have been a factor in the shift. The addition of the higher-order centre in Osaka implies that this new polity was composed of a four-tiered territorial hierarchy, assuming the original three levels represented in the Nara Basin as centres (large tombs), sub-centres (medium tombs) and villages were incorporated without modification.

The size of this coalescent polity that was focused on the Osaka plains is difficult to judge since we have no firm evidence of its boundaries. Known as the 'Yamato court' in the early Japanese chronicles (as opposed to the Chinese chronicles), it has traditionally been recognised as the only polity in Japan at the time and is therefore thought to have encompassed the entire area from modern Tokyo to Kyushu. However, some Japanese historians reject this view of a unified Japan in the fifth century (Hirano 1977). Friction between the Yamato court and Kyushu, in the form of the Iwai rebellion, is recorded in the *Nihon Shoki* chronicles (Aston 1896), and the Izumo area (modern Shimane Prefecture) on the Japan Sea coast was independent enough to have necessitated the incorporation of the local mythology into the Yamato pantheon. Finally, the third largest tomb in Japan was built in Kibi (Okayama Prefecture), rivalling the two great fifth-century tombs of the Kinai region, the Nintoku and Ojin mausolea on the southern Osaka plains. It is plausible, especially if considered within the framework of peer polity interaction, that separate polities may have existed in these areas of north Kyushu, Kibi and Izumo even though all written evidence presents only the traditions of the central Yamato area.

If, then, the Yamato polity occupied only the Kinai area and not all of western Japan, what was its size? The Kinai is described in the early chronicles as being delimited by four geographical points (Senda 1980: 109). This area is considered to have been the extent of direct Yamato authority in the early seventh century, although after the institution of the provincial system in the mid-seventh century, the Kinai came to be consonant with the 'five home provinces' (*gokinai*), a slightly larger area than that encompassed between the four geographical points. The earlier Kinai boundaries enclosed approximately 20,000 sq. km, with a nominal radius of 80 km (Fig. 6.7). This polity is contemporaneous with the Paekche and Silla polities in the southern Korean peninsula, which were probably comparable in size. There is at present no way of measuring the extents of those polities, but core areas of

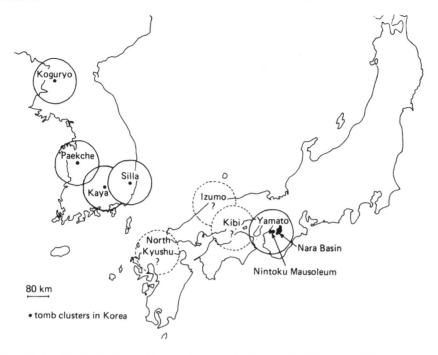

Fig. 6.7. Possible distributions of incipient state territories of c. 20,000 sq. km, fifth century AD.

20,000 sq. km are not unreasonable given the peninsular geography.

Thus the successive polity formations that we are dealing with in Japan are of two scales: a three-level hierarchy of territorial settlement extending over an estimated minimum of c. 225 sq. km during the second to fourth centuries AD, and a four-level hierarchy of territorial settlement in the fifth to sixth centuries AD extending over 20,000 sq.km. For Korea, a similar two-stage sequence of polity development has been discerned quite independently of this study (Lee 1982), and the fact that the results of these studies coincide reinforces my postulation of a co-ordinated developmental trajectory for Japan and Korea separate from that of China.

Symbols of élite identity and élite interaction

One of the propositions put forward in this chapter is that the formation of a supralocal élite grouping will be objectively symbolised through a homogeneous material culture denoting group membership. The first element of this proposition—the formation of a social élite—is irrefutably embodied in the mounded tomb evidence: social stratification is clearly implied by (i) the manipulation of mass labour to construct the tombs and (ii) access to both specialist labour and precious raw materials for the production of prestige goods. Second, it is undeniable that a homogeneous body of material objects was associated with the élite (Kondo, in press). These objects include the keyhole-shaped tombs themselves; the stone bracelets, triangular-rim bronze mirrors (Fig. 6.8), large cylindrical beads and curved *magatama* jewels deposited in the tombs; and the ceramic minijars and stands discovered in special-function rubbish deposits (Barnes 1983). What remains to be demonstrated is that

these objects were actually manipulated in the definition of élite social identity.

Supporting evidence is obtainable from the eighth-century *Nihon Shoki* chronicles (Aston 1896), which cover events of the fourth and fifth centuries. Several passages indicate how these prestige goods may have functioned to facilitate identity recognition and communication among the élite. The first tells of Emperor Keiko's travels from the Kinai region to the western part of the Inland Sea (20 days distant); his party is met by a local chieftain's ship bearing a white flag and a *sakaki* (*Cleyera japonica*) tree branch hung with the imperial regalia: a sword, a mirror and a jewel (Aston 1896, I: 193). Similar stories are related about Emperor Chuai, who also travels to the western Inland Sea and is met by two different chieftains, who erected *sakaki* branches on their ships and hung them with mirror, sword and jewel for the occasion (Aston 1896, I: 219–21). The second chieftain is said to have presented these materials to Emperor Chuai. Another passage illustrates how these objects also functioned in communicating with the gods as well as among the élite themselves. The sun goddess isolated herself in a cave, whereupon a *sakaki* branch was decorated with a mirror, jewel and tree bark fibres, and then a liturgy was recited to lure her out again (Aston 1896, I: 49). This story indicates the use of these objects in reconciliation and currying favour.

The inclusion of geographical referents in at least two of these stories makes it clear that identity recognition, facilitated by such special objects, occurred throughout the Inland Sea region; it therefore supports our interpretation of a 'supralocal' élite grouping. Such an interpretation, however, does not dictate the nature of the interaction within this

Fig. 6.8. Symbolic grave goods from a fourth-century AD keyhole tomb, Shikinzan, Osaka Prefecture: bronze mirrors, jasper and shell bracelets, curved and cylindrical beads, and spindlewhorl-like ornaments (photograph courtesy of Kodansha Publishing Company).

élite membership. There is a variety of archaeological and documentary data indicating both friendly and hostile inter-action, including warfare, marriage exchange, trade, gift exchanges and feasting.

One particular story is of interest since it illustrates simultaneously marriage alliance and hostility, and it may be one of the few literary references that can be co-ordinated with the archaeologically defined polities in Nara. In the *Nihon Shoki* story known as the 'Saho Uprising' (Aston 1896, I: 171–2), Prince Saho, brother of Emperor Suinin's consort, attempts to 'usurp the throne' by having his sister murder the emperor. She, however, reveals all to the emperor, who immediately raises troops and storms a temporarily constructed fortification, routing the prince after a one-month siege. The empress voluntarily joins her brother in immolation.

Emperor Suinin is known from the documents to have occupied a palace in the Makimuku area of the south-eastern Nara Basin; Saho, on the other hand, is the name of the river that flows through in the north-western part of the basin (Fig. 6.5). These are two general areas that we have identified, on the basis of concentrations of large keyhole tombs, as the central foci of the two polities in the Nara Basin during the Early Kofun period. Although the relationship between these two polities is cast as hierarchical in the literature (emperor and prince), no absolute differences are recognisable in the style of the tombs, their sizes or construction; thus we must give at least equal consideration to the possibility of peer status relations between them, based on the archaeological evidence.

Prestige goods production and exchange

In accounting for the development of peer polities in

Japan and the manipulation of material objects to symbolise group membership, we have seen that one of the most important questions concerns the controls over the production and distribution of prestige goods. In essence, two different strategies for obtaining the goods were pursued: long-distance importation and localised manufacture. These strategies were highly interrelated, since it can be seen from the Japanese case that objects which were initially imported were subsequently manufactured locally. Using modern market terminology, we can say that importation 'whetted the appetite' for an item, creating a demand that could only be met by initiating its local production.

Although I do not think that these were the actual dynamics of the process, which I call the 'localisation of production', localisation nevertheless entailed the transfor-mation and elaboration of the *local* productive system in response to the circulation of *exotic* goods. The eventual consequence of localised production was the devaluation of the exotic item into a more common consumer good. This pattern of 'conical diffusion', an archaeological version of 'trickle-down', can be traced with many craft goods in protohistoric and early historic Japan, including continental bronze mirrors, iron tools, bronze and iron weapons, grey stoneware, gilt bronze horse·trappings and dress ornaments, gold jewellery, and native ornamental stone bracelets and beads.

The process of localisation described here implies that production and exchange on the local and inter-regional levels are closely linked rather than being the independent spheres that they have previously been treated as being in the literature (Wright 1969; 1972; Wright and Johnson 1975). The Japanese case suggests that inter-regional trade volumes stimulate the intensification of local production volumes. Since importation is essentially *substitutive* while local craft production and specialisation are *additive*, the structural elaboration of a polity would be advanced more by the latter than by the former. The question we must ask, therefore, is which aspects of peer polity interaction would encourage the localisation of production?

The range of objects found in tombs and burials of the late third and early fourth centuries suggests the existence of a very elaborate production and trading network which has never been adequately elucidated. A possible example of one node in this trading network might be the unusual Late Yayoi burial at Tatesuki in Kibi (modern Okayama Prefecture); it was positioned on a high hill but without the large mound characteristic of later tombs. The burial facility consisted of a wooden coffin, which did not survive, but its estimated interior contained one jade *magatama* bead, 27 jasper and one agate large cylindrical beads, several hundred thin cylindrical beads and a similar number of glass beads, one iron sword and over 30 kilograms of vermilion, which was spread in the bottom of the coffin (Kondo 1980).

Major production areas of jasper beads and vermilion are known later in the protohistoric period from the Japan Sea coast north of Okayama and Nara respectively. Thus, it is possible that the Okayama region, represented by this chiefly burial, may have played an intermediary role in a procurement network, supplying jasper beads to the Kinai area and receiving vermilion in return. This hypothetical scheme suggests that some of the possibilities for the origin of goods and their movement lie in a supra-regional production and trade network within Japan. We also know that several goods were being imported into Japan from the continent: bronze mirrors from China and iron (Kiyonaga 1982) from the southern Korean peninsula. At this initial level of analysis, therefore, it appears that the network was based on the exploitation of regional resources and the exchange of finished products.

The relationship of the Tatesuki burial to the mounded tombs in temporal and functional terms is a difficult question, but one that is significant for our investigation of peer polity interaction. The excavator interprets the burial as a transitional form leading into the Mounded Tomb culture; his inference of an early date is based on the absence of a large mound, bronze mirrors and stone bracelets—all of which were characteristic of early fourth-century tombs. But, since we know that mounded tomb construction apparently began in the Nara region, spreading very quickly throughout the Inland Sea area to the west, there is another possible view: that the Tatesuki burial was contemporaneous with the very earliest tombs in Nara, and that the exchange of objects between these two areas, with their similar social development but different burial modes, was followed by the diffusion of mounded tomb construction to the west and cylindrical bead utilisation to the east. This homogenisation of the élite material culture (Kondo, in press), accomplished by combining regional elements into a pan-regional subculture, can then be viewed as the develop-

ment of the supralocal élite grouping predicted by our model of social stratification.

The initial extent of this grouping is described by Japanese archaeologists as having encompassed the Inland Sea region; it is interesting that one of the most important artefact categories in the early tomb assemblages of this core area— stone bracelets—was apparently manufactured outside the area. The few bead-making sites which have yielded evidence of bracelet manufacture are all in either the Japan Sea coastal region or the Kanto area around modern Tokyo (Teramura 1966). Presumably the élite of the core polities maintained exchange relations with the peripheral manufacturing centres to acquire these prestige objects. This situation is reminiscent of the models developed to describe the relationship of highland Oaxacan magnetite mirror-producing communities to the lowland Olmec consumers (Flannery 1968), and of the highland chlorite bowl-producing communities in Iran to lowland Mesopotamian consumers (Kohl 1978). These models utilise a core—periphery orientation in postulating the develop- mental elaboration of the peripheral societies through their institution of the production of consumer goods for the core élite. In Japan, it appears that these peripheral societies soon became incorporated in the élite network, since the Mounded Tomb culture had spread into the bead-making areas by the end of the fourth century. But by this time, stone bracelets had disappeared from the repertoire of élite objects, so the relations of production and exchange between core and periphery can be assumed to have been transformed during this expansion of the élite network.

A model of one-to-one regional production and exchange, whereby the élite of each region exploited a single precious resource and traded the product to élites of other regions, is much too simplistic. Nevertheless, the early tombs yield some evidence for the distributional control of certain products by particular local élites. Kobayashi (1961) has produced a model for the distribution of triangular-rim bronze mirrors with deity—beast designs. Of these mirrors excavated from the mounded tombs, 211 have been identified as products of 71 different casting moulds. Kobayashi plotted the geographical distribution of the mirrors cast from the same mould and found that significant numbers of each mould set are found in the Kinai region. The Otsukayama Tomb in Kyoto Prefecture yielded the greatest number of these mirrors as well as the greatest number of mould links to mirrors excavated from other tombs in the area; Kobayashi postulated, therefore, that the authority figure interred in the Otsukayama Tomb might have been the disburser of bronze mirrors as authority symbols to those subordinate units under Yamato power.

The triangular-rim deity—beast mirrors were made with such technical skill that it was originally thought they could be nothing but Chinese products; however, such mirrors are unknown in China itself. One of the current opinions on their manufacture is that they were made by Chinese craftsmen in Japan (Tanaka 1979). Unfortunately, the locus (or loci) of manufacture is not yet known, although a major manufacturing centre of Yayoi bronze bells is located only 20 km from Otsukayama Tomb, and a 'Mirror-making Shrine' (*Kagamizukuri Jinja*) occurs in the central Nara Basin near the Karako site, where clay moulds for casting bronze bells have also been recovered. Finally, a ceramic fragment from the Kazu site in the south-western Nara Basin appears to me to be the handle to a casting mould much like the one from Karako. I have previously included it when considering possible locations for bronze bell production (Barnes 1978; 1983), but the fragment, rather than curved as it should be for a bell, is quite flat in profile. That it is part of a mirror-casting mould is a possibility that should not be overlooked.

In the case of the mirrors, it can be hypothesised that one of the reasons for the localisation of production was to establish local control over the supply of mirrors and their distribution, rather than rely on the exchange network for their supply and be unable to control either their design or their distribution. This is one method of compensating for uncertainty or assuring competitive edge (Adams 1975). Localisation in this sense, however, does not imply the cessation of trade, since at least the raw materials for production must have been obtained through exchange or extraction. With localisation, therefore, a shift from trade in finished products to trade in raw materials might be expected.

Little is yet known about copper mining for bronze production in Japan, but iron and bead production in the fifth and sixth centuries do reflect such a shift. At the Soga and Furu sites in Nara, iron slag, crucibles, and jasper and talc flakes have been recovered dating to the mid-to-late fifth century—the first appearance of these crafts in the basin (Kashiwara 1983; Furu Iseki Han'i Kakunin Chosa Iinkai 1979: 61–3). And at the bead-producing site of Tamazukuri in Izumo (modern Shimane Prefecture), an estimated 95 per cent of the remains from its peak period of production in the sixth century consist of undrilled and unpolished blocky pieces (Maejima, personal communication), which I interpret as cylindrical bead blanks for export to finishing sites elsewhere. The Furu site has produced evidence for such finishing activities, but on talc rather than jasper beads. Most of the talc cylindrical bead remnants recovered from Furu are either circular flakes detached from the ends of the cylinders or beads damaged during the drilling of the central holes (personal observation).

We know from the early Japanese chronicles that prior to AD 645 many of the clan heads were delegated by the Yamato emperor to oversee certain élite craft manufacturing activities. What we do not know is how far back in time these administrative duties extended. However, it seems fairly clear that the fifth and sixth centuries saw a rapid initiation of local production of a variety of goods under élite control, the result of which was the gradual extension of administration over extractive activities as well (Barnes, in press). This is exemplified by the establishment in Izumo of a shrine dedicated to the head of the clan at court in charge of bead-making.

As we have seen from the tomb distribution data, the fifth century appears to have been a time of hierarchical consolidation in the Kinai region. With the growth and consolidation of a polity or polities in Japan, the focus of interaction on a peer basis also shifted from within Japan to beyond. The contents of fifth-century tombs indicate increased contact with Korea and the sharing of an élite material culture between the two areas, as we would expect with such interaction. There is also a movement towards the further localisation of production of continental goods, such as the hard-fired grey Sue ware and gilt bronze ornaments, following in the wake of bronze mirror production.

In summary, then, I hope to have established the necessity of specifying the changing relationships between local groupings of élites *vis-à-vis* the production and exchange of objects signifying their shared identity, in order to understand both the objectification of social élites through a material subculture and the organisational elaboration of polities through the localisation of production. It has been suggested here that competition and/or uncertainty over the procurement of goods important to maintaining identity relations prompted the elaboration of local productive systems.

Epilogue

I find it significant that although I have been able to discern patterns of multiple hierarchical polity formation in a sphere of East Asia distinct from that of northern China, I have been unable to exorcise core–periphery relationships from the important processes contributing to peer polity development. Asymmetrical relationships, especially between China and the southern Korean peninsula or the Japanese islands, can be eliminated from consideration as important causal mechanisms in institutional development within the latter areas; however, such relationships—and their material bases within Japan and Korea—apparently played crucial roles in organisational elaboration. The most noticeable asymmetrical relationships are those between core and periphery, redefined within Japan as the nuclear Inland Sea region on the one hand and the Japan Sea coastal areas and eastern Honshu on the other. Finer analyses of artefacts in terms of both style and raw material composition, accessible in the Japanese archaeological literature, must be integrated into the spatial and social context specified by peer polity interaction to elucidate further the nature of co-operative and competitive peer relations.

Note

1. These terms, printed in characters in Hirano's text but transliterated in Pinyin here, both imply good (*hao*) communications (*tong*) and ties (*jie*) between the peninsular and insular polities. Hirano's independent translation of these terms as 'peer relations' fits nicely with the thesis given here for peer polity interaction.

Chapter 7

Maya warfare: an example of peer polity interaction
David A. Freidel

Peer polity and the lowland Maya

The civilisation of the southern lowland Maya in south-eastern Mesoamerica (Fig. 7.1) provides a striking example of peer polity organisation (Sabloff, this volume: Ch. 8). The evidence of political and religious order reflected in material symbolism bolsters that from the archaeological record. From the Late Preclassic (350–1 BC) advent of public art and great centres (Freidel 1981a; Coe 1965) to the collapse in Terminal Classic times (AD 800–900), Maya civilisation registers a cohesive and pervasive charter of political power which is replicated and displayed in every major centre. Peerage among these polities was no doubt qualified by ties of royal inter-marriage (Marcus 1976), by temporary arrangements of alliance and subordination between major centres (Proskouriakoff 1960; Graham 1973), and by the ritual ranking of centres as a feature of élite interaction (Marcus 1973; Freidel 1983). Nevertheless, it is clear that southern lowland Maya civilisation never managed to transcend the peer polity mode and stabilise as a unified nation or empire (Cowgill 1979; Willey 1978b).

As documented by current research on Maya iconography and epigraphy (Robertson 1974; 1976; 1979), the royal dynasties of the Maya were all equally divine; all claimed descent from the same divine ancestors (Schele 1976). The mandate of heaven and the political justification of power were everywhere the same. By formal and public definition,

the myriad kings of the Maya formed a brotherhood of equals. Ranking between centres was left to secondary symbolic means. The charter of power provided no formal means of proclaiming a king of kings, and instead generated the remarkable cohesion binding a mosaic of polities into one of the largest and most enduring civilisations in Mesoamerica.

The interaction of lowland Maya polities was sustained and complex. The totality reinforced the local polity as a principle. Individual polities rose and fell, and sometimes rose again; but the advent of a new polity was heralded by the same charter of power found in all of the other polities. A dramatic example of this process is provided by the centre of Palenque, where a minor élite family rose to power late in Maya pre-history—during the Late Classic period (AD 600–900)—and announced its divinity with a very complete and detailed reiteration of the genesis myth of royal descent from the hero twin ancestors (Schele 1976; 1979). The family at Palenque displays all of the symbols of power devised by the Maya over the previous half millennium. The rulers of this polity claimed no special talent or charisma (although the founder, Pacal the Great, was no doubt a charismatic individual). Rather, they claimed to belong to the category of divine people broadly recognised among the southern lowland Maya. Maya religion and political ideology, then, provided a charter for the creation of peer polities, and only peer polities, throughout the history of the civilisation.

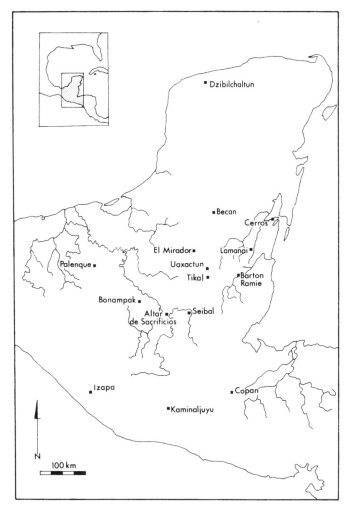

Fig. 7.1. Map of the Maya area showing important sites
mentioned in the text.

Imperium, unification, and war

While it is clear that Maya civilisation in the southern
lowlands never unified into an empire, there is reason to
believe that at least one major attempt at such unification
occurred, centred on the site of Tikal (Coe 1965; Willey
1978b). As described by Coggins (1975; 1979), the
community of Tikal attempted some radical revisions of the
political charter shared by all Maya. The degree of success
achieved by Tikal in establishing a distinctive state religion
remains a topic of controversy, but it is reasonable to suspect,
as Willey (1978b) does, that the motivation of Tikal in
establishing major alliances outside the lowlands was unification and hegemony over other Maya in the lowlands. The
strategy of changing the political charter and using outside
alliances finally worked among the Maya, at Chichen Itza in
the north (Sabloff and Andrews, in press); but the Tikal
experiment in the south failed. Instead of unification, collapse
finally overcame these southern lowland polities. Chichen
Itza evidently employed large-scale wars of conquest as a
means to unification (Andrews and Robles 1984). Why did not

warfare successfully override the peer polity charter in the
south?

The southern lowland Maya, once thought to be an
exceptionally peaceful folk, are known to have been as
militant as most ancient civilised peoples. The nature of their
warfare, however, remains a matter of some dispute and
discussion. Several recent positions are worth reviewing
before discussing how the Maya symbol system registers the
'emic' Maya view of how warfare worked—and did not work.

David Webster (1975; 1976; 1977) has developed the
most comprehensive model of Maya warfare. He sees the
development of military institutions in Maya society as an
early and gradual outcome of demographic pressure in
heavily settled areas on available vital resources, particularly
on land. Competition over land encouraged the development
of warfare as a means of boundary maintenance and of supple-
menting local supplies with booty and captives. Endemic
warfare of this kind, Webster suggests, encouraged the
establishment of leaders in the conduct of inter-polity
affairs—war lords—which formed the nucleus of the Maya élite-
to-be. Conquest is a factor, but more important in Webster's
model are the relationships of rank based upon military power
which would ensue from such competition. Such ranking
could have provided tribute to fuel an emergent élite. Finally,
Webster documents the importance of warfare in the Late
Preclassic period, when centres first arise in numbers, by
reference to an impressive ditch and rampart at the site of
Becan in the centre of the Yucatan peninsula.

Webster, fully aware of the lack of imperial development, views the primary war tactic as the raid or the brief
battle aimed at surprise attack and quick defeat rather than at
total conquest and subjugation. He argues that the importance
of the institution is in the initial establishment of the Maya
élite rather than in its long-term culmination in unification. He
sees a variety of ecological reasons as to why the Maya would
have been discouraged from attempting unification. Further,
he suggests that their polity size and internal political organisation were insufficient to mount successful full-scale war.

George Cowgill (1979) takes a different tack. He reasons
that warfare among the Maya was probably guided by the
same motivations found world-wide: power and aggrandise-
ment at the expense of neighbours. He points out that several
civilisations elsewhere in the world have experienced 'warring
states' periods, and that sometimes these episodes result in
unification; but sometimes they do not and instead lead to
internal weakening and outside invasion. Cowgill suggests that
the Maya were plainly civilised; that is, they enjoyed wealth
(surplus) and power. He doubts that the Maya lived so close
to the edge of economic or ecological disaster as implied by
Webster's model, and he rejects the notion that warfare must
be fuelled by demographic pressure. He points out that
warring states in civilisations elsewhere in the world are
interested in large populations to support political expansion.
Finally, he suggests that warfare in the Late Classic period
became directed at conquest and unification precisely because

the Maya were rich and powerful enough to attempt it. The fact that no victor emerged is an historical tragedy with precedents elsewhere in the ancient world.

These two cogent positions illustrate the paradoxes of the Maya case. Webster sees militarism as a central institution, but one in which conquest only plays a major role towards the beginning; warfare did not lead to either unification or collapse. Cowgill, on the other hand, does not regard militarism as a major factor in Maya evolution; but he does favour wars of conquest as a major factor in the Maya collapse. In neither case are we provided with an evolutionary argument for why Maya civilisation failed to unify. Perhaps such an argument is unwarranted, but it might be possible to develop an evolutionary perspective on this final hurdle to the imperial state if we can place warfare in a larger context of interaction among the Maya peer polities.

The conduct of war

A number of scholars have pointed out that the iconographic evidence for warfare among the Classic Maya suggests that it was an activity largely confined to the élite (Adams 1977a; Schele 1984). That is to say, while some visual charters in the ancient world, such as the reliefs of the neo-Assyrian period of unification (Winter 1981), are quite explicit about the role of warfare as an instrument of conquest and statecraft, the Maya focused on the capture, humiliation, and sacrifice of high-born individuals. While warfare appears to have been endemic among Maya polities, it existed as an aspect of a political charter—that is, a set of axiomatic and sacred propositions (Rappaport 1971) engendering and legitimising a particular definition of power and its institutional form—reinforcing peer polity organisation and a wide range of interaction.

Demarest (1978) has noted that, in terms of archaeological evidence in general, Maya settlements are dispersed and Maya centres of the Classic period are open and undefended. He postulates the existence of 'situational ethics', or rules of warfare constraining the circumstances and outcome of military encounters between Maya who regarded themselves as ethnically one group. He further suggests that the ditch and rampart at Becan might reflect the presence of a hostile zone between ethnically distinct Maya groups in the southern and northern peninsula. There are many scholars who have recognised the possibility of this division (Andrews IV 1965; Webster 1976a; Potter 1977; Ball 1977; Andrews V 1981; Freidel 1978). Between such distinct groups, Demarest reasons, total war could, and probably did, take place. The question becomes, what were the southern lowland Maya rules of war, how did they fit into the larger political and religious charter, and did they effectively hamper the internal development of conquest warfare?

Maya concepts of warfare

By the time the Spanish arrived in Yucatan, some five hundred years after the southern lowland collapse, the Maya had a history of conquest warfare (Roys 1962; Tozzer 1941). While the Maya themselves attributed the use of conquest warfare to foreign invaders from Mexico, archaeological evidence suggests that wars of conquest were quite popular in the Terminal Classic and Postclassic periods of the north (Webster 1976a; Kurjack and Andrews 1976; Andrews and Robles 1984). Warfare clearly played an important role in the rise of the state at Chichen Itza (Tozzer 1957) and is reputed to have been a factor in the founding of the last great Maya capital, Mayapan (Roys 1962). The Spaniards found the Maya polities in a condition of endemic war when they arrived, which nevertheless did not impede commerce, festival circulation, and other forms of peaceful interaction among them. Even with a history of conquest behind them, there is reason to suspect that the actual state of war at the time of the contact resembles what the Classic peer polities might have experienced.

As noted in one of the questionnaires sent back to the Crown from Yucatan:

> The reason they waged war with one another was to take their property from them and capture their children and wives, and because it was the custom among them to pledge what they possessed to each other; upon collection and payment they began to quarrel and attacked each other, and then the lord of that Pueblo armed his people against the other, and for that reason they waged war upon each other. (Tozzer 1941: 41)

The intriguing impression given in this account is that one factor in war was the breakdown between polities in expected exchange relationships, namely in gift-giving at festival occasions. Along with market trade and tribute, such festival sharing was a major factor in Maya production and consumption of goods (Tozzer 1941). But the motivation for war did not simply involve booty or the breakdown of cordial relations: 'In their wars they made great offerings of the spoils [to the gods], and if they made a prisoner of some distinguished man, they sacrificed him immediately' (Tozzer 1941: 123). Later, Tozzer continues:

> And so they never had peace, especially when the cultivation was over, and their greatest desire was to seize important men to sacrifice, because the greater the quality of the victim the more acceptable the service they did to god seemed to them. The number of people sacrificed was great. (Tozzer 1941: 217)

Endemic war was evidently not being fought for conquest at the time of the contact, but for booty, slaves and sacrificial victims. Many other people were sacrificed—orphans, purchased slaves and children, volunteers—but it is clear that the high-born victim was a singularly important category.

The conduct of war at the time of the Spanish Conquest was a highly sanctioned activity fully integrated into the ritual hierarchy and cycle of festivals. Leadership consisted of the hereditary chief or governor, *Batab*, and a heavily taboo warchief, *Nacom*, who was elected for three-year periods. The warchief was responsible for the actual battle and he presided over a special yearly festival in the month of *Pax*. In this festival he was treated as a god and military matters were discussed. Years presided over by *Muluc*, another divine apparition, involved a festival to the sun god, *Kinich Ahau*, for whom great war dances were enacted. Wars involved the temporary recruitment of soldiers from the community who were paid for the duration and then disbanded (Tozzer 1941).

One clear case for 'situational ethics' in the historical period is the saga of an amazing Spaniard, Aguilar, who was shipwrecked and captured by the ruler of Chetumal, a powerful polity on the coast of Belize. Aguilar managed to gain the confidence of the ruler and went to war for him, quite successfully. Other rulers in surrounding polities banded together to fight Chetumal, claiming that the use of a non-Maya infidel in warfare went against all established rules of conduct. They lost, and Aguilar went on to fight the Spanish for Chetumal. Yet clearly the rationale for war in this case was neigher booty nor territory (at least not openly), but the violation of the rules themselves. In general, however, booty and sacrificial victims ranked high on the list of motivations.

Classic Maya warfare and sacrifice

In a recent review of the epigraphic and iconographic materials bearing on sacrifice among the Classic Maya, Linda Schele (1984) confirms Demarest's notions of 'situational ethics' or a code of conduct for war. Briefly, Schele, and others such as Baudez and Mathews (1979), argue that the capture and sacrifice of highly ranked individuals is a pervasive theme in Maya public ritual. The focus is not on places taken, or even on dynasties subjugated (the emblems of dynasties and places are rarely mentioned in such contexts), but rather on the status of the victim, displayed in personal ornament, title or name. Although sacrifice occurs on a variety of important occasions (the naming of the royal heirs, the death of kings, important junctures in the sacred cycles) and not all victims can automatically be assumed to be war captives, the association of human sacrifice with warfare is an intimate one. The glyphs denoting war are frequently followed by glyphs denoting sacrifice (Schele 1984).

Mary Miller (1981) has thoroughly analysed a set of famous murals at the site of Bonampak. Dating to the Late Classic period, indeed right at the end of this site's history, the murals provide a complete cycle—of preparation, execution and culmination in sacrifice—of a Maya war. As Miller cogently argues (1981: 266), the purpose of the war was to provide suitable victims for the ritual sacrifice necessary for the naming of an heir to the throne. Inspection of the murals (Figs. 7.2–7.6) shows that they comprise a totality of which fragments are displayed on the more confined space of stone monuments at sites elsewhere. At the site of Yaxchilan, like Bonampak on the Usumacintla river, a series of well-preserved stone lintels show the same kinds of activity as seen at Bonampak. Correspondences include robing scenes as found in Room 1 at Bonampak and on Yaxchilan Lintels 26 and 4, where the battle gear appears in the hands of an attendant

and on the ruler (Figs. 7.7 and 7.8 (the gear includes the flexible rectangular shield and the scroll-topped jaguar helmet)). Formal confrontation of the ruler and his second-in-command occurs in Room 1 at Bonampak (Ruppert, Thompson and Proskouriakoff 1955: Fig. 27) and on Yaxchilan Lintels 3, 6 and 9 (Graham and von Euw 1977: Figs. 3.17, 3.23 and 3.29). The capture of victims, as seen in Room 2 at Bonampak (Fig. 7.3), is found on Yaxchilan Lintel 8 (*ibid.*: Fig. 3.27) and on many other stone monuments from the Usumacintla drainage. The humiliation of victims, seen in Room 2 at Bonampak (Fig. 7.5), is found on Yaxchilan Lintels 12 and 16 (*ibid.*: Figs. 3.33 and 3.41). Stela 20 at Yaxchilan (Fig. 7.9) also shows this scene, and as will be discussed further on, it is significant that both the captor and the victim wear the trappings of the jaguar. Auto-sacrifice by the ruler and his family is displayed in Room 3 at Bonampak (Ruppert *et al.* 1955: Fig. 29) and on many stone monuments. Finally, there is the display of the heir after naming and sacrifice, as in Room 3 at Bonampak (Fig. 7.6). Here the father is dancing with the bloody axe of sacrifice, associated particularly with Venus (Schele 1979), while his son stands on the steps below wearing a decapitated jaguar head-dress (an image which as a glyph has been associated by F. Lounsbury with the sun (cf. Schele 1984)) and carries the sceptre of royalty. Variations of these war-related scenes occur on numerous monuments in the lowlands. In sum, the Bonampak murals do not display a single war only; they display the charter for warfare—when, how and why to fight it.

The theology of sacrifice

The capture of high-born victims was a motivation in Maya warfare because sacrifice was central to the reproduction of the polity. Epigraphically, Schele has identified the public ritual of sacrifice, both auto-sacrifice and death-sacrifice, as *Nawah* (Schele 1984), a word with connotations of ecstatic dance, meritorious action, remembrance of the past, and humiliation. This complicated range of ideas is appropriate to an act that was a terrifyingly intimate confrontation of the ancestors and the supernatural (Furst 1976) in the public domain. The *Nawah* event occurs particularly in conjunction with important events in the life-cycles of royal persons. In sum, sacrifice is the evident means of transmitting divinity within Maya royal families. Schele (1984) has identified a glyph for the obsidian blood-letter of auto-sacrifice, and this glyph can represent both that act and the blood relationship between royal parent and child. Divine people reproduced through sacrifice. As the polity was embodied in the royal dynasty, the reproduction of the polity was also contingent on sacrifice.

This principle stems from the core of the political and religious charter for hierarchical organisation among the southern lowland Maya, which is first overtly displayed in the decorated architecture of the Late Preclassic period (350–1 BC) (Freidel 1981a). In brief, it is hypothesised that the Maya believed themselves to be descendants of hero twin

Fig. 7.2. The robing scene in Room 1, Bonampak.

Fig. 7.3. The battle scene in room 2, Bonampak, showing the engagement of the principals.

Fig. 7.4. The battle scene in Room 2, Bonampak, showing the wearing of the scroll-topped jaguar helmet by the defeated.

Fig. 7.5. The humiliation of the captives, Room 2, Bonampak.

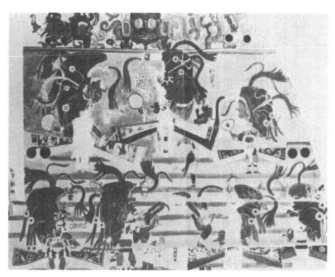

Fig. 7.6. Sacrifice and the designation of the heir, Room 3, Bonampak.

brothers born at the beginning of time (Coe 1978; Schele 1976; 1979; Freidel and Schele, in press). As recounted in the genesis of the royal line of the site of Palenque, these twins are the first and second-born of a set of triplets called the Palenque Triad (Berlin 1962; Kelley 1965; Schele 1976). The twins are represented in a variety of animal and human guises, and have youthful and aged aspects (Schele 1976). The third-born of the Palenque Triad, G II, is not represented as human except when living rulers impersonate him at death, at naming, or on important ceremonial occasions. The image of G II is polymorphic and a personification of the obsidian mirror, axe or blood-letter. This image, called God K or the manikin sceptre, characteristically displays a bifurcated scroll emanating from the forehead or from a mirror infixed in the forehead. While the scroll has been identified as smoke (Robicsek 1978), it is also represented by dots, such as those identified by Stuart (n.d.) as flowing blood. Reasons will be

Fig. 7.7. Lintel 26 at Yaxchilan (drawn by Ian Graham).

Fig. 7.8. Lintel 4 at Yaxchilan (drawn by Ian Graham).

presented further on for identifying the scroll which marks G II as the same bifurcated scroll which represents blood flowing from the mouth of several major icons. G II of the Palenque Triad, then, is the personification of divine blood, the bond between the twin brothers.

The Palenque Triad myth recounts the direct descent of the kings of this centre from both of these first ancestors. In Classic Maya theology, these brothers are apotheosised as Venus (older brother and G I) and the sun (younger brother and G III) (Schele 1976; Kelly 1965). The Triad glyph and the twins in glyphs, as regalia and as impersonated by rulers, occur throughout the corpus of Maya art in the Classic period. The assertion of direct descent is not peculiar to Palenque, but is evidently the categorical definition of élite and divine status for the lowland Maya.

The political charter focusing on the twins has sacrifice as a major component because the lateral blood-bond between the brothers was transformed into the statement of a parent–child relationship seen in the blood-letter glyph through sacrifice. In the version of this myth preserved in the oral history of the Quiche Maya of highland Guatemala, the *Popal*

Vu or Book of Council (Edmunson 1971), the hero twins harrow the gods of death and finally win immortality as the sun and moon. They are born of the sacrificed head of their father, who spits on the hand of their mother, blood maiden, and inseminates her. The twins in hell proceed to be sacrificed and rejuvenated, and sacrifice each other and rejuvenate each other. This cycle of sacrifice and rebirth allows brothers to stand in relationship to each other as parent to child. It was this lining-up of the brothers into a hierarchical relationship that allowed the Maya royalty to claim direct descent from them (Freidel and Schele, in press) and further allowed the Maya royalty to display physically that they replicated themselves, as the hero twins replicated each other. The transformation of a statement of brotherhood, a basically egalitarian idea, into a statement of hierarchy allowed the Maya élite to celebrate the existence of élite status overtly, beginning in the Late Preclassic period (Freidel 1981a; Freidel and Schele, in press). At the same time, the principle of brotherhood was maintained as the relationship between dynasties within the Maya lowlands. This was a reiteration of equality at the inter-polity level, tied to a charter of inequality within polities.

Fig. 7.9. Stela 20 at Yaxchilan (photograph by Teobert Maler).

Fig. 7.10. The Tablet of the Sun at Palenque (drawn by Linda Schele).

War and sacrifice: an iconographic complex

War for the purpose of capturing sacrificial victims can be shown to be an integral feature of the Maya political charter as displayed in iconography. There are probably several distinct but related complexes of images pertaining to warfare. One major complex of this kind can be traced from the Late Preclassic origins of southern lowland Maya art to the Bonampak murals at the time of the collapse. The central image in this complex is the jaguar, the zoomorphic aspect of the second-born of the twins, *Xbalan Ke* (Jaguar Deer), of the *Popol Vu* (Edmunson 1971; Schele 1976; 1979).

In the battle scene of Room 2 at Bonampak (Figs. 7.3 and 7.4), many varieties of war regalia are displayed. The major regalia of the winning side, as noted by Miller (1981), pertains to the jaguar. The ruler of Bonampak, as identified by Miller, is wearing a jaguar-head helmet marked with a forehead scroll and two tubes spouting feathers. This scroll-topped jaguar, also called the waterlily jaguar (Spinden 1913; Schele 1976), is a primary icon of war. The second-in-command, directly behind the ruler, also wears a jaguar-head helmet, but a full-figured one seated on a jaguar-skin pillow. This association of the jaguar with thrones is also a common image.

Both of these men are garbed in jaguar skins and have such skins on their spears. In the scene below (Fig.7.3), Miller (1981) has identified the ruler and his captains taking the opposing ruler captive. The winners are still garbed in jaguar skins. Miller suggests that only the winners are associated with jaguar icons (*ibid*.: 182). However, one clear loser (Fig. 7.4), who is defending a box with a tasselled baton, also wears a scroll-topped jaguar helmet. This suggests that while the winners are associated with the jaguar, so are the losers. In the humiliation scene which follows (Fig. 7.5), the ruler is again wearing jaguar skins and his two captains are both wearing scroll-topped jaguar helmets.

At the site of Yaxchilan, some of the previously mentioned lintels also display the scroll-topped jaguar regalia. On Lintel 26 (Fig. 7.7), the female attendant hands the ruler his shield and the scroll-topped jaguar helmet. On Lintel 4 (Fig. 7.8), the ruler wears the helmet and carries his battle shield. In both of these cases, the ruler carries the tip of his stabbing-spear. Finally, on Stela 20 at this site (Fig. 7.9), the ruler wears this helmet, carries his spear, and stands over a captive. The captive wears a shawl of jaguar skin and a vegetal scroll, possibly a waterlily, in his hair. It is clear here that the scroll-topped jaguar is associated with warfare and both the victor and his victim.

On the tablet in the Temple of the Sun at Palenque (Schele 1976; Fig. 7.10), the scroll-topped jaguar is again clearly associated with war. The jaguar occurs on a double-headed serpent bar, one of the sceptres of kingship, which is held up by two old gods. The full-faced jaguar shows the forehead scroll on each side emanating from the ear. Additionally, he has a large scroll formed by two side curls and a larger pendant element in his mouth. Finally, there is a bifurcated scroll on top of the jaguar's head emerging from a little face which is the glyph *Ahau* (lord, divine personage). This icon displays all of the elements on the scrolled jaguar.

Directly above the jaguar head is a round shield bearing the face of G III of the Palenque Triad, who is characteristically wearing a cruller (twisted loop) on the bridge of the nose and jaguar ears over his ear-plugs. This sun shield is another of the major insignia of royal power. Crossed spears frame the shield. The spear was the Maya weapon of choice, as displayed in the battle scene at Bonampak (Fig. 7.3). The scrolled jaguar is clearly associated with the implements of war. The god presiding over the occasion, as discussed in the accompanying hieroglyphic text, is G III of the Palenque Triad, and the event discussed is the naming of the son of Pacal the Great, *Chan Bahlum* (Snake Jaguar), as heir to the throne when he was a child, the same event displayed in Room 1 of Bonampak (Berlin 1962; Schele 1976; Ruppert *et al.* 1955. Fig. 27).

The tablet in the Temple of the Sun at Palenque shows images of Pacal, first great ruler of the polity, on the left, with his son, Chan Bahlum, on the right. Pacal (Schele 1976) is holding up a personified flint-and-shield motif. On the shield is a flayed face. Schele (1984: 100–2) suggests that this flint–shield motif, a replication of the implements in the centre of the scene, occurs as a glyph associated with war, capture and sacrifice. If this is the case, then the text accompanying another well-known example of the scroll-topped jaguar refers to war. This is the innermost of three lintels in the massive Temple I at Tikal, the greatest Classic period centre. Lintel 3 (Coe and Shook 1961; Fig. 7.11) shows a giant scroll-topped jaguar looming over a seated ruler. In the outstretched hand of the jaguar is a staff and at the top of the staff is another scroll-topped jaguar with a scroll-mouth as well. The staff is further decorated with bundled shields. It is clear visually that the ruler is under the aegis of the jaguar. The accompanying text refers to the bone variant (meaning *Bac*, capture) of the flint–shield glyph and its aftermath in blood sacrifice (Schele 1984: 106).

There are examples from the Late Classic corpus of the scroll-topped jaguar being associated with the implements of war elsewhere in the lowlands. Outside the Usumacintla drainage, however, narrative scenes are quite rare in monumental art. Hence, explicit scenes of warfare are generally lacking. Nevertheless, there are portraits which show the association of the scroll-topped jaguar not only with the implements of warfare, but also with the rest of the cycle found at Bonampak: capture, humiliation, and sacrifice. On Stela 33 at Naranjo (Graham 1978: Fig. 2.87), the ruler wears the scroll-topped jaguar helmet with the scrolled *Ahau* glyph above, carries a staff and stands upon a captive. On Stela 4 at Naranjo (Graham and von Euw 1975: Fig. 2.19), the ruler wears this helmet and carries a spear. On Stela 5 at Ixkun (Fig. 7.12), the ruler wears the helmet, carries a staff, stands

Fig. 7.11. Lintel 3 from Temple 1, Tikal (photograph by William R. Coe).

upon a captive and is making the 'casting' gesture which Stuart (n.d.) has identified as blood sacrifice. On Stela 4 at La Honradez (Morley 1937–8: Pl. 84f), the ruler is wearing the helmet, carrying a staff, and making the 'casting' gesture; but here there is no captive and the connotation of sacrifice is carried by the gesture. Finally, an earlier suggestion that the losers and winners are both associated with the scroll-topped jaguar may be supported by Lintel 12 at Piedras Negras (Morley 1937–8: Pl. 119c); the first of three bound captives kneeling before the ruler appears to be wearing the scroll-topped jaguar helmet.

The association of the scroll-topped jaguar with

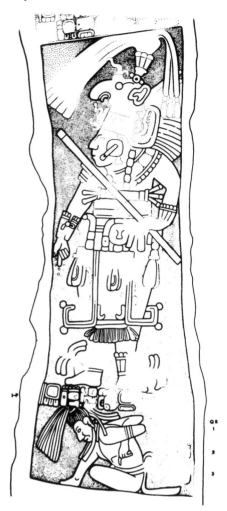

Fig. 7.12. Ixkun, Stela 5 (drawn by Ian Graham).

regalia, as costumes worn by rulers and principals, and as thrones. The distribution of the anthropomorphic version of the jaguar, G III, is even more widespread in the form of the sun shield and impersonation (Schele 1976: Appendix I). This war complex and its rationale are registered in the Late Preclassic beginnings of the Maya political charter and show continuous development into the Late Classic period.

Origins of the jaguar war complex

The earliest known expressions of the Maya political charter occur on Structures 5C-2nd at Cerros (Freidel 1981a) and E-VII Sub at Uaxactun (Ricketson and Ricketson 1937). The lower main masks on Structure 5C-2nd (Freidel 1981a: Figs. 6 and 7) are blunt-snouted feline polymorphs with the glyph for the sun, *Kin*, infixed on their cheeks. These images wear large, incurling scrolls on their helmets. When they are viewed in profile (Fig. 7.13), it is clear that these scrolls are the forehead scrolls worn by the scroll-topped jaguar. Here, as on the tablet in the Temple of the Sun at Palenque, two side-views are given of the forehead scroll. The image on Structure 5C-2nd is marked as the sun and as the scroll-topped jaguar. There are reasons to believe that the masks on the central terrace of Structure E-VII Sub (Fig. 7.14) also represent the scroll-topped jaguar and the sun. Here the

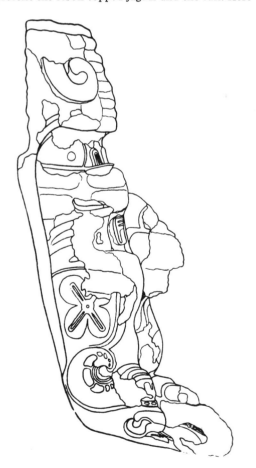

Fig. 7.13. Profile view of the Lower East main mask on Structure 5C-2nd at Cerros (drawn by Maynard Cliff).

sacrifice is explicit on an altar found in front of Stela F at Copan (Maudslay 1889–1902: Pl. 114f, g, h). Here, two scroll-topped jaguars are bundled in diving positions against a double-headed creature whose heads are the deity with three knots on his forehead. Joralemon (1974) has shown that this is the deity of the lanceolate blood-letter carried by Maya rulers or adorning their costumes. The composition at Copan bears a strong resemblance to the jaguar bar on the tablet in the Temple of the Sun at Palenque. The triple-knot-topped deity images and the flanking deity images on the Palenque bar carry the same bifurcated scrolls in their mouths (cf. Fig. 7.10).

To summarise, the Late Classic case for the scroll-topped, scroll-mouthed jaguar as an icon of war is as follows: (i) this is the primary image of war regalia worn by contenders in the battle scene at Bonampak; (ii) this image is a prominent feature of war regalia on narrative scenes at Yaxchilan; (iii) this is the central feature of the icons of war on the tablet in the Temple of the Sun at Palenque; and (iv) the icon is associated with hieroglyphic references to war, captives, war implements and sacrifice on numerous other monuments in the Maya lowlands. The scroll-topped and scroll-mouthed jaguar images occur in many other Late Classic contexts as ornaments or

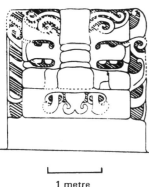

L———————————J
1 metre

Fig. 7.14. Stucco masks 9, 10 and 11 on Structure E-VII Sub at Uaxactun.

blunt-snouted feline images carry pointed teeth, characteristic of both the twins of the Palenque Triad and prominent on the sun shield image (Fig. 7.10). Several of these masks carry scrolls on their foreheads, generally emanating from the centre outwards. In some cases, these scrolls clearly depend from a central cartouche, as in the bifurcated scroll on top of the forehead scroll of the jaguar (Fig. 7.10). One of the Uaxactun cartouches bears a resemblance to the *Ahau* glyph. There are evidently two ways to display the scrolls at the beginning of Maya public art. One is to show the scrolls in profile view, incurling from the sides over the forehead; the other is to show two or more scrolls emanating from a medallion or cartouche in the centre of the forehead. On the jaguar icon in the Temple of the Sun at Palenque, both of these modes are displayed on the same image.

Within generations of the construction of Structure

5C-2nd at Cerros, a second building showing the jaguar was raised, Structure 29 (Freidel 1981a; Freidel, Robertson and Cliff 1982). Structure 29 faces west towards two ball courts and forms the apex of an equilateral triangle with them (Scarborough *et al.* 1982). The summit of Structure 29 supports three platforms, two facing inwards towards a central one decorated with jaguars. Each platform has panels flanking a central stairway. On the side platforms the panels display long-lipped creatures with humanoid masks emerging from their tops (Freidel 1981a: Figs. 11 and 12). These long-lipped creatures formally resemble the upper masks on Structure 5C-2nd (*ibid.*: Figs. 8 and 9) and the long-lipped creatures from which the feline masks on Structure 5C-2nd emerge (Fig. 7.13). Hence the jaguar here is flanked laterally, as it is sandwiched vertically on Structure 5C-2nd. The central platform on the north side is well preserved and shows a realistic jaguar (Fig. 7.15) with a great bifurcated scroll in the mouth and a skeletal mandibular process at the side along the cheek, showing that this creature has a skeletal jaw. Emerging from the jaguar is another humanoid head with in-set, in-curving fangs. This jaguar carries another motif of the jaguar sun, the scroll mouth as found on the icon in the Temple of the Sun at Palenque. The humanoid face is destroyed above the mouth region, so it is not possible to discern its diagnostic characteristics. From compositions of the Classic period, however, I predict that further examples of this Late Preclassic composition will display the cruller-eyed anthropomorphic version of G III of the Palenque Triad.

When the scroll-mouth occurs in polychrome paint, as in the series of jaguar-pawed creatures in the top line of Room 3 at Bonampak (Fig. 7.6), it is characteristically painted red. The scroll-mouth is also painted red on the flanking polymorphs of Structure 5C-2nd (Freidel 1981a: Figs. 6–9). For these and other iconographic reasons, the scroll-mouth can be identified with blood. The skeletal-jawed, bloody-mouthed jaguar image corresponds to a war practice described for the Maya at the time of Spanish contact: 'After the victory they took the jaw off the dead bodies and with the flesh cleaned off, they put them on their arms' (Tozzer 1941: 123).

An example of the skeletal-jawed jaguar occurs on a Late Preclassic structure at El Mirador, Guatemala (Matheny 1980). Structure 34 at El Mirador has one monumental mask, which is a skeletal-jawed jaguar with what appears to be the remains of a scroll element emanating below the jaw. The upper portion of this mask is badly damaged, but it is clearly marked as a jaguar by jaguar paw ear-flares (Richard Hansen, personal communication; Brigham Young University Project El Mirador 1981). Another variant of this image may have decorated Structure 5D-Sub 1-1st at Tikal (Coe 1965: 15), where two jawless jaguar masks flank the stairway. These masks bear some decoration on the forehead which might be the forehead scroll.

The association of Structure 29 at Cerros with ball

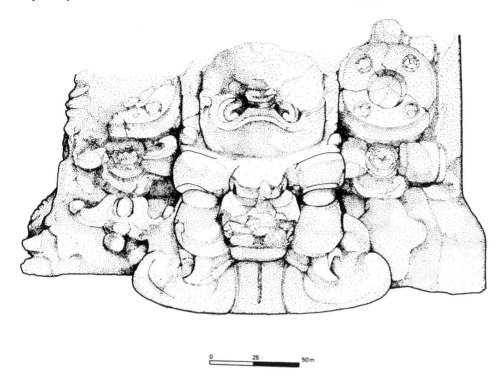

Fig. 7.15. Central Platform, North Panel, Stucture 29 at Cerros (drawn by Eleanor Powers).

courts is significant. As described in the *Popol Vu* (Edmunson 1971) and as displayed iconographically throughout Mesoamerica, the ball game is especially associated with decapitation sacrifice. Whether or not the ball game is regarded as a ritual form of combat related to warfare (several Late Classic reliefs show captives within the ball), the association with decapitation relates to a divergence of the skeletal-jawed and scroll-mouthed images of the sun which occurs between the Late Preclassic and the Early Classic periods.

At Kohunlich, Mexico, there is a structure decorated with mask panels which stylistically follow the Late Preclassic and precede the Early Classic programme (Stuart 1975). The uppermost panel (Fig. 7.16) shows a polymorphic image of the sun with the *Kin* glyph infixed in the forehead. This head is resting in a tripod bowl, clearly a decapitated head. The image has a skeletal jaw, like the jaguars at Cerros and El Mirador, and over the *Kin* glyph is a cartouche with scrolls emanating at either side. This is the cartouched scroll form used at Uaxactun on Structure E-VII Sub and found on Classic images above the forehead scroll. The nose area of this image is damaged, but enough remains to show that it bore an animal snout below the human nose, as found on the feline polymorphs of Structure 5C-2nd at Cerros.

This image of the sun as a skeletal-jawed, scroll-topped, decapitated head in a bowl becomes, in the classic period, a primary icon called the Quadripartite Badge. Schele (1976) has

Fig. 7.16. Uppermost panel on the decorated structure at Kohunlich (drawn by Linda Schele).

identified this icon as the sun and, more specifically, as the sun moving through the heavens and the underworld in a perpetual cycle of death at dusk and rebirth at dawn. The principle of rebirth through death embodied in the Quadripartite Badge is an image of the driving motivation behind war, capture and sacrifice.

In the course of the Classic period, the bowl which orginally held the head moves up to hold only the *Kin* glyph of the sun (Fig. 7.17). The *Kin* glyph in a covered bowl is known to read *Lekin* or *Likin* (east, the direction of the sun reborn) (Bricker 1983). Even in the Classic period, however, the original allusion to sacrifice is maintained. On Stela H at Copan (Fig. 7.18), the bowl is inverted over the head, which carries the *Kin* glyph infixed in its forehead as at Kohunlich. The head is thus covered by the bowl, as a skull offering would be covered, and the image is the flayed face of the sacrificial victim displayed on the flint–shield glyph of war (see Tozzer 1941: 122 for a discussion of the flayed faces of war captives).

The Quadripartite Badge, the decapitated sun, is explicitly shown in rebirth on the major celestial frame of the Classic Maya, the Celestial Monster (Schele 1976). In this image, a limbed and tailed monster with a long-lipped front head, marked *Lamat* (star or Venus), emerges from the earth bearing the decapitated head of the sun on its tail, upside-down. This is the movement of the sun and Venus across the sky, and the central image of rebirth following death sacrifice. The correspondence between the victim and the reborn is registered here and displays the mandate for the capture of other members of the category of divine people, in order that the divinity of the victor's line may be perpetuated through sacrifice.

The scroll-topped jaguar first appears in association with

a ruler on a bas-relief in Loltun Cave in Yucatan (A. Andrews 1981; Freidel and Andrews n.d.). Although this bas-relief does not have a hieroglyphic date, the style is clearly recognisable as Late Preclassic (Proskouriakoff 1950; A. Andrews 1981). Here the scroll-topped jaguar is worn as a girdle head, a position favoured in the Early Classic period for the sun. The association of the girdle position with the genitalia is physical and this position is associated with the deified blood-letter in the Classic period (Joralemon 1974). The placement of the sun here as a symbol of rebirth through sacrifice is a logical one. As noted by A. Andrews (1981) the Loltun figure is clearly carrying a war axe in his raised right arm. Here in the Late Preclassic, the scroll-topped jaguar is already associated with an implement of war.

Fig. 7.18. The reverse side of Stela H at Copan (after Maudslay 1889–1902).

Fig. 7.17. The panel from the Temple of the Cross at Palenque, showing the Quadripartite Badge (drawn by Linda Schele).

On Stela 29 at Tikal (Fig. 7.19), the earliest-dated stela at that site, the scroll-topped jaguar image is situated directly above the head of the cruller-eyed, jaguar-eared G III sun, which is held in the hand of the ruler. This position clearly denotes that the head is decapitated. The scroll-topped jaguar wears the bifurcated scrolled medallion on top of his forehead scroll. On Stela 36 at Tikal (Fig. 7.20), undated but regarded as very early in the Classic period, the scroll-topped jaguar image occurs twice. One head is between the knees of the seated ruler, in the groin area. Above the forehead scroll a very large bifurcated scroll arches over the outstretched hand of the ruler and then down in front of him. This large scroll is marked with dots and it is clear that the ruler is making the 'casting' gesture of sacrifice. As noted before, Stuart (n.d.) has identified the dots of the gesture as blood, and the bifurcated scroll is identified with flowing blood. On top of this large scroll rests the decapitated head of G III, the sun, who is

wearing as a headband ornament a second scroll-topped jaguar image. The image is one of sacrifice involving the decapitated head of the sun in his anthropomorphic aspect as G III and in his zoomorphic aspect as the scroll-topped jaguar.

The association of the anthropomorphic and jaguar-like aspects of G III of the Palenque Triad is given explicitly on Stela 31 at Tikal, also an Early Classic monument (Coe 1965: 33). Here the front girdle head worn by the ruler is anthropomorphic G III, and the rear girdle head is a jaguar head with a little jaguar-like figure on top in the curl position. Schele (1976) has shown that this little jaguar, actually a jaguar-pawed and -tailed anthropomorph, is a glyph for G III. This jaguar-pawed creature is clearly another aspect of the sun-jaguar, seen with the scroll-mouth on the top line of Room 3 at Bonampak (Fig. 7.6), and in this case the little jaguar specifies that the rear head is the zoomorphic aspect of the sun. As in earlier stelae at Tikal, this ruler carries a second disembodied head of G III in his arm. This cradled head carries the tubular top scroll seen on the jaguar helmet worn by the victorious ruler in Room 2 at Bonampak (Fig. 7.3). Another Early Classic stela at Tikal, 28, (Coe 1965: 32) shows a gaping scroll-topped jaguar on the left-hand side with the head of G III of the Triad in his mouth. Here the image of G III wears the forehead scroll and the bifurcated scroll cartouche normally found on his jaguar aspect. The jaguar in this case wears a clearly vegetal scroll. This will become the waterlily of the Late Classic period images. The evidence from Tikal shows the correspondence of the scroll-topped jaguar with his anthropomorphic aspect, G III of the Triad,

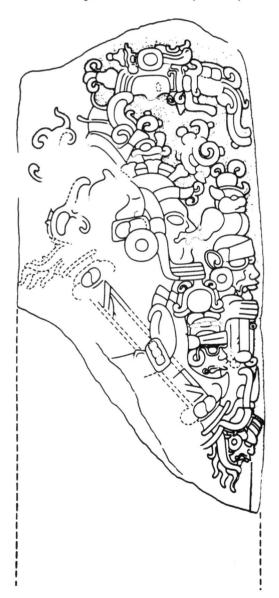

Fig. 7.19. Stela 29 at Tikal (drawn by William R. Coe).

Fig. 7.20. Stela 36 at Tikal (drawn by William R. Coe).

and the further association with the sun as the decapitated head of sacrifice as found in the Quadripartite Badge. Finally, it is clear that these images are central to royal power in the Early Classic period.

There are other examples of the scroll-topped and scroll-mouthed jaguar in the Early Classic corpus, and these generally occur, as at Tikal, on girdles, emerging from serpent bars, held in the hand, or otherwise decorating the costume of rulers. These symbolic displays of power persist through the Later Classic and there can be no doubt that the jaguar complex is central to the definition of royal status. Although the jaguar complex does not occur in explicit scenes of warfare until the Late Classic period (except on unprovenanced pottery vessels) several features of the earlier expression of the complex show that it, too, is associated with warfare and sacrifice. Firstly, there is the disembodied presentation of the head, a pan-Mesoamerican signal of sacrifice. Secondly, these disembodied heads are decorated with elaborate scrolls which are clearly flowing blood. It can be confidently hypothesised that the jaguar complex is, from the outset, associated with decapitation sacrifice. The Quadripartite Badge begins as an image of a skull in a bucket, the sun in a bucket, and is a literal expression of the jaguar sun as sacrifice. In Justeson's (personal communication, 1984) phonetic reading, however, this is *Likin* (east, the rising and new-born sun). The paradox of death sacrifice as a source of life is shown in this image, which can be stylistically dated to the Protoclassic period at Kohunlich and which shows iconographic continuities from the securely dated late Preclassic corpus.

The Quadripartite Badge, the scrolled jaguar, decapitation sacrifice are all inextricably tied to royal accession and warfare in the Late Classic period. That corpus shows little structural change from the earlier ones from which it evolved. Rather, it shows conservative retention of central icons combined with more elaborate and scenic displays of the ritual actions involving them. It is on the basis of the clear continuities linking the Late Classic corpus with the Late Preclassic one that I hypothesise that the decapitation sacrifice displayed in the Late Preclassic period required the same institutional means as found in the Late Classic: warfare.

Peace through war

Warfare among the polities of the southern lowland Maya is a problem which can be addressed through investigation of the rich material symbol system left by these people, as well as of traditional archaeological data on settlement patterns, artefacts and ecological factors. There are many additional dimensions to this problem which remain to be investigated iconographically and epigraphically. For example, the meaning and function of the scroll-topped jaguar as a glyph in texts remains to be elucidated. The association of G I, Venus, with warfare is likely and requires investigation in the iconographic material.

The jaguar complex is only one of several complexes alluding to the central institution of warfare. The point of this preliminary exercise is to illustrate the potential value of the symbolic record in elucidating problems posed by archaeologists, and to suggest a hypothesis concerning the nature and conduct of internecine conflict in one aggregate of peer polities. This hypothesis is that the Maya formally defined the principle of polity itself during their Late Preclassic breakthrough to a civilised way of life. War and sacrifice were no doubt already well-established features of Maya society, absorbed and controlled by the emergent political charter. Polity, hierarchy, war and the conduct of peaceful interaction were evidently features of a unitary political and religious charter focused upon the divinity of the Maya élite. In general, the definition of polity and the definition of inter-polity conduct appear as aspects of the same development.

The traditional view of the southern lowland Maya as a peaceful people was not based entirely on assumption. The generally open and dispersed settlement patterns of Maya communities are what archaeologists might expect of a society in which internecine warfare among the communities was a relatively minor factor. The steep-sided pyramids in centres are plausibly defensible, but Maya public places are normally open and accessible. Moreover, despite some variability, the artefact inventories from different Maya sites show an extraordinary cohesion in style, material and technology. This suggests sustained and complex exchanges of goods and services, as discussed by Sabloff (this volume: Ch. 8). No one would argue that such positive interaction can only occur in a peaceful society, but it does suggest that peaceful interaction was also central to Maya civilisation.

I have suggested that warfare and more peaceful interaction were probably conjoined. If the Maya élite were potentially victims of each others' sacrifice, how could such peaceful interaction take place? There are some clues in the Late Classic art that the congregation of élite members from different polities, in rituals preparatory for war and in rituals of sacrifice following war, involved truce sanctions and gifts, just as in the case of pilgrimages (Freidel 1981a). In Room 1 at Bonampak, the lords gather to witness the initial display of their heir to the throne. The costuming of these lords clearly signals their high rank (Miller 1981) and they wear insignia in their head-dresses suggesting that they are of the divine category, like the family of Bonampak. These lords wear a distinctive uniform: a long white mantle and a spondylus shell necklace. The uniform contrasts sharply with the diversity of loincloths and head-dresses. In Room 3 of Bonampak, the same uniform adorns the lords assembled to witness the sacrifice, and the transmission to the child of the divine blood. A Late Classic painted vessel from Tikal (Coe 1965: 42) shows the same uniform on lords who are offering gifts to a ruler (Linda Schele, personal communication). This same scene occurs on out-of-context vessels.

Both the old gods holding up the jaguar icon in the Temple of the Sun at Palenque (Fig. 7.10) wear long mantles and a shell necklace. On the left is God L (Schele 1976), primary god of the underworld; on the right, Kelley (1965)

identifies God M, *Ek Chuah* god of the merchants of the Maya.
at the time of Spanish contact. One of the portraits of Chan
Bahlum on the right-hand jamb of the doorway (Schele 1976:
Fig. 12) wears what Schele suggests is the backpack of these
merchants and he is carrying a staff. The gear of the merchant
and the garb of the pilgrim are displayed with the icons of
war in the Temple of the Sun. This evidence is merely
suggestive, but the ethnohistorical documents of the contact
period (Tozzer 1941; Scholes and Roys 1948) make it clear
that traders circulated on the peninsula in the guise of pilgrims
attending fairs at religious festivals (Freidel and Sabloff 1984;
Freidel 1981a) and that traders on the road operated under
heavy religious sanction. This notion—that the same rules
dictated the conduct of war and the conduct of peaceful
exchange under truce—is worth further investigation.

An implication of the hypothesis presented here is that,
by defining warfare as a prerogative of the élite and fought
primarily by the élite, the bulk of the population was neither
affected by, nor participated in, violent conflict. We have no
evidence for war zones in settlement data, except where there
is evidence of significant ethnic interfaces (Demarest 1978).
The zones between centres, where these have been investigated
(e.g. Rice and Puleston 1981), show dispersed residence. The
innovative definition of warfare introduced by the Maya
appears to have established peace and order through adjudi-
cation for the majority of the population. By containing
violent conflict and making it a means to reinforce the
principle of polity, the lowland Maya generated an internal
stability at the peer polity level of complexity.

This hypothesis is in line with the notion suggested by
Webster (1977) that Maya warfare was adaptive and a means
to further developments in their society. The timing of a
formal definition of war is also in concert with his model.
Conquest and the appropriation of surplus, while plausibly
features of the institution in practice, were not celebrated by
the Maya, and I suspect that they were incidental to the
primary goal. The hypothesis here would support Webster's
notion of the importance of boundary maintenance. Insofar
as populations may have been responding to stress in their
environment, it seems more likely that the internal order of
the polity was of primary importance. It does not seem
coincidental that the Late Preclassic breakthrough
witnesses the first evidence of intensification of production,
both through the construction of hydraulic systems, as in the
case of Cerros (Freidel and Scarborough 1982; Scarborough
1980), and through the mass production of widely circulated
artefacts, as at the stone-tool industrial site of Colha (Hester,
Shafer and Eaton 1982). In both of these cases, intensification
is associated with a centre. In the case of Cerros (Scarborough
1980), we have a small and possibly symbolic hydraulic system
of canals and fields. This system presumably provides an
allusion to the nearby river with its greater potential for
raised-field agriculture. Nevertheless, the Cerros system was
built as a public works project. The tremendous amount of
labour invested in public monumental buildings at such centres

as Cerros, El Mirador (Matheny 1980), Tikal (Coe 1965), and
Lamanai (Pendergast 1981) reflects social surplus and the
organisational efficiency of the emergent Maya polity. It seems
unlikely that the central organisation of labour was directed
solely to the construction of buildings. The largest Late
Preclassic centres, and presumably the largest polities, are in
the swamp-bound environments of the Peten, in Guatemala.
The northern Belizean river drainages and swamps show raised-
field agriculture, and this area participates in the Late Preclassic
breakthrough. I predict that the Peten will show equally pre-
cocious development of intensive agriculture in its Late
Preclassic polities.

In addition to the prospect of its facilitating an absolute
increase in production, it is plausible that the polity also
facilitated a more effective redistribution of resources within
the domain. An inhibition of conflict over resources within
polities would have been just as important in a stress situation
as the protection of resources from outside encroachment.
Although we have no clear idea as to how such redistribution
may have worked (but cf. Freidel and Sheets n.d.), given the
central focus on the family as the metaphor of the polity, it
seems likely that a metaphor of kinship obligations and rights
was the armature of the institution, as recently suggested by
Adams and Smith (1981). Boundary maintenance, effective
organisation of resources, and management of increased
production are adaptive features of the Maya polity.

War and collapse

Along with Cowgill (1979), I believe that the advent of
the hierarchically organised polity among the Maya did much
more than absolute stressful conditions in the environment
(Freidel 1981a). Whatever the factors leading to the
formation of this type of polity—and they were no doubt
many and complex (Freidel and Schele, in press)—the result
of such organisation was more than a simple survival level of
existence. The enormous surplus in labour registered in the
construction of Late Preclassic Maya centres must reflect
effective surplus in subsistence and other goods. The archaeological evidence for surplus production, long-distance trade
(Sabloff, this volume: Ch. 8) and building construction,
continues throughout Maya prehistory. Civilisation is predicated upon surplus, however conceived or manipulated,
and the Maya are no exception to this rule.

At the same time, the central organisation of labour
evinced in the Late Preclassic suggests that, at the very
beginning of Maya civilisation, polities could have fielded
armies in wars of conquest, had that been a feasible political
goal. The Late Classic polities may have been quantitatively
wealthier, but qualitatively they were not so different in
organisation that wars of conquest would have been more
practicable logistically.

What distinguishes the Terminal Classic from earlier
periods is that wars of conquest seem to emerge as a political
force generally in Mesoamerica (Webb 1973). The lowland
Maya of the northern peninsula appear to fortify centres

in increasing numbers in this period (but cf. Kurjack and Andrews 1976; Webster 1980). It is possible, as Cowgill (1979) suggests, that the southern lowland Maya polities attempted to adopt wars of conquest as an instrument of state, both to defend themselves from outsiders using this form of war, and as an avenue to power among themselves. I suspect, however, that this attempt, if it did occur, was doomed to failure as a consequence of a millennium of sacred warfare and its integration into a charter of political order and inter-polity interaction that included complex exchange under sanction. To violate the rules of war would, I suspect, have violated the rules of truce and the efficiency of an economy tied to exchange between polities. The role of truce and pilgrimage is aptly illustrated in this passage:

> 'And on account of this famine, the Xius, who are the lords of Mani, resolved to offer solemn sacrifice to their idols and brought them slaves of both sexes to throw them into the well of Chichen Itza. And they were obliged to pass by the town of the Cocom lords, who were their declared enemies, and thinking that at such a time they would not renew their old quarrels, they sent to ask permission to pass through their lands; and the Cocoms deceived them by a kind answer, and giving them lodging all together in a large house, they set it on fire and killed those who escaped. And this gave rise to great wars.' (Landa, in Tozzer 1941: 54)

Furthermore, movement to total war would have required the recruitment of the non-divine members of society, both as agents and as victims. If warfare had not only been an élite prerogative but also a central means of reinforcing hierarchical organisation within polities, such a move would have directly undermined the political charter and organisation within polities. Cowgill's hypothesis of a struggle for unity is plausible. But if such an episode occurred, it had immediate and disastrous consequences for the southern Maya polities. In the Terminal Classic period, the centres of the south are not fortified, but abandoned. The residual population indeed moved to nucleated organisation and defensible locations (Rice n.d.), but civilisation in this region had by this time already collapsed.

It is worth comparing the southern lowland experience with what occurred in an evidently successful conquest state in the north at Chichen Itza (Tozzer 1957). While the symbol system of the southern Maya focused intensely on the divine royal family as a metaphor for polity, the symbol system at Chichen Itza displays a celebration of many powerful people. While the southern Maya erected stone monumental portraits of their rulers and family, Chichen Itza displays the same stone medium but with hundreds of portraits of warriors, priests and lords. This vulgarisation of the Stela medium

makes sense in terms of a fundamental difference in political charter—from the definition of polity as family to the definition of polity as assembly. At Chichen Itza, the many agents necessary for wars of conquest, and the many victims to be assimilated rather than sacrificed, are displayed in the public domain. It would seem that the Maya of Chichen Itza and their Mexican allies were able to formulate a viable political charter for the conquest state employing iconographic and material mediums of the traditional Lowland social order. In the south, any such attempt met with failure. The Bonampak murals were never finished, and the collapse of that polity surrounded their creation (Miller 1981). They stand as a final, futile reiteration of the way of sacred warfare and of a way of life which became extinct rather than transformed.

Evolutionary implications

The lowland Maya of the southern peer polity aggregate developed an innovative formula for the conduct of warfare that was an integral aspect of their definition of polity, and it was an enduring and successful formula. It was also one that did not lend itself to modification to justify wars of conquest— a necessary step to unification and advancement to a higher level of social organisation. The Maya faced, in this instance, a structural impasse in their evolution. It was structural in both the social and ideological senses of the term, in that it pertained both to the social rules governing expectable conduct and to the rules by which the Maya perceived causality in the cosmos and possibility in the world of people. The nature of such an impasse is not environmental or logistical, although these can and do supply conditions of crisis at an impasse. The Maya case would suggest that consolidation of such a peer polity aggregate into an *imperium*, as an internal process, requires a new transformation of the structure underwriting the aggregate (cf. Winter 1981). This is a fundamental challenge to the ingenuity of people drawing upon an available cultural repertory. Ultimately, culture is indeed the means to adaptation and survival, but only as employed by self-reflecting people. A structural impasse dictates social transformation or extinction; the actual outcome depends on what people are willing to relinquish of the past in order to survive into the future.

Acknowledgements

The following are gratefully acknowledged as sources or as copyright holders for the illustrations to this chapter: Figs. 7.2–7.6, 7.9 and 7.14, Harvard University; Figs. 7.7, 7.8 and 7.12, Peabody Museum, Harvard; Figs. 7.11, 7.19 and 7.20, the Tikal Project; Figs. 7.10, 7.16 and 7.17, Linda Schele.

Chapter 8

**Interaction among Classic Maya polities:
a preliminary examination**
Jeremy A. Sabloff

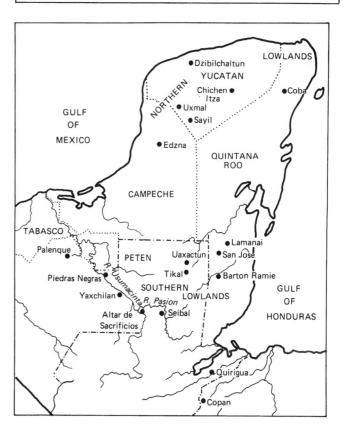

Fig. 8.1. Map of the Maya lowlands.

The Maya lowlands encompass an area of roughly
250,000 sq. km (according to Adams, Brown, and Culbert
1981), covering portions of modern-day Guatemala, Mexico,
Belize, El Salvador, and Honduras (Fig. 8.1). Between about
300 BC and the time of the Spanish Conquest in the sixteenth
century AD, a complex society flourished in the area (see
Henderson 1981 and Hammond 1982 for two excellent recent
overviews). The lowland Maya lived in and around political/
religious centres which minimally numbered in the several
hundreds and ranged in size from small villages with a very
limited amount of public architecture to relatively substantial
cities with populations in the many thousands and huge
investments in public works. During the period from AD 600
to 800, when the population may have reached its highest
point, the total population of the lowlands was almost
certainly in the millions, with one recent estimate suggesting
the possibility of a population as high as 14 million (Adams
et al. 1981: 1462).

Peer polities in the Maya lowlands
While there is a great degree of local and regional
variation to be observed among Mayan site plans, architecture,
ceramics, and other artefact classes, there is also a considerable
amount of similarity and continuity throughout the lowlands
relative to other areas. Some of this widespread similarity is
clearly the result of élite trade, although the mechanisms of
such trade are not yet clear. For example, obsidian and other

exotic stones were traded in from various sources in the adjacent highlands and distributed all over the lowlands, while polychrome vessels may have been manufactured at a limited number of centres and traded over wide distances (R.E. Smith, personal communication). Other similarities in architecture and in intellectual and religious paraphernalia are probably due to élite interactions and movements. Prior to AD 800, the quantity and nature of non-élite contacts and trade remain an open question. Goods of all kinds probably moved widely around major sites and their hinterlands (Rands 1967; Fry 1979; Fry and Cox 1974), and evidence now indicates that materials such as flint tools were traded regionally (Shafer 1981). But it is not all clear whether there were widespread movements of foodstuffs or other bulk goods on a regional or inter-regional basis, nor is it clear whether there were large market-places to facilitate such trade. After AD 800, however, there is better evidence for the movement of bulk goods.

Most sites probably had similar extensive agricultural practices and cultivated roughly the same crops. Through time, particularly in the Late Classic period from AD 600–800, a number of sites may have turned more and more to intensive techniques such as ridging, terracing, and raising fields in swampy zones, although such practices began in Pre-classic times prior to AD 300 (Harrison and Turner 1978). New areas were colonised, filling in land between sites, perhaps to relieve population pressure or bring new zones into cultivation.

The lowland Maya populations appear to have spoken and written the same, or closely related, languages. Although there are some regional differences, hieroglyphic writing, calendrics and mathematics are nearly identical from site to site. Religious symbolism (including presumably, observances) and recognisable deities are also similar across the lowlands (see Freidel, this volume: Ch. 7).

Let us consider briefly the site of Seibal during the Late Classic period (at about AD 700) as an example of the nature of interaction among various Classic Maya polities. The site was surveyed and excavated from 1965 through 1968 by the Peabody Museum of Harvard University, under the direction of Gordon R. Willey and A. Ledyard Smith (Willey, Smith, Tourtellot, and Graham 1975; Sabloff 1975; Willey 1978a; Smith 1982). Although Seibal was in close contact with other Late Classic centres, no clear inference can be made from the extant archaeological record that this sizeable site (probably more than 5,000 inhabitants) was not an independent political entity prior to AD 800. After a period of at least several centuries (AD 300–600), during which time Seibal's population dipped to a relative low point in the site's occupational history, there was an influx of population at the beginning of Late Classic times. It appears that these new settlers may have come from the north-east Peten, near Tikal and Uaxactun (Sabloff 1975; also Coggins 1979).

The site soon began to flourish and grow. It may have been resettled because of its proximity to the rich agricultural lands next to the Rio Pasión, which were intensively cultivated

through the use of artificial canals (Adams *et al.* 1981). It is possible that agricultural produce from these lands was traded by Seibal to the heavily populated zone in the north-east Peten. The Rio Pasión almost certainly served as an important trade route, too. The Maya inhabitants of Seibal had numerous ties to other sites. Their architecture and use of space closely resembled other centres (Fig. 8.2), as did the general layout of the site and its sustaining area. Their written language, as shown on their carved stelae, was nearly identical to that used at other sites (Fig. 8.3). The artisans involved in the building of various structures and the carving of monuments may have been sent for training at other centres or may even have come from outside Seibal. Although local potters made certain ritual items, such as incense burners, they were clearly familiar with *incensarios* from other Maya sites (Figs. 8.4 and 8.5). Moreover, the deities represented on these burners were identical to representations of the same deities over a large area of the lowlands. Even Seibal's utilitarian pottery reveals close resemblances to pottery from relatively distant lowland sites. Although studies by Rands (1967) and Fry (1979; Fry and Cox 1974) have indicated local marketing patterns for utilitarian pottery, movements of people among centres must have been frequent enough to cause the widespread dissemination of knowledge about ceramic forms and decorations. A variety of polychrome pottery forms, many of which had serving functions, were imported by the Seibal élite from different manufacturing places, particularly from the Tikal–Uaxactun area (Fig. 8.6). In addition, obsidian, among

Fig. 8.2. Ball courts for the playing of the ritually important ball game are found at numerous lowland polities. This photograph shows the sides of a ninth-century AD ball court at Seibal. The far playing wall is indicated by the number '1' (photograph courtesy of the Peabody Museum, Harvard University).

Interaction among Classic Maya polities   *111*

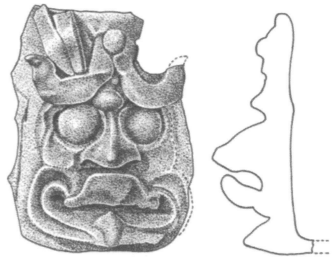

Fig. 8.4. Ceramic incense burners, such as this late Classic fragment from Seibal, were made locally at each peer polity. However, the depictions of deities which decorated these *incensarios* were uniform from polity to polity (drawing courtesy of the Peabody Museum, Harvard University).

Fig. 8.3. Carved monuments (or stelae) apparently served similar functions, had similar themes, and used the same hieroglyphic writing system throughout the lowlands. This Late Classic monument (Stela 5) from Seibal depicts a ball player (photograph courtesy of the Peabody Museum, Harvard University).

other materials, was traded into Seibal from the Guatemalan highlands (Fig. 8.7). Whether Seibal obtained it directly or from some lowland middleman is, to my mind, still uncertain.

The high level of intercommunication and exchange just described between Seibal and other lowland centres is clearly not unique to Seibal but could be replicated, in varying degrees (and in better detail), from site to site. From Altar de Sacrificios to Coba or Dzibilchaltun to Tikal, the cultural similarities are remarkable (for an area of 250,000 sq. km) and certainly outweigh the differences. Nevertheless, there are no clear data in the archaeological record which can be strongly linked with the inference that various sites *politically* controlled a number of other sites, particularly in regard to large sites controlling other large ones. In the realm of hieroglyphic inscriptions, for example, although provocative arguments have been made for hierarchies of sites and

Fig. 8.5. Ceramic figurines, such as this Late Classic example from Seibal, were usually manufactured locally at each peer polity and show great similarity from site to site (photograph courtesy of the Peabody Museum, Harvard University).

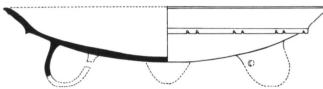

Fig. 8.6. Elaborately designed, but remarkably similar, polychrome ceramics were traded throughout the lowlands from a limited number of manufacturing centres. This particular plate was traded into Seibal from another polity in Late Classic times (drawing courtesy of the Peabody Museum, Harvard University).

regional groupings (see Marcus 1976 for a good example), the case for direct political control of large sites remains to be made. Moreover, the pictorial record in carvings and murals seems to indicate raiding among sites rather than political domination of a region by one centre. Finally, there is little evidence for the military conquest of many sites by one powerful centre. Thus, at the moment and given our limited interpretive controls, there are no convincing data which would allow one to argue against the assertion that the major lowland sites had a significant amount of political independence during the Classic period.

While lacking one or two dominant centres, the many hundreds of Maya polities throughout the Classic period were able rapidly to spread linguistic, religious, social, economic and architectural ideas, as well as material goods, over a relatively vast area. Obviously, it is extremely important for Maya scholars to understand the nature of such inter-site interaction in a much clearer and more rigorous manner than has so far been the case, since at present, despite a wealth of new data, archaeologists can often do little more than speculate about the processes involved. Although I can do no better

at this time, I would like to offer a few ideas which might point the way to future advances.

With this very brief background in mind, I shall argue that the southern Maya lowlands are a particularly significant and useful case for testing the utility of the concept of peer polity interaction (as set out in Ch. 1). If this concept is to prove of general utility, it must be concerned not only with the background and the reasons for the emergence of nation states and empires, but must also consider the reasons for the *failure* of such development. Renfrew's discussions of early state modules have emphasised their rise and how 'small states . . . emerged *together*, pulling each other up by the bootstraps' (this volume: 11). The strength of Renfrew's framework (as well as Price's (1977) model of cluster interaction) may be increased if it also has explanatory value for the decline of early state modules when the trajectory of their development does not lead to the rise of dominant central places, nation states and empires, or can explain why some ESMs endure and others do not. If we can understand the different parameters and constraints which cause these different trajectories, we shall have taken a first step on the road to building a body of theory about the development of complex societies. In order to reach this end, we can begin by trying to see if different repeated patterns can be observed.

The Classic period

I shall begin my examination with the established centres in the Early Classic period, with the rise of civilisation in the Maya lowlands. As already mentioned, there is considerable evidence in material goods, art style and use of space, as well as in hieroglyphic inscriptions, to indicate close interaction among the many polities of the lowlands. Although there are numerous local and regional differences among the various Maya sites, the great similarities over a relatively large area far outweigh the differences; in particular, I believe that the *differences* between the southern and northern lowlands have been overemphasised at the expense of the *resemblances*.

The conditions which Renfrew has described in his introductory statement (Ch. 1) seem to have great applicability to the lowlands, particularly the southern lowlands, which are often seen as the heartland of Classic Maya civilisation. I would argue that the environmental nature of the tropical rainforest lowlands (the southern lowlands), with their scattered Classic centres, is analogous to the island settings of the Aegean polities which stimulated Renfrew's thinking on peer polity interaction (Renfrew 1982d). While such an analogy might at first glance appear to be somewhat far-fetched, I believe it has some justification and potential utility for future comparisons between the two areas. Moreover, the Maya lowland centres appear to show the same kinds of 'push–pull' effects of independence which Renfrew has noted for the Aegean islands.

Relative to other parts of Mesoamerica, particularly the highlands, the southern Maya lowlands are a fairly

Fig. 8.7. Obsidian was traded to virtually all lowland polities from a very limited number of sources in the Guatemalan highlands. The tools manufactured from obsidian are nearly identical from polity to polity in the lowlands, although manufacturing usually appears to have been local (as was the case with these blades from Seibal) (photograph courtesy of the Peabody Museum, Harvard University).

homogeneous environment. Although this homogeneity may have been significantly overemphasised in the past (cf. Turner 1974; Sanders 1977), by and large the lowlands environment is repetitive. As Price (1977: 230) has argued:

> Concerning the implication that the cluster phenomenon in some fashion vitiates the impact of the environment, I do not see this as necessary. While no two environments are ever precisely identical in those parameters empirically determined to effect human occupation, some are specifically more similar than others. At each level, the environments exploited by cluster components tend to be relatively similar in those parameters affecting the numbers and densities of population. This is what is meant by the uniformitarian similarity of the cause—effect operation in all members. This need not, cannot, imply identity, which, did it exist, would militate against much interaction among members. Substantively the components are of course a little different.

Unlike the highlands, not many southern lowland sites had direct control of *strategic* resources which were unavailable to others. This situation contrasts with the relatively drier northern lowlands, as well as the Tabasco lowlands and northern Belize, where salt, cacao, cotton, and other materials were available or could be produced. Although sites which had

access to, and production control of, these goods may have traded them locally or regionally during much of the Classic period, I would argue that it was only with a growing long-distance demand after AD 770–800 that the strategic location of these sites was fully realised. Thus, the rainforest environment of the southern lowlands did not provide huge advantages to certain sites because of their location. Due to this circumstance, I would argue that no single site or group of sites emerged as dominant central places through time. Rather, a number of more or less equal, semi-autonomous centres arose. In other words, the *relatively* homogeneous environment allowed the major centres, along with their hinterlands, to act like islands with regular trails connecting them, just as regular sea-lanes linked the Aegean islands. Like islands, the centres and their hinterlands vary greatly in size: a site like Tikal apparently directly controlled an area of 120.5 sq. km (Jones, Coe, and Haviland 1981), while smaller sites might only have controlled a few sq. km. How far beyond their own hinterlands the major centres exercised direct political control is still unclear. While we know that the élite intermarried and traded goods, the strength of the political influence of a large site over nearby small ones still remains to be determined.

Throughout their development in Classic times, major

centres appear to have maintained a tension between autonomy and dependence, as appears also to have been the case in the Aegean. Henderson (1981: 119), for example, has stated:

> The emergence of a recognizable Maya world is the first stage of a remarkable process of coordinate evolution. The regions of the Maya world never lost their own distinctive cultural traditions, but they were never again entirely independent. Ideas and institutions developed in one region could spread to many distant communities. This interaction was the key process in the emergence of Maya civilization.

Traditionally, Maya archaeologists have argued that the Classic centres were more or less independent polities, which interacted with each other to varying degrees. Thompson (1966: 97), for instance, stated: 'I am inclined to think of the Maya lowlands during the Classic Period as a loose federation of autonomous city states.' Morley (1946: 50) offers an analogy to 'the city-states of classic Greece—Athens, Sparta, and Corinth—which were united by a common language, religion, and culture, but each of which was politically independent of the other' (cf. Thompson 1936: 13). Such views certainly fit in with Renfrew's (1975: 13) definition of the early state module:

> In most, perhaps all, early civilizations there function a number of autonomous central places which, initially at least, are not brought within a single unified jurisdiction. It is such autonomous territorial units, with their central places, which together constitute what we would term a civilization. They may be recognized as iterations of what I propose to call the *early state module* (ESM).

In sum, even with the wealth of new archaeological information which has been uncovered since Morley's and Thompson's overviews of ancient Maya civilisation, to my mind no convincing case has yet been made that the major centres were not at least semi-independent politically.

Demographic, political, and economic realignment from AD 800–1200 (the 'collapse')

During the Early Classic period (AD 300–600), a limited number of lowland Maya sites were significantly influenced by the expanding Teotihuacan state, either directly or through its satellites such as Kaminaljuyu. The nature of this influence is perhaps best known from the great site of Tikal (e.g. Coggins 1975), although its understanding by and large still remains unclear. Despite the patchiness of evidence for strong Teotihuacan influence throughout the Maya lowlands, I believe that Teotihuacan indirectly had a much more pervasive effect on ancient Maya civilisation. Through the numerous economic, political and social interchanges among the many Maya peer polities, Central Mexican ideas of economic organisation, which presumably were perceived as successful by the Maya at sites like Tikal, spread throughout the lowlands. Most particularly, the concepts of nucleation of population and the large scale of growth of craft specialisation, although known in the lowlands, were given strong impetus

through the emulation of Teotihuacan and the economic vacuum created by the withdrawal of Teotihuacan influence at the end of the Early Classic period (see particularly Cowgill 1979). Ultimately, such nucleation and the growth of specialist groups in and around the centres at the expense of rural agricultural groups led to the demise of certain centres (see Culbert 1977; Hosler, Sabloff, and Runge 1977; and Willey and Shimkin 1973, among others).

The decline of these centres. often labelled 'the Classic Maya collapse', can be seen in clearer perspective if the peer polity concept is used in the attempt to build an understanding of the collapse of such centres. In addition, the sphere of interaction must be seen as the whole lowlands, not just the southern portion—a point strongly made some years ago by E.W. Andrews IV (1973). For example, many hypotheses, especially those relating to environmental or agricultural factors, have often been negated by arguments that they are relevant to many sites (say those on the northeast Peten) but would not work for other sites (such as those located along rivers). Thompson (1966: 102), for instance, has stated:

> It has been suggested that Maya methods of agriculture . . . were so wasteful that in time and with an increase of population lack of food would have forced migration. To refute this theory, one can note that the soil around Quirigua, frequently fertilized by floodings of the Motagua River, is very rich, yet Quirigua was one of the earlier cities to cease functioning.

If the Maya polities had been closely linked socially, materially and symbolically on only an élite level, or on both élite and commoner levels, from the Late Preclassic (c. 300 BC) until just before the 'collapse' (AD 750), I would argue that the downfall of several principal members of the interacting peer group could also have brought about the fall of others because of the close interdependence of the group members.

Although there certainly was much competition among Maya polities during Late Classic times, there was also a growing degree of communication. As Willey and Shimkin (1973: 461) noted: 'During this two centuries of climax, Maya civilization in the south was integrated at the élite level in a more impressive fashion than ever before.' How much of this integration was forced by military threat or raid is not certain, but it certainly was one factor (Webster 1977). Some of the integration was clearly accomplished through kinship ties, as recent hieroglyphic research has indicated (see Coggins 1975; and Marcus 1976, among many others). There may have been movements of élite personages and their retainers, in part as results of marriages between élite individuals from different centres, and such ties could have led to emulation among distant centres. In addition, funerals may have been times at which inter-site élite contacts occurred, as suggested by Adams (1977b). Economic ties, probably closely related to kinship ties, may have been most important of all. Movements of élite merchants would obviously have fostered inter-site communication. Pilgrimage fairs, suggested by Freidel (1981b: 378–9), could also have strengthened communication and interdependence among both élite and non-élite alike. Finally, it should be noted that it would be impossible to separate religious or ideological ties from the social, economic, or political, since they were inextricably linked in the Maya world; but clearly there was considerable religious communication among far-flung Classic polities.

Malcolm Webb (1973) has formulated an argument for Classic growth and decline that is highly relevant to any consideration of peer polity interaction. In brief, Webb argues that a combination of economic and ideological links among the Classic Maya élite, which were reinforced by exotic materials obtained from neighbouring regions, both provided the support for Classic developments while making the élite vulnerable to disruption. Such vulnerability could have been exacerbated by internal stresses at several of the principal core sites (such as Tikal). In fact, as ecological stresses increased in strength throughout the Late Classic period—and by ecological stresses I broadly mean population increases, nucleation, and related pressures on the agricultural support base (Deevey *et al.* 1979)—peer interdependence may have increased con-comitantly, leaving the élite as a whole more vulnerable to disintegration than before.

In sum, it might be hypothesised that population pressures led to increasing ecological stress in Late Classic times. Such stresses may have led to growing élite inter-dependence as a means of buffering these stresses. However, such growing interdependence may ultimately have increased the vulnerability of the élite to external forces on whom they were dependent for exotic materials. The acceleration of internal stresses and a final *coup de grâce* from external forces may have brought disaster at one or several crucial centres, causing, in turn, the collapse of a number of closely inter-dependent sites. The lack of recovery in the southern lowlands, in contrast to the florescence of the polities in the northern lowlands, might well be attributed to the relative lack of exportable resources in the southern lowlands and the high cost of environmental improvement after the catastrophe in the eighth and ninth centuries. Clearly, these lines of reasoning deserve much further thought. It should be noted parentheti-cally that this discussion of the collapse is a descriptive statement, *not* an explanation; I believe the latter will be derived principally from consideration of, on the one hand, the internal stresses, both demographic and agricultural, and, on the other, the close interdependence of the major centres. Clearly, the peer polity framework has the potential to help us isolate those structural features of the Classic Maya polities which abetted the collapse of many centres in the southern lowlands. On the other hand, the contrast between the lack of recovery of a number of large sites in the southern lowlands after their collapse and the concomitant florescence seen in the northern lowlands is likely to be explained satisfactorily only by an understanding of external factors, with particular focus on shifting demands for resources among the wider Mesoamerican polities.

The aftermath of ecological disaster at certain key Classic Maya sites in the southern lowlands, such as Tikal, was the downfall of other peer centres which were closely allied to, and dependent to some degree upon, these sites, although the exact nature of such dependency remains to be understood. However, as the participants of a recent School of American Research Advanced Seminar on the later periods of ancient Maya civilisation have argued (Sabloff and Andrews V, in preparation), a number of sites in the lowlands, particularly in the north, in Belize, and in the lake and riverine areas of the Peten, continued to be occupied well after AD 800 and some, especially in the north, actually flourished between AD 800 and 1200.

If we can begin to discern some cross-cultural patterning in different peer polity interaction spheres, we can soon hope to be in a position to formulate hypotheses which will predict why the developmental trajectories of various related peer polities differ through time. What is the nature of the cultural ties among peer polities which allows some declining polities to drag down some along with them, while others avoid disaster? Given certain environmental and economic parameters, do those polities which have direct access to, or control over, desired bulk materials have a long-term advantage over those which produce goods from materials supplied to them? Although the industrial experience might appear to negate such a proposition, is the pre-industrial situation different? How direct and significant is the relationship between differential peer polity growth and external market demands?

I believe that continued research into peer polity situations (where no one centre dominates all its neighbours) will allow scholars to answer these and other related questions. Moreover, such research has the distinct potential to pull Maya studies from the seeming dead ends in which they are currently mired and to begin to allow some understanding of the pro-cesses which occurred in that crucial period in the Maya low-lands between AD 800 and 1200. There was no overall *collapse* at this time (as has often been argued in the past), but a major demographic, economic and political *realignment* among the various peer polities of the Late Classic period. The leads and stimuli provided by the editors and authors of this volume undoubtedly promise in the long run to shed new light on this realignment.

Discussion

Unfortunately, such promise will never be fulfilled and the kinds of preliminary thoughts presented above will be destined to remain 'just-so stories', unless some basic linkages between cultural behaviour and the archaeological record in the Maya lowlands and elsewhere are made in the very near future. Although this general point is also raised in the concluding chapters of this volume, it is crucial to point out that if talk about the potential utility of the peer polity concept in understanding the growth of ancient complex societies in the Maya lowlands is not to come to naught, then the very *first* question we must ask and begin to investigate is this: *How do we monitor peer polity interaction in the archaeological record*? The Maya, with their rich architectural, sculptural, hieroglyphic and ceramic remains, have the potential to be particularly useful in forging an answer to this crucial question.

By asking how we can link the statics of the modern archaeological record with past cultural dynamics, we are posing a general methodological problem which, I believe, should become one of the principal foci of archaeological research in the 1980s (see Binford 1977a; 1981; 1983; and also Willey and Sabloff 1980: 249–54; Sabloff 1981; 1983). The archaeological record we see today does not have any dynamic meaning, nor can we rigorously give it any simply by 'explaining' it through recourse to untested ethnographic or historic analogies. Only by developing middle-range or bridging theory, which predictably links past dynamic behaviour with the static remains we see today, will the discipline be able to break out of traditional model-building cycles, which accommodate new data but are unable to predict or explain.

The challenge of building middle-range theory is clearly evident in the case of peer polity interaction. We must be able to tie the interactions of the hypothesised peers to specific features of the archaeological record. The problem of linking ethnic groups, style and political boundaries is a crucial, but particularly difficult and vexing, problem. Renfrew (1975: 18), with some insight, points to one direction archaeologists might take, when he says:

> The flow of goods and information *between* the ESMs, what we may term the *intermediate trade,* is rarely discussed. Yet this is the exchange whose effect must have been to produce and maintain the uniformity of culture or civilization as a whole.

But, again, how are archaeologists to monitor this 'flow of goods and information'? Certainly, studies of culture trait distributions or trade items alone are not the answer. In the past, such studies have failed to show any 'cellular' distribution (in Childe's (1940) terms) of traits or trait complexes which corresponded regularly with social boundaries (Binford and Sabloff 1982; cf. Wissler 1914; Klimek 1935; Milke 1949; Clarke 1968; Hodder 1977a, among others). Perhaps the leads shown by Wright and Johnson (1975; cf. Johnson 1973; Flannery 1972), in studies attempting to monitor information flow in relation to political complexity, will prove rewarding. Nevertheless, whatever the means used, careful attention must be paid to this key question.

In other words, while those archaeologists who are concerned with the problem of linking the statics of the archaeological record with past cultural dynamics and who are studying hunter–gatherer groups have been able to focus much of their attention on understanding site function (see, for example, Binford 1978; 1981), those who are concerned with complex societies face much more difficult problems. How can the latter identify and monitor different organisational realms (subsystems, if you will) of culture such as the economic or political—as Lewis Binford (personal communication) has pointed out? Are different organisations or aspects thereof involved in peer interactions and local adaptations? Until we can conceptualise such problems carefully and begin to build bridging theory, our more elaborate models will remain as intellectual exercises divorced to an unknown degree from the reality of past processes. That is to say, the potential productivity of the concept of peer polity interaction will never be realised unless we first attempt to give meaning to the archaeological record. Ethnoarchaeological, or more importantly, historic studies, may well provide the means to begin to link dynamic cultural processes with the static record. I firmly believe that archaeologists will have to turn more and more to the historic record. What ethnoarchaeology has been in recent years to the study of hunter–gatherer groups, history will be, I predict, to research on complex societies.

In conclusion, if archaeologists wish to link the statics of the archaeological record with past dynamic processes in order to explain such processes, then new and more productive strategies and perspectives must be utilised. Archaeologists cannot be content to talk blithely about the new systems paradigm in archaeology and then proceed with 'business as usual', employing traditional concepts, methods and strategies. I can only hope that research and analysis stimulated by ideas stemming from the papers in this volume will produce new case materials which will make this wish a reality.

I further hope that this paper has indicated, in a very brief and preliminary fashion, some of the potential utility that the peer polity concept has for understanding the development of ancient Maya civilisation and, in turn, how archaeological data on the lowland Maya might lead to new refinements of the concept. Finally, I hope that my plea concerning the need for basic links between the processes of peer polity interaction and the modern archaeological record as a first step in future considerations of the peer polity concept will find some support.

Chapter 9

Midwestern Hopewellian exchange and supralocal interaction
David P. Braun

The concept of 'peer polity interaction' might seem inappropriate for examining changes in so-called tribal or non-hierarchical social systems; such systems usually lack anything that could be considered as 'polities' (Fried 1975; Braun and Plog 1982). Alternatively, however, when viewed on a large enough scale, regional tribal social networks can often be seen to consist of numerous overlapping, similarly organised, local residential networks, each focused on a single residential aggregate and possessing a slightly different identity within the whole (Peterson 1976; Blackburn 1976; Strathern 1969). The processes of communication and material transaction among such local networks can have profound cumulative effects on both local and regional social organisation. In simple, as in complex social systems, 'any communication process, once initiated and maintained, leads to the genesis of social structure—whether or not such structure is anticipated or deemed desirable' (Krippendorff 1971: 171).

The development of the so-called Hopewell interaction sphere and its sister phenomenon, the so-called Hopewell decline, in the prehistoric North American midlands, provide a case in point. When examined in terms of the processes of communication among local peer networks, the two phenomena appear not as unexpected events such that each interrupts the normal social character of the region, but rather as consequences of a single social—ecological process worked out over time.

Background

The Hopewell phase of exchange in the North American midlands, c. AD 1—200, stands out both in the diversity and quantity of goods circulated, and in the geographic range of this circulation. At the system's zenith, certain goods also take on a high degree of standardisation, both as exchanged goods and in local imitations (see the summary in Griffin 1967: 183—9). The zone of this exchange and local imitation covers most of the eastern Woodlands of the United States and south-eastern Canada (Fig. 9.1). Within this zone participation varied, with areas along the major waterways showing the greatest activity (see various papers in Brose and Greber 1979).

Two core areas are recognised: the Mississippi and Illinois river valleys in western Illinois, and the Scioto and Miami river valleys in southern Ohio (Fig. 9.1). These areas are marked by concentrations of 'Hopewell'-style finished goods and by evidence for an exceptional intensity of production of exchanged goods. Each of these two areas, one western and one eastern, appears to have stood at the centre of a large inter-regional network; they came to overlap each other, but never lost their broad distinctiveness (Struever and Houart 1972: 74—7).

Raw materials for the manufacture of exchanged goods were obtained over an even broader geographic zone, as well as from areas within the eastern Woodlands otherwise apparently lacking involvement in the exchange of élite

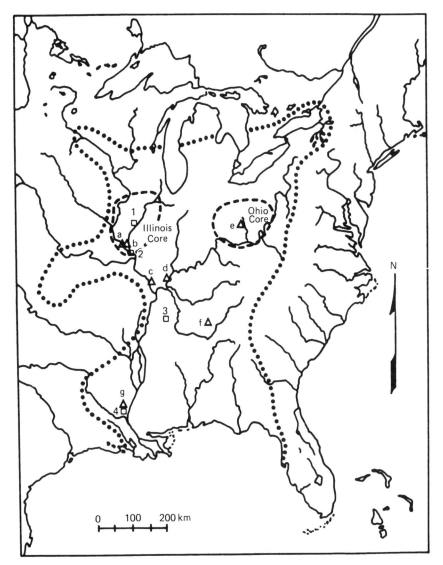

Fig. 9.1. Map of eastern North America showing the zone of participation in Hopewellian phenomena (outer bounded region) and the locations of the Illinois and Ohio core areas (inner bounded regions). Sites marked are those mentioned in the text or in Fig. 9.3. Earthen enclosures outside the Ohio area are: (1) Ogden Fettie; (2) Golden Eagle; (3) Pinson; (4) Marksville. Sites of recovery for artefacts illustrated in Fig. 9.3 are: (a) Snyders; (b) Klunk; (c) Twenhafel; (d) Rutherford; (e) Mound City; (f) Coffee County, Tennessee; (g) Crooks.

finished goods. Many of the exotic raw materials, in fact, appear to have been obtained either directly or preferentially by residents of the core areas or secondary areas, who concentrated and converted them into finished goods. The movement of these particular finished goods back into the larger local and regional networks, in turn, does not appear to have differed from the pattern of movement of goods made of local materials (Braun *et al.* 1982: 62–85; Griffin *et al.* 1969; Struever and Houart 1972).

The social context of exchange and imitative manufacturing has received increasing scrutiny. Several conclusions have been drawn. Many of the stylistically distinct goods, or goods of exotic material, ended their use-lives as burial offerings, most often in the interments of individuals otherwise marked as important members of their community (Buikstra 1976: 29–45; 1979: 230–2; Tainter 1977; 1980;

Braun 1979; Brown 1979; 1981; Greber 1979a; 1979b). This differential mortuary association of exchanged goods suggests that the interments involved are those of persons active in the manipulation of exchange. Such differentials, further, are most pronounced in the two core areas, perhaps even more so in Ohio than in Illinois. However, even in the core areas, none of the goods interred with individuals can as yet be identified as a consistent badge or symbol of any particular offices (Braun 1979: 70–2; Brown 1981: 36; Greber 1979a: 36–8). The data are consistent instead with a model of differential social dominance and privilege without symbolically distinct authority.

Recruitment of specific individuals to positions of social dominance appears closely tied to individual age, gender, and physical stature, rather than to any more complex form of ascription. This pattern appears to hold even at those sites exhibiting the most complex mortuary programmes in either Illinois (Buikstra 1976; see also Braun 1979; Brown 1981) or Ohio (Greber 1979a; 1979b). On a broader social scale, on the other hand, membership in parallel segmental divisions, which in turn differed in relative dominance, may have given *potential* access to positions of individual dominance in Ohio and in at least one community in Illinois (Greber 1979a: 36–8; Brown 1981: 34–6). The basis for membership in such segments is not known. Outside the core areas, evidence for such differential segmental dominance is unclear, and evidence of hierarchy is less pronounced (Griffin *et al.* 1970: 187–9; Brown 1979; Jefferies 1979).

Evidence for other forms of pan-residential social integration consists at present of evidence for communal ritual facilities, most notably in Ohio. Settlement patterns are as yet poorly understood.

The well-known geometric banked enclosures in Ohio appear to have been local centres for mortuary (and pre-sumably other) rituals within a relatively dispersed pattern of residence (Brown 1979: 213–15; see also Prufer 1965; 1975: 316; Baby and Langlois 1979). Greber (1979a; 1979b) also finds evidence that a tripartite geometric division of the enclosures, at two Ohio sites investigated, has parallels in a tripartite pattern of differentiation in the treatment and spatial arrangement of burials in their mortuary structures. Construction of the Ohio enclosures thus may have been organised along the social segmental lines mentioned earlier.

Outside Ohio, geometric enclosures occur only in adjacent portions of Indiana, at Pinson in Tennessee (Mainfort *et al.* 1982), at Marksville in Louisiana (Toth 1974), and at two scattered locations in Illinois (Fig. 9.1; Munson 1967; Struever and Houart 1972: 54). We do find elsewhere–in Illinois (Struever 1960; Struever and Houart 1972: 60–3; Buikstra 1976: 41–4; Asch *et al.* 1979: 82–3) and in Tennessee (Butler 1979)–sites that also apparently served as centres for ritual activity involving groups of adjacent settlements, but that lacked banked enclosures. This relative scarcity of evidence of facilities for formal pan-residential ritual outside the Ohio core area, of course, by no means indicates an absence of regular pan-residential congregation. The record is as yet simply mute.

Subsistence practices, in turn, are fairly well documented, at least in the core areas. Wherever appropriate analyses have been conducted, we find evidence of a regime based on harvesting diverse terrestrial and aquatic fauna, as well as wild nuts and other fruit and seeds, and on cultivating a modest range of garden crops (Asch *et al.* 1979: 82–4; Ford 1979).

Population densities, finally, were not high. Estimates for the lower Illinois valley, probably second only to the southern Ohio valleys in density, are of the order of only 40 people per 100 sq. km, with the larger villages containing no more than 50–100 people (Asch *et al.* 1979: 82; Buikstra 1979: 231). If perhaps more densely settled than their Illinois counterparts, the Ohio participants apparently resided in

smaller individual villages more dispersed across the valley bottoms (Prufer 1965; 1975).

The picture emerging of the local organisational base for the Hopewellian inter-regional network, then, is not one of great complexity. The ingredients–weakly to moderately developed village segmental organisation, weakly to moderately developed regular pan-residential ritual, personal dominance within and perhaps differential dominance among local social segments, an absence of consistent symbols of formal hierarchical gradation, a mixed hunting–gathering–gardening subsistence system, and modest densities of population residing in relatively small villages–are familiar ones, even if their patterns of combination here are peculiarly eastern North American.

To summarise the context of Hopewell in this manner, however, is to describe conditions only for the period of greatest inter-regional exchange. Yet the period from c. 150 BC to AD 400 witnessed a number of broad cultural changes, particularly in the Ohio and Illinois core areas, of which the aforementioned conditions were only an inter-mediate part. It is these broader changes that provide insight into the processes of interaction at work.

First, the regional exchange systems of the Hopewell period all had antecedents in the Eastern Woodlands extending back at least to c. 4000 BC (Brose 1979). Although antecedent, none of these earlier networks evolved continuously into a specific Hopewellian counterpart, with the possible exception of the Adena network in southern Ohio and vicinity (Dragoo 1964; Otto 1979). Each of these preceding networks was smaller than the overall Hopewellian network and covered a slightly different geographic range. Each of them also followed a cycle of expansion and dissolution (Fitting and Brose 1971; Stoltman 1978). This 'cyclicity' has attracted notice only in the Hopewellian case, yet each earlier network represents an incremental step towards the complexity of the Hopewellian systems. The diversity and number of distinctively but similarly styled goods circulated and the scale of local hierarchies of social dominance all increased, by steps, over time. Such parallels suggest a common set of social evolutionary processes at work, and less uniqueness about Hopewell.

Second, where settlement data are adequate, the Hopewellian upswing in exchange activity has been found to coincide with an aggregation of the participating populations into the valleys of the major waterways. Residence also appears to have become more nucleated and less mobile, particularly in Illinois and other western areas (Rackerby 1968: 80–5; Asch *et al.* 1979: 82–3; Black 1979; Johnson 1979: 86–8; Charles 1982). In western Illinois, at least, house floor areas also increase dramatically (Braun 1981a), as do indicators of the mean capacity for ceramic cooking vessels (Fig. 9.2; Braun 1985). Asch *et al.* (1979: 84) note, again at least for western Illinois where we have the appropriate data, that the cultivation of edible seeds and cucurbits also increased along with the trend of aggregation.

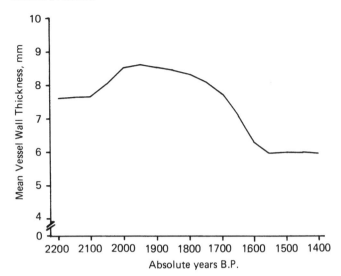

Fig. 9.2. Changes in mean wall thickness of domestic pottery over time, 2200 to 1400 BP, in western Illinois. Changes are related to changing cooking practices and possibly household size (after Braun 1985).

The onset of the Hopewell phase of exchange, then, witnessed not only increases in exchange activity and in the local social hierarchy, but trends of aggregation, decreasing mobility, and subsistence intensification. It appears reasonable to suggest that these trends did not coincide fortuitously, but were in fact highly mutually reinforcing. Whether some of the productive intensification arose through social demands for production beyond subsistence cannot as yet be evaluated. Whatever the specific details, however, the mutual reinforcement was intense. If we take the shift in ceramic cooking technology in Illinois (Fig. 9.2) as one indicator of the aggregation and of changes in the pattern of preparation of food bulk, its high rate of change between 150 BC and AD 1 suggests a rapid pace of cultural change.

Conditions during the peak in Hopewellian exchange (c. AD 1–200) were also not static. Differences in the distribution of temporal indicators among sites in both Ohio (Prufer 1968; Seeman 1977) and Illinois (Griffin *et al.* 1970; Braun *et al.* 1982; Morgan 1982) suggest that population movements and/or shifts in one particular group's social importance were marked among otherwise nominally contemporaneous sites. Local and inter-regional interactions were thus presumably quite fluid.

The 'decline' of Hopewellian phenomena (c. AD 200–400) reverses some, but (at least in the core areas) not all, of the preceding trends. The reverses include a decline in the quality of workmanship on exchanged and locally imitated goods; a decline in the preferential procurement of exotic raw materials and in the supralocal exchange of valuables in general; a decline in mortuary indicators of individual prestige; and the disuse of most earthen enclosures (Griffin 1967; Buikstra 1977: 74–83; Braun 1981b).

Decoration on domestic pottery, in some areas quite

elaborate during the period AD 1–200, becomes increasingly simple and homogeneous over large regions. Interestingly, this decline also involves an incorporation of most elements of the decorative style of the Hopewellian exchanged/imitated pottery into the local styles of the domestic pottery (Griffin *et al.* 1970: 8–9; Phillips 1970; Johnson and Johnson 1975; Kay and Johnson 1977; Benn 1978). I shall return to this point.

In contrast, the subsistence and demographic trends are not reversed, at least not in the Midwest, where data are available. The cultivation of crops for edible seeds in fact increases, particularly for several native species producing more starchy seeds. Due to problems of chronological control, the exact demographic trend remains unclear. However, no abrupt changes nor any reduction in settlement density have been detected, nor has evidence for major population movements, at least not in the most intensively studied regions such as western Illinois (Asch *et al.* 1979: 84; Buikstra 1977: 75–7). House floor areas decline significantly (Braun 1981a), again at least in western Illinois, but there is no evidence that overall village sizes declined as well (Asch 1979: 84). The exploitation of wild food resources continued as before and became even more locally intensive in some areas, possibly as a consequence of greater population densities (Styles 1981: 261–9). Further changes occur in the construction of ceramic cooking containers, which is again consonant with, and further indicates, the trends in diet and possibly household size (Fig. 9.2; Braun 1983; 1985).

Hopewellian peer polity interaction

With the foregoing in mind, we can turn to an examination of the processes of interaction evident in the Hopewellian cycle. In particular, we can ask: Why the increase in the intensity of exchange of valuables? Why the apparent standardisation among certain goods and their imitations? Why the eventual ebbing of decorative activity and the circulation of valuables? My argument is that these are all the consequences of peer polity interaction, one leading to the next, over time. This view contrasts with those already offered in the literature, which I shall first review from the following standpoints:

1   The initiation of the Hopewellian phase of exchange can be understood as a consequence of how local residential aggregates formed and how they adapted not only to the physical environment, but also to each other.

2   The inter-regional standardisation and imitation of style in valuables can be understood as a consequence of the process of symbolic communication among numerous increasingly interacting *local* residential aggregates.

3   The ebbing of certain symbolic hallmarks can be understood as a consequence of the *success* rather than the failure of the supralocal social interaction and integration they helped promote.

Initiation

The initiation of 'Hopewell' has been a subject more of speculation than analysis. Several authors, noting the four or more millennia of developments leading up to the Hopewellian systems, suggest that the exchanges throughout served as a form of supralocal social banking against local productive uncertainty (Ford 1974: 389–403; 1977; Brown 1977: 172–3; Brose 1979). The overall development in exchange activity, it is noted, parallels evidence for increasing population densities, decreasing mobility and increasing complexity in the scheduling of subsistence activities. Such changes would all have entailed a progressive localisation of subsistence activity, and hence of subsistence risk, the commonly cited stimulus for the seeking of supralocal ties of obligation.

Alternatively, others have suggested a primarily social stimulus for the overall development of exchange relations (e.g. Bender 1978). Demand for valuable goods by those seeking to manipulate positions of local social dominance is said to have led to the gradual reciprocal stimulation both of surplus production and of exchange activity wherever ecological and demographic conditions permitted.

Much has been made of a supposed contrast between the models of exchange underlying these two positions (e.g. Hodder 1980: 154–5). The contrast is superficial. There is no contradiction between recognising an ecological-selective stimulus for the establishment of reciprocal obligations among interacting residential units, and recognising the importance of exchange in the selective recruitment of personnel to positions of local leadership. We need only recognise, that is, the importance of local leaders in the negotiation of inter-community obligations (Dalton 1977), and the selective advantages accruing to communities that successfully produce effective leaders.

Factors conditioning the cross-cultural development of leadership or delegated decision-making appear to relate to the flow of information in decision-making structures (Johnson 1978; 1982). In particular, delegated or centralised decision-making becomes more efficient than consensual forms the greater the diversity of information requiring *constant* handling and *prompt* response (see also Peebles and Kus 1977: 427–30).

A cluster of positive feedback relationships among several variables can thus easily be visualised as leading to the initiation of Hopewell: increasing population densities, decreasing mobility, and increasing complexity of subsistence scheduling would have increased the local managerial woes of household and community, increased the ecological benefits of supralocal social obligations, and increased the relative advantages of both co-ordinated and delegated local decision-making. Eventually, the balance would have been tipped in favour of aggregated/more centrally co-ordinated residence as against dispersed/more consensually co-ordinated residence, in a few areas. We can then postulate an accelerating relationship among the aforementioned factors in those areas, with perhaps the addition of increased demands for production beyond subsistence to accommodate the competitive displays of would-be local leaders. The contagiousness of such changes can also be easily visualised (Bender 1978; 1982; Asch *et al.* 1979: 84).

From the standpoint of social and ecological theory then, the initiation of Hopewell can be modelled as a consequence of how residential aggregates formed and how they adapted not only to the physical environment, but also to the presence of each other. The ingredients of this social process—the stimuli for both supralocal co-operation and competition—may also be termed peer polity interaction.

Style

The development of stylistic standardisation and imitations among valuables has received both speculative and analytical attention. Several models have been proposed, none without serious weaknesses.

Several authors suggest the development of a single, relatively unified system of transactions among the participating regions (e.g. Prufer 1964; Struever 1964; 1965; Struever and Houart 1972). Both the stylistic standardisation of highly crafted goods—for example small ceramic jars and bowls with distinctive geometric and zoomorphic designs, carved stone pipes, copper earspools and panpipes, and ceramic figurines—and their widespread distribution along with certain exotic raw materials—for example obsidian, marine shell, copper and hornstone—are taken as evidence of this unity.

Analyses of the spatial distribution of exchanged goods and raw materials, however, contradict this image of unity. No transactional equivalences can be documented among any classes of goods or materials. Instead, each style of finished good and each raw material possesses a distinct and unique spatial distribution (Griffin 1965; Griffin *et al.* 1970: 98–114; Seeman 1979; Walthall *et al.* 1979; Braun *et al.* 1982: 82–5).

Further, the movements of exotic raw materials and of finished goods are not analytically equivalent social phenomena. As noted earlier, the movement of many exotic materials was highly directional or preferential. The movement of most finished goods, in contrast, appears to have been *local* and presumably roughly reciprocal (Struever and Houart 1972: 76; Seeman 1977; 1979). The movement of most exotic materials, in fact, appears to be accounted for most easily by the idea that deliberate expeditions were undertaken by a few residents of the core areas for the purpose of obtaining 'fuel' for local exchange activity back home (Griffin 1965). Such an interpretation is well in line with the entrepreneurial character of valuables exchange and exchange negotiators so commonly observed ethnographically in similar settings (e.g. Sahlins 1963; Vayda 1967; Harding 1967; Strathern 1971; Dalton 1977). With this in mind, it becomes important to treat only finished exchange goods as accurate markers of the social organisation of exchange. And when we do so, the suggested transactional unity of inter-regional relations seems even less likely (see also Toth 1977; 1983).

Other efforts to explain the standardisations and imitations have met similar difficulties. The stylistic standardisation of some goods, for example, has been attributed vaguely to the existence of a few highly productive artisans (Deuel 1952: 260–2). The incorporation of foreign decorative concepts into the manufacture of both domestic and exchanged goods in several regions has been attributed variously to undefined 'influences', to travelling artisans, or to the spread of an ideology (Deuel 1952; Prufer 1964; Hall 1977; 1979; Chapman 1980: 72–7). This citing of possible coincidental events still offers no insights into the processes at work.

Similarly, some writers have sought to explain the standardisations as evidence of a unified symbolisation of positions of authority (e.g. Deuel 1952: 258), or as a consequence of the use of the objects in the personal manipulation of prestige (e.g. Struever and Houart 1972: 77; Brown 1977: 172). In the former instance, as noted earlier, no analysis has yet identified the consistency in use and contextual association one would expect for symbols of authority and office. In the latter instance, the suggestion only redefines the problem. In the absence of any inter-regional social integration, why should the markers of prestige in one community be the same as those in another some hundreds of kilometres distant in which the populations followed only broadly similar ways of life?

An alternative explanation, advocated here, treats the stylistic phenomena among valuables as a consequence of certain basic characteristics of communications networks typical of peer polity interaction. The key, in this instance, is to recognise that the stylistic phenomena occurred during a period of residential nucleation, reduced mobility, and increasing supralocal exchange activity, and therefore of increasing intralocal and supralocal interaction and communication. My argument here follows in part from previous papers (e.g. Braun and Plog 1982), from the ideas of Wobst (1977) and others on the concept of 'style', and from theoretical treatments of the process of communication by Krippendorff (1971), C. Cherry (1978) and Rogers and Kincaid (1981).

All human interactions involve communication, whether or not intentionally. Moreover, communication involves a kind of mutual mapping-on of behaviour among the interacting parties—be they individuals or groups—as a result of the informational feedbacks necessarily involved. This development of mutual constraint takes place whether or not the specific contents of the interaction and the attendant communication vary. It also takes place without any one of the interacting parties deliberately seeking to impose structure on the interaction and communication. It appears to be a consequence of the processes of communication alone (Krippendorff 1971; Rogers and Kincaid 1981: 31–71).

This development of structure is especially evident in the development of means and channels of communication. Communication involves a process of encoding and decoding information from particular media or channels of transmission and reception (Weaver 1949). That is, communication requires the development of a code, a system of signs, between each pair of interacting parties.

Further, if a network of communication involves more than two mutually connected parties and/or a diversity of possible messages, successful communication will require the development of codes usable *by and for all*. With large numbers of parties communicating or messages being communicated, communications can become quite noisy, that is, distorted through cumulative errors. Under such circumstances, successful communication requires the development of increased redundancy in the system of signs involved, to reduce error. For example, we might see redundancy in the form of repetition, or in the use of multiple signs for the same information (see Cherry, C. 1978: 169–217, for one review). These developments would require no deliberate imposition of order by any would-be dominant party in the network, but can arise through selective processes affecting the network as a whole (e.g. Rogers and Kincaid 1981).

With these rather general ideas in mind, we can turn more specifically to a consideration of their application to exchange systems. Exchange, particularly the exchange of valuables, can be thought of as a form of meta-communication—that is, it serves to establish and maintain links between communities that, in turn, are used for more active communication and material transaction (Sahlins 1972: 185–230; Ford 1972; Dalton 1977). Further, exchange acts are acts of negotiation, expressing the activities of parties with distinct, but complementary, socio-economic interests. As Sahlins has noted (1972: 188–91), they both require and express the existence of a social difference between parties. Valuables exchange in particular tends to occur across pronounced social distances (Strathern 1971: 93–114; Sahlins 1972: 277–314; Dalton 1977).

According to the aforementioned expectations for networks of communication, we should expect, for networks of exchange, that as interaction, whether co-operative or competitive, develops among neighbouring parties across a region, there should develop an increasing consistency in the kinds of goods exchanged across the whole (mutual constraint). This consistency should develop first among sets of immediately neighbouring parties, but then increasingly include parties across larger geographic distances. Further, there should develop greater redundancy in exchange signs—that is, in the styles of the tokens of exchange.

These phenomena are well illustrated, if perhaps only relatively synchronically, in the ethnographic record. Mutual constraint is apparent in many regions, not only in widespread reciprocal (often competitive) demands for the circulating valuables for local social purposes, but also in reciprocal demands for the flow of commodities and/or for the local alliances of economic and political relations that the valuables exchanges are used to maintain (Dalton 1977). Redundancy in exchange signs, in turn, is apparent in the remarkable stylistic standardisation of the circulated valuables in these same regions. Raw material, artefact form, and, when present, decorative motif can be seen to constitute in each token an unmistakable identity as an exchange good of recognised value.

How do these concepts apply to Hopewellian exchange? The stylistic standardisation of exchanged valuables, such as the small ceramic containers, pipes, earspools and figurines, here developed simultaneously (as best we can tell) with the increase in the diversity and quantity of goods circulated and with the increase in the geographic range of the network (Griffin 1965; Griffin *et al.* 1970: 6–7, 82–7, 96–114; Seeman 1977; 1979; Toth 1977; 1979: 194; 1983; Braun *et al.* 1982: 82–5). The evidence for a simultaneously increased development of hierarchies of local personal social dominance is also compelling (Brown 1979). These apparently mutually reinforcing relationships are precisely what we should expect according to the concepts of communication and peer polity interaction discussed earlier. Moreover, as noted earlier, the underlying social trends were probably closely tied in with socio-demographic changes in settlement nucleation, residential mobility, and subsistence-productive intensity.

My argument, then, is that the stylistic standardisation and imitations arose as part of the development of structure and symbolic redundancy in exchange relations. As interaction among sets of overlapping communities increased, with the concomitant of increasing local exchange, selective advantages accrued to the use of exchange tokens that could be visually recognised and evaluated among large numbers of parties. Thus, in the case of specific decorative motifs, we need not speak of the spread of an ideology, but only of an evolving, convenient emphasis on symbols that evoked similar meanings among parties drawing upon broad, *already shared* ideational themes.

The styles of certain small ceramic vessels provide a specific illustration. From the earliest excavations of Hopewellian sites, archaeologists recognised a widespread 'ceremonial' ware distinct from the more common and regionally distinctive utility wares (Griffin 1952: 114–115). In the form of small, squat jars, morphologically and technically unlike the rest of the diverse local ceramic assemblages, this ware also exhibits a consistent and unique decorative treatment: a thickened or cambered vertical rim; a horizontal exterior band of finely incised cross-hatching immediately below the lip, followed immediately below by a band of horizontally applied hemiconical punctations, followed by a smoothed or polished band continuous to the throat inflection; and a body decoration consisting either of outlined curvilinear or geometric zones, or of a limited set of similarly outlined avian motifs. The birds appear either raptorial or spoon-billed, with a few straight-billed (Griffin

1952; Prufer 1964; Toth 1977; 1979; 1983; Braun *et al.* 1982: 62–3). Several examples of this ceramic style, from several regions, are illustrated in Fig. 9.3.

Despite efforts, no one has yet identified a single area of origin for this style. It does appear abruptly in such areas as the lower Mississippi (Marksville–Toth 1974; 1977; 1979; 1983) and central Missouri valleys (Kansas City Hopewell–Johnson 1979; Kay 1979), apparently coincidentally with their development of contacts with western Illinois. On the other hand, these same avian motifs are also found rendered in stone, bone, copper and shell in both western Illinois and southern Ohio (Webb and Snow 1974: 94; Dragoo 1964: 22–3; Braun *et al.* 1982: 89–90), as well as elsewhere, with neither region clearly stylistically primordial. Examples of renderings in several non-ceramic media, from several regions, are also illustrated in Fig. 9.3. Pottery specimens from the lower Illinois valley are today considered technically among the best executed, but are only occasionally found as imports at much distance (Braun *et al.* 1982: 76, 173). In fact, nearly all pottery specimens found in each region are rendered in locally typical pastes. The interment of a Roseate Spoonbill, a south-eastern native, in an élite burial facility in the lower Illinois valley (Parmalee and Perino 1971) represents one of the few known instances of possible inter-regional movement of any object related to the avian decorative motifs.

Our present image, then, is of a rapidly developed, concurrent use of visually similar symbols in several regions, but little actual flow of symbolic objects between regions–at least with respect to non-perishable materials (see also Griffin 1979: 278–9). This concurrence appears in the context of growing exchange activity within each region, aided and abetted by occasional interactions across much larger distances. The occurrence of similar avian motifs on several media and the occurrence of remains of the represented species as burial accompaniments (Webb and Snow 1974: 94; Griffin *et al.* 1970: Pls. 142a, 164) suggest a broadly similar ideational or ritual significance for parts of the decorative imagery.

It is important to note, finally, that the inter-regional uniformity occurs not merely in the renditions of the avian motifs, but in an entire decorative style overall. This condition suggests that the uniformity itself was something deliberately sought and maintained as a marker of participation in the developing network of social relations within and between regions.

'Decline'
The end of the Hopewellian phenomena has received much speculative, but as yet little analytical, attention. The apparent reversals of all that had seemed progressive–the inter-regional exchanges, the inter-regional art styles, the evidence of local co-operative monument building–gives an impression of a disruption, the cause of which many have sought in some widespread event. As yet, none has emerged (Buikstra 1977; Braun 1977: 35–48), although the search has

Fig. 9.3. Examples of the Hopewellian decorative style and use of avian motifs on pottery and other decorative media, from several regions. Sites of recovery are also indicated in Fig. 9.1: (a) Ceramic jar, 15 cm high, Klunk Mounds, Illinois (after Perino 1968: 91); (b) Ceramic jar, 14 cm high, Klunk Mounds, Illinois (after Perino 1968: 89); (c) Tetrapodal ceramic jar, 12 cm high, Mound City, Ohio (after Mills 1922: 511); (d) Ceramic jar, 14 cm high, Crooks Mound, Louisiana (after Ford and Willey 1940: 69); (e) Ceramic bowl, 20.5 cm wide at mouth, Twenhafel Site, Illinois (after Hofman 1979: 36); (f) Carved stone pipe, 6.1 cm beak to tail, Rutherford Mounds, Illinois (after Fowler 1957: 22); (g) Copper cut-out, 33 cm long, Mound City, Ohio (after Mills 1922: 533); (h) Copper plaque, 28 cm long, Mound City, Ohio (after Mills 1922: 534); (i) Carved stone pipe, size unknown, Coffee County, Tennessee (after Faulkner 1968: 20); (j) Engraved shell, 8.8 cm horizontal dimension, Snyders Mounds, Illinois (after Braun *et al.* 1982: 141–2).

been hampered by problems of local chronology (cf. Prufer 1964: 66–9; Tainter 1977; Braun 1981b).

Three alternative, processual models may be advanced, however, following suggestions by Tainter (1977), Bender (1978; 1982), Saitta (1982), and myself (Braun 1977; Braun and Plog 1982). All three models focus on organisational contradictions set in motion by the same factors that produced the antecedent Hopewellian phenomena–in a sense, by the same social processes.

1 Continued population growth, in part possibly encouraged by the continuing horticultural intensification, could have led to conflict over unevenly accessible resources (Tainter 1977). This model assumes that a limit was reached *and exceeded* in the capacity of social banking activities between local residential aggregates. Raiding thereby became a more viable means for acquiring less evenly accessible resources.

This model, however, does not explain the changes in exchange activity or local social hierarchy. We can as

easily argue that, under the circumstances, exchange and the importance of local leadership should have increased–for instance following ideas of Sahlins (1963) or Dalton (1977). In any case, evidence for internecine conflict during the period of 'decline' is highly ambiguous, and confined to southern Ohio alone (Braun 1981b; cf. Prufer 1964: 66–9).

2 Demands for more intensive horticultural production, encouraged by the trends in both exchange/ leadership and settlement patterns, could have led to the development of more successful systems of cultivation. Such systems would then have reduced the ecological incentives for both supralocal exchange and residential aggregation by reducing the effective variation in subsistence-productive potential across the local landscape (Bender 1978; 1982; Saitta 1982). From Illinois, for example, evidence for such changes as the accelerated use of cultivated seeds, the pattern of greater localisation of faunal procurement, and the

reduction in house floor areas would all fit into this model. Its predicted social consequences are the reduction in evidence for supralocal exchange and for local personal leadership. This model's utility, however, must be compared to that of the third.

3   Cultivation, while it may increase the subsistence-productive potential of land, also carries significant risks from temporal variation in productive conditions (see various articles in Barlett 1980, especially that by Cancian). As Voss (1980) and Braun and Plog (1982) have argued, we should not expect to see a population successfully increasing its vulnerability to temporal ecological variation without a compensating increase in the use of 'temporal averaging mechanisms' (Isbell 1978: 305) such as storage, diversified planting strategies, or ties of supralocal social obligation (see also Jorde 1977). We can argue, in fact, that such social changes were part of the processes that led to the Hopewellian phenomena to begin with. We can also argue that such changes in Illinois as the accelerated use of cultivated foods, the greater localisation of faunal procurement, and the shift to smaller households would not in fact have been possible without the continued development of such social averaging strategies.

Further, we should bear in mind that exchange acts involving valuables are generally acts of negotiation, establishing lines of obligation that can dissolve if not regularly reaffirmed. These lines stand in contrast to more long-term, stable forms of social obligation based on regular ritual and integrated systems of symbols and belief—what Sahlins (1972: 137) has called 'the anonymous and silent government of structure'. If the benefits of economic co-operation outweigh those of competition as incentives for the supralocal exchange of valuables, then we should see over time an evolution of more *continuous*, formal ties of supralocal obligation replacing the more unpredictable ties of negotiation. As with the aforementioned second model, we should again expect a reduction in the evidence for supralocal exchange and local personal leadership.

The verdict on the last two models is far from complete. I have argued elsewhere (e.g. Braun and Plog 1982) that changes over time in the diversity of decorative treatments on domestic pottery *within*, as opposed to *among*, localities in western Illinois support the third model. In contrast to the preceding two to three centuries, the period immediately after c. AD 200 witnessed both increasing decorative consistency between localities and decreasing decorative diversity within localities. Saitta (1982), however, argues that this pattern of domestic decorative change does not necessarily contradict the second model. Yet the widespread incorporation of the standardised decorative components from the distinctive Hopewellian pots into numerous domestic ceramic decorative complexes may also be taken as an indicator of increased formal supra-residential social integration. The stylistic codes of membership in the exchange system became the stylistic

codes of the domestic environment, as the interconnections of social and economic identity between neighbouring localities progressively increased.

While debate on these interpretations will continue, it appears at least plausible to explain the post-AD 200 changes in Hopewellian symbolic hallmarks as a consequence of the continuation, rather than the reversal, of many of the social processes they had initially helped promote. Such changes would also be examples of what has here been termed peer polity interaction—the symbolic, as well as the economic and social, consequences of interaction among large numbers of similarly organised local residential aggregates.

Conclusions

My purpose in this paper has not been simply to propose yet another model of Hopewell, but rather to help move the explanation of Hopewellian phenomena into the province of general social theory, and to help remove it from the culture-historical and event-oriented approaches of the past. In several ways, the concept of peer polity interaction provides a useful framework for relating several aspects of Hopewellian change to each other and to possible underlying social processes.

My theme throughout has been that, rather than coming as exogenous events disrupting the normal course of development in each region, the phenomena of Hopewell arose and faded precisely as a *result* of a normal course of development. That is, they arose and faded as a result of continuously increasing social interaction among large numbers of similarly organised or 'peer' local residential aggregates, across several ecologically similar regions. The changes in symbols, in supra-local exchange, in settlement organisation and in local social organisation have as much to do with how residential aggregates adapted to each other as with how they dealt with their physical environments.

Clearly, many of the topics raised require further work. Significant refinements in chronology are necessary to enable us to assess more precisely contemporaneity among deposits and lead/lag relationships among trends. Further, my argument emphasises the primacy of local stimuli for the observed regional and inter-regional trends. Yet much of our data comes from individual sites each taken as representative of an entire region, or from studies only of the inter-regional exchange. A better sampling of local variation and local exchange in several regions would greatly help clarify matters. Analyses of mortuary practices, subsistence practices, domestic decorative styles and other social—ecological indicators are also necessary in many areas to allow their comparison with the Illinois and Ohio core ideas.

Finally, I would offer a note of caution. Much of the difficulty in, as well as the feasibility of, dealing archae-ologically with relatively simple social systems arises from such systems' simplicity, their lack of segregation of functions (Sahlins 1976; Braun and Plog 1982: 506). This simplicity makes it easier to model gross change, but also more difficult to isolate material indicators of any one aspect of the system. We rely on the analysis of burial practices, settlement patterns, exchange connections or stylistic variation, for example, for our sociological information, yet the bridging interpretation of our analytical results remains controversial. This, more than a lack of appropriate social theory, may be what challenges us the most, as we try to apply concepts such as peer polity interaction to a large part of the archaeological record.

Acknowledgements

My thanks to Gregory Johnson, and to the editors and symposium discussants, for their comments and suggestions. Karen Schmitt, of the Southern Illinois University Office of Research Development Scientific Illustration service, deserves special thanks for preparing Fig. 9.3.

Chapter 10

The nature and development of long-distance relations in Later Neolithic Britain and Ireland
Richard Bradley and Robert Chapman

This paper stems from the perception of a contrast in emphasis in the approaches taken to the model of peer polity interaction in this volume. On the one hand, Renfrew argues that this model not only illuminates our understanding of the emergence of complex societies, as in the case of his Melos study (Renfrew 1982a), but also that it may be relevant to non-hierarchical societies. On the other hand, Barnes (this volume: Ch. 6) would prefer to restrict peer polity interaction to a model describing only interactions between hierarchically centralised units of distinct territorial scope, meaning chiefdom level and above. Such a conflict is, of course, not unusual when quite specific models are argued to represent a particular manifestation of a broader theory applicable beyond the data on which they were originally formulated — e.g. the models of central-place theory (Clarke 1977). Our case study, along with those of Braun and Shennan, provides an opportunity for assessing the utility of peer polity inter-action as an explanatory framework in the study of non-complex societies.

Some general discussion is necessary before we present our case study on interaction and social change in Britain and Ireland in the third millennium bc. A useful starting point is Renfrew's definition of peer polity interaction as 'the full range of interchanges taking place (including imitation and emulation, competition, warfare and the exchange of material goods and of information) between autonomous (i.e. self-governing and in that sense politically independent) socio-

political units which are situated beside or close to each other within a single geographical region' (this volume: 1). It is argued by Renfrew that this definition avoids stress upon relations of dominance and subordination and upon the analysis of socio-political units in isolation. This emphasis upon interaction provides a welcome counter to the post-diffusionist models of prehistoric Europe, which have developed explanations for change in autonomous socio-political units. So we begin by welcoming this emphasis upon interaction and communication.

The discussion of the nature of interaction and communication between polities and, by implication, the social context of innovation, adoption or rejection, also help to distinguish Renfrew's model from the diffusionism of the earlier twentieth century. In this context the peer polity interaction model is part of a wider examination of the scale and effects of interaction between social units and the results of this process in terms of stylistic diffusion (e.g. Davis 1983). We shall return to this point at the end of the paper.

In spite of this broad agreement with the peer polity interaction model, it is important that we specify differences in the nature and scale of our analytical units as compared with those presented in many other chapters of this volume, as well as in Renfrew's formulation.

The analytical units which we employ in this paper are by no means directly comparable to the early state module defined by Renfrew (1975) and exemplified in the Minoan and

Mycenaean states. Renfrew's empirical generalisation was that each module occupied an area of c. 1,500 sq.km, with a mean distance of 40 km (range 20–100 km) between the centres of contiguous modules. We would not claim that the 'core areas' which we use here, which appear in the archaeological record as higher densities of known artefacts and monuments, are spatially as bounded as the early state modules. However, our knowledge of the archaeological record leads us to argue that these areas may be treated as real centres of social interaction and cultural evolution within Later Neolithic Britain and Ireland. They are not all spatially contiguous, as in Renfrew's model, nor in a single geographical region. The largest distance between these 'core areas' is some 900 km, but the presence of intervening core areas may reduce these distances to c. 50–150 km (Fig. 10.1). In addition, it should be pointed out that we do not expect that the 'boundaries' of our core areas, as defined by the distribution of monuments and/or portable artefacts, will necessarily be identical to political boundaries. It is sufficient for this paper that the core areas be regarded as *centres* of polities.

It is also important to note that our core areas may be up to 100 km in diameter (Fig. 10.1) and may have been internally heterogeneous. By this we mean that in some cases it is possible to interpret a core area as a single polity, while in other cases it may reflect a series of internally interacting polities which we treat as an analytical unit at the larger scale. For example, there is evidence for inter-monument spacing within some core areas which is closely comparable to that postulated between early state modules: Wessex henge monuments have a mean spacing of 35 km, while within Ireland the major Passage Grave cemeteries have a mean spacing of 40 km. For the sake of applying the peer polity interaction model in this paper we have decided to work with the larger-scale core area as the basic analytical unit. In Renfrew's terms, the core area is treated as the 'highest-order social unit'.

A difference in temporal scale also characterises our case study. Renfrew stresses that the peer polity interaction approach must be concerned with the explanation of change through time and not just of trait distributions in space. Changes in the organisational complexity of societies through time must be archaeologically documented. There is an immediate contrast between the the fine-scale chronology witnessed, for example, in Snodgrass's paper, in which the measurement of competitive emulation in monument construction takes place within the decade, and our discussion of Late Neolithic Britain and Ireland, in which radiocarbon chronology gives us the century, or more, as the unit of analysis. Again such a difference in scale has an important implication for our theoretical approach. A temporal scale which encompasses three to four generations as the unit of analysis would seem of little utility in any attempt to test for the presence of individual competitive emulation using the archaeological record.

Given these contrasts in the definition, scale and spacing of our analytical units as compared with more complex polities, we now turn to our case study. This is presented in four sections: an introduction to the area and period of study; the archaeological evidence for third millennium bc development in each core area; the archaeological evidence for interaction between the core areas; and a discussion of the local contexts in which this evidence for interaction is found.

Archaeological case study

Introduction

This paper considers cultural change in Britain and Ireland between about 2700 bc and 2000 bc. Although we shall be referring to certain areas of western Europe (Iberia, Brittany and south Scandinavia), our study will concentrate on four areas of Britain (Wessex, east Yorkshire, south-east Scotland and the Orkneys) and one region in Ireland (the Boyne Valley) (Fig. 10.1). This list does not exhaust the total number of areas which participated in long-distance interaction, but it does include all the regions with an adequate amount of published information.

Five points are central to our argument.

1   Interaction took place between areas in which political evolution had entirely different emphases.

2   Interaction was a feature mainly of the later

Fig. 10.1. Distribution of core areas defined by large monuments and/or complex artefacts (solid) and major groups of Passage Graves (dotted): (1) Wessex, (2) east Yorkshire, (3) east Scotland, (4) Orkneys, (5) Boyne Valley.

phases of political evolution and for this reason cannot explain how developments in different regions started. On the other hand, it can account for the gradually increasing similarity in the archaeological record as these sequences proceeded.

3   The contexts of interaction varied between these different regions, but are best identified by the presence in the archaeological record of artefacts which lack a utilitarian function, by the sharing of specific symbols and by the adoption of similar forms of monument.

4   The most common elements were taken selectively from one network of interaction into another and appear in quite different contexts in different areas.

5   The assimilation of different areas into a wider network of contacts took place only gradually, and as it did so the newly incorporated areas showed evidence of increasingly complex monuments, copied from proto-types in other regions, but sometimes eclipsing them in scale and elaboration.

In geographical terms the poles of our study area are represented by the Orkneys in the north, the Boyne Valley in the west and Wessex in the south. It is 900 km from Wessex to the Orkneys and 450 km from Wessex to the Boyne Valley. All three of these areas have figured prominently in discussion of social change in prehistoric Europe. The megalithic tombs in Ireland and the Orkneys have been seen as copies of east Mediterranean prototypes, and one particular group of monuments, the Passage Graves, were regarded as the work of roving evangelists (e.g. Childe 1957; Mackie 1977). Similarly, it was suggested that Stonehenge, the most elaborate of the archaeological monuments in Wessex, was the work of a Mycenaean architect (Atkinson 1956). Because of the size and complexity of such structures, there seemed little alternative to an intrusive origin.

Not until the 1960s were these orthodoxies challenged in any detail. In 1968 Colin Renfrew reviewed the relationship between Wessex and Mycenae as one of the main examples of the diffusionist framework, and argued for its rejection. Sub-sequently he proposed an alternative model for the local evolution of the so-called Wessex Culture (Renfrew 1973). He saw the gradual emergence of a chiefdom in this area reflected by the building of increasingly massive earthwork monuments at the heart of four well-defined territories, each about the size of his early state module (Renfrew 1975: 12–21). In later phases, when still more ambitious monuments were being constructed, these separate territories may have combined to form a much larger unit. In the same way, he used data from the Orkneys to support his case for the local evolution of megalithic tombs from simple to complex forms in different parts of Europe. He suggested that initially such monuments had been used as territorial markers within segmentary societies (Renfrew 1976) and that social changes in the Orkneys might be monitored by the growing scale of the later Passage Graves (Renfrew 1979: 199). In a sense, both

areas showed a similar sequence of development, even though one culminated in a series of enclosed ceremonial centres (henge monuments) and the other in massive collective tombs. While such evolutionary schemes have gained a measure of acceptance, there remains an empirical problem which the theory of peer polity interaction may perhaps help to resolve. Given the case for entirely local development proposed by Renfrew for Wessex and the Orkneys, why do they have artefacts and monuments in common during the later stages of their evolution?

Evidence of autonomy

The areas discussed in this paper lack any real unity of culture or environment. All that they have in common are areas of outstandingly fertile land and an unusually rich and complex archaeological record (Bradley 1984: Ch. 3). They are also all connected by sea. Indeed, three of these areas played an equally prominent role during the period of Viking hegemony, with a powerful earldom in the Orkneys and major towns at York and Dublin.

During the third millennium bc, the five areas numbered in Fig. 10.1 show completely different archaeological sequences. During the earlier third millennium bc, the most prominent monuments in many parts of western Europe had been collective tombs, sometimes of considerable proportions. It seems likely that their importance in the archaeological record is connected with the special significance of ancestry among early agricultural communities, a point widely recognised in the ethnographic literature (e.g. Bloch 1975). On such sites, the remains of the dead were frequently introduced after they had received preliminary treatment elsewhere. One common practice was for the unfleshed bones of different individuals to be mixed together, or even arranged in elaborate formal patterns (Shanks and Tilley 1982). In many cases, grave goods were excluded from these tombs. The Passage Graves, which are such a notable feature of the Orkneys and the Boyne Valley, are perhaps the most elaborate and widely distributed type of monumental tomb. By the period considered in this paper the growing scale of certain of these monuments might well suggest that their construction formed a medium through which different communities might have competed with one another. A further clue to their distinctive role is given by the presence of elaborate artefacts—pins, pendants, maceheads or ceramics—whose distribution was virtually limited to these sites (Herity 1974; Fraser 1983). Here one might suspect that the construction and use of Passage Graves played a major part in political relations. This question has been considered in detail in Renfrew's study of Neolithic Orkney (1979: 199).

In two of the other study areas, Wessex and the Yorkshire Wolds, similar rites of collective burial were in abeyance by the time that this study begins, but even here there are signs that traditional funerary monuments retained enough of their significance to act as the focus for a whole range of later monuments, and for deliberate deposits of complex objects. In both of these regions one of the main forms taken by the earlier burial monuments had been long rectangular or trapezoidal mounds. Even when the practice of undifferentiated collective burial was effectively obsolete, communities seem to have continued to make use of the historical associations of these funerary sites. It was at this stage that enormous linear earthwork monuments were probably constructed, whose distinctive form is a massive elaboration of the character of the earlier burial places. Mounds up to 550 m long could be built in imitation of traditional funerary monuments, and open enclosures—the so called cursus monuments—could be even more elaborate, the largest single example running for 10 km and joining up a whole series of existing burial sites (Bradley 1984: 43–4). These tremendous linear monuments then formed the focus for a whole variety of later developments, including the deposition of exotic objects or the building of new types of monument.

To a large extent, these later developments took two alternative courses: either changing political relations were now displayed openly through the emergence of a distinctive rite of individual burial with grave goods, or power relations were still further obscured through the building of elaborate ceremonial monuments. The first of these developments is particularly characteristic of the Yorkshire Wolds, where we find the emergence of a distinctive type of burial monument and the appearance of a funerary rite involving the burial of complete bodies accompanied by a range of elaborate artefacts (Kinnes 1979; Pierpoint 1980). These burials occupied round mounds, sometimes of massive proportions, and were often those of older males. Although it is difficult to interpret the results of excavations which are frequently a century old, it is tempting to suggest that here we find the celebration of individual authority and achievement.

The alternative course is seen most clearly in Wessex, where, following the development of cursus monuments and bank barrows, we find the early development of the distinctive ceremonial centres known as henge monuments. These massive earthwork enclosures do not seem to have played a major domestic or funerary role but can be associated with large deposits of complex artefacts, some of exotic origin. A number of the henge monuments also contained circles of upright posts or stones, at times interpreted as the sites of massive buildings (Wainwright 1969). The scale of these centres is quite remarkable and it has been calculated that their earthworks alone may have required an investment of about 500,000 worker hours (Startin and Bradley 1981). Some of the sites are also accompanied by gigantic circular mounds, the largest of which made even more extravagant demands. The organisation of these efforts must have involved a strong measure of co-ordination, and Renfrew (1973) is surely correct in seeing their construction as some indication of the complexity of contemporary society. At the same time, there is little clear sign of differentiation in the evidence from contemporary settlements or burials in

Wessex, and it may be that power relations were mediated through the exercise of ritual authority (Thorpe and Richards 1984).

In summary, social developments in Later Neolithic Britain took place along sharply contrasting lines. In two areas there was a continuing emphasis on the construction of ancestral tombs, whilst elsewhere new and more elaborate monuments took on the traditional forms of earlier burial sites, although they may not have served the same functions. A second major development was the appearance of individual burials with grave goods, which seem to celebrate the roles of only one section of society. In other areas again, a different power structure is suggested by the building of huge ceremonial centres. All these sequences appear to have developed during the third millennium bc, but only in their later stages is there any evidence for close contacts between these different areas. At that stage the archaeological record in these separate areas starts to converge. The major links between these regions are summarised in Table 10.1.

Evidence of interaction

These different regional developments have a number of features in common. This evidence of interaction can be considered in three groups: monuments, portable objects and designs.

Monuments. Two types of monument can be considered here: the distinctive chambered tombs known as Passage Graves and the massive ceremonial enclosures described as henge monuments. Passage Graves are widely distributed in western Europe, whilst henge monuments appear to be specific to Britain and Ireland. The Passage Grave tradition extends from Iberia to southern Scandinavia (Fig. 10.2) and is best represented in two of the areas being considered here, the Boyne Valley and the Orkneys (Herity 1974; Fraser 1983), although other less impressive examples are known elsewhere, including parts of east Scotland (Henshall 1963: 20–39). In general, the distribution of Passage Graves follows the Atlantic coast, where the zenith of the Boyne tombs came around the mid-third millennium bc, several centuries before the main developments in the Orkneys (O'Kelly 1982; Renfrew 1979). By contrast, early henge monuments appear at scattered locations in England and Wales, although it seems significant that the most elaborate examples appear first in Scotland and the Orkneys and only later in Wessex and Ireland (Bradley 1984: 57–61). If henge monuments and Passage Graves represent the two most impressive groups of Neolithic monuments, there was only limited overlap between their distribution among our five study areas.

Portable artefacts. The development of artefact styles shows an equally complex pattern. These styles seem to stem from two main sources, the Boyne tombs and the single burials of Yorkshire. The Boyne tombs share several artefact

Table 10.1. *Archaeological evidence for interaction between the core areas*

	Passage graves	Cursus monuments	Complex single burials	Henge monuments	Complex artefacts
Wessex	–	*X*	x	X	X
Yorkshire Wolds	–	*X*	*X*	x	*X*
East Scotland	x	?	–	X	X
Orkneys	X	–	–	X	X
Boyne Valley	X	–	x?	X?	*X*

X : important component

x : minor component

? : no clear evidence

x or *X* : feature present at the start of the local sequence

types with Iberia, Brittany and possibly southern Scandinavia; within the British Isles their closest similarities are with the Orkneys. It seems clear that such connections are best witnessed towards the later stages of Passage Grave evolution (Bradley and Chapman 1984). Thus the stylistic similarities between artefacts in Ireland and other areas of the Passage Grave distribution almost all occur in the third millennium bc, despite the fact that tomb building in most of these areas had commenced appreciably earlier. For example, the types of carved bonework shared between Ireland and western Iberia

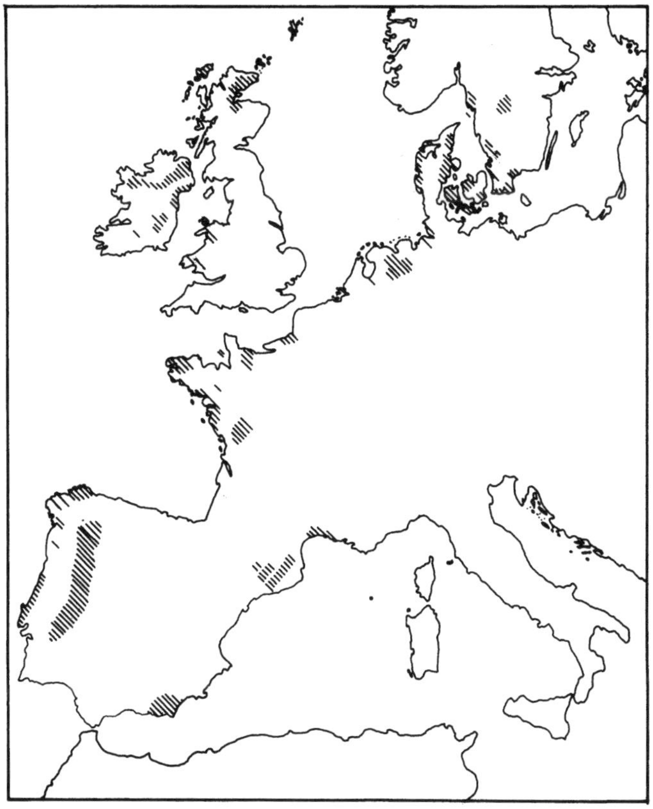

Fig. 10.2. Distribution of Passage Graves in western Europe (after Herity 1974).

are found only in the later tombs of the latter region (Nieto 1959). Similarly the Irish pins and pendants are claimed to represent types found in Danish Passage Graves (Herity 1973), but these monuments were not constructed until c. 2600–2450 bc, some five centuries after the beginnings of the burial mound tradition in that area.

The chronology of English single burials is rather more obscure, but it seems that the most elaborate grave goods do not appear in other contexts until the later third millennium bc. Although the ceramic chronology suggests that the burials of the Yorkshire Wolds began about 2800 bc (Kinnes 1979), the main similarities between these burials and finds from other areas are visible at a much later date. For example, most of the artefact types associated with these graves could have been present in Yorkshire before they became a regular feature of the archaeological record in Wessex (Bradley 1984: 57–61). Once adopted, they are found alongside a ceramic style–Grooved Ware–which shares its characteristic decoration with the art found in Irish Passage Graves (Shee Twohig 1981: 126–8). Again the connections between different areas come towards the end of the local sequence rather than at its beginning.

Design elements. Some of the similarities between these different regions are indicated by designs rather than portable objects. These similarities takes several forms. The characteristic features of mobile artefacts might be copied in another medium. Thus some Later Neolithic deposits in England contain stone maceheads, whilst the Boyne tombs contain miniature versions of these objects used as pendants; it is not known which type is the earlier in date (Roe 1968; Herity 1974). Again there are a few cases in which elaborate objects from English or Scottish sites can be decorated with motifs which make their first appearance in Irish Passage Grave art. Such objects may be found in ceremonial centres or in complete isolation, but in neither case do they seem to have played any utilitarian role (Simpson and Thawley 1972). Indeed, they can occur in areas in which pottery with similar

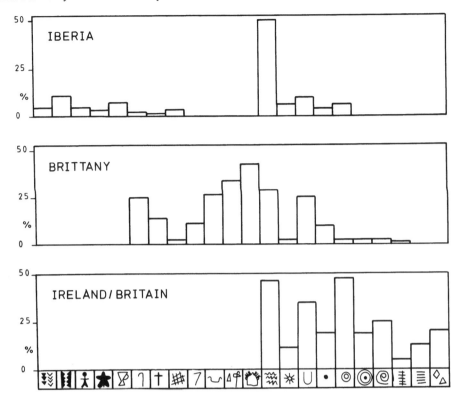

Fig. 10.3. Histogram of the percentage frequency of art motifs in Passage Graves in Britain/Ireland, Brittany and Iberia (after Shee Twohig 1981).

designs is absent. In the same way, the motifs of megalithic art in Iberia occur in other media, but for the most part this happens outside the distribution of Passage Graves.

The most striking pattern of this kind is the decoration of Later Neolithic Grooved Ware, with designs similar to those in megalithic art. Here the chronological sequence is particularly striking. The motifs in question belong to a broad tradition of decorated tombs extending down the Atlantic seaboard, but the great majority of these tombs are found in Ireland. Those few motifs found more widely are known in Brittany (Fig. 10.3), but again only in the later tombs in that area (Shee Twohig 1981: 136—8). Little or no Irish pottery shares the designs known in this tomb art and the earliest pottery to do so is the Grooved Ware of the Orkneys, which is contemporary with the Passage Graves in that area. Significantly, art is fairly rare in the Orkney tombs, although the same designs are known on portable objects and even in one excavated settlement there (*ibid.*: 127). It seems as if these particular motifs were transferred from monuments to portable artefacts.

The characteristic ceramics of the Later Neolithic in the Orkneys have a very wide distribution, extending as far south as Wessex and south-west England (Fig. 10.4), but the available chronology shows that this pattern may have developed only gradually. Grooved Ware was in use in the Orkneys throughout the second half of the third millennium bc, but in south-east Scotland and Yorkshire it was almost

certainly adopted at a later date. In Wessex it does not seem to be present much before 2000 bc. At the same time, the range of Grooved Ware associations increased as this style was adopted more widely, and gradually included some of the distinctive types of artefacts already in use in the single burials of northern England (Bradley 1982). The most widely distributed motifs on Grooved Ware ceramics are those shared with the Fourknocks style of megalithic art (Shee Twohig 1981). As we shall see, this pottery is often found in association with the types of monument considered earlier in this paper. Where it is rare or absent altogether, other types of portable object sometimes carry the same designs.

A possible chronology for these developments is summarised in Table 10.2.

The context of interaction

The evidence for interaction comes from a series of very specialised archaeological contexts. Now that we have enumerated some of the possible links, it is worth exploring their distinctive settings.

The sharing of designs taken from Passage Grave art is found in very restricted circumstances. Initially the motifs were associated with the burial of the dead in elaborate tombs, and it was only when such monuments were adopted in the Orkneys that they occurred widely in other contexts. The same designs were used to decorate settlements there, and even the planning of houses shows striking similarities

Table 10.2. *Approximate starting dates for interaction between core areas c. 2700–2000 bc*

	Yorkshire Wolds	East Scotland	Orkneys	Boyne Valley
Wessex	2700	2400–2200	2200?	2100–2000
Yorkshire Wolds		2700–2500	2400?	no information
East Scotland			2400?	uncertain
Orkneys				2700 or before

with the layout of contemporary tombs (Shee Twohig 1981: 127; Hodder 1982a: 221–6). They are also found on a restricted range of portable objects, including the distinctive stone plaques which carry engraved designs. Such plaques have been found at ceremonial centres and one example comes from a major axe quarry which supplied large areas of Britain during this period (Warren 1922).

The other sphere in which these patterns appear is on ceramics, but the Grooved Ware tradition has a rather restricted distribution. Although it may be divided into four substyles, these lack any regional identity, and are distributed discontinuously throughout the British Isles along a basically eastern axis, which complements the western distribution of the Passage Graves (Fig. 10.4).

Grooved Ware does not occur very widely and is found mainly in two types of context. It is found on a large number of the more elaborate henge monuments and could be mistaken for an entirely special-purpose ceramic. On the other hand, it can be found on a small number of settlement sites, but in these cases it often occurs together with unusually elaborate artefacts. For example, it is frequently associated with imported stone axes, even in areas with their own flint supply. In both henges and settlements it is regularly found with a high proportion of pig bones, suggesting an unusual level of meat consumption among its users (Bradley 1984: 50–3). An exception to this general pattern is its occurrence at the largest group of flint mines in Britain (Grimes Graves in Norfolk), which may well have been producing fine objects for exchange (Mercer 1981a: 39).

The more complex bone or stone artefacts of this period also have a restricted circulation. Most appear first in the burial record, but by the end of the third millennium bc they are associated mainly with Grooved Ware rather than other contemporary ceramics. They are commonly deposited inside or close to the larger ceremonial monuments of the period. Occasional examples are decorated with the same motifs as Grooved Ware and Irish Passage Graves (Simpson and Thawley 1972). In some cases these objects are again found with large deposits of meat bones. In such instances it is hard to regard them as chance losses (Bradley 1984: 55–7).

Another link between different regions is revealed by the adoption of different styles of large monument. Once again it seems most unlikely that any of these sites had a utilitarian

function. There were three main types during this period: henge monuments, large mounds and stone or timber circles. In spite of this variety, they have certain features in common. Apart from Passage Graves, very few of these sites seem to be associated directly with burials. All three classes of site are located in areas with elaborate objects and in many cases there is also evidence of large-scale food consumption. Not only does the construction of these monuments evidence the ability to mobilise and provision large labour forces, but some of these sites also show the ability to conceive complex architectural forms. Examples of three types of monument (passage graves, henge monuments and stone circles) also seem to incorporate astronomical alignments (Burl 1981).

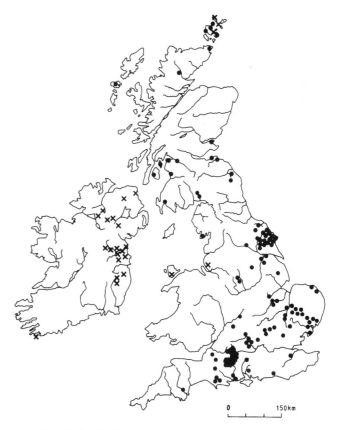

Fig. 10.4. Distribution of Passage Grave art (crosses) and Grooved Ware (filled circles) in Britain and Ireland (after Shee Twohig 1981; Manby 1974; Wainwright and Longworth 1971).

Although we have been able to suggest the sequence in which different types of monument were adopted, the detailed pattern of change is very different from the orderly transition characteristic of the diffusionist model. Rather, the evidence gives an impression of imitation, emulation, even confrontation. This can be seen in several aspects. There is the fact that the sequence of development may be much the same in different regions, even though these areas are some distance apart. For example, the sequence in the henge monuments in Wessex to some extent echoes that in eastern Scotland, rather than that in areas nearer at hand (e.g. the Yorkshire Wolds). In such cases it is not clear that these developments necessarily occurred at the same time. Indeed the Wessex sequence may have started some time later than that in Scotland. As we shall see, the monuments in Wessex were also conceived on an altogether larger scale.

At the same time, the adoption of new forms of monument from other areas could be remarkably abrupt, again suggesting something more complex than the gradual 'spread of ideas' implied in the literature. A recurrent pattern is the direct juxtaposition, or even superimposition, of different types of large monument. For example, important henges could be built over existing cursus monuments (Thomas 1955), just as a passage grave might be constructed inside an existing stone circle (Ashmore 1981). Stone circles were built on the sites of several timber circles, even when an appreciable interval separated the two phases (Catherall 1971), and on other sites large mounds without an obvious mortuary role were added to earlier henges (Wainwright 1971). In the Boyne Valley what may be a form of henge was imposed on a Passage Grave cemetery five hundred years after the original use of the site (O'Kelly 1982: 66–7, 230). In each case it is as if a monument of exotic type was deliberately annexed to an existing monumental tradition.

This becomes even clearer if we consider the human energy expenditure invested in these sites. The characteristic sequence in each area seems to show a series of increasingly complex monuments, normally culminating in one or more examples of remarkable scale and ostentation. For the most part, these have no immediate successors and the next large monuments to be built belong to the sequence in another area (Table 10.3). Thus first Ireland, then the Orkneys and east Scotland and finally southern England is pre-eminent. At the same time as the most impressive forms of monument are copied in one area after another, the scale of these undertakings tends to increase. The first great peak of activity is seen in Ireland, where the Passage Grave tradition culminated in the building of the largest monuments towards the middle of the third millennium bc. The labour investment has been estimated as about 3,500,000 worker hours (O'Kelly 1982: 117–18). The monuments of the Orkneys were much less demanding but have been thought to show a similar increase in the investment of human labour, culminating in monuments which may have taken nearly 100,000 worker hours to construct (Renfrew 1979). Henges were also built in this area and made rather similar demands (*ibid.*) Less is known about the east Scottish henges, but the same basic pattern is probably revealed by the reconstruction of timber monuments in stone (Mercer 1981b). Finally, there is the evidence from Wessex, where the first henge dates from about 2400 bc and represents a labour investment of only 11,000 worker hours, a similar estimate to those for the smaller Passage Graves. By about 2000 bc these sites had increased in scale considerably, until their earthworks alone required 500,000 worker hours. At the same time, gigantic circular mounds were being constructed, the largest of which needed an investment of about 4 million worker hours, roughly thirty times that found at the largest contemporary monument in the Orkneys, but a figure not very different from the estimate for

Table 10.3. *Labour estimates for the monuments of the Boyne Valley, the Orkneys and Wessex (in worker hours)*

	2750 bc	2500 bc	2250 bc	2000 bc
Boyne Valley Passage Graves				
Earlier phase	10,000			
Later phase		3,500,000		
Orkneys				
Passage Graves		3,000		
Henge monuments			80,000	
Wessex				
Early henge		11,000		
Later henge				500,000
Large mound				4,000,000

Sources: Data incorporated from Startin and Bradley 1981; O'Kelly 1982; Renfrew 1979; Fraser 1983.

the largest tombs in the Boyne Valley (Startin and Bradley 1981). Not only did the monuments of Wessex trump the efforts of communities in other areas: to some extent they did so by copying their characteristic monuments. In this case it may not be too much to talk of competitive emulation. The main labour estimates are summarised in Table 10.3.

Discussion

On a general level, we wish to enquire how far organisational change in different areas of the British Isles during the third millennium bc can be subsumed under a theory of purely autonomous evolution, and how far the peer polity interaction model may be applicable. This discussion is an attempt to answer this question.

First let us draw together our observations on organisational change in our core areas. The emergence of more complex societies has been discussed, primarily on the basis of monuments, for Wessex and Orkney by Renfrew (1973; 1979). In these studies, attention is focused upon the territorial implications of tomb location and the labour requirements of monument construction. Employing traits derived from Sahlins's and Service's discussion of ethnographic evidence, Renfrew suggested attributing a chiefdom level of organisation to both areas for the third millennium bc. Such an attribution to an undifferentiated 'type' of society is not without its problems, as Renfrew clearly recognised. Even allowing for some doubts over our ability to recognise the archaeological correlates of chiefdom societies in Later Neolithic Britain from the currently available data, there is still the problem of employing evolutionary types of society. In this respect the evidence and analysis of Late Neolithic Britain contrasts with the emphasis on social variability present in Braun's paper. On the other hand, recent work in Britain (e.g. Pierpoint 1980) has focused more precisely on social variability as reflected in attributes of the grave and grave goods rather than just those of the monuments.

We have traced the evidence for the emergence of more complex societies in the core areas. Regional differences in the rates of organisational change after agricultural colonisation in the fourth millennium bc have been proposed. In each area we can measure change in the energy expenditure and architectural complexity of monuments, whether or not such monuments were specifically associated with the dead. While some of the changes of monument may appear abrupt, there is no need to argue for intrusive populations. Radiocarbon dating has demonstrated that there are quite clear variations in the date of appearance of monument types and limited-circulation artefacts in different regions. At this point, the evidence for longer-distance interaction outweighs the evidence for autonomous development; it was only after several hundred years of local development that such inter-action between core areas can be said to have taken place.

Elsewhere (Bradley and Chapman 1984) we have argued that the polities centred upon our core areas had,

by c. 2700–2400 bc, approached the limits of expansion in their own areas. All these areas are physically circumscribed, the best example of this being the Orkneys, which are surrounded by sea! The archaeological record for areas such as Wessex and east Yorkshire reveals that it is not until the second millennium bc that more agriculturally marginal areas were brought into settlement and cultivation (Bradley 1978). Given such constraints on the production system and its relations with already expanding social systems, we argue that the emerging élites may have begun to develop political relations over greater distances, in effect going far beyond their own polities. With the growth of social complexity, the importance attached to access to exotic goods, non-utilitarian artefacts, special symbols and the orientation of communal activity around particular monument types may have increased. This would be particularly true if ritual and political power had been closely connected. The sharing of symbols, artefacts and monuments, as well as their adoption from other areas and clear examples of monument super-imposition, together suggest the use of polity interaction by local élites to develop their own political power. The sub-sequent spread through the British Isles of further limited-circulation artefacts in the form of the Beaker 'package' (Shennan, this volume: Ch. 11) would seem to us to fit this longer-term pattern of the establishment of larger-scale interaction networks between polities.

Elsewhere (Bradley and Chapman 1984) we have discussed the evidence for interaction between Ireland, Wessex, Orkney, Brittany, south Scandinavia and Iberia in the third millennium bc. Much depends upon the weighting of the individual evidence, but our conclusion was that the strongest interaction related those areas discussed in this paper, with the addition of Brittany. Another area not discussed in that paper was the Iberian peninsula, where similar core areas, in the south-east and the south-west, separated by a maximum linear distance of c. 500 km, witnessed changes in organisational complexity and interaction during the third millennium bc (Chapman 1982). We argue that interaction is better under-stood between such core areas (and, indeed, traces of less well-defined areas between them) within the peninsula than it is between the peninsula and Britain, Brittany and south Scandinavia, at least before the late third millennium bc. Briefly, the third millennium bc in Iberia witnessed an increase in the diversity and complexity of funerary monuments in the south-east and south-west of the peninsula and in the frequency and diversity of limited-circulation artefacts and raw materials—e.g. idols of various types, segmented bone pins (Nieto 1959), ivory, and ostrich eggshell (Harrison and Gilman 1977). This archaeological evidence of interaction has so far been treated solely within the framework of traditional diffusionism (e.g. Savory 1968) and would benefit from the approach discussed in this volume. Two interesting contrasts with Britain would deserve examination: first, the Beaker 'package' assumes a more important role in linking polities across the peninsula than it does in Britain, where it fitted into the longer-term development pattern described above; secondly, the peninsula did not witness the diversity, scale and succession of monument types seen in Britain.

Putting together these rather disparate observations on the archaeological record, we would argue that the third millennium bc witnessed important changes in the prehistory of western Europe. While a model of autonomous polities can be argued for the early agricultural societies, it is in the third millennium that an increase in organisational complexity to the chiefdom level became visible. This period was also characterised by the extension in scale of exchange networks, as evidenced in raw materials such as igneous stone and flint. The association of areas in which chiefdoms appear (e.g. our core areas in Britain, Brittany, and south-east and south-west Spain) with evidence for increased interaction between polities in the form of shared symbols, limited-circulation artefacts and more complex monuments supports the argument for a close link between ritual and political power.

The advantage of the peer polity interaction model in this context is that interaction and communication between such independent polities is removed from the assumptions of traditional diffusionism. As Davis has recently pointed out (1983), diffusionism has worked on a 'context-free' assumption. According to this, stylistic or other diffusion rates were proportional to geographical distance. Diffusionism took no account of the spatial distribution of potential donors and adopters, nor opportunities for communication, nor the use context of the innovation. It is this emphasis on communication and the social context of interaction which is one of the advantages of peer polity interaction.

In using this approach with our particular data from Late Neolithic Britain and Ireland, we have presented the archaeological evidence for change within the different core areas. In accordance with Renfrew's formulation we have tried to document the appearance of new institutional features,

such as monuments, symbolic systems and restricted-circulation artefacts, through time. However, our spatial and temporal units of analysis differ from those embodied in many of the papers in this volume. Specifically, our core areas are not all spatially contiguous and the evidence for evolution and interaction is measured in terms of centuries. An inevitable consequence is that there is a lack of clear distinction between the archaeological evidence of interaction and the evidence for the results of that interaction, in terms of shared monuments, artefacts and symbols. This is the problem of circularity to which Renfrew refers in this volume, but we note that in our case study there is evidence for differences in the starting dates both for interaction between our core areas and for the increase in energy expenditure and indeed the adoption of different types of monument.

In the light of our experience in using peer polity interaction as the framework for studying Late Neolithic Britain and Ireland (as well as their west European context), we conclude that it offers a better approach to the study of interaction than the diffusionism that had been applied previously. However, there clearly need to be modifications in the model to incorporate interactions between less complex systems than those for which it was devised. These must incorporate differences of scale. Braun's discussion of communication networks (this volume: Ch. 9) offers some useful predictions in this context, but until a more exact chronology can be compiled for Britain and Ireland this paper takes the discussion as far as it seems prudent to go.

Acknowledgements
We would like to thank Colin Renfrew and John Cherry for their invitation to write this paper, Averil Martin Hoogewerf for preparing the figures and Jan Chapman for typing the paper.

Chapter 11

Interaction and change in third millennium BC western and central Europe
Stephen Shennan

Introduction

In the study of prehistoric Europe perhaps more than in other parts of the world the definition and examination of those areas of material culture uniformity known as 'cultures' has played a central role. Indeed, the prehistory of the area has largely been written until recently in terms of their appearance and demise. When the first moves were made away from this approach in the 1960s and early 1970s they were marked by a concern with the autonomy of local developments in such spheres as social organisation and subsistence. In this, the study of material culture assemblages, earlier the backbone of the discipline, had little role to play, except insofar as it could be shown to be useful in the construction of measuring instruments for monitoring economic and social change.

The current concern with peer polity interaction represents an example of a wider trend towards a renewed concern with inter-regional connections as being relevant to the understanding of local situations, and with stylistic variation in material culture items as an appropriate area for study. But of course the theoretical perspective is very different. The unitary cultures which in earlier accounts of European prehistory acted as autonomous entities, expanding, contracting or submitting to outside influences, have been subjected to a process of deconstruction. This has been a critical advance, but it has left the study of the areas of material culture uniformity, which undoubtedly do

exist, without a role, whether as *explanans* or *explanandum*; in other words, in something of a theoretical vacuum. At the inter-regional level it has only been the process of exchange which has been amenable to incorporation within the standard models.

Peer polity interaction represents one attempt to develop a new framework, by raising the question of the link between the existence of material uniformities over space and the observed fact that the socio-economic developments which have been defined in many areas in recent years often occur more or less simultaneously over quite wide areas, without any obvious external stimulus or any clear priority for one particular region.

The case study: central and western Europe, 2500–1500 BC

The present study will consider the period from c. 2500 to 1500 BC in western and central Europe and will be largely concerned with the Bell Beaker phenomenon. It will begin with a description and a consideration of its significance and then try to show how it had a bearing on the trajectory of the individual regions within which it occurred.

Bell Beakers, of course, represent one of the most well-worn topics in the study of prehistoric Europe and there is no need to go into their interpretation as marking the trace of a wandering Beaker Folk all over the western half of Europe. This interpretation was based partly on biometric evidence

whose significance remains unresolved (see, for example,
Gallay 1981; Menk 1981), but much more on the prevailing
notion of cultures as unitary entities carried by peoples. When
the traditional view was attacked in the 1970s (Shennan
1975; 1976; 1977; Burgess and Shennan 1976), the criticism
was based on a detailed dissection of the entity, not least in
the light of Binford's criticisms of normative theory
(Binford 1962; 1965). This dissection emphasised that there
were many cross-cutting patterns of spatial variation in the
Beaker assemblage which had previously been largely ignored
(Shennan 1978). Much of the material associated with the
Bell Beakers could be shown to be local. The number of
widespread items was relatively restricted—most importantly
the decorated Bell Beaker vessel type and much smaller
numbers of such items as stone wrist-guards and tanged
copper daggers. The result of this work was an interpretation
of the Bell Beakers and other widespread items as prestige
goods, a view which, in accordance with the *Zeitgeist*, has
become virtually a new orthodoxy (Harrison 1980). In many
respects such a view remains attractive, but it does not really
go far enough. As Braun (this volume: Ch. 9) points out in
relation to Hopewell, to argue, or even to demonstrate, that
an item was a prestige good does not account for its use as
such in areas widely separated from one another.

The Bell Beaker phenomenon: a description

The most obvious characteristic of the Bell Beaker phase
is the standardisation of the pottery type known as the Bell
Beaker, both in shape and decoration. The type occurs in
varying quantities in a very large number of areas, from
north Africa to northern Scotland and from Ireland to
Hungary (Fig. 11.1). It used to be thought that there were
great variations between the different areas in the nature of
the initial Beaker occurrence, with complete assemblages,
including Beaker domestic pottery, in some areas and not
in others (see, for example, Clarke 1976). It is now becoming
clear, as more work is done on local sequences, that Bell
Beakers appeared initially almost universally as a new form
of fine pottery in the context of the local pottery assemblages
of particular regions. The inter-regional differences stem from
later developments within the different regions: in some areas
Beakers were taken up as the local domestic pottery and
underwent a considerable typological development, in others
their use was short-lived (Harrison 1980; Whittle 1981). Some
sequences from different regions are shown in Fig. 11.2. The
period over which a relatively high degree of standardisation
was maintained lasted from c. 2500 to c. 2200 BC. The
standardisation was based on imitation from area to area
of vessel shape and decoration, and presumably also on
exchange, although the work on pottery characterisation to
establish this has not yet been carried out.

In addition to the vessel, other attributes are also
regularly associated with the Bell Beakers over the area
indicated—copper daggers, stone wrist-guards, arrowheads

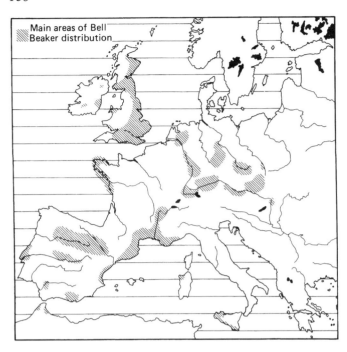

Fig. 11.1. The main concentrations of Bell Beakers in Europe
(after Harrison 1980).

and V-perforated buttons—all types whose standardisation
was again based to varying degrees on both exchange and local
imitation. However, standardisation was not restricted to the
material forms of artefacts. The mutual association of these
widespread items in burials also followed a fairly stereotyped
pattern (Fig. 11.3), while in many areas the appearance of the
assemblages was associated with a changed burial rite, not
just a new set of items in association with burials. In some
areas, such as central Europe, the change was only in burial
orientation; in others, for example much of western Europe,
it was associated with the introduction of single burial
accompanied by grave goods, in contrast to earlier collective
rites.

Within the overall region where the phenomenon occurs,
not all areas which have evidence of contemporary occupation
have equal evidence of connection with the Beaker
phenomenon; in some, very few Beaker traits occur. Outside
the region certain Bell Beaker elements have a wider
distribution; for example, Beaker motifs seem to occur on the
pottery of northern Europe, and stone wrist-guards are known
outside the area where Beaker vessels are found in east-central
Europe.

It should not be thought, however, that similarity in
content of a widespread phenomenon necessarily corresponds
to similarity in context or structure of association locally. A
detailed examination of the local trajectories of social change
in some of the Bell Beaker areas will be carried out below; at
this point, however, it is worth making some general points.
In particular, there are strong indications of differences in
the forms of local social organisation from region to region.

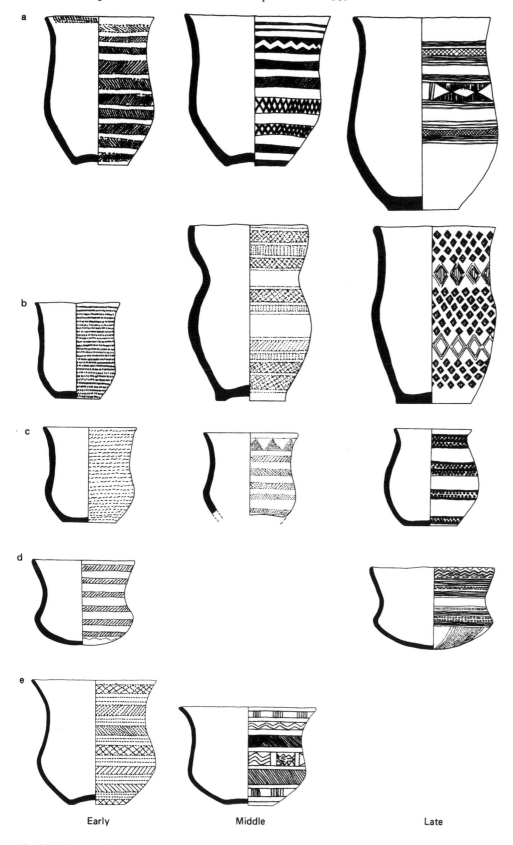

Fig. 11.2. Some Bell Beaker sequences in different parts of Europe: (a) the Middle and Upper Rhine area (after Harrison 1980); (b) Britain (after Harrison 1980); (c) Languedoc (after Harrison 1980); (d) Central Portugal (after Harrison 1980); (e) Bohemia.

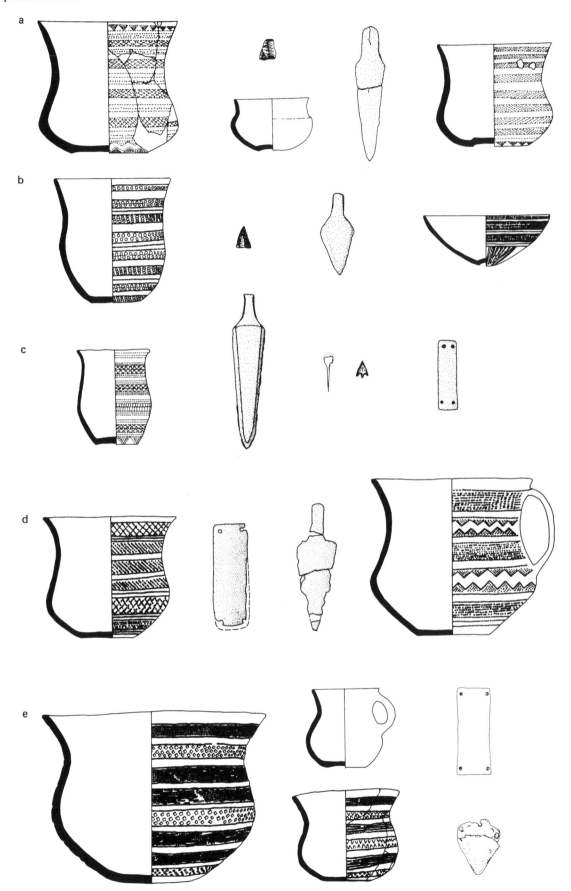

Fig. 11.3. 'Classic' Bell Beaker grave inventories from different parts of Europe: (a) Spain, Miguel Ruiz sandpit, Madrid (after Harrison 1977); (b) Southern France, Tumulus de Soyons, Soyons, Ardèche (after Bill 1973); (c) Britain, Roundway, Wilts. (after Clarke 1970); (d) Hungary, Bekasmegger, Budapest (after Schreiber 1976); (e) Moravia, Letonice. For Lower Rhine, see Fig. 11.6.

In central Portugal Bell Beakers appear in a context where the existence of elaborate fortifications and large megalithic tombs with considerable quantities of exotic grave goods suggest some degree of local social differentiation and probably local warfare (Harrison 1977; 1980; Sangmeister 1976). In the Wessex area of southern England, as we shall see below, Bell Beakers appear at a time when the landscape is dominated by large-scale ceremonial monuments (Renfrew 1973; Burgess 1980), and a case can be made for strong ritually based authority and differentiation. In continental north-west and central Europe, on the other hand, there is no evidence of any such phenomena at this time, but only of a dispersed and undifferentiated settlement pattern.

Thus it seems clear that regions whose forms of organisation were very different were taking part in the Bell Beaker phenomenon: exchanging and imitating Bell Beaker pottery and other items, but also to varying degrees following new modes of burial practice whose appearance was associated with Bell Beaker material.

It is, of course, in the context of burials that Bell Beaker items are very often, in some places almost exclusively, found. It has already been noted that most recently these items have been interpreted as prestige goods, the basis of this inference being their exotic or special nature and, for such items as the copper daggers at least, the limited number of occurrences. Given the very different contexts indicated above, a number of questions must be asked for which answers are not readily available at present: whether the items had a similar role, whether similar types of status were being symbolised, and whether control of the items had a creative or only a symbolic role in defining status. If in one area Bell Beakers were being used as a grave good in a system of contrasts and distinctions with other local types, how does one relate the patterning to that in other areas, where the local material assemblage with which the Beakers form a system of distinctions is completely different in structure? Unfortunately, in the one case where a secure basis for comparison exists in principle—the relationship between the presence of Bell Beaker material and the physical attributes of the individual with whom it was buried—the available skeletal information in most regions is poor, and even when it exists it has not been exploited to its full extent.

There are clearly some marked similarities between the Bell Beaker phenomenon as described above and the Hopewell (Braun, this volume: Ch. 9), but whereas the Hopewell coincides with trends towards population aggregation and subsistence intensification, an association which Braun regards as highly significant, nowhere can it be shown that the Bell Beakers are associated with major subsistence–settlement changes of this kind. Settlement patterns remain the same—a pattern of dispersion in most areas. Evidence for subsistence in most regions is hard to come by, but is not suggestive of major changes and certainly not of any new pattern of intensification. What might be considered the one possible exception—the indication of an association between Bell Beakers and the appearance of the domestic horse in western Europe (Shennan 1977)—is more likely to be of social rather than subsistence significance.

The end of the Bell Beaker phase

In his examination of the Hopewell, Braun rightly notes that there is a tendency in archaeology to consider the 'rise' of phenomena but not to pay too much attention to their 'decline', when in fact this is just as much in need of explanation. What happens in the case of the Bell Beaker 'decline'? Most obviously, it is to be defined in terms of the disappearance of ceramic uniformity over the wide area noted above. In many parts of western Europe this involves the development of regionally specific Bell Beaker styles, which also come into domestic use from c. 2100 BC (Harrison 1980; Whittle 1981; van der Waals and Glasbergen 1955). However, in most parts of Europe east of the Rhine where Bell Beakers occur (with the possible exception of central Germany), they went out of use relatively quickly, by c. 2100 BC, and the local pottery with which they had been associated continued alone, with minor typological developments. In terms of ceramic uniformity, this eastern area remained a relatively coherent unit, fairly distinct from the areas to the west, which were somewhat diverse in their own ceramic traditions.

Other Beaker phenomena also either disappear (e.g. the wrist-guard) or increase in local diversity (e.g. the V-perforated buttons). Single grave burial accompanied by grave goods continues, but the grave good associations are much more locally specific, and considerable local variation occurs in such features as grave orientation and rules concerning the side on which the individuals in crouched burials are lying in the grave (see, for example, Tuckwell 1975).

On the other hand, this does not mean that interregional contacts cease. Certain parts of the Beaker network do become relatively isolated, Portugal for example (Schubart 1975; 1976; Harrison 1977), but this is by no means universally true. The considerable uniformity which continues in the regions east of the Rhine has already been noted, but there are also wider links between this zone and areas further west and north, not least Wessex and Brittany; these links may be seen in the metalwork, even though ceramic uniformity disappears. Typological innovations, for example in daggers, are reflected, albeit often weakly, in areas further west, and metal analyses indicate that exchange was also involved, since metal of central European origin appears to reach southern England (Northover n.d.). In fact, the extent of these contacts and exchanges continues down into the early second millennium BC, as more areas come to share in them. The overall orientation of this network of contacts changes, no longer corresponding to the area of Bell Beaker ceramic similarity, but in particular expanding to include Denmark and incorporating amber as well as metalwork into a system which no doubt involved many other commodities, such as textiles, which are not archaeologically visible.

Finally, it should be said that nowhere does the evidence support suggestions of a decrease in the extent of hierarchical

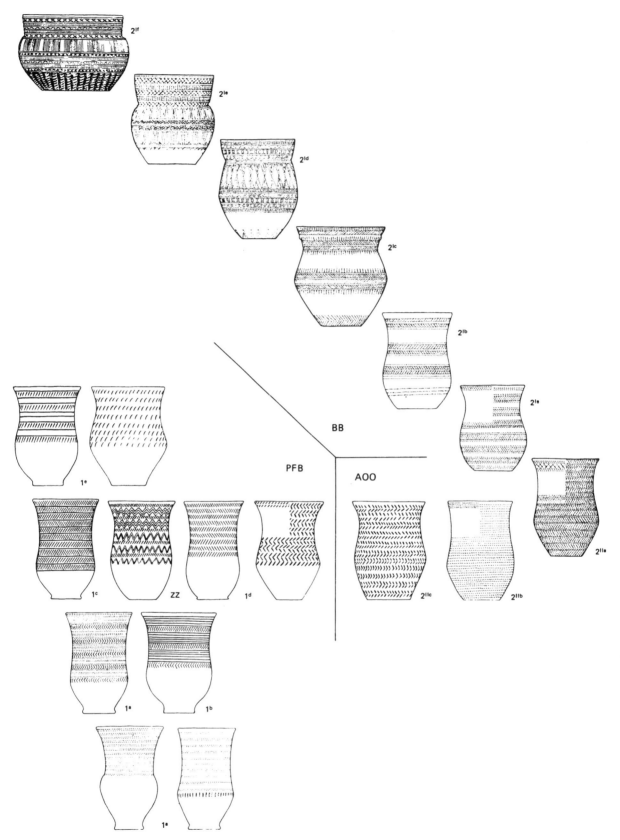

Fig. 11.4. The typological development of Beakers in the Netherlands (from Lanting and van der Waals 1976), showing the transition from Corded Ware (PFB), through All-Over-Ornamented Beakers (AOO) to Bell Beakers (BB). Earliest forms are at the bottom, most recent at the top.

differentiation in the post-Beaker phase, and in some areas at least, the trend seems to be towards an increase; nor is there any indication of marked subsistence–settlement changes associated with the end of widespread Bell Beaker contacts.

The origins of the Bell Beaker phenomenon

Having given a descriptive account of the Bell Beakers and their distribution, I shall now consider the processes which may be involved in the Beaker case, and how these relate to the concept of peer polity interaction. This inevitably involves providing what is in some sense an historical account, beginning with the question of origins.

Through an outstanding programme of detailed archaeological analysis in the late 1960s and early 1970s Dutch scholars demonstrated that the Bell Beaker vessel type originated in the Lower Rhine area, where both it and the remains of the burial ritual in whose context it is largely found show a clear pattern of continuity from the preceding Corded Ware (see especially Lanting and van der Waals 1976). The sequence is shown in Fig. 11.4. The Corded Ware 'culture group' is another widespread phenomenon, similar in type to the Bell Beakers. It is defined by certain kinds of pottery and stone shaft-hole 'battle-axes', as well as by aspects of burial ritual, but is found largely in northern Europe and only overlaps with what was later to be the Bell Beaker distribution area in a narrow zone in north-west and west-central Europe (Fig. 11.5).

I have argued elsewhere (Shennan, in press), in terms very similar to those used by Braun for the Hopewell, that the reasons for the appearance of the Corded Ware lie in the social response to very widespread processes of settlement dispersion and expansion following on the establishment of a newly

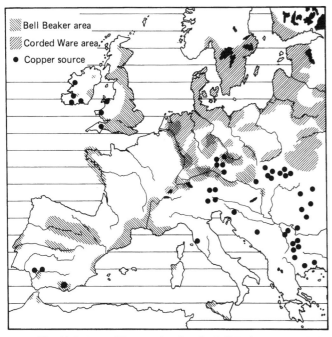

Fig. 11.5. Map of Europe showing the Bell Beaker and Corded Ware distributions, together with copper sources.

integrated mixed farming strategy affecting much of central and northern Europe. Expansion and population growth meant the breakdown of existing networks of communities and a much greater mixing-together of groups with no well-defined relation to one another. In the preceding period ceramic assemblages and other artefact types showed a pattern of more localised variation, whereas in the Corded Ware phase widespread uniformities in certain material items existed. These represented one aspect of the creation of a common idiom which arose as a basis for relating groups to one another. Furthermore, settlement units at this time had become much smaller than previously, while some of the environments being occupied were less stable for long-term exploitation than the areas of earlier occupation. Both these factors would have tended to increase the risk of disaster for individual communities and provided another source of pressure for the establishment of amicable inter-community relations (cf. Halstead and O'Shea 1982; Braun, this volume: Ch. 9). The uniformities in material culture seen in the archaeological record, it was argued, refer to items involved in the communication of personal (generally male) status. Throughout this area, however, status differentiation was very limited and based mainly on gender and age differences.

It was in one part of this milieu that the Bell Beaker originated, as a new form of the Beaker vessel type which was the most widespread form of the Corded Ware ceramic inventory (Lanting and van der Waals 1976). But this was not the only change. It has been noted for some time that copper daggers do not occur in the earliest Bell Beaker phase of north-west Europe, but come in with the second Bell Beaker phase. What is interesting, however, and its full significance has not been adequately appreciated, is that some of the later Corded Ware burials and some of the earliest Bell Beaker burials do contain daggers, as well as, or instead of, the previously current battle-axes; the daggers, however, are made of flint, of a colour very similar to that of copper, from Grand Pressigny, several hundred kilometres away in central France. In summary, the Corded Ware male status kit was changing at this time in the Lower Rhine area (Fig. 11.6).

The appearance of the flint daggers is significant from two points of view, apart from the demonstration of long-distance contact with the Grand Pressigny mines across cultural boundaries. It would appear to indicate that some-where at least, if not in the Lower Rhine area, there was a knowledge of the existence of copper daggers and a desire to imitate them, suggesting that they were held in high regard. It also points to a process of emulation at work in this area since only this would provide a context in which a new potential status item would be of interest. In the Lower Rhine region, then, we have what are initially some minor develop-ments in an already existing system with established structuring principles, involving, apart from the aspects already mentioned, the use of single inhumation burials in which inter-individual distinctions, predominantly those based on age and sex, were marked.

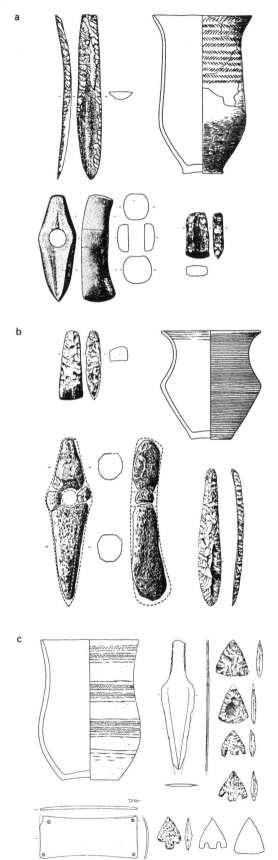

If this is so, the obvious question is why this local development had such enormous ramifications spatially. More specifically, why did the distribution take the curious form it did, not affecting most of the Corded Ware/Battle-Axe area of northern Europe, except marginally and relatively late, but expanding enormously in other areas, across the North Sea and along the Atlantic coast in particular, into societies organised very differently from those of the Corded Ware area? Indeed, the way the material of the Corded Ware/Battle Axe complex did not penetrate societies very different from the context in which it arose, whereas the Bell Beaker complex did, is one of the most interesting contrasts between the two. In order to investigate it, it is necessary to consider one of the societies in question.

Late Neolithic and Early Bronze Age Wessex

One area where such Bell Beaker penetration did occur, and where the sequence of development has recently been the subject of extensive analysis and discussion is the Wessex area of southern England (Renfrew 1973; Burgess 1980; Whittle 1981; Shennan 1982; Thorpe and Richards n.d.; Braithwaite n.d.).

From early in the third millennium BC in Wessex there is evidence of the construction of large-scale monuments, including henges, requiring the input of very large amounts of labour and reasonably regarded as ceremonial centres for what seems to have been a dispersed population (Fig. 11.7). Although there has recently been criticism of Renfrew's original labour input figures and their implications (Renfrew 1973; Startin and Bradley 1981; Whittle 1981), there remains a strong presumption that these societies must have been in some way centrally organised if such constructions were to be realised, even if it is by no means clear exactly what sort of control was being exercised. Recently, too, attention has been drawn to the independent evidence for the special nature of many of these sites in the distinctive material assemblage associated with them, particularly Grooved Ware pottery (see, for example, Thorpe and Richards n.d.), while the activities within them also seem to have been of a non-domestic nature (see, for example, Wainwright and Longworth 1971).

The assumption made here is that Late Neolithic Wessex was characterised by a hierarchically based form of social organisation involving a considerable use of material culture in the creation and definition of social distinctions and ritual as the basis of power. On the other hand, although burials are known, there is little sign in Wessex of the

Fig. 11.6. Late Corded Ware, All-Over-Ornamented, and Bell Beaker grave groups from the lower Rhine area: (a) Eext, Late Corded Ware; (b) Garderen, All-Over-Ornamented Beakers (also 34 amber beads, not shown); (c) Ede-Ginkelse Heide, Bell Beaker (all from Lanting and van der Waals 1976).

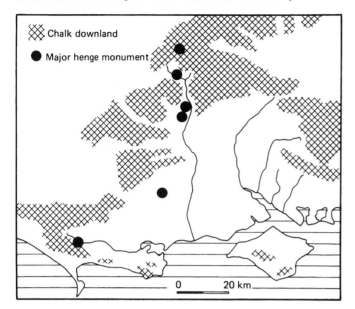

Fig. 11.7. The distribution of major henge monuments in Wessex (after Bradley and Ellison 1975).

representation of rank and status variation in terms of grave goods.

The first appearance of individual burials with variations in grave goods potentially interpretable in such a way occurs on the periphery of the monument complexes (Whittle 1981; Thorpe and Richards n.d.), and they are of Bell Beaker type. Bell Beaker material is not found within the monuments in their early phases, but this position changes and about 300 years later, near the end of the third millennium BC, Grooved Ware pottery has disappeared and a phase of reuse associated with Bell Beaker pottery occurs at a number of monuments.

The typologically early Bell Beaker burials had virtually no associations apart from the vessel itself. It was only with the appearance of the Wessex/Middle Rhine type (Clarke 1970) that what is always regarded as the 'typical' Bell Beaker grave assemblage of decorated Bell Beaker, copper dagger and stone wrist-guard first appears, stereotyped but in fact extremely rare. The deposition of individual burials associated with grave goods continued until well into the second millennium BC, but in the course of time the items found within them changed. In particular, the decorated Bell Beaker went out of funerary use and new types of dagger and other items appeared. The most striking feature of the developed Early Bronze Age in the Wessex area, at the end of the third and early in the second millennium BC (Burgess's Overton phase), is the rich burials of the so-called 'Wessex Culture' (Piggott 1938). By this time monument construction had generally ceased, with the exception of Stonehenge.

The view taken here (cf. Thorpe and Richards n.d.; Shennan 1982; Renfrew 1974–his distinction between 'group-oriented' and 'individualising' chiefdoms) is that by this time the ritually based hierarchy prevalent half a millennium earlier had finally ceased to exist. The Wessex burials represent the existence of hierarchical differentiation which had a different

basis, in which control of the circulation of such items as the copper daggers and amber beads which appear in the burials played an important role; competition for that control would then have become a significant part of social life.

Why did these changes occur? Elsewhere in this volume (Ch. 10) Bradley and Chapman demonstrate the considerable evidence for social change in the British Isles as a whole in the course of the third millennium, even before the Bell Beakers appeared. In some places at least, perhaps Yorkshire in particular, differentiation at burial in terms of grave goods seems to have developed, while inter-regional contacts on a wide scale within the British Isles were increasingly important. The argument in this paper sees the appearance of Bell Beakers in Wessex as associated with the introduction of a new ideology of power into the areas. In an earlier publication (Shennan 1982), it was suggested that this was a move by those controlling the existing authority structure away from an ideology based on rituals involving the collective labour of the community and towards one depending on the consumption in burial of prestige items and symbols obtained by means of contacts with high-ranking groups elsewhere; the latter would have been seen as providing a more secure basis for power. Such a model, however, overemphasises the egalitarian nature of the ceremonial monuments; it fails to take into account the material culture distinctiveness associated with many of them, and the fact that Beakers are excluded from the early phases of monuments, even though it is clear from radiocarbon dates that they must have been contemporary with one another. Thorpe and Richards (n.d.) have suggested that Beakers were adopted by those who were excluded from the ritual system and were on its peripheries. Thus they came to be introduced into a social environment very different from that of their origin because they had something to offer in the context of conflicts of interest in the local societies. Bradley and Chapman's paper (this volume: Ch. 10) emphasises the wide-ranging contacts which existed in Britain before Bell Beakers appeared, so there is no reason to believe that Corded Ware material and burial ritual were unknown; they were simply not taken up.

However, contacts with Europe were not restricted to a single phase. They were maintained for a considerable period and may be seen in the way that typological changes in the pottery involving the use of new motifs and new arrangements of the decoration on the vessel can be seen across a large area, including the Rhine valley and southern Britain. These contacts were also the basis for the introduction of new, ultimately central European, metalwork traditions, again involving both exchange and imitation. At the same time, it was into a newly Beaker-influenced social context of central-north European origin that the metallurgical innovations were introduced, and in which they found at least part of their use–for the production of daggers and ornaments–as an element of a process of emulation within the area. In the course of this process earlier prestige goods were successively devalued and replaced by other forms, in particular new metal types.

The presence of a later Beaker phase at a number of the major henges represents a coming-together of the earlier tradition of ritual power and the new structure of prestige associated with the Bell Beaker network (Thorpe and Richards n.d.), or perhaps rather a takeover of the former by the latter, since it is the prestige goods tradition which dominates the remaining part of the Early Bronze Age.

The argument, then, is that the Bell Beaker tradition existed as a local development within the Rhine area which was taken up not just as a result of the widening network of interaction demonstrated by Bradley and Chapman (this volume: Ch. 10) for the British Later Neolithic, but because the innovations it represented had a role to play in the local situation in Wessex, as described above. This was the critical step, because once Wessex had become connected to a system in which prestige was defined in terms of control of material goods, in particular exotic ones, and once emulation had become an important principle, it then in effect remained automatically locked into the wider network. Thus, we see Wessex continuing to have contacts with continental Europe, particularly on an axis reaching along the Rhine and into central Europe, essentially as the recipient and emulator of innovations originating in central Europe, but also connected through the exchange of such materials as copper and amber. The second phase, after the initial Beaker link, involves typological changes in the decorated Bell Beaker and the appearance of the tanged copper dagger and stone wrist-guard. In later phases it is changes in metalwork and ornaments which filter through, as well as the actual materials just mentioned.

Ever since the pre-eminent position of Wessex in the Earlier Bronze Age of England, in terms of the richness of its burial record, was recognised, the question has arisen as to why this should have been the case (e.g. Piggott 1938). The answer offered here depends on two main assumptions: first, that the greater deposition of exotic objects in this area is associated with a greater control over their circulation, and second, that the model already outlined to account for the introduction of Bell Beakers and their significance is essentially correct in nature. That is to say, their introduction marked the penetration of a principle by which prestige and rank were not simply represented in terms of objects, but the objects themselves could actually be used to create a position and thus acquired an intrinsic value, so that there emerged a medium for competition which had not previously existed. It may be that a system dependent on such a principle had already begun to develop elsewhere in Britain, for example in Yorkshire (Bradley and Chapman, this volume: Ch. 10), but it had not penetrated Wessex with its much stronger ritual system (Thorpe and Richards n.d.), and in any event the Beaker network offered much wider possibilities.

Since the ability to maintain exotic links had become so important, competition led to an emphasis on the active seeking-out of distant contacts. Thus, for those involved in local prestige competition in areas distant from the sources of innovation and exotic materials, both of which were playing the same prestige role, to become linked to the inter-regional exchange system was vital to success. This would no doubt have required the establishment of appropriate alliances, which itself may have involved the competitive mobilisation of subsistence resources by local kin groups, in the struggle to become sufficiently influential to join the inter-regional system. It is suggested here that Wessex owed its special position in this system to its exceptional ritual developments of the Late Neolithic, and for two reasons. First, there was prestige attached to having links with groups associated with ritual power and esoteric knowledge; second, as a result of the earlier developments and the organisation associated with them, more local resources could be mobilised here to establish a pre-eminent position. It may be that the expansion of settlement around the fringes of chalkland Wessex into new areas, many of which were on sandy soils and degenerated swiftly to heathland following clearance, was a result not of population increase but of the need for production beyond subsistence.

I have sketched a trajectory to account for the apparent 'richness' of Wessex in terms of the control of exotic materials at the end of the third and early in the second millennium; it remains important to consider its loss of this position, as Braun has pointed out in discussing the rise and decline of the Hopewell (this volume: Ch. 9). Bradley (1981) has suggested that the decline in importance of Wessex in the mid-second millennium may have been due, at least in part, to soil exhaustion as a result of overexploitation in connection with the demands of production beyond subsistence. It may also be suggested, however, that as time went on and metal became more important for prestige items, weapons and tools, Wessex—initially part of the system as a result of the exceptional ritual developments discussed above, but without special exchangeable resources of its own—became increasingly peripheralised. This is seen not just in the much smaller quantities of goods deposited in the ground but also in the growing lack of contact which Wessex had with the typological development in central European metalwork, and in its apparent severance from central European sources of metal—and its use of Welsh ones instead—early in the Middle Bronze Age (Northover n.d.).

The impact of the Bell Beaker network elsewhere in western and central Europe

The preceding section has offered an account of the way in which Bell Beakers came to be adopted in Wessex, an area very different in its local organisation from the Corded Ware zone in which they developed, and secondly of the subsequent history of the linkage of Wessex to the inter-regional system. But although it has offered one example of the processes involved in the incorporation of such an area into the Beaker network, it should not necessarily be considered in any sense as 'typical'. In the Tagus area of Portugal, for example, it would appear that, initially at least, Bell Beakers simply represent the appearance of a new fine ware in the local Vila Nova de São Pedro culture (Harrison 1977; 1980). Here there is strong evidence both for warfare, in the existence of fortified strongholds, and for social differentiation and its material representation, in the rich grave goods found in the local megalithic tombs. Given the pre-existing emphasis on the obtaining of exotic materials such as ivory and callais (Harrison and Gilman 1977), it may be that emulation of prestige items was already a factor operating in the societies around the Tagus estuary. Here, then, the trigger for the taking-up of the new fine ware style, the early Bell Beaker, would simply have been its appearance in an area with which these communities already had connections—in this case Brittany, which has indications of long-standing contacts with Portugal, including during the Beaker period (Giot *et al.* 1979).

The aim of this paper, however, is not to give an account of all the various regional trajectories. It is now necessary to consider the second curious aspect of the Bell Beaker distribution—the fact that it was not more widespread in northern Europe—before returning to the more general issues raised by the Bell Beakers as an example of peer polity interaction.

The relative uniformity of burial rite, status representation and certain material aspects of the Corded Ware culture over large areas of continental northern Europe has already been mentioned and it is clear that an established pattern of information exchange lay behind it. Given that this is the case, it is natural to ask why the innovations which had appeared in the Rhine area were not adopted more widely. It may be that the emulation process which we have suggested as being behind the Dutch developments was limited to certain societies only, but even if this were true it would only postpone the problem of explanation. More likely, the orientation of the new network was the result of a concern to establish alliances along an axis which would provide access to supplies of metal, a suggestion based on two lines of argument. The first of these is the evidence discussed above that the late Corded Ware and early Bell Beaker burials of the Lower Rhine area show a concern with metal, even before its appearance in the archaeological record there, in the context of a desire for emulation associated with the representation of inter-individual differences by material means, which characterises the Corded Ware culture. The second is the fact that those parts of central Europe which do become included in the Bell Beaker network are those settled areas which are adjacent to the central European metal sources, while northern Europe, which does not have its own metal sources, is excluded (Fig. 11.5).

Other aspects of the evidence may also be fitted into this framework. In continental north-west Europe, and Britain as well, the second Beaker phase does show evidence of access to metal supplies (Fig. 11.6c). Furthermore, within central Europe itself an examination of the pattern of change in the third millennium BC (Shennan, in press) suggests that in the Bell Beaker phase copper items were much more closely bound up with the representation of higher status than they had been

in the preceding Corded Ware period, and that a change took place at this time to a system in which status relations were actually based much more than before on competition for the control of prestige goods, and metal in particular.

It was this pattern crystallising in central Europe which became crucial for subsequent developments. Within that region the new emphasis on metal prestige goods led to the growth of the Early Bronze Age metal industry and an associated growth of social differentiation, which worked itself out differently in different parts of the region, depending, in part at least, on the possibility of establishing local monopolies (Shennan, in press). At the same time, the development had wide ramifications spatially. In north-west Europe the process of emulation which we have argued as being critical for the establishment of the link between Bell Beakers and metal in the first place continued, with the adoption of central European innovations in prestige kits. But what gave the link between these north-western areas and central Europe an added cohesion was the considerable dependence they had on central European metal supplies for the production of metal items (Northover n.d.; Butler and van der Waals 1966). The position of some of the other areas where Bell Beakers were in circulation was different. In Iberia, for example, even if one accepts that emulation and the control of prestige items were important, and there is certainly clear evidence that second-phase Beaker innovations of central European origin did penetrate into the Iberian peninsula (Harrison 1977), copper and other metals were available locally. As Schubart (1975; 1976) has pointed out, although there is some evidence of contact between the two centres of Iberian Earlier Bronze Age metallurgy—southern Portugal and south-east Spain—the area as a whole remains isolated from developments elsewhere in Europe and the Mediterranean until the beginning of the first millennium BC. In other words, the presence of a common basis of prestige and emulation was not sufficient to keep Iberia integrated into the wider pattern initially defined by the Beakers. Because it was not dependent on the maintenance of exchange links for the continued supply of metal and other prestige goods it gradually relapsed into isolation.

Conclusion

The preceding account of the Bell Beaker network has been concerned with two related tasks: to offer an account of the meaning of the phenomenon and to examine its effect in particular local situations. It is the first of these which has received the most attention. Nevertheless, conclusions about its effect in particular situations have a considerable impact on explanations of its significance. As far as peer polity inter-action is concerned, the key question is whether the parallel developments in a number of adjacent regions have any connection between them, and whether they would have been different if the connection had not been present.

This is not to say that the regions themselves represent

polities. One of the major problems in this particular case is that of defining polities at all. Even in the Wessex area, where large ceremonial monuments exist, there is no reason to believe that these are necessarily the centres of polities in the sense discussed by Renfrew (this volume: Ch. 1). Over continental northern and central Europe at this time there are no indications of any such centres. If accepted at face value, as it probably should be, this could be taken to suggest that the highest-order political unit was very localised indeed. But in such relatively egalitarian social contexts as those inferred here, the whole notion of a highest-order political unit may be open to question in any event, since it is characteristic of many such societies to be organised on a segmentary basis, so that exactly what represents an operationally relevant unit is defined relativistically, with reference to a particular situation. Perhaps all that can be said in this particular case is that the regions referred to are so large in scale that they must have included a number of units, even if we presuppose the units of interest to be high-level ones rarely mobilised for any purpose. Although individual hunter—gatherer or nomadic pastoralist groups may occupy very large territories, those of mixed agriculturalists are several orders of magnitude smaller; even the 'early state module' is in fact extremely small in scale.

In effect, then, although the degree of social complexity of the polities considered in this paper is slight compared with most of those described elsewhere in this volume, the spatial scale in the Beaker example is very much larger. Whereas the other contributors to this volume are generally considering the relations between recognisably distinct polities within a region, this paper has been examining the relations *between* regions presumptively containing a number of 'polities', to whose definition we do not have access.

Whether it is meaningful to include these different situations under the single rubric of 'peer polity interaction' is doubtful; it appears to stretch an already protean concept beyond its limits of usefulness. Although the significance of the issues raised by the peer polity interaction model, and of many of the individual processes included within it, remains undeniable even in the Beaker case, it is more appropriate to attempt to describe those processes for the specific situation being considered than to subsume it under a label.

In the Bell Beaker case the argument is that the Beaker network was associated with the spread of a form of organisation in which social relations and political activity were expressed in terms of the control of prestige goods. Thus, it was not simply new prestige goods which were introduced to a number of areas but also the social context of their use. In Wessex this represented a major break with pre-existing traditions and it occurred because of a local conflict of interest. In central Europe the change was not so marked because many aspects of the preceding north European tradition, out of which the Bell Beakers had arisen in the first place, continued. Nevertheless, the emphasis on the importance of the control of prestige items was something new here, too. In both areas it had a profound effect on subsequent developments, in particular defining the pattern of social change which one sees culminating in both areas in the rich burials of the Early Bronze Age, and in central Europe representing an important driving force in the growth of the metal industry.

The system developed in the Earlier Bronze Age as it did because over large areas local societies were now playing by similar rules and, as a result of this, had to maintain linked patterns of exchange to obtain the prestige goods that were locally necessary; where independent exchange systems could be set up, as in Iberia, the links were not maintained. At the very large scale over which for about 300 years the Bell Beakers had their period of currency, the type of more generalised uniformity and integration identified by Braun with the Hopewell 'decline' never grew up. Relations remained at the level of inter-societal exchanges and the imitation and exchange of higher-ranking goods.

Local conditions were a key factor in whether or not particular areas became incorporated within the Beaker network; the initial impetus behind it, however, was a concern with emulation, and one of the reasons behind its enormous impact was its association with very striking innovations. It was the same process of emulation which saw its 'decline', because in the new social context of prestige competition with which the Bell Beakers were associated, changes in the fashionable forms of prestige item were assured.

Chapter 12

Epilogue and prospect
John F. Cherry and Colin Renfrew

The opening chapter of this volume provides an explicit statement of the general approach and specific theoretical constructs that inform the case studies that follow it. Each of them was written with this statement to hand and—drawn as they are from a wide range of temporal, geographical, and socio-political contexts—they offer some immediate assessment of the extent to which the peer polity interaction approach (hereafter abbreviated as PPI) has proved illuminating when faced with empirical data. A number of the contributions have also noted some of the practical difficulties that arise in the application of the concept, and they have suggested aspects of it which might benefit from further methodological or theoretical elaboration. These chapters can speak for themselves, and it is accordingly not our intention here to attempt any fundamental critique of PPI (nor are we the people to do so.) Rather, the concluding remarks that follow are intended to help place the notion in its wider context and to explore, albeit briefly, some of its potential implications.

An initial point requiring emphasis is that the idea of PPI is not an intellectual foundling. In recent years there has been a marked shift in work on the development of early complex societies away from what might be termed the 'monopolity' approach (i.e. a form of methodological individualism in which it is regarded as valid to study the evolution of states or other types of political units in splendid isolation) and towards the wider horizons offered, for instance, by approaches such as 'world systems', which focus on complex patterns of simultaneous interaction and change among polities spread throughout a macro-region. The germ of such a development can be seen clearly in Fried's (1967: 232) suggestion that groups of stratified agricultural societies developed 'in tandem' via processes that led to the emergence of pristine states. A few years later, Renfrew (1975) drew attention to the recurrent tendency of small-scale, formative complex societies (or 'early state modules') to exhibit a certain amount of spatial regularity and institutional redundancy, although that paper went only so far as to assert that trade (in its widest sense and implying interactions of various sorts and at differing scales) must be one of the mechanisms responsible.

Undoubtedly, the closest precursor of the ideas developed in the present volume is Price's 'cluster-interaction' model for considering shifts in organisation and production, initially with reference to prehistoric Central Mexico (Price 1977). Price's model offers a number of detailed points of similarity with the framework adopted here. Writing of changes in the agricultural mode of production and of the emergence of ranking and the state, she noted that such developments occurred in clusters: the rise, for instance, of several more or less simultaneous pristine states, rather than a single one (1977: 210). In her view, the most important definitional feature of cluster components is their close comparability—in size range, institutional structure, relative power and mode of production—irrespective of their level of 'socio-political integration'. Such close correspondences, it is claimed, arise from a basic similarity in adaptive processes, enhanced by the fact that cluster components interact regularly with each other and that such interaction accentuates the resemblances already existing among them. Price emphasises two principal forms of interaction which have an intensifying effect (by disseminating innovations and accelerating the overall processes of cultural evolution):

> 1   exchange or 'economic interchange' *sensu lato*, often stimulated by microecological differentiation both within and between polities, and
> 2   competition and/or warfare.

In short:

> While selection pressure operates at the level of the individual components . . . it also appears to operate in some way upon the cluster as a whole: the cluster *per se* can be analyzed as some sort of unit. If the components, in systems-theory terms, constitute essentially autonomous—if open—systems, then the cluster must be treated as a unitary—similarly open—and inclusive super-system . . . it is epistemologically illegitimate to attempt within the cluster to assign either chronological priority or direction of influence (Price 1977: 210).

It should be apparent that Price's formulation and our own share numerous points of contact and overlap. At the same time, there are some important contrasts, perhaps most notably in our emphasis on structural and formal homologies resulting from interactions of a strongly *symbolic* nature. Nonetheless, certain epistemological and methodological assumptions common to both constructs would merit further careful consideration.

One such assumption is that a PPI or cluster-interaction approach is applicable—in principle, at least—to societies at markedly different levels of complexity. According to Price (1977: 210), 'cluster components may all be egalitarian hunting—gathering bands, or ranked societies, or states: the point is their comparability'. Likewise, Renfrew (this volume: 2–4) emphasises how the term 'polity' need not, and should not, suggest any specific scale of organisation, but rather should be reserved for the highest-order socio-political unit, whether a hunter—gatherer band or an early state, in the region in question. This eminently simple definition, though sweeping in its applicability, does impose some limits on the relevant universe of study. For instance, a ranked society or early state comprising a central place with subordinate satellite units would not qualify, although a number of comparable, territorially defined groupings in interaction would do so. Since the fundamental criterion is the existence of demonstrably autonomous synchronic polities in contact with each other, many instances of highly asymmetric power relationships must also be ruled out. One important class of such cases would be secondary state formation, since a cluster consisting of a developed state and a number of peripheral, less institutionally differentiated societies in reality constitutes

a single hierarchically arranged unit, parts of which are subject to the jurisdiction of a single higher locus of power. Thus, PPI should not be considered a generally applicable model for the growth of political complexity, and it must be distinguished clearly, for instance, from 'core—periphery' or 'world system' approaches (Kristiansen *et al.*, in press).

Yet, as several of the papers in this volume demonstrate, this ostensibly straightforward definition of 'polity' is often difficult to apply in practice. In the case of Minoan Crete (Cherry, this volume: Ch. 2), for example, it is a simple matter to recognise in the archaeological record evidence for a number of highest-order central places, whose spatial separation implies the existence of comparable, hierarchic, territorially based units. But the assertion that those units are both politically equivalent and autonomous is one for which hard archaeological data are in short supply, however plausible it may seem. The difficulty, of course, arises from the necessity to infer political status from the mute evidence of the size, location, and functional differentiation of settlements. Instances in the modern world where the use of such criteria could be misleading spring readily to mind (e.g. Washington DC). There may be procedures, however, for dealing with the phenomenon of the 'disembedded capital' (Willey 1979). A peer polity analysis is often likely to be most solidly anchored when dealing either with historically documented societies, such as Archaic and Classical Greece (Snodgrass, this volume: Ch. 3), Anglo-Saxon England (Hodges, this volume: Ch. 5), or the Classic Maya (Freidel and Sabloff, this volume: Chs. 7 and 8); or with polities on the periphery of, and in contact with, literate societies, as is the case in parts of Later Iron Age Europe (T. and S. Champion, this volume: Ch. 4; Champion 1985). As Barnes's data on third century AD polities in Japan reveal (this volume: Table 6.2), in favourable circumstances historical sources may indicate very clearly not only the names and territorial extents of equivalent polities, but also the titles of their respective rulers and subordinate officials, the names of satellite communities, population figures, instances of dynastic intermarriage of high-ranking kin, prestige gift-giving between the élites of different polities, and so on. Sabloff predicted in his paper (this volume: Ch. 8) that historical archaeology would have the same importance for theory building and the growth of methodological sophistication in studies of complex societies that ethnoarchaeology has had for work on prehistoric hunter—gatherers—a point also made recently by Binford (1977b). It seems likely, to judge from this collection of papers, that the potential and problems of the PPI approach are most readily evaluated in historically well-documented contexts; operational difficulties encountered in such cases may often be greatly exacerbated as we move back into fully prehistoric settings.

Written records, of course, come into existence to serve the increased communication/decision-making needs and political self-consciousness of polities. It follows that the literate contexts in which PPI can best be tested will be those of early states, and it was indeed with such cases primarily in mind that the approach was developed (Renfrew 1982a). Some may feel, therefore, that its application should be restricted to the nature, internal dynamics and growth of large chiefdoms and early states, and that its extension to 'polities' of a markedly lower order of complexity and hierarchy involves too catholic a definition; the same comment, obviously, applies with equal force to Price's cluster-interaction model. Would the concept not then become indistinguishable from the ideas enshrined in much previous writing on 'communication networks' and 'interaction spheres' in prehistory (see, for instance, references in Braun, this volume: Ch. 9)? And is it not the case that the range of specific structural homologies, whose explanation constitutes one of the chief attractions of the approach, is then necessarily much reduced? How well can 'polities' be defined archaeologically in such circumstances?

We feel that, while PPI is perhaps particularly well suited to illuminating homologous institutional, ideological and socio-economic developments in early states, it does have a role to play in studies of non-hierarchical or non-complex societies, too. There is, after all, a problem demanding explanation—namely, the relationship between the manifest occurrence of material uniformities in space and the apparently simultaneous socio-political developments taking place over remarkably wide areas, without clear indications of external stimuli or of any clear priority in the diffusion of innovations from one particular region. The problem has become the more acute with the collapse of traditional diffusionist frameworks and the subjection of the concept of 'archaeological cultures' to a process of deconstruction. Much recent discussion of 'interaction spheres' has not helped fill this theoretical vacuum, since it generally either recasts in new terminology a loosely diffusionist approach, or else focuses narrowly on processes of exchange at the macro-regional level.

PPI can make some contribution here by dealing with both the existence, and the impact on socio-political developments, of a far wider range of forms of interaction than has hitherto been the case. Certainly, the authors of the three papers in this volume (Ch. 9–11) which are concerned with non-hierarchical societies have found that the concept does offer a better approach to the study of interaction than the diffusionism that had been applied previously in these cases. Interestingly, however, they have also found it necessary to relax at least one of the definitional criteria set out in Chapter 1, that of the scale of the 'highest-order political unit'. Shennan (this volume: 147–8), pointing out how hard it is to recognise such centres, pertinently questions the validity of the notion with respect to relatively egalitarian social contexts where 'it is characteristic of many such societies to be organised on a segmentary basis, so that exactly what represents an operationally relevant unit is defined relativistically, with reference to a particular situation'. In any event, the units of analysis (whether or not they be termed 'polities') are not individual residential settlements or

segmentary 'tribal' units, but whole 'core' regions or culture areas. Thus, while the degree of social complexity is slight, the spatial scale is extremely large—quite the converse of the case with 'early state modules'. This seems to be a problem not of archaeological recognition, but rather of the ontological status of the units in question. What stands out clearly, however, are the advantages accruing from the emphasis in the peer polity framework on the *social context and impact* of interaction and communication, aspects that diffusionist thought conspicuously fails to handle adequately (Ericson and Earle 1982). Only further studies at varying scales, and in different times and places, drawing on the insights gained in historically well-grounded uses of the concept, will reveal the potential contribution of PPI in non-hierarchical, non-literate situations of this sort. One possible area in which further illumination may be anticipated is that of the emergence of concepts of ethnicity, together with the development of linguistic groups; we shall return to this later.

Another contentious issue emerges from the methodological stance that is a feature both of the cluster-interaction model and of the concept of PPI, namely that shifts in complexity (such as state formation) are properly intelligible only on a multi-unit or multi-regional basis. We feel less than happy when Price (1977: 210) speaks of 'selection pressure' operating at this 'supersystem' level. It is surely on the individual members of different polities, each with their own social persona, their own degree of access to resources and power, and their own social strategies, that the most important determinants and constraints operate, though naturally it is possible to study interactions between such individuals only in aggregate through the archaeological record—for instance by considering the different kinds of interaction that must have taken place both between individuals and between whole polities. Nonetheless, the insistence that causal questions about the development of complexity are most profitably considered at the multi-polity level, despite the fact that individual polities may themselves be organised as emergent states, represents a parting of the ways with several state origins theorists. Scholars such as Carneiro (1970; 1977) maintain that it is incorrect to suppose that one cannot study the evolution of one polity apart from the rest, even if many such polities in fact evolved together: 'we cannot understand how states developed in general unless we can show how states developed individually' (1977: 222). To Renfrew's suggestion (this volume: 11) that peer polities 'emerged *together*, pulling each other up by the bootstraps, as it were', one might oppose Carneiro's opinion (*ibid.*) that the adoption of a polity interaction model is 'akin to saying that states arose by "taking in each other's washing"'!

As the present volume demonstrates, such a view seems to us ill-considered. The empirical facts indicate quite clearly that both states and other less hierarchical forms of polity regularly develop in groups or clusters; the very redundancy of that evolutionary process both invites a cross-cultural (and cross-polity) approach, and virtually guarantees that there must exist some causal aspects to be seen in the context of their emergence. If it is legitimate to consider such batches of interacting polities as bound together into some sort of larger system, then it follows that the net behaviour of that supersystem will not simply reflect the sum of the behaviours of its individual constituent polities; that is an axiom of systems thinking. On the contrary, there must exist complex, multidimensional networks of communication and interaction, operating with both beneficial and negative effects (depending on one's position in the system), within and between such societies. It is in understanding the development of such channels of communication—the emergence of structure, in fact—that we believe the PPI approach has something to contribute. And, as discussed in Chapter 1, it is precisely because such communications were to a large extent effected by means of material symbols that the approach offers the archaeologist a tangible means of tackling seemingly abstract problems of socio-political process; these are 'symbols in action' (cf. Hodder 1982a).

It may be noted in passing that this distinction between studies of *individual* polities versus studies of *groups* of comparable polities cannot simply be dismissed as a semantic quibble about the operational question of systems boundary definition. Drawing the line between what is external and what internal to a given system is a common problem which has obfuscated many a discussion of, for instance, the role of long-distance trade or of warfare in early state formation (Claessen 1984: 365–6). The wish to obviate the problem no doubt partly underlies the current popularity of 'world systems' analyses in archaeology, although there is a considerable price to be paid in terms of the fuzziness of the analysis that inevitably results from operating under that paradigm. We would maintain, on the contrary, that there do exist important classes of behaviour, to which adequate attention has not hitherto been paid, at scales intermediate between those typically adopted in studies of individual polities and those necessary when considering large-scale imperial systems and their dealings with peripheral societies. Furthermore, since individual polities can be well understood only in the context of the growth of comparable institutions nearby, and since mature states and empires arise from the differential survivorship of polities when some are institutionally absorbed into others as a consequence of competitive imbalances over time, it can be concluded that PPI should occupy a critical central position between studies of small- and large-scale socio-political systems. This is ultimately an argument about the essential locus or level of causality.

There are other senses, too, in which PPI provides a bridge between existing schools of thought. Its primary emphasis on interaction as both context and stimulus for social and political elaboration finds, of course, many echoes in earlier literature. In fact, it forms an integral part of the currently prevalent conceptualisation of the state as an organisation in which there is a differentiated and specialised communications, or decision-making, subsystem that regulates variable exchanges and interactions among other subsystems and with other systems (Wright 1978: 56). But the focus here is quite distinctive, and not merely a reformulation in new language of well-tried ideas. For the range of interactions dealt with in the PPI approach is much wider than that customarily considered, being in effect a major extension of Renfrew's earlier discussion (1975) of trade as an information carrier implying 'action at a distance'. 'Interaction' is here taken to include everything from exchanges within and between polities of matter, energy, information and symbolic ideas, through processes of imitation and competitive emulation, to acts of a more negative and hostile character, including outright warfare.

Such a broad view has the virtue of making it possible to sidestep the (to us) unnecessary distinctions made in so much of the literature on state formation between models that stress *conflict* and *exploitation* and those emphasising *co-operation* and *mutual benefit* (Service 1978; cf also 1975: 266–308). On which side of this divide individual archaeologists fall seems to be a function of their fundamental political and philosophical beliefs about past societies—whether they were run by benign altruists or despotic entrepreneurs (Binford 1983: 215–20)—rather than of any inherent characteristics of the data under consideration. No such professions of belief are required here. There are many instances described in this volume where competitive or hostile relations between polities actively foster collaborative or co-operative behaviour within them. Likewise, the rise of agonistic relations between various societal segments within a polity often serves to encourage closer and mutually beneficial interactions between the élites in different polities—for instance the establishment of alliances, through intermarriage, to ensure military support when required, or the acquisition of prestige items and symbolic knowledge with which to astound the populace and legitimise the *status quo*.

Such instances, of course, have already received much attention from archaeologists in a wide variety of settings. PPI, however, specifies the *systemic level* of such interchanges very much more precisely than is usually the case. Again, it bridges established approaches which have not previously been satisfactorily unified. For the principal emphasis here is neither on long-distance exchanges between partners often of markedly different organisational complexity, nor on purely intra-polity mobilisation, redistribution and intensification, but rather on what we might term the *intermediate* flows (Renfrew 1975: 18) of objects, energy and information of all sorts *between* local but independent polities as a result of their interaction. We believe this is a class of behaviour that has not hitherto been adequately treated, either in a descriptive or an explanatory sense. Naturally, the latter is far more difficult to put into practice than the former, just as is the case with exchange/interaction models at other levels. There may be those who feel that the case studies in this volume, while giving some insight into the mechanisms by which certain distributional aspects of the archaeological record at certain scales came into being, have not answered many 'why' questions and display an uncomfortable degree of circularity of reasoning. We feel more optimistic, for two reasons.

First, while the recognition and definition of widespread archaeological traits or features will very often provide the *point de départ* for a PPI analysis, that alone is not the point of the exercise. It is socio-political change and shifts in the degree of organisational complexity of past societies for which we wish to account; there must therefore be some chronological patterning, some temporal dynamic, as well as mechanisms which relate interactions, prior to any observed changes, to the very occurrence of those changes. Some specific predictions which become possible when such criteria are met are laid out in Chapter 1 (pp. 7–8). The fact that not all the case studies included here have found it possible to meet these criteria fully in no way impugns the applicability of the concept of PPI itself, for the difficulties encountered often appear to stem not from *lacunae* in the archaeological record, but from the neglect of certain lines of approach. As is often the case, the very act of asking a question in a different way may lead to fresh and unexpected insights.

Second, we feel encouraged by the ways in which PPI returns us to important unfinished business in the development of archaeological thinking. The recognition of spatial patterning in material culture at different scales is a fundamental aspect of the descriptive, taxonomic activities of all archaeologists. Yet to relate such purely archaeological taxa satisfactorily to the intersecting social, political, ethnic, linguistic and genetic units that must lie behind them has proved a far more difficult task. By far the clearest expression, in recent years, of the problems involved is to be found in the late David Clarke's seminal chapter on 'Group Ethnology' in his book *Analytical Archaeology* (1978: 363–408). It must surely be the case that interactions between loosely related yet politically independent entities give rise both to larger institutional units (such as the nation state itself) and to ethnic and linguistic groupings which cross-cut such units.

J.F.C.

It may be appropriate to return, in the concluding pages of this 'Epilogue', to three or four items of the 'unfinished business' to which a review of the PPI concept and of the papers in this volume have naturally led us. In doing so it is possible to do no more than single out problems which require more thorough treatment in the future, but the exercise will in itself be a useful one if it does indeed encourage such further treatment, so that what we have written here becomes a 'Prospect' towards further work rather than simply a commentary on what has gone before.

The concept of the state in state formation

Snodgrass (this volume: 58) has stressed the role of PPI as a *conscious* process in his discussion of the development of the Greek city state. Indeed, when the PPI model was first introduced, this point was raised (Renfrew 1982a: 289): 'The specific state is legitimised in the eyes of its citizens by the existence of other states which patently do function along comparable lines.' There is the germ of an idea here which is perhaps relevant, in many cases, to the issue of early state formation. But there is also the accompanying difficulty which faces any archaeologist when an attempt is made to consider not only what people did, but also the manner in which they were thinking.

Certainly the question of legitimacy is important in any political system. In some cases the discussion centres upon the legitimacy of an individual person as the holder of an office of power or responsibility within a particular organisation. Was this ruler a duly appointed chief, was that magistrate properly nominated to office? But the underlying question is, more generally, whether the system itself is an appropriate or acceptable form of government. Should the succession always be by primogeniture? In what cases can an official be removed from office? This same issue is implicit in much of the discussion by Hodges (this volume: Ch. 5) with respect to Anglo-Saxon England.

It may be that in the process of initial state formation—that is to say during the development of a state-organised society in an area where such societies have not been seen before—this question of the legitimation of a new societal form is of central importance. For in the extensive discussions which many scholars have undertaken about what it is precisely which distinguishes a state society from other, generally less complex organisational forms, they have perhaps undervalued this particular factor. What is crucial to state government, as opposed to other forms of leadership, is that the members of the society in question do consciously *regard* it as a state society—that there can exist an organisation which confers various powers upon the ruler and other officers of state, while at the same time limiting those powers in well-defined ways, which can often validly be set down and codified. It is in this way that the institutions of state government are needed, since power is no longer exercised in an arbitrary way. Members of the society in question thus recognise that they are part of a society of a particular kind, and see themselves as members of it.

For some time it has been recognised that in the early days of a new system of centralised government, there is often considerable expenditure of wealth, often magnifying the importance of the ruler, or of labour devoted to public works which may have served to consolidate central power (Cherry, J.F. 1978: 431); Egyptian pyramids and Maya ceremonial centres have been seen in this light. These have been interpreted, generally, as operating within the polity in question, serving to emphasise, by grandiloquent statement, the stability and legitimacy of government. But the importance of their influences on other polities should not be underestimated. For the success of such a governmental form in one polity makes its adoption in a neighbouring one very much more likely. This adoption of a comparable form of government in the second polity may in turn serve to reinforce its legitimacy in the first polity in the eyes of its own citizens, and of others.

The extent to which the governmental form of an early state society can be made to gain in legitimacy for its own citizens and those of other polities through conforming to an acceptable norm is well illustrated by the Kingdom of Tonga in the nineteenth century AD. Until that time, Tonga had been a complex society of a kind which in Polynesia is often called a 'chiefdom', yet which anthropologists in Africa would certainly call a state. Be that as it may, the ruler of Tonga, King George Tupou I, wished to establish his status as the ruler of a state society. He appointed as his 'Prime Minister' a shrewd New Zealander, the Rev. Shirley Baker, who saw that amongst other things Tonga should have a state seal, a coat of arms and a flag. Although Tonga was not an independent state at that time, having come within the jurisdiction of the British Empire, the deliberate move to statehood measuring up to European criteria of the state undoubtedly allowed Tonga to avoid the status of a directly administered colony and to become instead a dependent state within the Empire, and later within the Commonwealth, and a member of the United Nations (Thomson 1894).

The discussion here of the legitimacy of state society, as a social form consciously recognised by its members, is related to Freidel's reference (this volume: Ch. 7) to the 'situational ethics' which were notionally at work among the Lowland Maya in respect of their conduct of warfare. Certain kinds of conduct were regarded as appropriate in war, and others were not. Once again, we are familiar with such issues in modern times, where the 'situational ethics' of war were formalised in the Geneva Convention under the auspices of the League of Nations. What is of interest in the present discussion, however, is the way in which the interactions between peer polities can and do result in unwritten conventions in areas of experience which it is outside the power of any one of them to regulate. For while the ultimate sanction among polities which disagree about the proper regulation of interactions between them is to go to war, it is precisely in reference to the rules of war that this sanction cannot operate.

These are abstract matters. From the archaeological point of view there are widely recognised risks in working too freely with concepts which are difficult to recognise in the archaeological record. The sort of issues which we are discussing here, namely the picture which individuals carry within their own heads of the organisational nature of their own society, might well be thought the kind of unobservable entity which archaeologists would do best to avoid. This is a difficult issue, which we are only now beginning to explore. But it is certainly one which is raised by the question of the role of PPI in state formation.

It has been argued (Renfrew, in press, a) that in order effectively to model the working of human societies, it may also be necessary to model aspects of cognitive behaviour. One way of doing this is to postulate that each individual carries an internalised mental map of the world which in part governs behaviour. For the actions of the individual are not made simply in response to external stimuli or internal needs, but are made after reference to this internalised map. The use of the term 'mental map' is not here restricted to the representation of spatial relationships, as in the use to which some geographers have put it (Gould and White 1974), since the mapping of relationships by which individuals make coherent their view of the world extends to social relationships also. Within this framework, a crucial aspect of the emergence of state society would be not simply the development of various new power relationships within the community, but their institutionalisation. This institutionalisation must involve first the formulation of new concepts descriptive of these new relationships, concepts which can take their place in the mental maps of individual citizens. These internalised concepts can later be made external and evident in the material form by which these institutions are expressed or symbolised.

To speak in these terms may seem needlessly concrete to some historians. Why, they may ask, specify a hypothetical entity, a mental map, in order to speak of perfectly straight-forward processes of thinking with which, as human beings, we are all familiar—an exercise in pointless reification! Many archaeologists, on the other hand, will criticise the approach from precisely the opposite standpoint, seeing this talk of concepts within mental maps as embracing a needlessly 'idealist' approach, inviting a discussion written in precisely that language of 'palaeopsychology' which the processual archaeologist has sought to avoid. To the first, however, the answer must be that the essence of good modelling is to make explicit and open to careful discussion that which was previously implicit, and taken as obvious, as a given feature: that there are problems here which cannot be ignored. To the latter, the materialist archaeologist, the answer must be that cognitive archaeology is concerned with the human use of symbols, and that material symbols do not have an independent origin of their own; they are the product of human cognitive processes which are located in the brain. They may not be directly observable by the archaeologist, but nor is it expected of a theoretical entity that it should be. The resolution of this problem seems to us an important one for the development of archaeology and a necessary step if a constructive cognitive archaeology is to be arrived at by coherent methodological procedures. These are needed if it is to advance beyond those purely intuitive and subjective insights which seem to form the stock-in-trade of what is sometimes termed 'structuralist archaeology'.

Although such mental maps may indeed be regarded as theoretical entities, their consequences can be documented archaeologically. Any depiction of the world may be regarded as a form of mapping. So a painting of an animal on the wall of a cave must be regarded as the representation or transformation of an internalised concept if it is painted not from life but from memory. The early topographic maps surviving from the ancient Near East are further suggestive of coherent ordering, this time of spatial relationships. And when we see, on a Greek vase of the fifth century BC, a whole range of gods and goddesses from the Olympian pantheon, accompanied by their names in alphabetic script, we are looking at a map of transcendental relationships.

The consequences of mental maps extend, however, well beyond simple depictions which we can regard as in some sense transformations of them. Any projection of a prior ordering has a comparable status. When we are discussing state society, any degree of urban planning which we may perceive in the principal town centre of the state offers a case in point. In the case of ancient Greece, many city states had features which go beyond the obvious necessities of town walls and reservoirs, which we might think of as features of almost any urban centre in such an environment. Often they had their own theatre and perhaps their own stadium, too, as well as one or more temples conforming to quite a well-defined plan. These are features of the Greek city as such. As we have seen, their wide distribution can be seen as the product of PPI operating within the Aegean. Yet when we begin to consider in detail the manner in which such processes as emulation and symbolic entrainment, discussed in Chapter 1, in fact operate, we shall find it necessary to give some consideration to mental mapping.

Here, then, is just one way in which the consideration of PPI brings forward fresh problems rather faster than it disposes of old ones.

System collapse

Similar issues can arise when we are discussing the collapse of complex societies—a phenomenon which, as Sabloff has pointed out (this volume: Ch. 8), can be as interesting in processual terms as their emergence.

It is interesting that the process of PPI often seems to play a highly significant role here. For often polities do not collapse singly, but in groups. Naturally, single complex entities do collapse; this may be true of the single nation state, or the fall of an empire. But in other cases we see several polities collapsing within a relatively short space of time. This is certainly so of the various polities of Mycenaean Greece, and appears to be the case with the Classic Maya collapse.

Now in some cases we may become aware of some major causal factor which, acting upon each polity individually and in isolation, would cause it to collapse. Most of the traditional monocausal explanations for collapse are of this kind. Were the collapse of one brought about by a cataclysmic volcanic eruption, resulting in widespread ash fall, the same might be true for all. A disastrous plague or a severe and widespread drought could, in the same way, affect neighbouring polities equally and bring about the collapse of each. But in most cases the evidence which we have for system collapse militates against simple, monocausal explanations of this kind.

In certain other cases, the polities might be strongly interdependent in economic terms, to the extent that the collapse of one would make the others no longer viable. If one

should collapse, as a consequence of purely local causes, this could result in a more widespread system collapse—the phenomenon which Flannery (1972) has described as 'hypercoherence'. Something comparable to this, namely a general scarcity of bronze, perhaps the product of difficulties in the Near East, may have contributed to the demise of Mycenaean civilisation.

But this explanation would not explain the simultaneous collapse of polities which were less tightly integrated into a commercial complex of this kind.

In both the Mycenaean and Maya cases, the analysis has to go rather further, as Tainter (in press, Ch. 6) has pointed out. For in neither does there seem to have been a dominant outside cause for the collapse, the external catastrophe which some commentators have sought. Neither is it easy to see the phenomenon as the result of economic difficulties among the neighbouring polities brought about by the collapse of a single one. Instead, there would seem to be some interaction process at work which it is appropriate to consider in PPI terms.

Emulation can have destructive as well as constructive effects—that is precisely why the potlatch is such a fascinating phenomenon. And symbolic entrainment can be as effective in propagating affronts to authority as in disseminating new governmental forms. And, rather obviously, while warfare between peer polities can result in stronger leadership and higher centralised organisation in each, it can also deplete resources of manpower and materials, so that the stability of the individual polities may be gravely endangered, even if none is actually victorious over its neighbours.

The most important factor, however, may be that of confidence. For just as in the last section we were employing the rather abstract concept of legitimacy, so here it may again be relevant to think in terms of what appears to the individual members of the states as possible and viable. The collapse of state organisation in one polity could have significant effects upon its neighbours. For it may alter the perception of what is feasible, of what is *thinkable*.

This is already a rather familiar thought when one is considering revolts against centralised government within different provinces of a single large polity; it is a commonplace that revolts spread 'like wildfire', even when they entirely lack centralised organisation. It is tempting to make comparisons here with the 'student revolts' in different countries across the world in the later 1960s. Although these were hardly, except perhaps in Paris, as serious as full-scale revolutions, it is difficult to avoid the conclusion that a process of PPI was at work. Politics is, after all, the art of the possible. The best way of recognising that something is possible is to observe that it has, somewhere, already happened.

Networks in non-hierarchical societies

At several points in this volume, there has been discussion as to how far the PPI concept is applicable to societies which do not show a very high degree of ranking. Barnes (this volume: Ch. 6) was doubtful of its applicability, and we have noted earlier how convenient for interpretive purposes is some supplementation of the archaeological evidence by written documentation. Shennan (this volume: Ch. 11) has indicated that the task of definition of the polities themselves is not an easy one, and Bradley and Chapman (this volume: Ch. 10) have deliberately and informatively dealt with what they view as 'core areas', which are sometimes territorial units of quite considerable extent.

This care over the definition of the appropriate units of analysis is a very necessary one. It is certainly a difficulty which is not generally seen for state societies. These almost invariably possess an organising centre, which helps the process of definition. In many cases, state societies were territorially defined anyway—that is to say that membership of the polity was in some cases automatically extended to those persons born within the state territory.

Yet even if the 'polities' in question were very small ones, in some cases little more than residence units, the consequences of interaction and the nature of the interaction certainly remain of comparable interest. It is indeed likely that the further investigation of these interactions will lead in different directions than does the study of the relations between early state societies. But there remain certain basic realities about processes of interaction which have not yet been sufficiently investigated.

Shennan (this volume: Ch. 11; 1982; 1985) has considered the network of interactions between local communities which he sees as responsible for the Bell Beaker phenomenon, and Braun (this volume: Ch. 9) has given an illuminating discussion of the Hopewell interaction sphere in network terms. They have brought out well that what is at issue here is not simply the distribution of certain exotic goods. It is rather that the very notion of exotic goods (or at least certain new ways of perceiving goods as valuable, desirable and capable of conferring prestige), is seen in the relevant areas for the first time. Shennan (1982) has spoken of these things in ideological terms, and this is perhaps warranted. Certainly we could usefully ask here what was the place of such goods and that of their rightful use and ownership within the mental map of social relationships of those participating in the network. It seems perfectly appropriate here to speak of emulation and of symbolic entrainment. In north-western Europe this is the first time (if we bring the Corded Ware assemblage into the discussion also) that we can use these terms about individual artefacts which we can establish, through the archaeological record, as the property of recognisable individuals.

The role of the interactions along the network in spreading this perception of the way that material goods can operate in the world was clearly a crucial one. There is an interesting parallel here with the question of when specific materials were first recognised as commodities— of having, that is, real value in their own right, as materials (Renfrew, in press, b). These, although rather abstract questions, have immediate and concrete implications. It can be argued, at

least for Europe, that this process of commoditisation did not really get under way until metal objects were becoming available (although the large-scale extraction of flint through mining in the British Neolithic should not be overlooked). It has been suggested (Torrence 1986) that the extraction of obsidian on the island of Melos in prehistoric times was not controlled by a local Melian population, who therefore did not exercise proprietary rights over the quarry areas. This carries with it, perhaps, the notion that obsidian was not regarded there as a valuable resource in the commercial sense, that is to say as a fairly high-value commodity. In the Aegean also such a concept may not have made its appearance until the onset of the Bronze Age. There, too, it is likely to have been propagated by interactions like those which we have been describing. Indeed, the discussion emphasises that one of the likely outcomes of a network of peer polity interactions is indeed a common system of values, although not necessarily a standardised one.

Once again, further discussion will need to centre upon the appropriate means of operationalising these concepts in archaeological terms. In some cases at least, this is not an excessively ambitious aspiration. Petruso (1979) has shown the existence of weight and counting systems in the Late Bronze Age Aegean which exhibit at least some degree of standardisation and serve to document a widely operating system of values.

The emergence of ethnicity

One of the characteristics of the traditional archaeology of the early years of this century was to think very easily in ethnic terms when dealing with prehistoric materials. For Gordon Childe it was a relatively straightforward matter to define an archaeological 'culture' in operational terms, and 'cultures' were soon equated with 'peoples'. This approach is well exemplified by Rouse (1972: 62), for whom the first question that the prehistorian attempts to answer by means of his research is: 'Who produced the archaeological remains under study, that is, to which ethnic groups did the producers belong?' It now seems, however, that ethnicity should not be treated as a given, something universal to all human societies. As noted earlier, it is very much a matter for investigation, and one of the most important consequences of the PPI approach may be the framework which it offers for this, whether in state or in non-state societies.

In talking of ethnicity, we are talking of groups which recognise themselves as distinct, of what may be regarded as a cultural interpretation of descent. It is convenient to use the definition offered by the Russian ethnologist, Dragadze (1980: 162):

> Ethnos can be defined as a firm aggregate of people, historically established on a given territory, possessing in common relatively stable particularities of language and culture, and also recognising their unity and differences from other similar formations (self-awareness) and expressing this in a self-appointed name.

It should, however, be noted that *ethnicity is a matter of degree*. Some ethnic groups are very conscious of their separateness and emphasise it in all manner of ways, some of them employing material culture, for instance in dress and distinguishing decoration (see Hodder 1982a). But others are less aware of 'belonging' and take no special care to distinguish themselves from other groups. They may not be aware of languages other than their own and may have no special name to distinguish what outsiders—such as colonial administrators or visiting anthropologists—regard as an ethnic group. The West African group known as the LoWiili (Goody 1967) offers a very good example here of what seems to be, to a large extent, an externally bestowed ethnicity.

Ethnic questions and linguistic questions are closely related. But it should be noted that ethnicity does not automatically correlate with language: a single ethnic unit can employ more than one language and several distinct ethnic units can speak the same language.

It is clear that concepts of ethnicity can have a considerable bearing upon the nature and scale of interactions between polities. The Greeks, for instance, distinguished between themselves and others, whom they categorised as 'barbarians'. And 'Greek', at the time in question (for example in the seventh and sixth centuries BC), was purely an ethnic term, the political reality being an assemblage of city states and of various loose tribal groupings, as Snodgrass has discussed (this volume: Ch. 3). These tribes were themselves ethnic groups, within the terms of Dragadze's definition, but collectively they regarded themselves, along with the Greek city states, as sharing a higher-order ethnicity, that of being Greek. It was this, for instance, which conferred the right of participating in pan-Hellenic festivals such as the Olympic games.

Here, then, at this time, we see what appears to have been (and was certainly then interpreted as) a pre-existing ethnic grouping, which certainly had a determining role in determining the nature of the PPI which took place. Indeed, at this time the city state in the Aegean was (in ethnic terms) essentially a Greek phenomenon.

Yet if we go back to an earlier era, it is likely that we shall come ultimately to a time, perhaps in the Neolithic period, when there were no ethnic groupings of comparable scale in the area. Ethnicity is thus likely to have grown up partly as a result of patterns of prolonged interaction, which we can regard as one kind of PPI, although occurring long before the formation of the city states. The discussion at this point cannot be separated from linguistic problems. For if one were to accept the notion of the 'coming of the Greeks', one might well imagine that many basic elements of Greek ethnicity were pre-formed, as it were, outside the Aegean region and brought thither by an intrusive, Greek-speaking population. The alternative view of the Greek language would be that it developed within the Aegean, by a process of differentiation, from a pre-existing, Indo-European linguistic base.

These are complicated issues, not to be resolved in an Epilogue, still less in a Prospect. But the discussion does illustrate, we hope, whatever view be taken of the Greek case itself, that the causal links can operate in either direction. In some cases, where well-defined ethnic groups already exist, the ethnic background is likely to have a significant role in shaping the subsequent patterns of interaction (as in Greece in the first millennium BC). In other cases, where the degree of ethnicity is very much less, or virtually non-existent, it is the patterns of interaction which are themselves, in some cases, likely to have been decisive in the process of ethnic formation. It is not difficult to imagine the Corded Ware network or the Beaker network acting in this way. It may be, indeed, that some of the 'core areas' identified by Bradley and Chapman (this volume: Ch. 10) came ultimately to have an ethnic identity. Their own formation may well have been through a process of PPI.

These at present seem very hypothetical matters. But this is not necessarily because they are not susceptible to archaeological investigation. There must indeed be relationships between the extent of ethnic units and of style zones, as they can be determined by careful examination of the variation and distribution of artefactual forms, decorative forms and by other aspects of material culture. The trouble is that earlier workers have often not seen this as a difficult area of discussion where the relevant questions require very careful formulation. All too frequently they have assumed the existence of ethnic units, and even defined their extent, without examining the underlying concepts with sufficient care. It is our hope that questions of ethnic formation can, in favourable instances, be approached archaeologically and that the PPI concept may offer a preliminary framework, in some cases, for that undertaking.

Travel in the ancient world

A final question which, in the light of the discussions in this book, certainly merits further investigation, is the actual mechanism of contact involved in the interactions between the polities under review. A polity, as defined here, is a spatially well-defined entity. Interactions between polities imply action at a distance. In some cases, of course, traded goods may in themselves be highly significant in the interactions, carrying a symbolic message with them. This must have been so in the case of the networks considered above. It would hold for the development of coinage, where knowledge of the use of coins may well have travelled with coins themselves. It might well be true, also, when new commodities were introduced—not necessarily new materials, but materials which for the first time came to be regarded as substances of value.

Even in these cases, however, the traded goods do not move of their own accord. It is necessary to consider in some detail the movements of the traders who carried them.

In some of the cases under discussion, however, we have not been talking here of traded goods or other movable objects, but of major monuments and other localised features.

In such cases we need to enquire very much more closely into the nature of the 'interaction'. Who was doing the travelling? Who was bringing back word of what other polities were doing and thus propagating knowledge of significant innovations? In some cases, no doubt, the informants were traders or others motivated by the acquisition of resources not locally available. But these were probably not the most influential of travellers. The travels of the decision-makers may have been more important, some undertaken, no doubt, in the course of arranging marriage alliances, or simply in gift exchange.

Naturally, for the historical period, there are rich written sources, and we know a good deal of the geography of the Classical world from the *periploi* of early traders and the early geographers themselves. In the first millennium AD the travels of early missionaries and of Church officials may have been highly significant. It has always seemed to us a remarkable thing that King Alfred the Great, king of Wessex in southern England from 871 AD, should have visited Rome in his childhood. In such cases as this the locus of PPI at the individual level may not be difficult to recognise.

In earlier times, too, there are sometimes signs of considerable mobility, as indicated already for the Later Neolithic period of north-western Europe by Bradley and Chapman (this volume: Ch. 10). Where major ritual sites are involved, as in this case, it may not be inappropriate to think in terms of early pilgrimages (see Renfrew 1985: 255). In any case, the question of travel, in non-hierarchical as well as hierarchical societies, is an important one which seems to have been considered relatively little. Yet when we are talking about the way symbolic structures in one polity had an influence upon those of another, the existence of interaction and its mechanism is of crucial relevance. Here again the existence of meeting places at the supra-polity level is an important theme: we have already seen the major role played by Delphi, Olympia and the other pan-Hellenic sanctuaries within the Greek world. It is a matter for investigation how far comparable mechanisms operated in other cultures.

A.C.R.

The contentious nature of the questions spelt out here illustrates how much we have still to learn, not only about the subject matter of archaeology, but also about the most appropriate ways of tackling the problems. In many cases a necessary first step is the reformulation of those problems in such a way that data can be sought which will be relevant to them. But at least we are now beginning to see that the problems do exist and that some of the assumptions made by earlier workers have served to obscure rather than clarify them.

It is on this note that we would like to leave the reader: with an acute sense of problem, yet with the clear and optimistic feeling that the basic materials of archaeology can in some cases provide data that are capable of answering such issues. We would like to see this as an open-ended book. Not a great deal has been proved, but some issues have, we hope, been clarified and perhaps a framework established by which some of them may be approached. We hope that it will indeed prove to be a Prologue to further work.

BIBLIOGRAPHY

Adams, R. E. W. 1977a. *Prehistoric Mesoamerica*. Boston, Little, Brown and Company.
  1977b. Comments on the glyphic texts of the 'Altar vase'. In N. Hammond (ed.), *Social Process in Maya Prehistory*, pp. 412–20. London, Academic Press.
Adams, R. E. W., Brown, W. E. Jr. and Culbert, T. P. 1981. Radar mapping, archaeology, and ancient Maya land use. *Science* 213: 1457–63.
Adams, R. E. W. and Smith, W. D. 1981. Feudal models for Classic Maya civilisation. In W. Ashmore (ed.), *Lowland Maya Settlement Patterns*, pp. 335–49. Albuquerque, University of New Mexico Press.
Adams, R. McC. 1974. Anthropological reflections on ancient trade. *Current Anthropology* 15: 239–58.
  1975. The emerging place of trade in civilizational studies. In J. A. Sabloff and C. C. Lamberg-Karlovsky (eds.), *Ancient Civilisation and Trade*, pp. 451–66. Albuquerque, University of New Mexico Press.
Adcock, F. E. 1957. *The Greek and Macedonian Art of War*. Berkeley and Los Angeles, University of California Press.
Addyman, P. V. 1972. The Anglo-Saxon house: a new review. *Anglo-Saxon England* 1: 273–307.
Alcock, L. 1972. *Arthur's Britain*. Harmondsworth, Penguin.
Alden, J. 1979. A reconstruction of Toltec period political units in the Valley of Mexico. In C. Renfrew and K. L. Cooke (eds.), *Transformations: Mathematical Approaches to Culture Change*, pp. 169–200. New York, Academic Press.
Alexiou, S. 1979. Teiche kai akropoleis ste minoike Krete. *Kretologia* 8: 41–56.
Allen, D. F. 1980. *The Coins of the Ancient Celts*. Edinburgh, University Press.
Allen, P. M. 1982. The genesis of structure in social systems: the

paradigm of self-organisation. In C. Renfrew, M. J. Rowlands and B. A. Segraves (eds.), *Theory and Explanation in Archaeology: The Southampton Conference*, pp. 347–76. New York, Academic Press.
Ammerman, A. J. and Cavalli-Sforza, L. L. 1979. A population model for the diffusion of early farming in Europe. In C. Renfrew and K. L. Cooke (eds.), *Transformations: Mathematical Approaches to Culture Change*, pp. 275–94. New York, Academic Press.
Anderson, J. K. 1954. A topographical and historical study of Achaea. *Annual of the British School of Archaeology at Athens* 49: 72–92.
Andreou, S. 1978. Pottery Groups of the Old Palace Period in Crete. Ph.D. Dissertation, University of Cincinnati.
Andrews, A. P. 1981. El 'Guerrero' de Loltun: commentario analitico. *Boletin de la Escuela de Ciencias Antropologicas de la Universidad de Yucatan* 48–9: 36–50.
Andrews, A. P. and Robles C. F. 1984. Chichen Itza and Coba: an Itza-Maya standoff. In A. Chase and P. Rice (eds.), *Lowland Maya Postclassic: Questions and Answers*, pp. 62–72. Austin, University of Texas Press.
Andrews, E. W. IV 1965. Archaeology and prehistory in the northern Maya lowlands. In G. Willey (vol. ed.), *Handbook of Middle American Indians, Vol. II*, pp. 288–330. Austin, University of Texas Press.
  1973. The Development of Maya civilization after the abandonment of the southern cities. In T. P. Culbert (ed.), *The Classic Maya Collapse*, pp. 243–68. Albuquerque, University of New Mexico Press.
Andrews, E. W. V 1981. Dzibilchaltun. In J. A. Sabloff (vol. ed.), *Supplement to the Handbook of Middle American Indians, Vol. I: Archaeology*, pp. 113–41. Austin, University of Texas Press.

Arnold, C. J. 1980. Wealth and social structure: a matter of life and death. In P. Rahtz, T. Dickinson, and L. Watts (eds.), *Anglo-Saxon Cemeteries 1979* (BAR 82), pp. 81–142. Oxford, British Archaeological Reports.

1982. Stress as a stimulus for socio-economic change: Anglo-Saxon England in the seventh century. In C. Renfrew and S. Shennan (eds.), *Ranking, Resource and Exchange*, pp. 124–31. Cambridge, University Press.

Arnold, C. J. and Wardle, P. J. 1981. Early medieval settlement patterns in England. *Medieval Archaeology* 25: 145–9.

Asch, D. L., Farnsworth, K. B. and Asch, N. B. 1979. Woodland subsistence and settlement in west-central Illinois. In D. Brose and N. Greber (eds.), *Hopewell Archaeology: The Chillicothe Conference*, pp. 80–5. Kent, Ohio, Kent State University Press.

Ashmore, P. 1981. Callanish. *Discovery and Excavation in Scotland (1981)*: 49–50.

Aston, W. G. 1896. *Nihongi: Chronicles of Japan from the Earliest Times to AD 697*. Tokyo, Tuttle (1972).

Atkinson, R. J. C. 1956. *Stonehenge*. London, Hamish Hamilton.

Baby, R. S. and Langlois, S. M. 1979. Seip Mound State Memorial: nonmortuary aspects of Hopewell. In D. Brose and N. Greber (eds.), *Hopewell Archaeology: The Chillicothe Conference*, pp. 16–18. Kent, Ohio, Kent State University Press.

Ball, J. W. 1977. The rise of the northern Maya chiefdoms: a socioprocessual analysis. In R. E. W. Adams (ed.), *The Origins of Maya Civilisation*, pp. 101–32. Albuquerque, University of New Mexico Press.

Barlett, P. F. (ed.). 1980. *Agricultural Decision-Making*. New York, Academic Press.

Barnes, G. L. 1978. The Yamato state: steps towards a developmental understanding. *Bulletin of the Indo-Pacific Prehistory Association* 1: 103–28.

1983. Yayoi–Kofun Settlement Archaeology in the Nara Basin, Japan. Ph.D. Dissertation, University of Michigan. Ann Arbor, University Microfilms. To be published as *Protohistoric Yamato*, Museum of Anthropology and Center for Japanese Studies, University of Michigan.

in press. The role of the *be* in state formation. In T. Earle and E. Brumfiel (eds.), *Production, Exchange and Complex Societies*. Cambridge, University Press.

Barnes, J. A. 1969. Graph theory and social networks: a technical comment on connectedness and connectivity. *Sociology* 3: 215–32.

Baudez, C. F. and Mathews, P. M. 1979. Capture and sacrifice at Palenque. In M. G. Robertson (ed.), *Tercera Mesa Redonda de Palenque*, Vol. IV, pp. 31–40. Palenque (Chiapas, Mexico), Pre-Columbian Art Center.

Beeser, J. 1983. Der kouro-keltos von Hirschlanden. *Fundberichte aus Baden-Württemberg* 8: 21–46.

Bender, B. 1978. Gatherer–hunter to farmer: a social perspective. *World Archaeology* 10: 204–22.

1982. Emergent tribal formations in eastern North America: a study in gatherer–hunter intensification. Paper presented at the annual meeting of the Society for American Archaeology, Minneapolis, Minnesota.

Benn, D. W. 1978. The Woodland ceramic sequence in the culture history of northeastern Iowa. *Midcontinental Journal of Archaeology* 3: 215–83.

Bennet, D. J. L. in prep. Archaeological and Textual Approaches to the Structure of the Administration of Late Minoan II-III Crete. Ph.D. Dissertation in preparation, University of Cambridge.

Berlin, H. 1962. The Palenque Triad. *Journal de la Société des Americanistes* n.s. 52: 91–9.

Berve, H. and Gruben, G. 1963. *Greek Temples, Theatres and Shrines*. London, Thames and Hudson.

Betancourt, P. (ed.) 1984. *The Scope and Extent of the Mycenaean Empire* (Temple University Aegean Symposium 9). Philadelphia, Temple University.

Betts, J. H. 1967. New light on the Minoan bureaucracy. *Kadmos* 6: 15–40.

Biddle, M. 1975. 'Felix urbs Winthoniae': Winchester in the age of monastic reform. In D. Parsons (ed.), *Tenth-Century Studies*, pp. 123–40. Chichester, Phillimore.

1976. The towns. In D. M. Wilson (ed.), *The Archaeology of Anglo-Saxon England*, pp. 99–150. London, Methuen.

Biel, J. 1982. Ein Fürstengrabhügel der späten Hallstattzeit bei Eberdingen-Hochdorf, Kr. Ludwigsburg (Baden-Württemberg). *Germania* 60 (1): 61–104.

Bikaki, A. 1984. *Ayia Irini: The Potters' Marks* (Keos IV). Mainz-on-Rhine, Philipp von Zabern.

Bill, J. 1973. *Die Glockenbecherkultur und die frühe Bronzezeit im französischen Rhonebecken und ihre Beziehungen zur Südwestschweiz*. Basel, Schweizerische Gesellschaft für Ur- und Frühgeschichte.

Binford, L. R., 1962. Archaeology as anthropology. *American Antiquity* 28: 217–25.

1965. Archaeological systematics and the study of culture process. *American Antiquity* 31: 203–10.

1977a General introduction. In L. R. Binford (ed.), *For Theory Building in Archaeology*, pp. 1–10. New York, Academic Press.

1977b Historical archaeology: is it historical or archaeological? In L. Ferguson (ed.), *Historical Archaeology and the Importance of Material Things* (The Society of Historical Archaeology Special Publication Series, 2), pp. 13–21. Charleston, South Carolina, The Society for Historical Archaeology.

1978. *Nunamiut Ethnoarchaeology*. New York, Academic Press.

1981. *Bones: Ancient Men and Modern Myths*. New York, Academic Press.

1983. (ed. J. F. Cherry and R. Torrence). *In Pursuit of the Past: Decoding the Archaeological Record*. London, Thames and Hudson.

Binford, L. R. and Sabloff, J. A. 1982. Paradigms, systematics and archaeology, *Journal of Anthropological Research* 38: 137–53.

Bintliff, J. L. 1977. New approaches to human geography. Prehistoric Greece: a case study. In F. Carter (ed.), *An Historical Geography of the Balkans*, pp. 59–114. London, Academic Press.

1984. Structuralism and myth in Minoan studies. *Antiquity* 58: 33–8.

Black, D. B. 1979. Adena and Hopewell relations in the lower Hocking valley. In D. Brose and N. Greber (eds.), *Hopewell Archaeology: The Chillicothe Conference*, pp. 19–26. Kent, Ohio, Kent State University Press.

Blackburn, T. C. 1976. Ceremonial integration and social interaction in aboriginal California. In L. J. Bean and T. C. Blackburn (eds.), *Native Californians: A Theoretical Retrospective*, pp. 225–43. Ramona, California, Ballena Press.

Bloch, M. 1975. Property and the end of affinity. In M. Bloch (ed.), *Marxist Analyses and Social Anthropology*, pp. 203–28. London, Malaby Press.

Boissevain, J. and Mitchell, J. C. (eds.) 1973. *Network Analysis Studies in Human Interaction*. The Hague, Mouton.

Bonfante, L. 1980. *Out of Etruria: Etruscan Influence North and South* (BAR S103). Oxford, British Archaeological Reports.

Bonís, E. B. 1969. *Die Spätkeltische Siedlung Gellerthegy-Taban in Budapest* (Archaeologia Hungarica 47). Budapest, Akadémiai Kiadó.

Bradley, R. J. 1978. *The Prehistoric Settlement of Britain*. London, Routledge and Kegan Paul.

1981. 'Various styles of urn'–cemeteries and settlement in southern England c. 1400–1000 BC. In R. W. Chapman, I. A. Kinnes and K. Randsborg (eds.), *The Archaeology of Death*, pp. 93–104. Cambridge, University Press.

1982. Position and possession: assemblage variation in the British Neolithic. *Oxford Journal of Archaeology* 1: 27–38.

1984. *Social Foundations of Prehistoric Britain.* Harlow. Longman.

Bradley, R. J. and Chapman, R. W. 1984. Passage Graves in the European Neolithic: a theory of converging evolution. In G. Burenhult (ed.), *The Archaeology of Carrowmore* (Theses and Papers in North European Archaeology 14), pp. 348–56. Stockholm.

Bradley, R. and Ellison, A. 1975. *Rams Hill: A Bronze Age Defended Enclosure and its Landscape* (BAR 19). Oxford, British Archaeological Reports.

Braithwaite, M. n.d. Prestige, ritual and social change. Paper presented at the conference 'The Neolithic and Early Bronze Age in Southern England–Recent Applications of Theory and Methodology', Cardiff, March 1983.

Branigan, K. 1965. The origin of the hieroglyphic sign 18. *Kadmos* 4: 81–3.

1966. Byblite daggers in Cyprus and Crete. *American Journal of Archaeology* 70: 123–6.

1968. *Copper and Bronze Working in Early Bronze Age Crete* (Studies in Mediterranean Archaeology 19). Göteborg, Paul Åström.

1969. The earliest Minoan scripts: the pre-palatial background. *Kadmos* 8: 1–22.

1970. *The Foundations of Palatial Crete: A Survey of Crete in the Early Bronze Age.* London, Routledge and Kegan Paul.

1973. Crete, the Levant and Egypt in the early second millennium BC. *Proceedings of the Third International Cretological Congress* (Rethymnon, 1971), Vol. I, pp. 22–7. Athens.

1981. Minoan colonialism. *Annual of the British School of Archaeology at Athens* 76: 23–33.

Braudel, F. 1975. *The Mediterranean and the Mediterranean World in the Age of Philip II.* London, Fontana.

Braun, D. P. 1977. Middle Woodland–Early Late Woodland Social Change in the Prehistoric Central Midwestern US. Ph.D. Dissertation, University of Michigan. Ann Arbor, University Microfilms.

1979. Illinois Hopewell burial practices and social organization: a re-examination of the Klunk-Gibson mound group. In D. Brose and N. Greber (eds.), *Hopewell Archaeology: The Chillicothe Conference*, pp. 66–79. Kent, Ohio, Kent State University Press.

1981a. Illinois Woodland social change as organizational transformation. Paper presented at the annual meeting of the Society for American Archaeology, San Diego, California.

1981b. A critique of some recent North American mortuary studies. *American Antiquity* 46: 398–416.

1983. Pots as tools. In J. Moore and A. Keene (eds.), *Archaeological Hammers and Theories*, pp. 107–34. New York, Academic Press.

1985. Absolute seriation: a time-series approach. In C. Carr (ed.), *For Concordance in Archaeological Analysis: Bridging Data Structure, Quantitative Technique, and Theory*, pp. 509–39. Kansas City, Missouri, Westport Publishers.

Braun, D. P., Griffin, J. B. and Titterington, P. F., 1982. *The Snyders Mounds and Five Other Mound Groups in Calhoun County, Illinois* (University of Michigan Museum of Anthropology Technical Report 13). Ann Arbor, University of Michigan Museum of Anthropology.

Braun, D. P. and Plog, S. 1982. Evolution of 'tribal' social networks: theory and prehistoric North American evidence. *American Antiquity* 47: 504–25.

Bricker, V. R. 1983. Directional glyphs in Maya inscriptions and codices. *American Antiquity* 48 (2): 347–53.

Brooks, N. 1971. The development of military obligations in eighth- and ninth-century England. In P. Clemoes and K. Hughes (eds.), *England before the Conquest*, pp. 69–84. Cambridge, University Press.

Brose, D. S. 1979. A speculative model of the role of exchange in the prehistory of the eastern Woodlands. In D. Brose and N. Greber (eds.), *Hopewell Archaeology: The Chillicothe Conference*, pp. 3–8. Kent, Ohio, Kent State University Press.

Brose, D. S. and Greber, N. (eds.) 1979. *Hopewell Archaeology: The Chillicothe Conference.* Kent, Ohio, Kent State University Press.

Brown, J. A. 1977. Current directions in midwestern archaeology. *Annual Reviews in Anthropology* 6: 161–79.

1979. Charnel houses and mortuary crypts: disposal of the dead in the Middle Woodland period. In D. Brose and N. Greber (eds.), *Hopewell Archaeology: The Chillicothe Conference*, pp. 211–19. Kent, Ohio, Kent State University Press.

1981. The search for rank in prehistoric burials. In R. Chapman, I. Kinnes, and K. Randsborg (eds.), *The Archaeology of Death*, pp. 25–37. Cambridge, University Press.

Buikstra, J. E. 1976. *Hopewell in the Lower Illinois Valley: A Regional Study of Human Biological Variability and Prehistoric Mortuary Behavior* (Northwestern University Archaeological Program Scientific Papers 2). Evanston, Northwestern University Archaeological Program.

1977. Biocultural dimensions of archaeological study: a regional perspective. In R. L. Blakely (ed.), *Biocultural Adaptation in Prehistoric America* (Southern Anthropological Society Proceedings 11), pp. 67–84. Athens, Georgia, University of Georgia Press.

1979. Contributions of physical anthropologists to the concept of Hopewell: a historical perspective. In D. Brose and N. Greber (eds.), *Hopewell Archaeology: The Chillicothe Conference*, pp. 220–33. Kent, Ohio, Kent State University Press.

Burgess, C. B. 1980. *The Age of Stonehenge.* London, Kent.

Burgess, C. B. and Shennan, S. J. 1976. The beaker phenomenon: some suggestions. In C. B. Burgess and R. Miket (eds.), *Settlement and Economy in the Third and Second Millennia BC* (BAR 33), pp. 309–31. Oxford, British Archaeological Reports.

Burl, A. 1981. By the light of the cinerary moon: chambered tombs and the astronomy of death. In C. Ruggles and A. Whittle (eds.), *Astronomy and Society in Britain during the Period 4000–1500 bc* (BAR 88), pp. 243–74. Oxford, British Archaeological Reports.

Butler, B. M. 1979. Hopewellian contacts in southern Middle Tennessee. In D. Brose and N. Greber (eds.), *Hopewell Archaeology: The Chillicothe Conference*, pp. 150–6. Kent, Ohio, Kent State University Press.

Butler, J. J. and van der Waals, J. D. 1966. Bell Beakers and early metal working in the Netherlands. *Palaeohistoria* 12: 41–139.

Cadogan, G. 1976. *Palaces of Minoan Crete.* London, Barrie and Jenkins.

1983. Early Minoan and Middle Minoan chronology. *American Journal of Archaeology* 87 (4): 507–18.

Caldwell, J. A. 1964. Interaction spheres in prehistory. In J. R. Caldwell and R. L. Hall (eds.), *Hopewellian Studies* (Illinois State Museum Papers 12, No. 6), 133–43.

Campbell, J. (ed.) 1982. *The Anglo-Saxons.* London, Phaidon.

Carneiro, R. L. 1970. A theory of the origin of the state. *Science* 169: 733–8.

1977. Comment on B. Price, Shifts in production and organization: a cluster-interaction model. *Current Anthropology* 18: 222–3.

Cartledge, P. 1983. 'Trade and politics' revisited: Archaic Greece. In P.D.A. Garnsey, K. Hopkins and C. R. Whittaker (eds.), *Trade in the Ancient Economy*, pp. 1–15. London, Chatto and Windus.

Catherall, P. 1971. Henges in perspective, *Archaeological Journal* 51: 177–239.

Catling, H.W. and Karageorghis, V. 1960. Minoika in Cyprus. *Annual of the British School of Archaeology at Athens* 55: 108–27.

Catling, H. W. and MacGillivray, J. A. 1984. An Early Cypriot III vase from the palace at Knossos. *Annual of the British School of Archaeology at Athens* 78: 1–8.

Chadwick, J. 1972. The Mycenaean documents. In W. A. McDonald and

G. R. Rapp Jr. (eds.), *The Minnesota Messenia Expedition: Reconstructing a Bronze Age Regional Environment*, pp. 100–16. Minneapolis, University of Minnesota Press.

1976. *The Mycenaean World*. Cambridge, University Press.

Champion, S. T. 1982. Exchange and ranking: the case of coral. In C. Renfrew and S. Shennan (eds.), *Ranking, Resource and Exchange*, pp. 67–72. Cambridge, University Press.

Champion, T. 1985. Written sources and the study of the European Iron Age. In T. C. Champion and J. V. S. Megaw (eds.), *Settlement and Society: Aspects of West European Prehistory in the First Millennium BC*, pp. 10–25. Leicester, Leicester, University Press.

Chaney, W. 1973. *The Cult of Kingship in Anglo-Saxon England*. Manchester, University Press.

Chang, K.-C. 1980. *Shang Civilization*. New Haven, Yale University Press.

Chapman, C. H. 1980. *The Archaeology of Missouri*, Vol. II. Columbia, University of Missouri Press.

Chapman, R. W. 1982. Autonomy, ranking and resources in Iberian prehistory. In C. Renfrew and S. Shennan (eds.), *Ranking, Resource and Exchange*, pp. 46–51. Cambridge, University Press.

Chapoutier, F. 1930. *Les Ecritures minoennes au palais de Mallia* (Etudes crétoises 11). Paris. L'Ecole française d'Athènes.

Charles, D. K. 1982. Subsistence-settlement in west-central Illinois: contributions from the archaeology of mortuary sites. Paper presented at the annual meeting of the Society for American Archaeology, Minneapolis, Minnestoa.

Cherry, C. 1978. *On Human Communication: A Review, a Survey, and a Criticism* (3rd edn). Cambridge, Mass., MIT Press.

Cherry, J. F. 1977. Investigating the political geography of an early state by multidimensional scaling of Linear B data. In J. L. Bintliff (ed.), *Mycenaean Geography*, pp. 76–83. Cambridge, British Association for Mycenaean Studies.

1978. Generalisation and the archaeology of the state. In D. Green, C. Haselgrove and M. Spriggs (eds.), *Social Organisation and Settlement* (BAR S47), pp. 411–37. Oxford, British Archaeological Reports.

1980. Diachronic Island Archaeology in the Aegean: A Case Study on Melos. Ph.D. Dissertation, University of Southampton.

1981. Pattern and process in the earliest colonisation of the Mediterranean islands. *Proceedings of the Prehistoric Society* 47: 41–68.

1983a. Evolution, revolution and the origins of complex society in Minoan Crete. In O. Krzyszkowska and L. Nixon (eds.), *Minoan Society*, pp. 33–45. Bristol, Bristol Classical Press.

1983b. Putting the best foot forward. *Antiquity* 57: 52–6.

1984. The emergence of the state in the prehistoric Aegean. *Proceedings of the Cambridge Philological Society* 30: 18–48.

Childe, V. G. 1936. *Man Makes Himself*. London, Watts.

1940. *Prehistoric Communities of the British Isles*. London, W. and R. Chambers.

1956. *Piecing Together the Past*. London, Routledge and Kegan Paul.

1957. *The Dawn of European Civilisation*. London, Routledge and Kegan Paul.

Claessen, H. J. M. 1984. The internal dynamics of the early state. *Current Anthropology* 25. 365–79.

Claessen, H. J. M. and Skalník, P. (eds.) 1978. *The Early State*. The Hague, Mouton.

1981. *The Study of the State*. The Hague, Mouton.

Clarke, D. L. 1968. *Analytical Archaeology*. London, Methuen.

1970. *Beaker Pottery of Great Britain and Ireland*. Cambridge, University Press.

1976. The beaker network–social and economic models. In J. N. Lanting and J. D. van der Waals (eds.),

Glockenbechersymposion, Oberried 1974, pp. 459–76. Bussum–Haarlem, Fibula–van Dishoeck.

1977. Spatial information in archaeology. In D. L. Clarke (ed.), *Spatial Archaeology*, pp. 1–32. London, Academic Press.

1978. *Analytical Archaeology* (2nd edn., revised by R. Chapman). London, Methuen.

Coe, M. D. 1978. *Lords of the Underworld: Masterpieces of Classic Maya Ceramics*. Princeton, University Press.

1981. Religion and the rise of Mesoamerican states. In G. D. Jones and R. R. Kautz (eds.), *The Transition to Statehood in the New World*, pp. 157–71. Cambridge, University Press.

Coe, W. R. 1965. Tikal: ten years of study of a Maya ruin in the lowlands of Guatemala. *Expedition* 8(1): 5–56.

Coe, W. R. and Shook, E. M. 1961. *The Carved Wooden Lintels of Tikal* (Tikal Report 6). Philadelphia, The University of Pennsylvania Museum.

Coggins, C. C. 1975. Painting and Drawing Styles at Tikal. Ph.D. Dissertation, Harvard University.

1979. A new order and the role of the calendar: some characteristics of the Middle Classic period at Tikal. In N. Hammond and G. R. Willey (eds.), *Maya Archaeology and Ethnohistory*, pp. 38–50. Austin, University of Texas Press.

Cohen, A. 1974. *Two-Dimensional Man: An Essay on the Anthropology of Power and Symbolism in Complex Society*. London, Routledge and Kegan Paul.

Collis, J. R. 1975. *Defended Sites of the Late La Tène* (BAR S2). Oxford, British Archaeological Reports.

1976. Town and market in Iron Age Europe. In B. Cunliffe and T. Rowley (eds.), *Oppida: the Beginnings of Urbanisation in Barbarian Europe* (BAR S11), pp. 3–23. Oxford, British Archaeological Reports

Cooke, K. L. and Renfrew, C. 1979. An experiment in the simulation of culture changes. In C. Renfrew and K. L. Cooke (eds.), *Transformations: Mathematical Approaches to Culture Change*, pp. 327–48. New York, Academic Press.

Cowgill, G. L. 1979. Teotihuacan, internal militaristic competition, and the Fall of the Classic Maya. In N. Hammond and G. R. Willey (eds.), *Maya Archaeology and Ethnohistory*, pp. 51–62. Austin, University of Texas Press.

Cramp, R. 1976. Monastic sites. In D. M. Wilson (ed.), *The Archaeology of Anglo-Saxon England*, pp. 201–52. London, Methuen.

Culbert, T. P. 1977. Maya development and collapse: an economic perspective. In N. Hammond (ed.), *Social Process in Maya Prehistory*, pp. 509–30. London, Academic Press.

Dalton, G. 1975. Karl Polanyi's analysis of long-distance trade and his wider paradigm. In J. A. Sabloff and C. C. Lamberg-Karlovsky (eds.), *Ancient Civilization and Trade*, pp. 63–132. Albuquerque, University of New Mexico Press.

1977. Aboriginal economies in stateless societies. In T. K. Earle and J. E. Ericson (eds.), *Exchange Systems in Prehistory*, pp. 191–229. New York, Academic Press.

Dämmer, H.-W. 1978. *Die bemalte Keramik der Heuneburg* (Römisch-Germanische Forschungen 37). Mainz, Philipp von Zabern.

Date, M. 1963. Iseki bumpu yori mita kodai chiiki no kosai: Nara bonchi no baai (Treatise on protohistoric regionalism as seen in the distribution of archaeological sites: the case of the Nara Basin). In Kashiwara Kokogaku Kenkyujo (ed.), *Kinki Kobunka Ronko*, pp. 51–84. Tokyo, Yoshikawa Kobunkan.

Davies, W. and Vierck, H. 1974. The contexts of Tribal Hidage: social aggregates and settlement patterns. *Frühmittelalterliche Studien* 8: 223–93.

Davis, D. D. 1983. Investigating the diffusion of stylistic innovation. In M. B. Schiffer (ed.), *Advances in Archaeological Method and Theory*, Vol. VI, pp. 53–89. New York, Academic Press.

Davis, E. N. 1979. The silver kantharos from Gournia. In P. Betancourt (ed.), *Gournia, Crete: The 75th Anniversary of the Excavations*

(Temple University Aegean Symposium 4), pp. 34–45. Philadelphia, Temple University.

Davis, R. H. 1982. Alfred and Guthrum's frontier. *English Historical Review* 97: 803–10.

De Atley, S. P. and Findlow, F. J. (eds.) 1984. *Exploring the Limits: Frontiers and Boundaries in Prehistory* (BAR S223). Oxford, British Archaeological Reports.

Deevey, E. S., Rice, D. S., Rice, P. M., Vaughan, H. H., Brenner, M. and Flannery, M. S. 1979. Mayan urbanism: impact on a tropical karst environment. *Science* 206: 298–306.

Demarest, A. A. 1978. Interregional conflict and 'situational ethics' in Classic Maya warfare. In M. Giardino, B. Edmunson and W. Creamer (eds.), *Codex Wauchope: A Tribute Roll*, pp. 101–11. New Orleans, Human Mosaic, Tulane University.

Deuel, T. 1952. The Hopewellian community. In T. Deuel (ed.), *Hopewellian Communities in Illinois* (Illinois State Museum Scientific Papers 5), pp. 249–70. Springfield, Illinois, Illinois State Museum.

Dinsmoor, W. B. 1950. *The Architecture of Ancient Greece.* London, Batsford.

Dixon, P. 1982. How Saxon is the Saxon house? In P. J. Drury (ed.), *Structural Reconstruction: Approaches to the Interpretation of the Excavated Remains of Buildings* (BAR 110), pp. 275–88. Oxford, British Archaeological Reports.

Doumas, C. (ed.) 1978. *Thera and the Aegean World*, Vol. I. London, Thera and the Aegean World.

Dragadze, T. 1980. The place of 'ethnos' theory in Soviet anthropology. In E. Gellner (ed.), *Soviet and Western Anthropology*, pp. 161–70. London, Duckworth.

Dragoo, D. W. 1964. The development of Adena culture and its role in the formation of Ohio Hopewell. In J. R. Caldwell and R. L. Hall (eds.), *Hopewellian Studies* (Illinois State Museum Scientific Papers 12), pp. 1–34. Springfield, Illinois, Illinois State Museum.

Edmunson, M. S. 1971. *The Book of Counsel: the* Popol Vu *of the Quiche Maya of Guatemala* (Middle American Research Institute Publication 35). New Orleans, Tulane University.

Edwards, I. E. S. 1961. *The Pyramids of Egypt.* Harmondsworth, Penguin.

Egami, N. 1964. The formation of the people and the origin of the state in Japan. *Memoirs of the Research Department of Toyo Bunko* 23: 35–70. Tokyo, Toyo Bunko.

1967. *Kiba Minzoku Kokka: Nihon kodaishi e no apurochi* (The Nation of Horseriders: an Approach to Japanese Protohistory). Tokyo, Chuo Koronsha.

Ehrenberg, V. 1969. *The Greek State* (2nd edn.). London, Metheun.

Ericson, J. E. and Earle, T. K. 1982. *Contexts for Prehistoric Exchange.* New York, Academic Press.

Evans, A. J. 1909. *Scripta Minoa*, Vol. I. Oxford, Clarendon Press.

1921–35. *The Palace of Minos at Knossos*, Vols. I–IV. London, Macmillan.

Evans, J. D. 1971. Neolithic Knossos: the growth of a settlement. *Proceedings of the Prehistoric Society* 37 (Part II): 95–117.

1972. The Early Minoan occupation of Knossos. *Anatolian Studies* 22: 115–28.

1973. Islands as laboratories of culture change. In C. Renfrew (ed.), *The Explanation of Culture Change*, pp. 517–20. London, Duckworth.

Faulkner, C. H. 1968. *The Old Stone Fort.* Knoxville, University of Tennessee Press.

Faure, P. 1969. Sur trois sortes de sanctuaires crétois. *Bulletin de correspondance héllénique* 93: 174–213.

Fiandra, E. 1961–2. I periodi struttivi del primo palazzo di Festos. *Kretika Khronika* IE′–IST′ (A′): 112–26.

1968. A che cosa servivano le cretule di Festos. *Proceedings of the Second International Cretological Congress* (Chania, 1966), Vol. I, pp. 383–97. Athens.

1975. Ancora a proposito delle cretule di Festos: connessione tra i sistemi amministrativi centralizzati e l'uso delle cretule nell'età del bronzo. *Bollettino d'Arte* 60: 1–25.

Fisher, A. R. 1985. The early state module: a critical assessment. *Oxford Journal of Archaeology* 4: 1–8.

Fitting, J. E. and Brose, D. S. 1971. The northern periphery of Adena. In B. K. Swartz (ed.), *Adena: The Seeking of an Identity*, pp. 29–55. Muncie, Indiana, Ball State University Press.

Flannery, K. V. 1968. The Olmec and the Valley of Oaxaca: a model for inter-regional interaction in Formative times. In E. P. Benson (ed.), *Dumbarton Oaks Conference on the Olmec*, pp. 79–110. Washington DC, Dumbarton Oaks.

1972. The cultural evolution of civilisations. *Annual Review of Ecology and Systematics* 3: 399–426.

Flannery, K. V. and Marcus, J. 1976. Formative Oaxaca and the Zapotec cosmos. *American Scientist* 64: 374–83.

Ford, J. A. and Willey, G. 1940. *Crooks Site, A Marksville Period Burial Mound in La Salle Parish, Louisiana* (Louisiana Department of Conservation, Geological Survey, Anthropological Study 3). Baton Rouge, Louisiana Department of Conservation.

Ford, R. I. 1972. Barter, gift, or violence: an analysis of Tewa intertribal exchange. In E. N. Wilmsen (ed.), *Social Exchange and Interaction* (University of Michigan Museum of Anthropology Anthropological Papers 46), pp. 21–45. Ann Arbor, University of Michigan Museum of Anthropology.

1974. Northeastern archaeology: past and future directions. *Annual Review of Anthropology* 3: 385–413.

1977. Evolutionary ecology and the evolution of human ecosystems: a case study from the midwestern USA. In J. N. Hill (ed.), *Explanation of Prehistoric Change*, pp. 153–84. Albuquerque, University of New Mexico Press.

1979. Gathering and gardening: trends and consequences of Hopewell subsistence strategies. In D. Brose and N. Greber (eds.), *Hopewell Archaeology: the Chillicothe Conference*, pp. 234–8. Kent, Ohio, Kent State University Press.

Forrest, W. G. 1957. Colonisation and the rise of Delphi. *Historia* 6: 160–75.

Fowler, M. L. 1957. *Rutherford Mound, Hardin County, Illinois* (Illinois State Museum Scientific Papers 7(1)). Springfield, Illinois, Illinois State Museum.

Frankel, D. 1974. Inter-site relationships in the Middle Bronze Age of Cyprus. *World Archaeology* 6(2): 190–208.

Frankenstein, S. and Rowlands, M. J. 1978. The internal structure and regional context of early Iron Age society in south-western Germany. *Bulletin of the Institute of Archaeology, University of London* 15: 73–112.

Fraser, D. 1983. *Land and Society in Neolithic Orkney* (BAR 117). Oxford, British Archaeological Reports.

Freidel, D. A. 1978. Maritime adaptation and the rise of Maya civilisation: the view from Cerros, Belize. In B. Stark and B. Voorhies (eds.), *Prehistoric Coastal Adaptations*, pp. 239–65. New York, Academic Press.

1981a. Civilisation as a state of mind: the cultural evolution of the lowland Maya. In G. D. Jones and R. R. Kautz (eds.), *The Transition to Statehood in the New World*, pp. 188–227. Cambridge, University Press.

1981b. The political economics of residential dispersion among the lowland Maya. In W. Ashmore (ed.), *Lowland Maya Settlement Patterns*, pp. 371–82. Albuquerque, University of New Mexico Press.

1983. Political systems in lowland Yucatan: dynamics and structure in Maya settlement. In E. Z. Vogt and R. M. Leventhal (eds.), *Prehistoric Settlement Patterns: Essays in Honor of Gordon R. Willey*, pp. 375–86. Albuquerque, University of New Mexico Press.

n.d. The monumental architecture at Cerros. In R. A. Robertson and D. A. Freidel (eds.), *Investigations at Cerros, Belize: An Interim Report*. Dallas, Southern Methodist University.

Freidel, D. A. and Andrews, A. P. n.d. Evidence of kingship in the Late Preclassic Maya lowlands from Loltun Cave, Yucatan. Unpublished paper.

Freidel, D. A., Robertson, R. A. and Cliff, M. B. 1982. The Maya city of Cerros. *Archaeology* 35 (4): 12–21.

Freidel, D. A. and Sabloff, J. A. 1984. *Cozumel: Late Maya Settlement Patterns*. New York, Academic Press.

Freidel, D. A. and Scarborough, V. L. 1982. Subsistence, trade and the development of the coastal Maya. In K. V. Flannery (ed.), *Maya Subsistence: Studies in Memory of Dennis E. Puleston*, pp. 131–55. New York, Academic Press.

Freidel, D. A. and Schele, L. in press. Symbol and power: a history of the lowland Maya cosmogram. Princeton, University Press.

Freidel, D. A. and Sheets, P. D. n.d. Obsidian in the Maya lowlands: utilitarian luxury or ritual necessity. In P. Netherly and D. A. Freidel (eds.), *Pathways to Power: New Models for the Political Economy of Pre-Columbian Polities*.

Frey, M. 1935. Eine spätgallische Töpfersiedlung in Sissach. *Tätigkeitsbericht der naturforschenden Gesellschaft Baselland* 10: 70–82.

Fried, M. H. 1967. *The Evolution of Political Society*. New York, Random House.

1975. *The Notion of Tribe*. Menlo Park, California, Benjamin-Cummings.

Friedman, J. 1982. Catastrophe and continuity in social evolution. In C. Renfrew, M. Rowlands and B. Segraves (eds.), *Theory and Explanation in Archaeology*, pp. 175–9. London, Academic Press.

Friedman, J. and Rowlands, M. J. 1977. Notes towards an epigenetic model of the evolution of 'civilisation'. In J. Friedman and M. J. Rowlands (eds.), *The Evolution of Social Systems*, pp. 201–76. London, Duckworth.

Fritz, J. M. 1978. Palaeopsychology today: ideational systems and human adaptation in prehistory. In C. L. Redman *et al.* (eds.), *Social Archaeology: Beyond Subsistence and Dating*, pp. 37–59. New York, Academic Press.

Fry, R. E. 1979. The economics of pottery at Tikal, Guatemala: models of exchange for serving vessels. *American Antiquity* 44: 494–512.

Fry, R. E. and Cox, S. E. 1974. The structure of ceramic exchange at Tikal, Guatemala. *World Archaeology* 6: 209–55.

Furst, P. D. 1976. Fertility, vision quest and auto-sacrifice: some thoughts on ritual blood-letting among the Maya. In M. G. Robertson (ed.), *The Art, Iconography and Dynastic History of Palenque*, Part III, pp. 181–93. Pebble Beach, California, Pre-Columbian Art Research, the Robert Louis Stevenson School.

Furu Iseki Han'i Kakunin Chosa Iinkai (Committee for the Investigation of the Areal Extent of the Furu Site) (ed.), 1979. *Furu Iseki Han'i Kakunin Chosa Hokokusho* (Report on the Investigation of the Extent of the Furu Site). Nara, Tenri-shi Kyoiku Iinkai.

Gall, P. L. and Saxe, A. A. 1977. The ecological evolution of cultures: the state as predator in succession theory. In T. K. Earle and J. Ericson (eds.), *Exchange Systems in Prehistory*, pp. 255–68. London, Academic Press.

Gallay, A. 1981. Le phénomène campaniforme: une nouvelle hypothèse historique. In R. Menk and A. Gallay (eds.), *Anthropologie et archéologie: le cas des premiers âges des métaux* (Archives suisses d'anthropologie générale 43 (2)), pp. 231–57. Geneva, Département d'anthropologie de l'Université de Genève.

Gersbach, E. 1976. Das Osttor (Donautor) der Heuneberg bei Hundersingen (Donau). *Germania* 54 (1): 17–42.

Gilman, A. 1981. The development of social stratification in Bronze Age Europe. *Current Anthropology* 22: 1–8.

Giot, P., Briard, J. and Pape, L. 1979. *Protohistoire de la Bretagne*. Rennes, Ouest-France.

Gledhill, J. and Rowlands M. 1982. Materialism and socio-economic process in multi-linear evolution. In C. Renfrew and S. Shennan (eds.), *Ranking, Resource and Exchange*, pp. 144–9. Cambridge, University Press.

Godart, L. and Olivier, J.-P. 1976. *Recueil des inscriptions en Linéaire A* (Etudes crétoises 21). Paris, L'Ecole française d'Athènes.

Goody, J. 1967. *The Social Organisation of the LoWiili*. Oxford, University Press.

Gould, P. R. 1969. *Spatial Diffusion* (Association of American Geographers, Commission on College Geography Publications, Resource Paper 4). Washington DC, Association of American Geographers.

Gould, P. and White, R. 1974. *Mental Maps*. Harmondsworth, Penguin.

Graham, I. 1978. *Corpus of Maya Hieroglyphic Inscriptions, Vol. II, Part II: Naranjo, Chunhuitz, Xunantunich*. Cambridge, Mass., Peabody Museum, Harvard University.

Graham, I. and von Euw, E. 1975. *Corpus of Maya Hieroglyphic Inscriptions, Vol. II, Part 1: Naranjo*, Cambridge, Mass., Peabody Museum, Harvard University.

1977. *Corpus of Maya Hieroglyphic Inscriptions, Vol. III, Part 1*. Cambridge, Mass., Peabody Museum, Harvard University.

Graham, J. A. 1973. Aspects of non-Classic presences in the inscriptions and sculptural art of Seibal. In T. P. Culbert (ed.), *The Classic Maya Collapse*, pp. 207–19. Albuquerque, University of New Mexico Press.

Graham, J. W. 1960. The Minoan unit of length and Minoan palace planning. *American Journal of Archaeology* 64: 335–41.

1964. The relation of the Minoan palaces to the Near Eastern palaces of the second millennium. In E. Bennett (ed.), *Mycenaean Studies*, pp. 199–215. Madison, University of Wisconsin Press.

1969. *The Palaces of Crete* (2nd edn.). Princeton, University Press.

Greber, N. 1979a. Variations in social structure of Ohio Hopewell peoples. *Midcontinental Journal of Archaeology* 4: 35–78.

1979b. A comparative study of site morphology and burial patterns at Edwin Harness Mound and Seip Mounds 1 and 2. In D. Brose and N. Greber (eds.), *Hopewell Archaeology: The Chillicothe Conference*, pp. 27–38. Kent, Ohio, Kent State University Press.

Green, S.W. and Perlman, S. M. (eds.) 1985. *The Archaeology of Frontiers and Boundaries*. New York, Academic Press.

Griffin, J. B. 1952. Some early and middle Woodland pottery types in Illinois. In T. Deuel (ed.), *Hopewellian Communities in Illinois* (Illinois State Museum Scientific Papers 5), pp. 93–130. Springfield, Illinois, Illinois State Museum.

1965. Hopewell and the dark black glass. *Michigan Archaeologist* 11 (3–4): 115–55.

1967. Eastern North American archaeology: a summary. *Science* 156: 175–91.

1979. An overview of the Chillicothe Hopewell conference. In D. Brose and N. Greber (eds.), *Hopewell Archaeology: The Chillicothe Conference*, pp. 266–79. Kent, Ohio, Kent State University Press.

Griffin, J. B., Flanders, R. E. and Titterington, P. F. 1970. *The Burial Complexes of the Knight and Norton Mounds in Illinois and Michigan* (University of Michigan Museum of Anthropology Memoir 2). Ann Arbor, University of Michigan Museum of Anthropology.

Griffin, J. B., Gordus, A. A. and Wright, G. A. 1969. Identification of the sources of Hopewellian obsidian in the middle West. *American Antiquity* 34: 1–14.

Gschnitzer, F. 1971. Stadt und Stamm bei Homer. *Chiron* 1: 1–17.

Haas, J. 1982. *The Evolution of the Prehistoric State*. New York, Columbia University Press.

Hägg, R. and Marinatos, N. (eds.) 1984. *The Minoan Thalassocracy:*

Myth and Reality. Stockholm, Swedish Institute of Archaeology at Athens.

in press. *The Function of the Minoan Palaces.* Stockholm, Swedish Institute of Archaeology at Athens.

Haggett, R. and Chorley, R. J. 1969. *Network Analysis in Geography.* London, Edward Arnold.

Hall, R. L. 1977. An anthropocentric perspective for eastern United States prehistory. *American Antiquity* 42: 499–518.

1979. In search of the ideology of the Adena–Hopewell climax. In D. Brose and N. Greber (eds.), *Hopewell Archaeology: The Chillicothe Conference,* pp. 258–65. Kent, Ohio, Kent State University Press.

Hallager, E. 1977. *The Mycenaean Palace at Knossos* (Medelhavsmuseet Memoir 1). Stockholm, Medelhavsmuseet.

Halstead, P. L. J. 1981. From determinism to uncertainty: social storage and the rise of the Minoan palaces. In A. Sheridan and G. Bailey (eds.), *Economic Archaeology: Towards an Integration of Ecological and Social Approaches* (BAR S96), pp. 187–213. Oxford, British Archaeological Reports.

1982. The relevance of evolutionary theory to archaeology. Paper read to the Theoretical Archaeology Group, Durham.

1985. Strategies for Survival: An Economic Approach to Social and Economic Change in the Early Farming Communities of Thessaly, North Greece. Ph.D. Dissertation, University of Cambridge.

Halstead, P. and O'Shea, J. 1982. A friend in need is a friend indeed: social storage and the origins of ranking. In C. Renfrew and S. J. Shennan (eds.), *Ranking, Resource and Exchange: Aspects of the Archaeology of Early European Society,* pp. 92–9. Cambridge, University Press.

Hammond, N. 1982. *Ancient Maya Civilization.* New Brunswick, Rutgers University Press.

Hammond, N. G. L. 1967. *A History of Greece to 322 BC* (2nd edn.). Oxford, Clarendon Press.

Harding, T. G. 1967. *Voyagers of the Vitiaz Strait.* Seattle, University of Washington Press.

Härke, H. G. H. 1979. *Settlement Types and Settlement Patterns in the West Hallstatt Province* (BAR S57). Oxford, British Archaeological Reports.

Harris, M. 1968. *The Rise of Anthropological Theory.* New York, Crowell.

Harrison, P. D. and Turner, B. L. II. (eds.) 1978. *Pre-Hispanic Maya Agriculture.* Albuquerque, University of New Mexico Press.

Harrison, R. J. 1977. *The Bell Beaker Cultures of Spain and Portugal* (American School of Prehistoric Research Bulletin 35). Cambridge, Mass., Peabody Museum of Archaeology and Ethnology.

1980. *The Beaker Folk.* London, Thames and Hudson.

Harrison, R. J. and Gilman, A. 1977. Trade in the second and third millennia BC between the Maghreb and Iberia. In V. Markotic (ed.), *Ancient Europe and the Mediterranean,* pp. 90–104. Warminster, Aris and Phillips.

Helm, J. (ed.) 1968. *Essays on the Problem of the Tribe.* New York, American Ethnological Society.

Henderson, J. S. 1981. *The World of the Ancient Maya.* Ithaca, Cornell University Press.

Henshall, A. 1963. *The Chambered Tombs of Scotland,* Vol. I. Edinburgh, University Press.

Herity, M. 1973. Irish Sea and Scandinavian Passage Graves: some comparisons. In G. Daniel and P. Kjaerum (eds.), *Megalithic Graves and Ritual,* pp. 129–35. Moesgård, Jutland Archaeological Society.

1974. *Irish Passage Graves.* Dublin, Irish Universities Press.

Hester, T. R., Shafer, H. J. and Eaton, J. D. 1982. *Archaeology at Colha, Belize: The 1981 Interim Report.* San Antonio, Center for Archaeological Research, the University of Texas at San Antonio.

Hill, J. N. 1977. Systems theory and the explanation of change. In J. N. Hill (ed.), *Explanation of Prehistoric Change,* pp. 59–104. Albuquerque, University of New Mexico Press.

Hiller, S. 1977. *Das minoische Kreta nach den Ausgrabungen des letzten Jahrzehnts.* Wien, Österreichische Akademie der Wissenschaften.

Hills, C. 1979. The archaeology of Anglo-Saxon England in the pagan period: a review. *Anglo-Saxon England* 8: 297–329.

Himmelmann-Wildschütz, N. 1963. Über einige gegenständliche Bedeutungsmöglichkeiten des frühgriechischen Ornaments. *Abhandlungen der Geistes- und Sozialwissenschaftlichen Klasse, Akademie der Wissenschaften und der Literatur, Mainz* 7: 261–346.

Hirano, K. 1977. The Yamato state and Korea in the fourth and fifth centuries. *Acta Asiatica* 31: 51–82.

Hodder, I. 1977a. Some new directions in the spatial analysis of archaeological data at the regional scale. In D. L. Clarke (ed.), *Spatial Archaeology,* pp. 223–351. London, Academic Press.

1977b. The distribution of material culture items in the Baringo district, W. Kenya. *Man* 12: 239–69.

1978. (ed.). *The Spatial Organisation of Culture.* Cambridge, University Press.

1980. Trade and exchange: definitions, identifications and function. In R. E. Fry (ed.), *Models and Methods in Regional Exchange* (Society for American Archaeology Papers 1), pp. 151–5. Washington DC, Society for American Archaeology.

1982a. *Symbols in Action.* Cambridge, University Press.

1982b. Theoretical archaeology: a reactionary view. In I. Hodder (ed.), *Symbolic and Structural Archaeology,* pp. 1–16. Cambridge, University Press.

Hodges, R. 1982a. *Dark Age Economics.* London, Duckworth.

1982b. Method and theory in medieval archaeology. *Archeologia Medievale* 9: 7–39.

in press. The imported pottery and its European context. In K. Wade, Excavations in Ipswich 1974–78, *East Anglian Archaeology* (forthcoming).

Hodges, R. and Cherry, J. F. 1983. Cost-control and coinage: an archaeological approach to economic change in Anglo-Saxon England. *Research in Economic Anthropology* 5: 131–84.

Hodges, R. and Whitehouse, D. 1983. *Mohammed, Charlemagne and the Origins of Europe.* London, Duckworth.

Hofman, J. L. 1979. Twenhafel, a prehistoric community on the Mississippi, 500 BC–AD 1500. *The Living Museum* 41(3): 34–8.

Hood, M. S. F. 1973. *The Minoans.* London, Thames and Hudson.

1983. The 'country house' and Minoan society. In O. Krzyszkowska and L. Nixon (eds.), *Minoan Society,* pp. 129–35. Bristol, Bristol Classical Press.

Hood, M. S. F. and de Jong, P. 1952. Late Minoan warrior-graves from Ayios Ioannis and the New Hospital site at Knossos. *Annual of the British School of Archaeology at Athens* 47: 243–77.

Hood, M. S. F. and Smyth, D. 1981. *Archaeological Survey of the Knossos Area* (Annual of the British School of Archaeology at Athens, Supplement 14). London, British School of Archaeology at Athens.

Hood, M. S. F. and Taylor, W. 1981. *The Bronze Age Palace at Knossos* (Annual of the British School of Archaeology at Athens, Supplement 13). London, British School of Archaeology at Athens.

Hooker, J. T. 1977. *Mycenaean Greece.* London, Routledge and Kegan Paul.

Hope Simpson, R. and Dickinson, O. T. P. K. 1979. *A Gazetteer of Aegean Civilisation in the Bronze Age, Volume I: The Mainland and the Islands* (Studies in Mediterranean Archaeology 52). Göteborg, Paul Aström.

Hope Simpson, R. and Lazenby, J. F. 1970. *The Catalogue of Ships in Homer's Iliad.* Oxford, Clarendon Press.

Hope-Taylor, B. 1977. *Yeavering: an Anglo-British Centre of Early*

Northumbria. London, Department of the Environment.

Hosler, D., Sabloff, J. A. and Runge, D. 1977. Simulation model development: a case study of the Classic Maya collapse. In N. Hammond (ed.), *Social Process in Maya Prehistory*, pp. 553–90. London, Academic Press.

Hult, G. 1983. *Bronze Age Ashlar Masonry in the Eastern Mediterranean* (Studies in Mediterranean Archaeology 66). Göteborg, Paul Åström.

Irwin-Williams, C. 1977. A network model for the analysis of prehistoric trade. In T. Earle and J. Ericson (eds.), *Exchange Systems in Prehistory*, pp. 141–52. New York, Academic Press.

Isbell, W. H. 1978. Environmental perturbations and the origin of the Andean State. In C. Redman *et al.* (eds.), *Social Archaeology: Beyond Subsistence and Dating*, pp. 303–13. New York, Academic Press.

Jacobi, G. 1974a. *Werkzeug und Gerät aus dem Oppidum von Manching*. Wiesbaden, Franz Steiner.

1974b. Zum Schriftgebrauch in keltischen Oppida nördlich der Alpen. *Hamburger Beiträge zur Archäologie* 4: 171–81.

Jacobsthal, P. 1944. *Early Celtic Art*. Oxford, University Press.

Jefferies, R. W. 1979. The Tunacunnhee site: Hopewell in northwest Georgia. In D. Brose and N. Greber (eds.), *Hopewell Archaeology: The Chillicothe Conference*, pp. 162–70. Kent, Ohio, Kent State University Press.

Jeffery, L. H. 1976. *Archaic Greece: the City-States, c. 700–500 BC*. London, Methuen.

Joffroy, R. 1954. *Le Trésor de Vix (Côte d'Or)* (Monuments et mémoires Piot 48-1). Paris, Presses universitaires de France.

1960. *L'Oppidum de Vix et la civilisation hallstattienne finale dans l'est de la France* (Publications de l'université de Dijon 20). Paris, Société des belles lettres.

Johnson, A. E. 1979. Kansas City Hopewell. In D. Brose and N. Greber (eds.), *Hopewell Archaeology: The Chillicothe Conference*, pp. 86–93. Kent, Ohio, Kent State University Press.

Johnson, A. E. and Johnson, A. S. 1975. K-means and temporal variability in Kansas City Hopewell ceramics. *American Antiquity* 40: 283–95.

Johnson, G. A. 1973. *Local Exchange and Early State Development in Southwestern Iran* (Anthropological Papers 51). Ann Arbor, University of Michigan Museum of Anthropology.

1978. Information sources and the development of decision-making organisations. In C. L. Redman *et al.* (eds.), *Social Archaeology: Beyond Subsistence and Dating*, pp. 87–112. New York, Academic Press.

1982. Organizational structure and scalar stress. In C. Renfrew, M. Rowlands and B. A. Segraves (eds.), *Theory and Explanation in Archaeology: The Southampton Conference*, pp. 389–421. New York, Academic Press.

Jones, C., Coe, W. R. and Haviland, W. A. 1981. Tikal: an outline of its field study (1956–1970) and a project bibliography. In J. A. Sabloff (vol. ed.), *Supplement to the Handbook of Middle American Indians, Vol. I: Archaeology*, pp. 296–312. Austin, University of Texas Press.

Joralemon, P. D. 1974. Ritual blood-sacrifice among the ancient Maya: part I. In M. G. Robertson (ed.), *Primera Mesa Redonda de Palenque*, pp. 59–76. Pebble Beach, California, Pre-Columbian Art Research, the Robert Louis Stevenson School.

Jorde, L. B. 1977. Precipitation cycles and cultural buffering in the prehistoric Southwest. In L. R. Binford (ed.), *For Theory Building in Archaeology*, pp. 385–96. New York, Academic Press.

Kashiwara (Kokogaku Kenkyjo) 1983. *Kashiwara-shi Soga Iseki* (The Soga Site, Kashiwara City). Nara, Nara Kenritsu Kashiwara Kokogaku Kenkyujo.

Kay, M. 1979. On the periphery: Hopewell settlement of central Missouri. In D. Brose and N. Greber (eds.), *Hopewell Archaeology: The Chillicothe Conference*, pp. 94–9. Kent, Ohio, Kent State University Press.

Kay, M. and Johnson, A. E. 1977. Havana tradition chronology of central Missouri. *Midcontinental Journal of Archaeology* 2: 195–217.

Keatinge, R. W. 1981. The nature and role of religious diffusion in the early stages of state formation: an example from Peruvian prehistory. In G. D. Jones and R. R. Kautz (eds.), *The Transition to Statehood in the New World*, pp. 172–87. Cambridge, University Press.

Kelley, U. 1965. The birth of the gods at Palenque. *Estudias de cultura Maya* 5: 93–134.

Kemp, B. J. and Merrillees, R. S. 1980. *Minoan Pottery in Second Millennium Egypt*. Mainz-on-Rhine, Philipp von Zabern.

Kent, J. P. C. 1975. The date of the Sutton Hoo hoard. In R. L. S. Bruce-Mitford, *The Sutton Hoo ship burial*, Vol. I, pp. 588–607. London, British Museum.

Kimmig, W. 1969. Zum Problem späthallstättischer Adelssitze. In K.-H. Otto and J. Herrmann (eds.), *Siedlung, Burg und Stadt: Studien zu ihren Anfängen*, pp. 96–113. Deutsche Akademie der Wissenschaften zu Berlin, Schriften der Sektion für vor- und Frühgeschichte 25. Berlin.

1975. Early Celts on the Upper Danube: the excavations at the Heuneburg. In R. L. S. Bruce-Mitford (ed.), *Recent Archaeological Excavations in Europe*, pp. 32–64. London, Routledge and Kegan Paul.

Kimmig, W. and von Vacano, O.-W. 1973. Zu einem Gussform-Fragment einer etruskischen Bronzekanne von der Heuneburg a. d. oberen Donau. *Germania* 51: 72–85.

Kinnes, I. 1979. *Round Barrows and Ring Ditches in the British Neolithic*. London, British Museum.

Kiyonaga, Y. 1982. *Nara-ken shutsudo no tetsu rikken no bunseki* (The Analysis of Iron Swords and Daggers Unearthed in Nara Prefecture). Yasugi, Hitachi Metals Company, Metallurgical Laboratory.

Klimek, S. 1935. The structure of California Indian culture, *University of California Publications in American Archaeology and Ethnology* 37: 1–70.

Kobayashi, Y. 1961. *Kofun Jidai no Kenkyu* (Research on the Kofun Period). Tokyo, Aoko Shoten.

Kohl, 1978. The balance of trade in southwestern Asia in the mid-third millennium BC. *Current Anthropology* 19(3): 463–92.

Kondo, Y. 1980. *Tatesuki Iseki* (Tatesuki Site). Okayama, Sanyo Shimbunsha.

in press. The keyhole tumulus and its relationship to earlier forms of burial. In R. Pearson *et al.* (eds.), *Windows on the Japanese Past: Studies in Archaeology*. Ann Arbor, Center for Japanese Studies.

Krippendorff, K. 1971. Communication and the genesis of structure *General Systems* 16: 171–85.

Kristiansen, K., Larsen, M. and Rowlands, M. J. (eds.) in press. *Centre–Periphery Relations in the Ancient World*. Cambridge, University Press.

Kurjack, E. B. and Andrews, E. W. V 1976. Early boundary maintenance in northern Yucatan. *American Antiquity* 44: 318–25.

Lanting, J. N. and van der Waals, J. D. 1976. Beaker culture relations in the lower Rhine basin. In J. N. Lanting and J. D. van der Waals (eds.), *Glockenbechersymposion, Oberried 1974*, pp. 1–80. Bussum–Haarlem, Fibula–van Dishoeck.

Laviosa, C. 1973. L'abitato prepalaziale di Haghia Triada. *Annuario della Scuola Archeologica di Atene* 50–1: 503–13.

Lawrence, A. W. 1957 *Greek Architecture*. Harmondsworth, Penguin.

Ledyard, G. 1975. Galloping along with the horseriders: looking for the founders of Japan. *Journal of Japanese Studies* 1(2): 217–54.

Lee, J.-W. 1982. Relations among Lolang, Samhan and Wa. Paper presented at the association for Asian Studies Annual Meeting, Chicago.

Lekson, S. H. 1981. Cognitive frameworks and Chacoan architecture. *New Mexico Journal of Science* 21: 27–37.

Levi, D. 1958. L'archivo di cretule a Festos. *Annuario della Scuola Archeologica di Atene* 35–6: 7–192.

1969. Sulle origine minoiche. *Parola del passato* 127: 241–64.

1976. *Festos e la civiltà minoica*. Rome, Edizione dell'Ateneo.

Levison, W. 1946. *England and the Continent in the Eighth Century*. Oxford, University Press.

Llewellyn Smith, M. 1965. *The Great Island*. London, Longmans.

Mackie, E. W. 1977. *The Megalith Builders*. Oxford, Phaidon.

Maier, F. 1970. *Die bemalte Spätlatènekeramik von Manching*. Wiesbaden, Franz Steiner.

Mainfort, R. C., Broster, J. B. and Johnson, K. M. 1982. Recent radiocarbon determinations for the Pinson Mounds Site. *Tennessee Anthropologist* 7: 14–19.

Majewski, K. 1955. Nouvelles formes du culte en Crète à la fin de la période MA III et au début de la période MM I. *Studi e materiali di storia delle religioni* 27: 60–70.

Manby, T. G. 1974. *Grooved Ware sites in Yorkshire and the North of England* (BAR 9). Oxford, British Archaeological Reports.

Mansfeld, G. 1973. *Die Fibeln der Heuneburg 1950–1970: Ein Beitrag zur Geschichte der Späthallstattfibel*. (Römisch-Germanische Forschungen 33). Berlin, de Gruyter.

Marcus, J. 1973. Territorial organisation of the lowland Classic Maya. *Science* 180(4089): 911–16.

1976. *Emblem and State in the Classic Maya Lowlands: An Epigraphic Approach to Territorial Organization*. Washington DC, Dumbarton Oaks.

Marinatos, S. 1934. Zur Orientierung der minoischen Architektur. *Proceedings of the First International Congress of Prehistoric Sciences* (London, August 1932). Oxford.

1974. *Thera VI: Colour Plates and Plans*. Athens, Bibliotheke tes en Athenais Archaiologikes Etereias.

Maruyama, M. 1963. The second cybernetics: deviation amplifying mutual causal processes. *American Scientist* 51: 164–79.

Matheny, R. T. 1980. El Mirador, Peten, Guatemala: an interim report. In R. T. Matheny (ed.), *Papers of the New World Archaeological Foundation, No. 45*. Provo, Utah, Brigham Young University.

Maudslay, A. P. 1889–1902. *Biologia Centrali Americana: Or Contributions to the knowledge of the Fauna and Flora of Mexico and Central America* (5 vols. ed. F. D. Godman and O. Salvin). London.

Megaw, J. V. S. 1970. *Art of the European Iron Age*. Bath, Adams and Dart.

Menk, R. 1981. Le phénomène campaniforme: structures biologiques et intégration historique. In R. Menk and A. Gallay (eds.), *Anthropologie et archéologie: le cas des premiers âges des métaux* (Archives suisses d'anthropologie générale 43 (2)), pp. 259–83. Geneva, Département d'anthropologie de l'Université de Genève.

Mercer, R. J. 1981a. *Grimes Graves, Norfolk: Excavations 1971–72*, Vol. I. London, HMSO.

1981b. The excavation of a late Neolithic henge-type enclosure at Balfarg, Markinch, Fife, Scotland. *Proceedings of the Society of Antiquaries of Scotland* 111: 63–171.

Milke, W. 1949. The quantitative distribution of cultural similarities and their cartographic representation. *American Anthropologist* 51: 237–52.

Miller, M. E. 1981. The Murals of Bonampak, Chiapas, Mexico. Ph.D. Dissertation, Yale University.

Miller, R. A. 1967. *The Japanese Language*. Chicago, University of Chicago Press.

Miller, W. 1964. *The Latins in the Levant: A History of Frankish Greece (1204–1566)* (Reprint of 1903 edn). Cambridge, Speculum Historiale.

Mills, W. C. 1922. Exploration of the Mound City Group. *Ohio State Archaeological and Historic Quarterly* 31(4): 423–584.

Molloy, J. P. and Rathje, W. L. 1974. Sexploitation among the Late Classic Maya. In N. Hammond (ed.), *Mesoamerican Archaeology. New Approaches*, pp. 431–43. London, Duckworth.

Morgan, D. T. 1982. Middle Woodland ceramic variation within the lower Illinois Valley. Paper presented at the annual meeting of the Midwest Archaeological Conference, Cleveland, Ohio.

Morley, S. G. 1937–8. *The Inscriptions of the Peten* (5 vols.). Washington, DC, Carnegie Institution of Washington.

1946. *The Ancient Maya*. Palo Alto, Stanford University Press.

Mountjoy, P.-A., Jones, R. E. and Cherry, J. F. 1978. Provenance studies of the LM IB/LH IIA Marine Style. *Annual of the British School of Archaeology at Athens* 73: 143–71.

Munson, P. J. 1967. A Hopewellian enclosure earthwork in the Illinois River Valley. *American Antiquity* 32: 391–3.

Myres, J. N. L. 1977. *A Corpus of Anglo-Saxon Pottery*. Cambridge, University Press.

Nakane, C. 1970. *Japanese Society*. Berkeley, University of California Press.

Nara-ken Kyoiku Iinkai (Nara Prefectural Board of Education) (ed.), 1974. *Nara-ken Iseki Chizu* (Maps of Sites in Nara Prefecture). Nara, Nara Prefecture.

Nash, D. 1976a. Reconstructing Poseidonius' Celtic ethnography: some considerations. *Britannia* 7: 111–26.

1976b. The growth of urban society in France. In B. Cunliffe and T. Rowley (eds.), *Oppida: the Beginnings of Urbanisation in Barbarian Europe* (BAR S11), pp. 95–133. Oxford, British Archaeological Reports.

1978a. Territory and state formation in central Gaul. In D. Green, C. Haselgrove and M. Spriggs (eds.), *Social Organisation and Settlement* (BAR S47), pp. 455–75. Oxford, British Archaeological Reports.

1978b. *Settlement and Coinage in Central Gaul, c. 200–50 BC* (BAR S39). Oxford, British Archaeological Reports.

Niemeier, W.-D. 1979. The master of the Gournia octopus stirrup jar and a Late Minoan IA workshop at Gournia exporting to Crete. In P. Betancourt (ed.), *Gournia, Crete: The 75th Anniversary of the Excavations*, pp. 18–26 (Temple University Aegean Symposium 4). Philadelphia, Temple University.

1982. Mycenaean Knossos and the age of Linear B. *Studi Micenei ed Egeo-Anatolici* 22: 219–87.

Nieto, G. 1959 Colgantes y cabezas de alfiler con decoración acanalada: su distribución en la Peninsula Ibérica. *Archivo de Prehistoria Levantina* 8: 125–44.

Nilsson, M. P. 1950. *The Minoan–Mycenaean Religion* (2nd edn.). Lund, University of Lund.

Northover, P. n.d. Lecture presented at a symposium on Hallstatt. Institute of Archaeology, London, April 1982.

O'Kelly, M. J. 1982. *Newgrange:Archaeology, Art and Legend*. London, Thames and Hudson.

Otto, M. P. 1979. Hopewell antecedents in the Adena heartland. In D. Brose and N. Greber (eds.), *Hopewell Archaeology: The Chillicothe Conference*, pp. 9–14. Kent, Ohio, Kent State University Press.

Ozanne, A. 1962. The Peak dwellers. *Medieval Archaeology* 6: 15–52.

Pader, E. 1981. *Symbolism, Social Relations and the Interpretation of Mortuary Remains* (BAR S130). Oxford, British Archaeological Reports.

Page, D. 1959. *History and the Homeric Iliad*. Berkeley, University of California Press.

Parmalee, P. W. and Perino, G. 1971. A prehistoric archaeological record of the Roseate Spoonbill in Illinois. *Central States Archaeological Journal* 18: 80–5.

Parsons, D. (ed.) 1975. *Tenth-Century Studies*. Chichester, Phillimore.

Peacock, D. P. S. 1971. Roman amphorae in pre-Roman Britain. In M. Jesson and D. Hill (eds.), *The Iron Age and its Hill-forts,* pp. 161–88. Southampton, University of Southampton Archaeological Society.

Pearson, R. 1979. The role of Lolang in the rise of Korean chiefdoms and states. *Journal of the Hong Kong Archaeological Society* 7: 77–90.

Peatfield, A. A. D. 1983. The topography of Minoan peak sanctuaries. *Annual of the British School of Archaeology at Athens* 78: 273–9.

in press. Palace and peak: the political and religious relationship between palaces and peak sanctuaries. In R. Hägg and N. Marinatos (eds.), *The Function of the Minoan Palaces.* Stockholm, Swedish Institute of Archaeology at Athens.

Peebles, C. S. and Kus, S. M. 1977. Some archaeological correlates of ranked societies. *American Antiquity* 42: 421–48.

Pelon, O. 1980. *Le Palais de Malia: V, 2* (Etudes crétoises 25). Paris, École française d'Athènes.

1982–3. L'épée à l'acrobate et la chronologie maliote. *Bulletin et correspondance hellénique* 106: 165–90 and 107: 679–703.

Pendergast, D. 1981. Lamanai, Belize: a summary of excavation results, 1974–80. *Journal of Field Archaeology* 9: 29–53.

Pendlebury, J. D. S. 1939. *The Archaeology of Crete.* London, Methuen.

Perino, G. H. 1968. The Pete Klunk Mound Group, Calhoun County, Illinois: the Archaic and Hopewell occupations. In J. A. Brown (ed.), *Hopewell and Woodland Site Archaeology in Illinois* (Illinois Archaeological Survey Bulletin 6), pp. 9–124. Urbana.

Pernier, L. 1935. *Il Palazzo minoico di Festos I.* Rome, Istituto d'Archeologia e Storia dell'Arte.

Peterson, N. (ed.) 1976. *Tribes and Boundaries in Australia.* Atlantic Highlands, New Jersey, Humanities Press.

Petruso, K. 1979. Reflections on Cycladic and Minoan petrology and trade. In J. L. Davis and J. F. Cherry (eds.), *Papers in Cycladic Prehistory* (Institute of Archaeology UCLA Monograph 14), pp. 135–42. Los Angeles, University of California.

Phillips, P. 1970. *Archaeological Survey in the Lower Yazoo Basin, Mississippi, 1949–1955* (Papers of the Peabody Museum of Archaeology and Ethnology. Harvard University, 60). Cambridge, Mass., Peabody Museum, Harvard University.

Pierpoint, S. 1980. *Social Patterns in Yorkshire Prehistory* (BAR 74). Oxford, British Archaeological Reports.

Piggott, S. 1938. The early bronze age in Wessex. *Proceedings of the Prehistoric Society* 4: 52–106.

Pingel, V. 1971. *Die glatte Drehscheiben-Keramik von Manching.* Wiesbaden, Franz Steiner.

Planck, D. 1982. Eine neuentdeckte keltische Viereckschanze in Fellbach-Schmiden, Rems-Murr Kreis. *Germania* 60 (1): 105–72.

Platon, N. 1974. *Zakros: To neon Minoikon Anaktoron.* Athens.

Potter, D. F. 1977. *Maya Architecture of the Central Yucatan Peninsula, Mexico* (Middle American Research Institute Publication 44). New Orleans, Tulane University.

Press, L. 1973. On the origin of Minoan palatial architecture. *Archeologia* (Warsaw) 24: 1–11.

Price, B. J. 1977. Shifts in production and organisation: a cluster interaction model. *Current Anthropology* 18: 209–34.

Proskouriakoff, T. 1950. *A Study of Classic Maya Sculpture* (Carnegie Institution of Washington Publication 593). Washington DC, Carnegie Institution of Washington.

1960. Historical implications of a pattern of dates at Piedras Negras, Guatemala. *American Antiquity* 25 (4): 454–75.

Prufer, O. H. 1964. The Hopewell Complex of Ohio. In J. R. Caldwell and R. L. Hall (eds.), *Hopewellian Studies* (Illinois State Museum Scientific Papers 12), pp. 35–83. Springfield, Illinois, Illinois State Museum.

1965. *The McGraw Site: A Study of Hopewellian Dynamics.* (Scientific Publication of the Cleveland Museum of Natural History 4(1)). Cleveland, Ohio, Museum of Natural History.

1968. *Ohio Hopewell Ceramics: An Analysis of the Extant Collections.* (University of Michigan, Museum of Anthropology Anthropological Papers 33). Ann Arbor, University of Michigan Museum of Anthropology.

1975. The Scioto valley archaeological survey. In O. H. Prufer and D. H. McKenzie (eds.), *Studies in Ohio Archaeology* (revised edn), pp. 267–328. Kent, Ohio, Kent State University Press.

Rackerby, F. 1968. *Carlyle Reservoir Archaeology: Final Season.* (Southern Illinois University Museum Research Records, Southern Illinois Studies, Series 68S(1)A). Carbondale, Southern Illinois University.

Rahtz, P. 1976. Buildings and rural settlement. In D. M. Wilson (ed.), *The Archaeology of Anglo-Saxon England,* pp. 49–98. London, Methuen.

Rands, R. L. 1967. Ceramic technology and trade in the Palenque region, Mexico. In C. L. Riley and W. W. Taylor (eds.), *American Historical Anthropology,* pp. 137–51. Carbondale, Southern Illinois University Press.

Rappaport, R. A. 1971. The sacred in human evolution. *Annual Review of Ecology and Systematics* 2: 23–44.

Rathje, W. L. 1973. Models for mobile Maya: a variety of constraints. In C. Renfrew (ed.), *The Explanation of Culture Change: Models in Prehistory,* pp. 731–60. London, Duckworth.

Renfrew, C. 1972. *The Emergence of Civilisation: The Cyclades and the Aegean in the Third Millennium BC.* London, Methuen.

1973. Monuments, mobilisation and social organisation in Neolithic Wessex. In C. Renfrew (ed.), *The Explanation of Culture Change,* pp. 539–58. London, Duckworth.

1974. Beyond a subsistence economy: the evolution of prehistoric social organisation in prehistoric Europe. In C. B. Moore (ed.), *Reconstructing Complex Societies* (Supplement to the Bulletin of the American Schools of Oriental Research 20), pp. 69–95. Cambridge, Mass.

1975. Trade as action at a distance: questions of integration and communication. In J. A. Sabloff and C. C. Lamberg-Karlovsky (eds.), *Ancient Civilisation and Trade* pp. 3–59. Albuquerque, University of New Mexico Press.

1976. Megaliths, territories and populations. In S. J. de Laet (ed.), *Acculturation and Continuity in Atlantic Europe.* pp. 198–220. Bruges, De Tempel.

1977. Retrospect and prospect. In J. L. Bintliff (ed.), *Mycenaean Geography,* pp. 108–19. Cambridge, British Association for Mycenaean Studies.

1978a. Space, time and polity. In J. Friedman and M. J. Rowlands (eds.), *The Evolution of Social Systems,* pp. 89–112. London, Duckworth.

1978b. Phylakopi and the Late Bronze I period in the Cyclades. In C. Doumas (ed.), *Thera and the Aegean World,* Vol. I, pp. 403–21. London, Thera and the Aegean World.

1978c. The anatomy of innovation. In D. Green, C. Haselgrove and M. Spriggs (eds.), *Social Organisation and Settlement* (BAR S47), pp. 89–117. Oxford, British Archaeological Reports.

1979. *Investigations in Orkney.* London, Society of Antiquaries.

1982a. Polity and power: interaction, intensification and exploitation. In C. Renfrew and J. M. Wagstaff (eds.), *An Island Polity: The Archaeology of Exploitation in Melos,* pp. 264–90. Cambridge, University Press.

1982b. *Towards an Archaeology of Mind* (Inaugural Lecture, University of Cambridge). Cambridge, University Press.

1982c. Explanation revisited. In C. Renfrew, M. Rowlands, and B. Segraves (eds.), *Theory and Explanation in Archaeology,* pp. 5–23. London, Academic Press.

1982d. Peer polity interaction and socio-political change. Paper presented at the 47th annual meeting of the Society for American Archaeology, Minneapolis, Minnesota, 16 April 1982.

1985. Epilogue. In C. Renfrew (ed.), *The Prehistory of Orkney*, pp. 243–62. Edinburgh, University Press.

in press, a. Problems in the modelling of socio-cultural systems.

in press, b. Varna and the emergence of wealth in prehistoric Europe. In A. Appadurai (ed.), *Commodities and Culture: the Social Life of Things*. Cambridge, University Press.

Renfrew, C. and Wagstaff, J. M. (eds.) 1982. *An Island Polity: The Archaeology of Exploitation in Melos*. Cambridge, University Press.

Rice, D. S. n.d. Classic to Postclassic Maya household transitions. Paper delivered at a symposium entitled 'Mesoamerican Houses and Households', 48th annual meeting of the society for American Archaeology, Pittsburgh, 1983.

Rice, D. S. Puleston, D. E. 1981. Ancient Maya settlement patterns in the Peten, Guatemala. In W. Ashmore (ed.), *Lowland Maya Settlement Patterns*, pp. 121–56. Albuquerque, University of New Mexico Press.

Rice Holmes, T. 1899. *Caesar's conquest of Gaul*. London, Macmillan.

Ricketson, O. G. and Ricketson, E. B. 1937. *Uaxactun, Guatemala, Group E, 1926–1937* (Carnegie Institution of Washington, Publication 477). Washington DC, Carnegie Institution of Washington.

Riek, G. and Hundt, H-J. 1962. *Der Hohmichele* (Römisch-Germanische Forschungen 25). Berlin, de Gruyter.

Riesenberg, S. H. 1968. *The Native Polity of Ponape* (Smithsonian Contributions to Anthropology 10). Washington DC, Smithsonian Institution Press.

Robertson, M. G. (ed.) 1974. *Primera Mesa Redonda de Palenque*, Part II (A Conference on the Art, Iconography and Dynastic History of Palenque). Pebble Beach, California, Pre-Columbian Art Research, the Robert Louis Stevenson School.

1976. *The Art, Iconography and Dynastic History of Palenque*, Part III (Proceedings of the Segunda Mesa Redonda de Palenque). Pebble Beach, California, Pre-Columbian Art Research, the Robert Louis Stevenson School.

1979. *Tercera Mesa Redonda de Palenque*, Vol. IV (Proceedings of a Conference on the Art, Hieroglyphics and Historic Approaches of the Late Classic Maya, 11–18 June 1978). Palenque (Chiapas, Mexico), Pre-Columbian Art Research Center.

Robicsek, F. 1978. *The Smoking Gods: Tobacco in Maya Art, History and Religion*. Norman, University of Oklahoma Press.

Roe, F. 1968. Stone mace-heads and the latest Neolithic cultures of the British Isles. In D. Simpson and J. Coles (eds.), *Studies in Ancient Europe*, pp. 145–72. Leicester, University Press.

Rogers, E. M. and Kincaid, D. L. 1981. *Communication Networks: Toward a New Paradigm for Research*. New York, The Free Press.

Rouse, I. 1972. *Introduction to Prehistory: a Systematic Approach*. New York, McGraw Hill.

Roys, R. L. 1962. Literary sources for the history of Mayapan. In H. E. D. Pollock, R. L. Roys, T. Proskouriakoff and A. L. Smith, *Mayapan, Yucatan, Mexico* (Carnegie Institution of Washington Publication 619), pp. 25–86. Washington, DC, Carnegie Institution of Washington.

Ruppert, K., Thompson, J. E. S. and Proskouriakoff, T. 1955 *Bonampak, Chiapas, Mexico* (Carnegie Institution of Washington Publication 602). Washington, DC, Carnegie Institution of Washington.

Rutkowski, B. 1972. *Cult Places in the Aegean World*. Warsaw, Polish Academy of Sciences.

Rutter, J. B. and Zerner, C. W. 1984. Early Hellado-Minoan contacts. In R. Hägg and N. Marinatos (eds.), *The Minoan Thalassocracy: Myth and Reality*, pp. 75–83. Stockholm, Swedish Institute of Archaeology at Athens.

Sabloff, J. A. 1975. *Excavations at Seibal: Ceramics* (Memoirs of the Peabody Museum, Harvard University, 13 (2)). Cambridge, Mass., Peabody Museum, Harvard University.

1981. When the rhetoric fades: a brief appraisal of intellectual trends in American archaeology during the past two decades. *Bulletin of the American Schools of Oriental Research* 242: 1–6.

1983. Classic Maya settlement pattern studies: past problems, future prospects. In E. A. Vogt and R. M. Leventhal (eds.), *Prehistoric Settlement Pattern Studies: Retrospect and Prospect*, pp. 413–22. Albuquerque, University of New Mexico Press.

Sabloff, J. A. and Andrews, E. W. V (eds.) In press. *Late Lowland Maya Civilization: Classic to Postclassic*. Albuquerque, University of New Mexico Press.

Sahlins, M. D. 1963. Poor man, rich man, big-man, chief: political types in Melanesia and Polynesia. *Comparative Studies in Society and History* 5: 285–303.

1972. *Stone Age Economics*. Chicago, Aldine.

1976. *Culture and Practical Reason*. Chicago, University of Chicago Press.

Saitta, D. J. 1982. The explanation of change in egalitarian society: a critique. Paper presented at the 47th annual meeting of the Society for American Archaeology, Minneapolis, Minnesota.

Sakellarakis, J. A. 1967. Mason's marks from Arkhanes. In *Europa* (Festschrift für E. Grumach), pp. 277–88. Berlin.

Sanders, W. T. 1977. Environmental heterogeneity and the evolution of lowland Maya civilization. In R. E. W. Adams (ed.), *The Origins of Maya Civilization*, pp. 287–98. Albuquerque, University of New Mexico Press.

Sangmeister, E. 1976. Das Verhältnis der Glockenbecherkultur zu den einheimischen Kulturen der iberischen Halbinsel. In J. N. Lanting and J. D. van der Waals (eds.), *Glockenbechersymposium, Oberried 1974*, pp. 423–38. Bussum–Haarlem, Fibula–van Dishoeck.

Savory, H. N. 1968. *Spain and Portugal*. London, Thames and Hudson.

Saxe, A. 1977. On the origin of evolutionary processes: state formation in the Sandwich Islands. In J. N. Hill (ed.), *Explanation of Prehistoric Change*, pp. 105–52. Albuquerque, University of New Mexico Press.

Scarborough, V. L. 1980. The Settlement System in a Late Preclassic Maya Community: Cerros, Northern Belize. Ph.D. Dissertation, Southern Methodist University, Dallas.

Scarborough, V. L., Mitchum, B., Carr, S. and Freidel, D. A. 1982. Two Late Preclassic ballcourts at the lowland Maya center of Cerros, northern Belize. *Journal of Field Archaeology* 9(1): 21–34.

Schele, L. 1976. Accession iconography of Chan Bahlum in the group of the Cross at Palenque. In M. G. Robertson (ed.), *The Art, Iconography and Dynastic History of Palenque*, Part III, pp. 9–34. Pebble Beach, California, Pre-Columbian Art Research, the Robert Louis Stevenson School.

1979. Genealogical documentation on the tri-figure panels at Palenque. In M. G. Robertson (ed.), *Tercera Mesa Redonda de Palenque*, Vol. IV, pp. 41–70. Palenque (Chiapas, Mexico), Pre-Columbian Art Research Center.

1984. Human sacrifice among the Classic Maya. In E. Boone (ed.), *Ritual Human Sacrifice in Mesoamerica*, pp. 6–48. Washington DC, Dumbarton Oaks.

Scholes, F. and Roys, R. L. 1948. *The Maya Chontal Indians of Acalan-Tixchel: A Contribution to the History and Ethnography of the Yucatan Peninsula* (Carnegie Institution of Washington Publication 560). Washington DC, Carnegie Institution of Washington.

Schreiber, R. 1976. Die Probleme der Glockenbecherkultur in Ungarn. In J. N. Lanting and J. D. van der Waals (eds.), *Glockenbecher-*

symposion Oberried 1974. Bussom–Haarlem, Fibula–van Dishoeck, 184–215.

Schubart, H. 1975. *Die Kultur der Bronzezeit im Südwesten der iberischen Halbinsel.* Berlin, de Gruyter.

1976. Eine bronzezeitliche Kultur im Südwesten der iberischen Halbinsel. In S. J. de Laet (ed.), *Acculturation and Continuity in Atlantic Europe mainly during the Neolithic Period and the Bronze Age,* pp. 221–34. Bruges, De Tempel.

Schwappach, F. 1973. Frühkeltisches Ornament zwischen Marne, Rhein und Moldau. *Bonner Jahrbücher* 173: 53–112.

Schwarz, G. T. 1964. Gallo-römische Gewichte in Aventicum. *Schweizer Münzblätter* 13–14: 150–7.

Seeman, M. F. 1977. Stylistic variation in Middle Woodland pipe styles: the chronological implications. *Midcontinental Journal of Archaeology* 2: 47–66.

1979. *The Hopewell Interaction Sphere: The Evidence for Interregional Trade and Structural Complexity* (Indiana Historical Society Prehistory Research Series 5 (2)). Indianapolis, Indiana Historical Society.

Senda, M. 1980. Territorial possession in ancient Japan: the real and the perceived. In The Association of Japanese Geographers (eds.), *Geography of Japan,* pp. 101–20. Tokyo, Teikoku-Shoin.

Service, E. R. 1978. Classical and modern theories of the origin of government. In R. Cohen and E. R. Service (eds.), *Origins of the State: The Anthropology of Political Evolution,* pp. 21–34. Philadelphia, Institute for the Study of Human Issues.

1975. *Origins of the State and Civilization.* New York, Norton.

Shafer, H. J. 1981. Maya lithic craft specialization in northern Belize. Paper presented at the 80th annual meeting of the American Anthropological Association, Los Angeles, California.

Shanks, M. and Tilley, C. 1982. Ideology, symbolic power and ritual communication: a reinterpretation of Neolithic mortuary practices. In I. Hodder (ed.), *Symbolic and Structural Archaeology,* pp. 129–54. Cambridge, University Press.

Shaw, J. W. 1973a. Minoan architecture: materials and techniques. *Annuario della Scuola Archeologica di Atene* 49: 7–256.

1973b. The orientation of the Minoan palaces. In *Antichità cretesi: studi in onore di Doro Levi* (Cronache di archeologia 12), pp. 47–59. Catania, Università di Catania Istituto de Archeologia.

1973c. The Chrysolakkos façades. *Proceedings of the Third International Cretological Congress (Rethymnon, 1971),* Vol. I, pp. 319–31. Athens.

1983. The development of Minoan orthostates. *American Journal of Archaeology* 87: 213–16.

Shee Twohig, E. 1981. *The Megalithic Art of Western Europe.* Oxford, Clarendon Press.

Shennan, S. J. 1975. Die soziale Bedeutung der Glockenbecher. *Acta Archaeologica Carpathica* 15: 173–80.

1976. Bell Beakers and their context in central Europe. In J. N. Lanting and J. D. van der Waals (eds.), *Glockenbechersymposion, Oberried 1974,* pp. 231–9. Bussom–Haarlem, Fibula–van Dishoeck.

1977. Bell Beakers and their Context in Central Europe: A New Approach. Unpublished Ph.D. Dissertation, University of Cambridge.

1978. Archaeological 'cultures': an empirical investigation. In I. Hodder (ed.), *The Spatial Organisation of Culture,* pp. 113–39. London, Duckworth.

1982. Ideology, change and the European Early Bronze Age. In I. Hodder (ed.), *Symbolic and Structural Archaeology,* pp. 155–61. Cambridge, University Press.

1985. Settlement expansion and socio-economic change. In T. Champion, C. Gamble, S. Shennan and A. Whittle, *Prehistoric Europe,* pp. 153–96. New York, Academic Press.

in press. Central Europe in the third millennium BC: an evolutionary trajectory for the beginning of the European Bronze Age. In K. Kristiansen, M. Larsen and M. J. Rowlands (eds.), *Centre–Periphery Relations in the Ancient World.* Cambridge, University Press.

Shepherd, J. 1979. The social identity of the individual in isolated barrows and barrow cemeteries in Anglo-Saxon England. In B. C. Burnham and J. Kingsbury (eds.), *Space, Hierarchy and Society* (BAR S59), pp. 47–80. Oxford, British Archaeological Reports.

Sherratt, A. n.d. The Aegean Bronze Age and the east Mediterranean: political structures and external trade. Unpublished paper.

Simpson, D. and Thawley, J. 1972. Single Grave art in Britain. *Scottish Archaeological Forum* 4: 81–104.

Skoufopoulos, N. 1971. *Mycenaean Fortifications* (Studies in Mediterranean Archaeology 22). Göteborg, Paul Åström.

Smith, A. L. 1982. *Excavations at Seibal: Architecture* (Memoirs of the Peabody Museum, Harvard University, 15 (1)). Cambridge, Mass., Peabody Museum, Harvard University.

Smith, C. A. 1976. Exchange systems and the spatial distribution of elites: the organisation of stratification in agrarian societies. In C. A. Smith (ed.), *Regional Analysis,* Vol. II, pp. 309–74. New York, Academic Press.

Snodgrass, A. M. 1971. *The Dark Age of Greece.* Edinburgh, University Press.

1980. *Archaic Greece: The Age of Experiment.* London, Dent.

1985. The new archaeology and the classical archaeologist. *American Journal of Archaeology* 89: 1–7.

Soja, E. W. 1971. *The Political Organisation of Space* (Association of American Geographers, Commission on College Geography Publications, Resource Paper 8). Washington DC, Association of American Geographers.

Spinden, H. J. 1913. *A Study of Maya Art: Its Subject Matter and Historical Development* (Peabody Museum Memoirs 6). Cambridge, Mass., Peabody Museum, Harvard University.

Starr, C. G. 1955. The Minoan thalassocracy re-examined. *Historia* 3: 282–91.

Startin, W. and Bradley, R. J. 1981. Some notes on work organisation and society in prehistoric Wessex. In C. Ruggles and A. Whittle (eds.), *Astronomy and Society in Britain during the Period 4000–1500 bc* (BAR 88), pp. 289–96. Oxford, British Archaeological Reports.

Stoltman, J. B. 1978. Temporal models in prehistory: an example from eastern North America. *Current Anthropology* 19: 703–29.

Strathern, A. 1971. *The Rope of Moka: Big-men and Ceremonial Exchange in Mount Hagen, New Guinea.* Cambridge, University Press.

Strathern, S. 1969. Descent and alliance in the New Guinea Highlands: some problems of comparison. *Proceedings of the Royal Anthropological Institute of Great Britain and Ireland for 1969:* 37–52.

Struever, S. 1960. The Kamp Mound Group. Unpublished M. A. Thesis, University of Chicago.

1964. The Hopewell interaction sphere in riverine-western Great Lakes culture history. In J. Caldwell and R. L. Hall (eds.), *Hopewellian studies.* (Illinois State Museum Scientific Papers 12), pp. 85–106. Springfield, Illinois, Illinois State Museum.

1965. Middle Woodland culture history in the Great Lakes riverine area. *American Antiquity* 31: 211–23.

Struever, S. and Houart, G. L. 1972. An analysis of the Hopewell interaction sphere. In E. N. Wilmsen (ed.), *Social Exchange and Interaction* (University of Michigan Museum of Anthropology Anthropological Papers 46), pp. 47–79. Ann Arbor, University of Michigan Museum of Anthropology.

Stuart, D. n.d. The iconography of blood and the symbolism of Maya rulership. Paper presented at the Princeton Conference on the Origins of Maya Iconography, October 1982.

Stuart, G. E. 1975. The Maya riddle of the glyphs. *National Geographic* 148 (6): 769–95.

Stucynski, S. L. 1982. Cycladic imports in Crete: a brief survey. *Temple University Aegean Symposium* 7: 50–9.

Styles, B. W. 1981. *Faunal Exploitation and Resource Selection: Early Late Woodland Subsistence in the Lower Illinois Valley* (Northwestern University Archaeological Program, Scientific Papers 3). Evanston, Northwestern University Archaeological Program.

Szczesniak, B. 1952. The Kotaio monument. *Monumenta Nipponica* 7: 242–68.

Tainter, J. A. 1977. Woodland social change in west-central Illinois. *Midcontinental Journal of Archaeology* 2: 67–98.

1980. Behavior and status in a Middle Woodland mortuary population from the Illinois valley. *American Antiquity* 45: 308–13.

in press. *The Collapse of Complex Societies*.

Tanaka, M. 1979. *Kokagami* (Ancient Mirrors). Tikyo, Kodansha.

Taus, M. 1963. Ein spätlatènezeitliches Schmied-Grab aus St Georgen am Steinseld, p.B. St Polten, NÖ. *Archaeologia Austriaca* 34: 13–16.

Teramura, K. 1966. *Kodai Tamazukuri no Kenkyu* (Research on Ancient Bead-Making). Kokugakuin Daigaku Kokogaku Kenkyu Hokoku, Vol. 3. Tokyo, Yoshikawa Kobunkan.

Thomas, N. 1955. The Thornborough Circles, near Ripon, North Riding. *Yorkshire Archaeological Journal* 38: 425–45.

Thompson, J. E. S. 1936. *Civilization of the Mayas* (3rd edn.) (Anthropology Leaflet 25), Chicago, Field Museum of Natural History.

1966. *The Rise and Fall of Maya Civilization* (2nd edn.). Norman, University of Oklahoma Press.

Thomson, B. 1894. *The Diversions of a Prime Minister.* London, Dawsons.

Thorpe, I. and Richards, C. 1984. The decline of ritual authority and the introduction of Beakers into Britain. In R. J. Bradley and J. Gardiner (eds.), *Neolithic Studies: A Review of Some Current Research* (BAR 133), pp. 67–84. Oxford, British Archaeological Reports.

Tierney, J. J. 1960. The Celtic ethnography of Posidonius. *Proceedings of the Royal Irish Academy* 60: 189–275.

Torrence, R. 1986. *Production and Exchange of Prehistoric Stone Tools.* Cambridge, University Press.

Toth, A. 1974. *Archaeology and Ceramics at the Marksville Site* (University of Michigan, Museum of Anthropology Anthropological Papers 56). Ann Arbor, University of Michigan Museum of Anthropology.

1977. Early Marksville phases in the lower Mississippi valley: a study of culture contact dynamics. Unpublished Ph.D. Dissertation, Harvard University.

1979. The Marksville connection. In D. Brose and N. Greber (eds.), *Hopewell Archaeology: The Chillicothe Conference*, pp. 188–99. Kent, Ohio, Kent State University Press.

1983. The chronological implications of early Marksville ceramics. In W. H. Marquardt (ed.), *Southeastern Archaeological Conference, Bulletin 20*, pp. 196–204 (Proceedings of the 33rd Southeastern Archaeological Conference, Tuscaloosa, Alabama, 4–6 November 1976). Gainesville, Florida, Southeast Archaeological Conference.

Tourtellot, G. and Sabloff, J. A. 1972. Exchange systems among the Maya. *American Antiquity* 37: 126–35.

Tozzer, A.M. (ed.) 1941. *Landa's Relacion de las Cosas de Yucatan, a Translation* (Papers of the Peabody Museum 18). Cambridge, Mass., Peabody Museum, Harvard University.

Tozzer, A. M. 1957. *Chichen Itza and its Cenote of Sacrifice: A Comparative Study of Contemporaneous Maya and Toltec* (Memoirs of the Peabody Museum 11, 12). Cambridge, Mass., Peabody Museum, Harvard University.

Tsunoda, R. and Goodrich, L. C. 1951. *Japan in the Chinese Dynastic Histories.* South Pasadena, P. D. and Ione Perkins.

Tuckwell, A. 1975. Patterns of burial orientation in the round barrows of East Yorkshire. *Bulletin of the Institute of Archaeology, University of London* 12: 95–123.

Turner, B. L. II 1974. Prehistoric intensive agriculture in the Maya lowlands, *Science* 185: 118–24.

Ullman, W. 1969. *The Carolingian Renaissance and the Idea of Kingship.* London, University Press.

Van der Waals, J. D. and Glasbergen, W. 1955. Beaker types and their distribution in the Netherlands. *Palaeohistoria* 4: 5–46.

Van Effenterre H. 1980. *Le Palais de Mallia et la cité minoenne* (Incunabula Graeca 76). Rome, Edizione dell'Ateneo.

Vayda, A. P. 1967. Pomo trade feasts. In G. Dalton (ed.), *Tribal and Peasant Economies*, pp. 494–500. New York, Natural History Press.

Ventris, M. and Chadwick, J. 1973. *Documents in Mycenaean Greek* (2nd edn.). Cambridge, University Press.

Voss, J. A. 1980. Tribal Emergence during the Neolithic of Northwestern Europe. Ph.D. Dissertation, University of Michigan. Ann Arbor, University Microfilms.

Wailes, B. 1972. Plow and population in temperate Europe. In B. Spooner (ed.), *Population Growth: Anthropological Implications*, pp. 154–80. Cambridge, Mass., MIT Press.

Wainwright, G. J. 1969. A review of henge monuments in the light of recent research. *Proceedings of the Prehistoric Society* 35: 112–33.

1971. The excavation of a Late Neolithic enclosure at Marden, Wiltshire. *Antiquaries Journal* 51: 177–239.

Wainwright, G. J. and Longworth, I. H. 1971. *Durrington Walls: Excavations 1966–1968.* London, Society of Antiquaries.

Walberg, G. 1976. *Kamares: A Study of the Character of Palatial Middle Minoan Pottery* (Boreas 8: Uppsala Studies in Ancient Mediterranean and Near Eastern Civilisations). Uppsala, University of Uppsala.

1978. *The Kamares Style: Overall Effects* (Boreas 10: Uppsala Studies in Ancient Mediterranean and Near Eastern Civilisations). Uppsala, University of Uppsala.

1983. *Middle Minoan Provincial Pottery.* Mainz-on-Rhine, Philipp von Zabern.

Wallace-Hadrill, J. M. 1971. *Early Germanic Kingship in England and on the Continent.* Oxford, Blackwell.

Wallerstein, I. 1974. *The Modern World System.* London, Academic Press.

Walthall, J. A., Stow, S. H. and Karson, M. J. 1979. Ohio Hopewell trade: galena procurement and exchange. In D. Brose and N. Greber (eds.), *Hopewell Archaeology: The Chillicothe Conference*, pp. 247–50. Kent, Ohio, Kent State University Press.

Warren, H. 1922. The Neolithic stone axes of Graig Lwyd, Penmaenmawr. *Archaeologia Cambrensis* 77: 1–26.

Warren, P. 1973a. Crete, 3000–1400 BC: immigration and the archaeological evidence. In R. A. Crossland and A. Birchall (eds.), *Bronze Age Migrations in the Aegean*, pp. 41–9. London, Duckworth.

1973b. The beginnings of Minoan religion. *Antichità cretesi: studi in onore di Doro Levi* (Cronache di archeologia 12), pp. 137–47. Catania, Università di Catania Istituto di Archeologia.

1975. *The Aegean Civilisations.* London, Phaidon.

1981. Knossos and its foreign relations in the Early Bronze Age. *Proceedings of the Fourth International Cretological Congress* (Iraklion, 1976), *Vol I.* pp. 628–37. Athens.

in press. The genesis of the Minoan palace. In R. Hägg and N. Marinatos (eds.), *The Function of the Minoan Palaces.* Stockholm, Swedish Institute of Archaeology at Athens.

Watrous, L. V. in press. The role of the Near East in the rise of the Cretan palaces. In R. Hägg and N. Marinatos (eds.), *The*

Function of the Minoan Palaces. Stockholm Swedish Institute of Archaeology at Athens.

Weaver, W. 1949. The mathematics of communication. *Scientific American* 181: 11–15.

Webb, M. C. 1973. The Peten Maya decline viewed in the perspective of state formation. In T. P. Culbert (ed.), *The Classic Maya Collapse*, pp. 367–404. Albuquerque, University of New Mexico Press.

1975. The flag follows trade: an essay on the necessary interaction of military and commercial factors in state formation. In J. A. Sabloff and C. C. Lamberg-Karlovsky (eds.), *Ancient Civilisation and Trade*, pp. 155–209. Albuquerque, University of New Mexico Press.

Webb, W. S. and Snow, C. E. 1974. *The Adena People* (Reprint of 1945 edn). Knoxville, University of Tennessee Press.

Webster, D. L. 1975. Warfare and the evolution of the state: a reconsideration. *American Antiquity* 40: 464–70.

1976a. *Defensive Earthworks at Becan, Campeche, Mexico. Implications for Maya Warfare* (Middle American Research Institute Publication 41). New Orleans, Tulane University.

1976b. On theocracies. *American Anthropologist* 78: 812–28.

1977. Warfare and the evolution of Maya civilization. In R. E. W. Adams (ed.), *The Origins of Maya Civilization*, pp. 335–72. Albuquerque, University of New Mexico Press.

1980. Spatial bounding and settlement history at three walled northern Maya centers. *American Antiquity* 45 (4): 834–44.

Wells, P. S. 1980. *Culture Contact and Culture Change: Early Iron Age Central Europe and the Mediterranean World*. Cambridge, University Press.

Werner, J. 1954. Die Bronzekanne von Kelheim. *Bayerische Vorgeschichtsblätter* 20: 43–73.

Wheatley, P. 1971. *The Pivot of the Four Quarters: A Preliminary Enquiry into the Origins and Character of the Ancient Chinese City*. Chicago, Aldine.

Whitelaw, T. M. 1983. The settlement at Fournou Koriphi Myrtos and aspects of Early Minoan social organisation. In O. Krzyszkowska and L. Nixon (eds.), *Minoan Society*, pp. 333–6. Bristol, Bristol Classical Press.

Whitelock, D. (ed.) 1955. *English Historical Documents*, Vol. I. London, Eyre and Spottiswoode.

Whittle, A. 1981. Later neolithic society in Britain: a re-alignment. In C. Ruggles and A. Whittle (eds.), *Astronomy and Society in Britain during the Period 4000–1500 BC* (BAR 88), pp. 297–342. Oxford, British Archaeological Reports.

Wiener, M. H. in press. Trade and rule in palatial Crete. In R. Hägg and N. Marinatos (eds.), *The Function of the Minoan Palaces*. Stockholm, Swedish Institute of Archaeology at Athens.

Willey, G. R. 1978a. *Excavations at Seibal: Artifacts* (Memoirs of the Peabody Museum, Harvard University, 14 (1)). Cambridge, Mass., Peabody Museum, Harvard University.

1978b. Developmental stages in ancient Mesoamerican society: reflections and impressions. In M. Giardina, B. Edmunson and W. Creamer (eds.), *Codex Wauchope: A Tribute Roll*. New Orleans, Human Mosaic, Tulane University, 155–62.

1979. The concept of the 'disembedded capital' in comparative perspective. *Journal of Anthropological Research* 35: 123–37.

Willey, G. R. and Sabloff, J. A. 1980. *A History of American Archaeology* (2nd edn.). San Francisco, W. H. Freeman.

Willey, G. R. and Shimkin, D. B. 1973. The Maya collapse: a summary view. In T. P. Culbert (ed.), *The Classic Maya Collapse*, pp. 457–501. Albuquerque, University of New Mexico Press.

Willey, G. R., Smith, A. L., Tourtellot, G. III and Graham, I. 1975. *Excavations at Seibal: Introduction, the Site and its Setting* (Memoirs of the Peabody Museum, Harvard University, 13, (1)). Cambridge, Mass., Peabody Museum, Harvard University.

Wilson, A. L. 1977. The place-names in the Linear B tablets from Knossos: some preliminary considerations. *Minos* 16: 67–125.

Winter, I. J. 1981. Royal rhetoric and the development of historical narrative in neo-Assyrian reliefs. *Studies in Visual Communication* 7 (2): 2–38.

Wissler, C. 1914. Material cultures of the North American Indians. *American Anthropologist* 16: 447–505.

Wobst, H. M. 1977. Stylistic behavior and information exchange. In C. Cleland (ed.), *For the Director: Research Essays in Honor of James B. Griffin* (University of Michigan Museum of Anthropology, Anthropological Papers 61), pp. 317–42. Ann Arbor, University of Michigan Museum of Anthropology.

Wormald, P. 1977. 'Beowulf' and the conversion of the Anglo-Saxon aristocracy. In R. T. Farrell (ed.), *Bede and Anglo-Saxon England*, pp. 32–95. Oxford, British Archaeological Reports.

1982. Hegemonies. *London Review of Books* 21 October–3 November: 22–3.

Wright, H. T. 1969. *The Administration of Rural Production in an Early Mesopotamian Town*. Anthropological Papers, Museum of Anthropology, University of Michigan, 58.

1972. A consideration of inter-regional exchange in greater Mesopotamia. In E. Wilmsen (ed.), *Social Exchange and Interactions*, pp. 95–106. Anthropological Papers, Museum of Anthropology, University of Michigan, 46.

1977a. Recent research on the origin of the state. *Annual Review of Anthropology* 6: 379–97.

1977b. Toward an explanation of the origin of the state. In J. N. Hill (ed.), *Explanation of Prehistoric Change*, pp. 215–30. Albuquerque, University of New Mexico Press.

1978. Toward an explanation of the origin of the state. In R. Cohen and E. R. Service (eds.), *Origins of the State: The Anthropology of Political Evolution*, pp. 49–68. Philadelphia, Institute for the Study of Human Issues.

Wright, H. T. and Johnson, G. A. 1975. Population, exchange and early state formation in southwestern Iran. *American Anthropologist* 77: 267–89.

Wyss, R. 1974. Technik, Wirtschaft, Handel und Kriegswesen der Eisenzeit. In W. Drack (ed.), *Ur- und frühgeschichtliche Archäologie der Schweiz, IV: Die Eisenzeit*, pp. 105–38. Basel, Schweizerische Gesellschaft für Ur- und Frühgeschichte.

Xanthoudides, S. 1924. *The Vaulted Tombs of Mesara*. London, Hodder and Stoughton.

Yorke, B. A. E. 1981. The vocabulary of Anglo-Saxon overlordship. In D. Brown, J. Campbell and S. C. Hawkes (eds.), *Anglo-Saxon Studies in Archaeology and History*, Vol. II (BAR 92), pp. 171–200. Oxford, British Archaeological Reports.

Young, J. 1958. *The Location of Yamatai: A Case Study in Japanese Historiography, 720–1945*. Baltimore, the Johns Hopkins Press.

Yu, Y.-S. 1967. *Trade and Expansion in Han China*. Berkeley, University of California Press.

Zoes, A. 1982. Gibt es Vorläufer der minoischen Paläste auf Kreta? Ergebnisse neuer Untersuchungen. In D. Papenfuss and V. M. Strocka (eds.), *Palast und Hütte: Beiträge zum Bauen und Wohnen im Altertum von Archäologen, Vor- und Frühges-chichtlern* pp. 207–15. Mainz-on-Rhine, Philipp von Zabern.

Zürn, H. 1970. *Hallstattforschungen in Nordwürttemberg* (Veröffentlichungen des staatlichen Amtes für Denkmalpflege Stuttgart, Reihe A, 16). Stuttgart, Müller and Gräff.

INDEX

An Island Polity

The Archaeology of Exploitation in Melos
Edited by Colin Renfrew and Malcolm Wagstaff

'The abiding impression left on the reader, and reinforced by
chapter after chapter of the book, is one of freshness and
challenging quality of approach.'

The Times Literary Supplement

'The real achievement of this volume lies . . . in integrating
different disciplines in both the arts and the sciences, and in
the seamless interpenetration of theory with precise data
collection. This is our new standard of progressive inter-
disciplinary scholarship, and its rapid publication will have an
immensely beneficial effect on Mediterranean archaeological
and historical research.'   *Journal of Historical Geography*

Island Societies

Archaeological Approaches to Evolution and Transformation
Edited by Patrick Kirch

Concentrating their attention on the Pacific Islands, the
contributors to this book show how the tightly focused social
and economic systems of islands offer archaeologists a series
of unique opportunities for tracking and explaining prehistoric
change. Over the last thirty years excavations in Fiji, the
Marianas, and Hawai'i have revolutionised Oceanic archaeology
and, as the major problems of cultural origins and island
sequences have been resolved, archaeologists have come
increasingly to study social change and to integrate newly
acquired data on material culture with older ethnographic and
ethnohistorical materials. The fascinating results of this work,
centring on the evolution of complex Oceanic chiefdoms into
something very much like classic 'archaic states', are authori-
tatively surveyed here for the first time.

New Directions in Archaeology

Approaches to the Archaeological Heritage

Edited by Henry Cleere

'Truly international books about cultural resource management
and monuments conservation are a rarity, indeed few archaeologists have ever thought about these problems on anything
more than a local, or national, scale. Henry Cleere realizes this,
so he has edited a series of essays on monuments conservation
in twelve countries, each of them written by a scholar with
first-hand experience of local problems. The result is a fascinating, and depressing, look at the crisis facing archaeologists
everywhere . . . a mine of valuable and thought-provoking
information.'   *Antiquity*

'This volume should be read by anyone concerned by the wide
range of threats to our cultural heritage. Legislators and
administrators, in particular, will benefit from learning of the
strengths and weaknesses of the measures and systems adopted
by other countries.'   *British Book News*

New Direction in Archaeology

Hunters in Transition

*Mesolithic Societies of Temperate Eurasia and their Transition
to Farming*
Edited by Marek Zvelebil

Hunters in Transition analyses one of the crucial events in
human cultural evolution: the emergence of postglacial hunter-
gatherer communities and the development of farming.
Traditionally, the advantages of settled agriculture have been
assumed and the transition to farming has been viewed in
terms of the simple dispersal of early farming communities
northwards across Europe. The contributors to this volume
adopt a fresh, more subtle approach. Farming is viewed from a
hunter-gatherer perspective as offering both advantages and
disadvantages, organisational disruption during the period of
transition and far-reaching social consequences for the existing
way of life. The hunter-gatherer economy and farming in fact
shared a common objective: a guaranteed food supply in a
changing natural and social environment. Drawing extensively
on research in eastern Europe and temperate Asia, the book
argues persuasively for the essential unity of all postglacial
adaptations whether leading to the dispersal of farming or the
retention and elaboration of existing hunter-gatherer strategies.

New Directions in Archaeology

Prehistoric Quarries and Lithic Production

Edited by Jonathon E. Ericson and Barbara A. Purdy

The papers in this volume represent the first systematic study
of archaeological sites which served as quarries for stone tools,
showing that amongst prehistoric quarries and workshops
there exist tremendous variations in the associated cultures
and social organisations. The volume links prehistoric production of lithic materials to the wider aspects of society, to
technology, to exchange, labour and the management of
resources in an exciting and innovative manner.

'. . . the ideas put forward [in this collection] will be of interest
to all archaeologists concerned with stone tools, whatever their
field of specialization, and the book is strongly recommended
to them'.   *Geological Journal*

New Directions in Archaeology

Printed in Great Britain
by Amazon.co.uk, Ltd.,
Marston Gate.